Margaret Laurence & Jack McClelland, Letters

McCLELLAND

Publishers 25 Hollinger Road

CABLES: Emandess TE

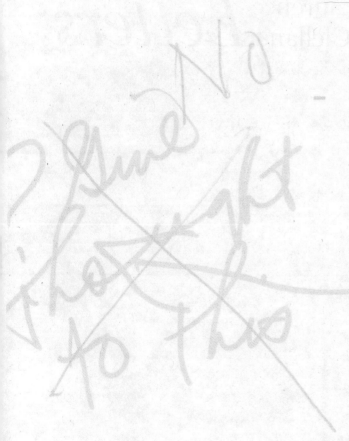

- the only other
that I made was
sold on the hea
not referring h
passage" which
is an obvious h
I mean that I a
terms like "mem
"inner film".
prejudice becau
liked this type
allowances for
I would say tha
and maybe a typ
a workable alte

In putting togethe
that, any good or competen
certain to achieve some ap

Edited and with an Introduction by
Laura K. Davis & Linda M. Morra

Margaret Laurence & Jack McClelland *Letters*

THE UNIVERSITY OF ALBERTA PRESS

Published by

The University of Alberta Press
Ring House 2
Edmonton, Alberta, Canada T6G 2E1
www.uap.ualberta.ca

LIBRARY AND ARCHIVES CANADA CATALOGUING IN PUBLICATION

Margaret Laurence and Jack McClelland, letters / edited and with an introduction by Laura K. Davis & Linda M. Morra.

Includes bibliographical references and index.
Issued in print and electronic formats.
ISBN 978-1-77212-335-7 (softcover).—
ISBN 978-1-77212-394-4 (EPUB).—
ISBN 978-1-77212-395-1 (Kindle).—
ISBN 978-1-77212-393-7 (PDF)

1. Laurence, Margaret, 1926–1987—Correspondence. 2. McClelland, Jack, 1922——Correspondence. 3. Novelists, Canadian (English)—20th century—Correspondence. 4. Publishers and publishing—Canada—Correspondence. I. Davis, Laura K., editor II. Morra, Linda M., editor III. Laurence, Margaret, 1926–1987 . Correspondence. Selections. IV. McClelland, Jack, 1922– . Correspondence. Selections. V. Title.

PS8523.A86Z48 2018 C813'.54 C2017-907562-4
C2017-907563-2

First edition, first printing, 2018.
First printed and bound in Canada by Houghton Boston Printers, Saskatoon, Saskatchewan.
Copyediting and proofreading by Kirsten Craven.
Indexing by Stephen Ullstrom.

The University of Alberta Press is committed to protecting our natural environment. As part of our efforts, this book is printed on Enviro Paper: it contains 100% post-consumer recycled fibres and is acid- and chlorine-free.

The University of Alberta Press gratefully acknowledges the support received for its publishing program from the Government of Canada, the Canada Council for the Arts, and the Government of Alberta through the Alberta Media Fund.

This book has been published with the help of a grant from the Canadian Federation for the Humanities and Social Sciences, through the Awards to Scholarly Publications Program, using funds provided by the Social Sciences and Humanities Research Council of Canada.

Canada

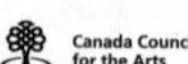

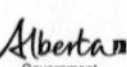

Lines of Encouragement to J.G. McClelland

Roses are red
Violets are blue
One of your authors
Has faith in McStew.

Violets are blue
Roses are red
I don't believe
You've got rocks in your head

Violets are blue
Roses are pink
Let nobody say
As a bookman you stink

Violets are mauve
Or purple or worse
In two hundred years
Who'll give you a curse?

Roses are crimson
And green is the chive
Whatever your troubles
I know you'll survive

Roses are red
Violets are blue
Be heartened old buddy
I'm betting on you

—MARGARET LAURENCE

Contents

Preface

IT IS DIFFICULT *not* to be seduced by Margaret Laurence and Jack McClelland's correspondence, as we were when we first started research on this project. We sat in the archives, surrounded by boxes and files, and read through the proliferation of letters exchanged between the writer and her publisher. From this moment onward, we brought our unique but complementary perspectives and sets of scholarly expertise related, respectively, to Laurence's life and writing and to women's archives to bear on their discussions about the developments of English-Canadian literature from the 1960s. Laurence and McClelland were committed to the *idea* of Canadian literature, which was at that time in its formative years as a nationally recognized corpus; they set out to foster it by supporting the writing of Canadian authors through publications, literary dinners, promotions, and collaborations with other writers. They engaged in disagreements, shared frustrations, and planned celebrations. McClelland frequently praised Laurence for her "great dedication to Canada and Canadian letters" (28 Feb. 1978), and Laurence as frequently commended McClelland for his vast contributions: "I ... hope," she stated, "as I have been telling you for years and years, that you accept how much you have done for publishing in Canada and for our writers" (30 July 1986).

If we are to consider the correspondence between Laurence and McClelland in the context of the history and rise of Canadian literature, then it is also important to consider them *as letters*. In other words, we must pay heed to the form they assume as well as their content. As Marlene Kadar, Linda Warley, and Jeanne Perrault explain, the autobiographical can be found in "traces of text" and "unlikely documents" (2). Business letters might not appear to represent life stories, but the letters here constitute an evocative form of life writing because they demonstrate how the lives of individuals can have a significant impact on the business of publishing, the importance of literary culture, and understandings of the national imaginary.

To echo Kadar, Warley, and Perrault's words, we are "tracing" the autobiographical in our presentation of these letters. To "trace" is to draw and make visible by copying or outlining, as in tracing a pattern, or it is to investigate and discover, as in tracing footsteps to find one's whereabouts. For Jacques Derrida, a "trace" is that which remains but eludes the visible or the enunciated at the moment when meaning is made. It is differentiated from the sign, but it is still related and attached to it. Until now, the letters in this book were left in the archives: they were the remainders of major published works on (or by) Laurence and McClelland. *Margaret Laurence and Jack McClelland, Letters* frames and makes public these traces of their professional lives by compiling an inventory, contextualizing their letters, bringing them to the fore, and enunciating their meaning.

That Laurence's letters were preserved marks a significant shift in the history of the preservation of documents. In *Unarrested Archives: Case Studies in Twentieth-Century Canadian Women's Authorship*, Linda M. Morra observes how, before the twentieth century, women's papers were often refused a place in official archival repositories, since women were not recognized as full citizens, much less as authors. "What is included within a repository," she explains, "determines and limits potential enunciations of personhood" (4). In her well-known feminist manifesto, *A Room of One's Own*, written in 1929, Virginia Woolf had observed how women themselves were excluded from physically entering archival centres in England, unless accompanied—only to confront the relative absence of women's papers therein.

These practices that occasioned the neglect of women's papers, when contrasted with the voluminous and carefully preserved letters by Laurence, show how much has changed for women writers—and how much Laurence strove to make a place not only for her writing but also for that of other women authors. She did benefit from being a best-selling author and living at a time and in a place when women writers could be taken seriously: her papers were valued and solicited by archival centres. Indeed, Laurence was conscious of the value their correspondence would hold for posterity, a fact she acknowledged in several of her missives to McClelland and one that McClelland confirmed in his. So Laurence wrote to say that she had placed one of his letters in her filing system, which resembled the "tombs of the pharaohs" and which would only be "opened by future generations" (28 June 1982). At times, both acknowledged they would likely see each other before the said letter would arrive, but, they affirmed, that letter was largely "for the record" (4 July 1980). Pragmatically, McClelland noted, "Our mutual correspondence is saleable at both ends. I sell your letters. You should be selling mine" (17 June 1982).

But the historical and material conditions that enabled Laurence to archive her papers should not be forgotten. An example of one such condition that facilitated the preservation of Laurence's archival records was her close friendship with Clara Thomas. Thomas was a prominent English professor at York University, Toronto, when it was not common for women to hold such positions. She was instrumental in persuading Laurence not only to house her papers at York University but also to grant scholars of her work access to them. Writing to Laurence about the working agreement between Laurence and York University on the preservation of her papers, Thomas stated,

> *It seems to me that you have covered everything except access for serious scholars ... who might well have very valid reasons for wanting access. ... Research on Canadian writing in the 60s and 70s is as good and as valid as any. Such a collection as yours is priceless documentation about our literary history, as much as, or*

more than, it is documentation about individual writers. I would therefore hope that you would add a clause to your mini-will, and put into your final agreement ... "Research scholars will be given access to the collection at the discretion of ... [the] Archivist of York University." (Margaret Laurence Fonds, William Ready Division, Box 11, File 6)

That Thomas anticipated the value of "research on Canadian writing in the 60s and 70s" and Canadian "literary history" demonstrates her foresight; that Laurence eventually concurred suggests she too came to recognize the importance of her papers in this context. What Thomas did not explicitly say, but what held equally true for her and for Laurence, was that they were both women in male-dominated professions. If they did not explicitly reference this situation, however, their life's commitments demonstrated how they expressly wished to see greater representation for women in the arenas of writing and scholarship.

Laurence had great respect for many scholars, such as Thomas and Malcolm Ross, but she was also wary of literary critics and the harm they could inflict, specifically, to a writer's reputation and place in the writing community and, generally, to book sales. As a friend and a woman in the male-dominated field of literary criticism, Thomas was able to mitigate Laurence's anxieties. She wrote,

This is very hard for me, dear Margaret, because I feel as if I'm on the wrong end of your understandable, but perhaps mistaken mistrust of scholars. Your agreement is set up to protect you and your correspondents from what you sometimes see, I think, as a ravening horde. In fact, they are not. Not even a miniscule percentage of them are like that. That is what all the discipline training of PHD students is all about—what I spend my life at, as you know. (Margaret Laurence Fonds, William Ready Division, Box 11, File 6)

Laurence was eventually swayed by Thomas's counsel and allowed scholars to access her papers. The dynamics at play here between Laurence and Thomas contributed to the creation of her archive and, specifically, to scholarly access to Laurence's unpublished work, and more largely demonstrated how women were beginning to hold more prominent positions and to be valued on the Canadian literary scene.

Laurence's papers at both York and McMaster universities have been accessible to scholars for some time now; many researchers have consulted and discussed them in publications. McClelland's papers, however, were restricted until twenty-five years after acquisition, and therefore have only recently been opened to viewing by scholars. For the first time, then, we can consider more fully both sides of the correspondence. Each set of archival papers is already framed in particular ways, by year and by correspondent. As such, the framing of the letters facilitates research on Laurence's and McClelland's relationships with individuals. *Margaret Laurence and Jack McClelland, Letters* constitutes another reframing: most of Laurence and McClelland's letters to each other are included in this volume, which are historically contextualized by our introduction and annotations to tell the story of the unfolding of their personal and professional dynamics in the building of Canadian literature.

If this book, as we have suggested, "traces the autobiographical" and disseminates more broadly what was only previously available to a select few in the archives, then it also leaves its own traces for others. There is that which is gestured at but still remains mostly unspoken in the letters: for instance, Ann Nelles was the financial manager at McClelland & Stewart during the first two decades of this correspondence, and her name is mentioned a few times in these letters. McClelland praises her in a letter to Laurence on 6 April 1978, in which he observed that she "has taken over our Royalty Department and is one of the most competent individuals I have ever dealt with in business. If you haven't met her yet, you will love her." But Nelles is not mentioned anywhere in literature about the publishing house, not even in James King's comprehensive biography of McClelland. Her personality and the extent of her influence at McClelland & Stewart, as one example, remain largely unrecorded.

The letters, however, do otherwise have broad reach. There are approximately four hundred letters that were exchanged between Laurence and McClelland, now preserved in the Clara Thomas Archives and Special Collections at York University, Toronto, and the William Ready Division of Archives and Research Collections at McMaster University, Hamilton. The correspondence begins with a letter of invitation from McClelland to Laurence on 4 March 1959 to submit her manuscript, and concludes on 10 December 1986 with another letter from him to her—a month before she died with, as Donn Downey noted in the *Globe and Mail* on 6 January 1987, her reputation "secure" (A11). We initially planned to include all of their exchanges in this book, and to make it a comprehensive volume of letters between the writer and her publisher. After careful consideration, we decided to remove some of them: those that are short and do not give pertinent information about Laurence and McClelland or their interactions; those that are simply requests to review a manuscript; and those that are simple acknowledgements that letters, documents, or manuscripts have been received. We have included most of the other letters; we have not removed any letters that would alter their story or shed light on their relationship or the development of Canadian literature. Some letters are simply missing, as we often indicate in endnotes, or have been answered through an alternate means—by telephone or in person. Occasionally, we have omitted phrases or sentences from some of the letters, and we have indicated so with ellipsis points. In these instances, information was redundant or irrelevant. We have not included the enclosures to which Laurence and McClelland occasionally refer in these letters. In some cases, these were not available to us in the archives; in others, the enclosures were explained sufficiently in the letters, or it was not practical or relevant to include them. We have divided the manuscript into three discrete parts, largely by decade (1960s, 1970s, and 1980s), to showcase the trajectory of their evolving friendship and the major decisions that characterize their professional relationship. The first decade showcases the beginnings of their professional relationship; the second decade, Laurence's growing confidence as an author and her deepening friendship with McClelland; and the last decade, the legacy of a friendship that even outstrips their professional association.

Little about the individual letters included in this volume has been changed: some light punctuation has been added to make clear that a question is being raised or to break up an overly long sentence. We largely respected idiosyncratic spellings, such as "yr," "yrself," "migod," "goddsake," and so forth. We maintained their abbreviations for countries, such as "Eng" or "Engl" for England and "Can" for Canada, and for cities, such as "Tor" for Toronto and "P'borough" for Peterborough. At times, we corrected mistaken punctuation (McClelland incorrectly added an apostrophe to *The Olden Days Coat*, the title of one of Laurence's children's books). Titles of books that Laurence and McClelland sometimes wrote in capital letters have been italicized instead for consistency. Addresses on the letters have been abbreviated. Laurence and McClelland often underlined words or phrases for emphasis, and in those cases we italicized, rather than underlined, the text. We have annotated the letters where relevant, often adding significant detail. If the letters published tell a persuasive story and trace the professional lives of the writer and her publisher, the rise of Canadian literature, and the shaping of a Canadian national identity through arts and letters from the 1960s through the 1980s, then our extensive annotations serve the purpose of highlighting the important players in this story and the remarkable history that undergirds this correspondence. This book in total represents an important piece of Canadian literary history. As their correspondence clearly shows, Laurence and McClelland's efforts to build Canadian literature were part of a larger impetus in Canada to create and preserve arts and letters; they themselves were important contributors, individually and as collaborators, in such efforts.

Acknowledgements

THIS BOOK could not have come together without key players and support in the production of the manuscript: archivists, executors of the Jack McClelland and Margaret Laurence estates, researchers and research assistants, and university and federal support. We were graciously assisted by Suzanne Dubeau, Michael Moir, Anna St. Onge, Julia Holland, and Heather Pitka at the Clara Thomas Archives and Special Collections at York University, and by Rick Stapleton, Renu Barrett, Beverly Bayzat, Myron Groover, Olga Perkovic, and Bridget Whittle at the William Ready Division of Archives and Research Collections at McMaster University. We owe thanks to the executors of Jack McClelland's and Margaret Laurence's estates: McClelland's daughter, Suzanne Drinkwater, and Laurence's children, the late Jocelyn Laurence and David Laurence—all of whom were enthusiastic about this project from its beginnings. We thank Dianne Woodman, who agreed to be interviewed about her work at McClelland & Stewart in the 1960s and 1970s. Her knowledge gave us important background information for this book. We give sincere thanks to the anonymous reviewers of the manuscript who provided us with valuable feedback. We are grateful to the employees at the University of Alberta Press, in particular, Peter Midgley, Linda Cameron, Mary Lou Roy, Duncan Turner, and Alan Brownoff for their enthusiasm for this project and their hard work in bringing the manuscript into publication. We owe a special debt of gratitude to our research assistant, Nirupama Raghavan, for her unflagging devotion, research, support, and sense of humour, as we ploughed through the manuscript and, at times, chased down elusive details about figures or newspaper articles that were referenced therein.

We are also thankful to our respective research offices and their employees, particularly Alicia Cafferata and Eric Kokko at Red Deer College and Julie Fredette and Sylvie Côté at Bishop's University, who showed support as we worked through the peculiarities of applying for and executing a SSHRC Insight Development grant. The grant supported our work in the archives, several conference papers, and, evidently, the material production of this book. Without such financial support from our respective institutions, Red Deer College and Bishop's University, and from SSHRC, this book would never have come to fruition. Laura K. Davis thanks her mentor and former professor, Nora Foster Stovel, for the insightful knowledge she passed on to her about Margaret Laurence and her work. She also thanks her colleagues and students for their continuing inspiration. She would like to give special thanks to her parents, Ken and Wendy Strong, who sparked in her an interest in Margaret Laurence and Canadian literature at an early age; to her brother, Greg Strong; and to her husband Roger Davis, and children, Rachael, Kai, and Clara Davis, for their ongoing love and support through early mornings and late nights of work on this book. Linda M. Morra is immensely grateful to her parents, Anthony and Jessie Morra, for the consistency of their love and support for all her projects, and to Anna Sedo, Kate Ready, Caroline Van Der Meer, Marc Fortin, Teresa Petruzzo, Jennifer Andrews, Tina Trigg, Chantal Lavoie, Elise Moser, Lori Schubert, Deanna Reder, Mark Morra, Gabriella McCloskey, Ben and Leo Morra, Sue Morra, and Louis-Georges Harvey for their sustenance and balm during this project, for their nourishing words of friendship, love, and kindness.

Introduction

THIS BOOK IS PRIMARILY about the dynamic and intriguing relationship between one of Canada's most prominent writers and one of its most important publishers: Margaret Laurence and Jack McClelland. Unlike any other existing publication, the correspondence between these two figures sheds light on both their unique decision-making process related to publishing matters in Canada and the sweeping implications for the English-Canadian literary scene as a result of some of these decisions. Their letters trace how they consistently manifested respect for and trust in each other as they settled on particular issues—sometimes in spite of their vast differences of opinion. During the 1980s, for example, when McClelland & Stewart encountered a period of financial trouble, Laurence declared, "My loyalty to you and to the firm will never be in question" (4 Oct. 1984). Other writers, she added, had apparently been pursuing what they believed to be greener publishing pastures and savvier literary agents, but she was never "one of them": "The vultures were gathering, and I say to hell with them" (4 Oct. 1984). McClelland was equally loyal and admiring. In lauding her achievements as a writer, he exclaimed, "God, Margaret!"—to which he added, "I don't know why I keep inserting that comma" (30 Sept. 1985).

The letters trace how their relationship shifted from a professional to a personal one and thus also provide a hitherto rare view of and insight into their private lives from Laurence's pronouncements on motherhood and her divorce, to McClelland's struggles with depression and anxiety. They shared some of these more intimate details because they were confident, not only in their professional rapport, but also in their evolving friendship. Moments in their letters are reminders of the humanity of these figures—when traces of their problems erupted or at least became visible—and make their struggle for the establishment of arts and letters in Canada seem ever more poignant. More markedly, the letters demonstrate how much Laurence matured as an author and learned to come into her own in a professional capacity. They poured themselves into their careers, so their personal and professional tribulations were often intertwined. Both author and publisher experienced highs and lows in these careers: Laurence's books hit bestseller lists at a time when McClelland was deemed, by Anna Porter, "the Prince of Publishers, the most persistent and imaginative publisher to have erupted onto the world stage" (MacSkimming 118); later, Laurence was to be plagued by censorship controversies surrounding *The Diviners* and her other Manawaka books, while McClelland lamented the sale of his firm and eventually handed over the title of president and publisher to Linda McKnight. To read these letters is therefore to immerse oneself in both the professional and private lives of these two animated people, who not only cared deeply about Canadian literature but were also actively engaged in creating and sustaining it.

The Beginnings: Contributions to Arts and Letters in Canada

McClelland first wrote to Laurence upon hearing from a mutual friend, Gordon Elliott, that she had written a novel about Africa. A professor for whom she marked papers at Simon Fraser University, Elliott correctly ascertained how McClelland would respond: he hoped Laurence would submit her manuscript to McClelland & Stewart. The year was 1959, a significant moment in English-Canadian culture and publishing. Just a few years before, in 1952, and at thirty years of age, McClelland took over McClelland & Stewart from his father, John McClelland, and his business partner, George Stewart (MacSkimming 123)—a period when many Canadian authors chose not to publish in Canada at all. Indeed, prior to 1959, Archibald Lampman's 1891 proclamation that Canadian literature did not exist (421) still held sway. But when McClelland wrote his first letter to Laurence, the Canadian literary landscape was ready for a transformation. The Massey Commission, which had been led by Vincent Massey and set forth policy to support the development of Canadian arts and letters, was pivotal to the beginnings of that change. Introduced in 1951, the commission produced a report, *The Royal Commission on National Development in the Arts, Letters, and Sciences*, that articulated the importance of the arts in Canada, "changed the nature of Canada and the role of government in modern Canadian society," and led to funding councils for authors and academics, such as the Canada Council for the Arts and the Social Sciences and Humanities Research Council (Lorimer 70–71). As Rowland Lorimer observes, "even if few saw it this way at the time, Canada began to wend its way towards a cultural awakening" (70). Laurence and McClelland thus began their working relationship at a time when literature in Canada would begin to flourish, largely made possible by the Massey Commission and the subsequent establishment of the Canada Council.

If the Massey Commission evoked a "cultural awakening" in Canada, then it was people such as McClelland who facilitated and mobilized it. As the letters make plain, McClelland suggested to Laurence as early as 1960 that she write fiction about Canada, rather than Africa. His suggestion was also related to the interests of another important figure in Canadian culture, Robert Weaver, a broadcaster with CBC (Canadian Broadcasting Corporation) Radio: "Have you done, or do you plan to do, any short stories with a Canadian background? ... It is entirely likely that Bob Weaver of the C.B.C. will be writing to you shortly looking for such a story. He has an interesting project under way in which we are involved, and if he does write you, he will offer a fairly substantial fee" (7 Jan. 1960). Since Weaver's project focused on Canadian-content literature and offered respectable financial compensation, it attracted writers who devoted their attention to the literary scene in Canada. The proliferation of such economic, socio-political, and cultural opportunities undergirded the production of Canadian literature. Although her response to this particular request does not survive, it was not long after it that Laurence began to write about Canada: her first novel, *The Stone Angel*, was set in Canada and published in 1964.

Clearly, then, this correspondence encompasses considerably more than the personal and professional lives of Laurence and McClelland. The letters extend well beyond that to reveal the authority they held in relation to English-Canadian literary life, moments related to the rise of Canadian literature, the creation of Canadian funding agencies for literature and the humanities, the history of censorship and English curricula in Canadian schools, the shifting dynamics of Canadian feminism, and the rise of Canadian nationalism and multiculturalism. Writing about the history of book publishing in Canada, Rowland Lorimer observes there are periods when "talented creators and entrepreneurs coalesce around the writing and publishing of books" (69). That coalescence can lead to "a rich and generative interaction and an emergent identity ... when opportunities exist for change" (69). The letters here, spanning nearly three decades, from 1959 to 1986 exemplify such "generative interaction." Their work undoubtedly contributed to the distinct shaping of "emergent identit[ies]"—for themselves, for the body of English-Canadian literature as they conceived it, and, arguably, for the Canadian national imaginary itself. The correspondence also generally reveals how the production of English-Canadian literature, as a body of literary texts and as a discipline for university study, was influenced by their interventions and contributed to the national imaginary; how the socio-political culture of the time contributed to the creation of English-Canadian literature and to the practice of studying it; and how gender played a role with respect to their creation and navigation of the English-Canadian publishing scene.

Although relatively little has been written about the crucial interaction between these two figures, considerably more has been written about them as individuals: Laurence as an important national literary figure and McClelland as one of Canada's most important publishers. To date, there are three biographies on Laurence: *The Life of Margaret Laurence* by James King, *Alien Heart: The Life and Work of Margaret Laurence* by Lyall Powers, and *The Making of a Writer: Margaret Laurence* by Donez Xiques. Critical works have proliferated around her and her literary accomplishment—from the first books on Laurence's writing by Clara Thomas, *Margaret Laurence* and *The Manawaka World of Margaret Laurence*, to Nora Foster Stovel's *Divining Margaret Laurence*, to Laura K. Davis's *Margaret Laurence Writes Africa and Canada*. In terms of her letters, only approximately five of those exchanged between her and McClelland have already been previously published in the volume edited by Sam Solecki, *Imagining Canadian Literature: The Selected Letters of Jack McClelland*. Solecki's volume demonstrates the range of McClelland's contacts and the rise and end of his career as a publisher; however, no real comparison can be made between Solecki's book and the volume of letters included here in all their richly textured depth and quality and in the kind of evidence they provide for the long-lasting effects and the reach of decisions Laurence and McClelland made.

The material about McClelland has been as voluminous. His biographer, James King, has taken a wide view of both his personality and the publishing house in *Jack: A Life with Writers*. Janet Friskney's *New Canadian Library* and Roy MacSkimming's *The Perilous Trade*, as examples, focus respectively on aspects of McClelland's company and on the shape his personality gave to its publication trajectory. This book, however, is the first to address Laurence and McClelland's personal and professional relationship extensively, to examine and showcase their investments in the English-Canadian literary world, and to do so by making their letters public. It is also the first book to reveal the degree of influence these two wielded in the English-Canadian literary scene as they collaborated together and operated with a specific agenda: to create their vision of a national literature and of a national—even international—publishing house.

Laurence's own novels were a part of that vision. Her most popular books are the five she wrote about the fictional Canadian prairie town of Manawaka, based on her hometown of Neepawa, Manitoba, and known as the Manawaka cycle. The Manawaka cycle, in its entirety, was eventually inducted into the New Canadian Library Series (NCL). Her support for and contributions to writing in Canada, however, extended well beyond McClelland & Stewart. Indeed, her commitments also encompassed advocacy for women, for the writing community, and for Indigenous peoples, and manifested themselves in various ways: she was a founding member of the Writers' Union of Canada and the Writers' Trust of Canada (Atwood, Margaret Laurence Lecture Series 315), a pacifist who fought for disarmament, and an advocate for women's rights and Indigenous self-government (see King, *The Life of Margaret Laurence*).

If Laurence supplied some of the content for what was to be considered quintessentially Canadian literature in the period, McClelland was to give it its shape. Jack McClelland's father, John McClelland, and his business partner, Frederick Goodchild, established the Canadian publishing company in 1906. In 1913, George Stewart became a third partner in the firm. Goodchild left the firm in 1918, at which point the firm became known as McClelland & Stewart (Friskney, *New Canadian Library* 29). McClelland's leadership of the company, which began in the 1950s and rose to its height during the following three decades, was radically different from that of his father and the practices of other publishers in Canada. Unlike other publishers, he promoted and published almost exclusively Canadian rather than British or American authors, and to great success (see also King, *Jack*). His decisions effectively altered and eventually reshaped the terrain of Canadian publishing, and brought many of those who would come to be recognized as Canada's best writers to the fore.

At times, Laurence directly participated in the process by which some writers would be included as part of his stable of "great authors"—what she referred to as "evangelizing for Can literature" (11 Apr. 1978)—and then helped to promote those who were published with the firm. She and McClelland discussed the merits—and sometimes the foibles—of Farley Mowat, Adele Wiseman, Pierre Berton, Rudy Wiebe, Al Purdy, Pat Blondal, Margaret Atwood, Marian Engel, Mordecai Richler, and many others. About Rudy Wiebe's *The Temptations of Big Bear*, for which he later won the Governor General's Award, she wrote, "I think it is the best book he has ever written." She actively supported his nomination for the Royal Society of Canada's Lorne Pierce Medal. She pushed McClelland to invest more money in advertising the novel, because she had "a terrible and sinking thought" that "Upper Canadians" (by which she meant English Canadians from Ontario) would see the book as of chief interest to western Canada. Instead, she believed the novel had "meaningful things" to communicate to all Canadians and, as such, could extend in interest "beyond geographical boundaries" (7 Oct. 1973). Other writers of the time were concerned with seeing how the local could productively engage a larger audience. In his 1975 essay, "On Being an Alberta Writer," for example, Robert Kroetsch insisted on the importance of writing the local, even or especially when that place had not been valued or grounded in a Western literary tradition. Laurence's emphasis on specifically western Canadian literature illustrated her belief in the projects of other prairie writers, such as Wiebe and Kroetsch, even as she saw them as making broader claims for the national imaginary.

Cultivating the National Imaginary and Canadian Literature

Laurence's view about the general importance of a national literature was nourished by her interactions with McClelland. Their brand of nationalism often focused on geography and history as its more significant components, and was made clear even in the company's publishing trajectory. Pierre Berton's *The National Dream* and *The Last Spike* are evidence of the particular manifestations of a self-celebratory English-Canadian national identity of the period that McClelland & Stewart valorized. Yet Laurence too felt herself drawn towards writing about the country she learned to love. In one instance, for example, she wrote to McClelland from England to say that, albeit somewhat ironically, "I feel deep sentiments towards my home and native land, especially when I am not there" (16 June 1963). In a subsequent letter, she offered a corrective, more sincere in nature: "I said I liked my home and native land best when I was away from it. Actually, that is not true, as I see now when I read *Hagar* [*The Stone Angel*]. Perhaps reading it again has made me homesick—I don't know. But when the chips are down, there is only one country in the world that I really give a damn about, and I see now how right it was to stop writing about people other than my own" (29 June 1963). Such a sense of devotion to the country continued to inform her work, not just her views of the books of other authors for whom she showed support.

Indeed, that *The Stone Angel* was published to such immediate acclaim shows how powerful and how widely appealing Laurence and McClelland's conceptions of nationalism were for citizens in Canada. Margaret Atwood was to later emphasize the significance of *The Stone Angel* at the moment it was published in Canada. She claimed that when she first read it, she felt that, finally, "The impossible, dreamed of thing could be done. [One] could write a novel about Canada—which at that time did not exist as a force in the international literary world, and pretty much did not exist as a force in Canada itself. [One] could write a novel about Canada that was real, and strong, and authentic, and smart, and moving" (Atwood, Margaret Laurence Lecture Series 316). As her statement suggests, Laurence's groundbreaking book opened opportunities not only for the writer herself but also for a younger generation of writers who could see and read what was now possible for literature produced in Canada.

McClelland saw the importance and power of Laurence's writing about Canada. She focused on her "own people" in her novels about Canada, but she was sensitive to and accommodated political differences within Canada. This aspect of her work did not go unnoticed by McClelland. He emphasized this sensitivity in his response to her upon first reading the manuscript of her 1974 novel, *The Diviners*—a novel that extensively addresses the history of the Métis and their leader, Louis Riel, in the Red River area of Manitoba. He wrote, "You have confronted yourself with the formidable problem of relating the two streams of heritage" (12 June 1973). The coming together of the "two streams" of which McClelland here spoke—the Anglo-Scots and the Métis—corresponded to some facets of a more contemporary national identity being espoused by Prime Minister Pierre Elliott Trudeau (although his 1969 White Paper suggested his wish to devolve federal responsibility for Indigenous matters to the provinces, rather than showcasing support for Indigenous communities). This new national vision, still in the early stages of development, at least embraced and highlighted Canada's multicultural history rather than its historical and imperial ties to Britain and the United States. Yet *The Diviners* was released in 1974, just three years after Trudeau implemented multiculturalism as a state policy in Canada. Announced by Trudeau on 8 October 1971, in response to the Royal Commission on Bilingualism and Biculturalism, Canadian multiculturalism was written into the Charter of Rights and Freedoms in 1982 and became the official Multiculturalism Act in 1988. Here, emerging visions of nationalism were aligned: between the English-Canadian state, the writer, her publisher, and the Canadian public. Laurence was equally inspired by Indigenous histories, which compelled her to write to McClelland about Wiebe's book, *The Temptations of Big Bear*, in 1973, as she was writing *The Diviners*. The Cree history and the Métis history about which Wiebe and Laurence respectively wrote occurred simultaneously and were interrelated: his novel takes up the history of the Plains Cree in western Canada in the late nineteenth century, when an imperial presence pushed treaties upon them—despite Chief Big Bear's resistance. Her novel addresses Métis history in the Red River area of Manitoba and addresses settler-Métis relations. Wiebe and Laurence were thus engaged in a similar project: to address Indigenous-settler relations in early western Canadian history and to demonstrate its significance. Laurence's influence on McClelland's publication and promotion of certain authors and books was neither a matter of personal choice nor informed by an elitist notion of what constitutes great literature. Rather, she supported authors who, like Wiebe, provided important perspectives on Canadian places and histories and could articulate the limits and possibilities of cross-cultural understanding and human communication. In so doing, she shaped the Canadian literary landscape and the authors who were to become a central part of it.

Specifically, Laurence and McClelland agreed about Mordecai Richler's novel, *The Apprenticeship of Duddy Kravitz*: they regarded it as an exceptional example of what Canada's best writers could produce and believed it should be used as a key textbook in schools.[1] That McClelland also saw these two exceptional writers on equal footing is rendered clear by the fact that he made a point of introducing her to Richler in a letter to the latter in January 1963: "One of my favourite writers, a gal by the name of Margaret Laurence, is now living in London. ... I'd be grateful if you and Florence would have her over some evening and introduce her to a few people" (Solecki 67). To underscore her accomplishment and value, he added, "She's won several University of Western Ontario President's Medals for her short stories, which have been published in *Tamarack, Prism,* etc., and also *Saturday Evening Post*." Laurence needed no persuading about Richler's accomplishment.

However much they appreciated the merits of Wiebe's and Richler's writing, Laurence and McClelland both agreed in their assessment of Alistair MacLean's *Ice Station Zebra*: it was a poor example of Canadian literary achievement that was yet regrettably required reading in some educational institutions. He scoffed at its adoption in high school classes: "I find the use of his book in English courses in Canada or anywhere else totally inexcusable, even for slow learners" (17 Feb. 1976). Published in 1963, the novel is set against the background of the space race and the Cold War between the United States and the Soviet Union, and it is about a fictional British meteorological station in the Arctic that undergoes a disaster. Although the novel might have had content that appealed to teachers of Canadian high school curricula—an Arctic setting with British characters and evocations of contemporary international politics—the exchanges between McClelland and Laurence reveal their shared conviction that such content was not enough to warrant its status as good writing about Canada.

In light of the subject matter and content of the books Laurence and McClelland discussed, it is intriguing that they agreed that Wiebe's and Richler's books were more impressive than those of MacLean. It demonstrates the kind of influence they were wielding in terms of the books they valorized: Wiebe wrote about Indigenous identities, and Richler about Jewish identities, which corresponded to more complex and multiple notions of Canadian nationalism in the period. MacLean, by contrast, wrote about Canada in relation to British and Arctic landscapes, an older formulation of nationalism that was predicated on "elsewhere" as the source of identity. One might argue, then, that their assessment of Canadian literature took into consideration the author's subject matter and its fit within the Canadian national imaginary contemporary with the period. This interpretation highlights the dynamic nature of the national imaginary: visions of Canada shift and change, influenced as much by literature as by state-driven forces and sociological factors. As is clear from Laurence and McClelland's discussions of these literary works, they sought to influence both the body of literature produced in the country and the literary canon that was taught in schools—and, in so doing, to shape what its citizens would come to think of the nation. To a certain extent, McClelland, if not Laurence, had some influence on school curricula. His decisions related to the books that would be published in paperback by the New Canadian Library show his concern that school systems, both at the high school and university levels, could afford to purchase them as textbooks. In this sense, he especially had an impact on the national imaginary through the production of literature and its dissemination.

The sense of English-Canadian nationalism that Laurence and McClelland espoused was shifting at the very moment their letters were written—from a sense of being tied to or rooted in British cultural traditions, to breaking from that ideal and defining Canada as constituted in and through multiculturalism. Laurence believed Canada should distinguish itself from Britain and the practice of British cultural traditions—but also from those of the United States. For example, in her essay, "Ivory Tower, Or Grass Roots? The Novelist as Socio-Political Being," she refers to the cultural domination of the United States over Canada. She asserts that Canada "had been under the colonial sway of Britain once and is now under the colonial sway of America" (15). Such a statement recalls the Massey Commission's emphasis on the creation and establishment of Canadian arts and letters apart from Britain and the United States. In her published writing and in her correspondence, "Laurence acknowledged Canada's history as a colony of Britain but also paid heed to how settlers colonized Aboriginals and how Aboriginal people and immigrants continued to be oppressed. She valued the break from Britain but also knew and resisted Canada's ongoing imperialist practices" (Davis, *Margaret Laurence Writes Africa and Canada* 10). McClelland wholeheartedly endorsed Laurence's perspective. He asserted that *The Diviners* was powerful because it addressed how "the two streams of heritage" (Anglo-Scottish and Métis) could be understood against the backdrop of the nationalist ideology of the time, namely, official Canadian multiculturalism and the loosening of strict immigration policies. Thus, through the creation and publication of literature, Laurence and McClelland not only adhered to some facets of the national ideology of the period but also contributed to its making.

For McClelland, then, this national imaginary was to assume a particular shape. For example, he lamented the harm he perceived Atwood's *Survival* would cause to the field of Canadian literary studies and criticism: "that book has done a disservice to Canadian Lit. as a whole" (9 Sept. 1977). In *Survival*, published by House of Anansi Press in 1972, Atwood proposed that the will to survive was the primary mode of thought that dominated Canadian literature—a thesis that McClelland clearly impugned. He confessed to Laurence that the financial success of Atwood's book was wholly uninteresting to him: "But I do care," he added, "that some balanced, reliable guide be available to undo some of the damage that book has done" (6 Apr. 1978). It is possible, too, that he felt threatened by this young woman writer, for Atwood was just thirty-two years old when the book was published. Moreover, her book, which was an immediate bestseller, co-opted McClelland's own project to shape and define Canadian literature. *Survival* was influential and hotly debated at the time, and has come under attack in recent years for making overgeneralizations about literature in Canada and for excluding minority Canadian voices. Threatened or not, he also clearly felt that the thesis delineated in her book did not recognize the richness and diversity of Canadian literature. Through his company's directives, he set out to demonstrate the value and diversity of Canadian literature and to show that it had gone well beyond shallow imitations of British and American literary forms.

McClelland specifically tried to counter *Survival*'s influence on the Canadian canon and Canadian school curricula, in part by organizing the 100 Authors Conference, that is, the University of Calgary conference that listed the one hundred most "significant" books and that took place on 6 April 1978. His attempt to shape literature in Canada through the 1978 Calgary conference was problematic because—like Atwood's *Survival*—it seemed exclusionary. As Laurence noted, the books that had been highlighted and the people invited to the event seemed to privilege McClelland & Stewart, its agenda, and its authors—and therefore came across as an act of shameless self-promotion for the firm. Laurence regarded the event as potentially injuring the firm's reputation rather than forwarding the interests of Canadian literature as a whole. She was reassured when he explained who had been invited and how a "cross-section of 250 at least—scholars, academics, critics, etc." were involved in selecting the titles, and these would not be exclusively those related to his firm (9 Sept. 1977). The argument would surface later, when the New Canadian Library Series, which began with the 1978 Calgary conference, came to the fore of their discussions. Still, his assessment of Atwood's book was to be prophetic: he believed the book did not accurately or fairly convey the thematics of literature in Canada, a view of the book to which many scholars of Canadian literature adhere today.

Although her response to McClelland's assessment of Atwood's book does not survive, several of Laurence's show how she might agree—or vociferously disagree—with him on other occasions, and, in particular, how she coaxed him to publish the work of others, especially women and younger writers. In particular, the letters bear witness to how several Canadian women writers directly benefitted from the kind of weight her opinion carried with McClelland. He put her suggestions into action when he deemed them fit. In several letters, for example, she extensively praised Adele Wiseman's novel, *Crackpot*, and urged him to consider bringing it out through his firm: "It should be published; it's a crime that it is not published" (7 Oct. 1973). Similarly, Laurence suggested that McClelland publish Wiseman's book about Wiseman's mother, *Old Woman at Play*. She argued it was "a part of our heritage which should not get lost" (7 Oct. 1973). Eventually, and no doubt in some measure because of her urgings, he did indeed publish *Crackpot* in 1974, although he refused *Old Woman at Play*, which was published by Clarke, Irwin and Company in 1978. Yet he was suitably impressed by her scouting out of talent and how she used it to serve the interests of the firm, such that he began to search for a means by which she could become integrated into its operations: "I have some thought that you should become Chairman of an Editorial Committee or Publications Committee or something of that sort for McClelland and Stewart" (28 Nov. 1973). Perhaps made only in half-earnest at the time, this kind of offer would later translate more seriously into proposing to Laurence a place on the firm's board of directors—yet another way in which, through her decision-making authority, she would contribute to the shape of the Canadian literary scene.

Women in the Canadian Literary and Publishing Scene

It was certainly not Wiseman alone for whom Laurence advocated: it was women writers as a whole and, indeed, it was even potential female employees for the firm. Just as earlier women authors made her literary success possible, so too Laurence made possible the success of women authors who followed her—in part through her debates and negotiations with McClelland. It is not an overstatement, therefore, to assert that she began to wield considerable influence in terms of the shape of Canadian literature. The correspondence shows she did not assume such a role at the outset of her working relationship with McClelland, but she eventually came to weigh in on matters of national importance. Gradually, by the early 1970s, her confidence noticeably grew, such that she began to recommend potential female editors for his firm, including Phyllis Bruce (3 Aug. 1971), Alice Frick (13 Mar. 1972), and Leslie Cole (12 Oct. 1978), and then, as already observed, potential women authors for his consideration.

One of the most important writers Laurence championed was Alice Munro, new on the Canadian literary scene in this period. Dianne Woodman, who worked for McClelland & Stewart in the 1960s and 1970s, noted that Laurence was a big supporter of Munro (personal interview). Robert Thacker, Munro's biographer, explains that Laurence offered Munro support in 1968 to help publish her first collection of short stories, *Dance of the Happy Shades* (*Alice Munro* 208). Laurence's support for Munro is not surprising, since, in many ways, the content of their work is similar, especially their focus on small towns: Laurence's major works are set in the fictional town of Manawaka, based on her hometown of Neepawa, Manitoba, while Munro's major works are set in the fictional town of Jubilee, based on her hometown of Wingham, Ontario. But it was more than just the content of Munro's writing that Laurence valued. She believed Munro had talent, even though the latter would not gain significant recognition from the Canadian public until some years later. She felt an affinity with Munro when their respective books, *The Diviners* and *Lives of Girls and Women*, were under attack by censors. In a letter to McClelland, she expressed her frustration that she could not publicly support Munro with respect to the censorship scandal: "I ... can't, unfortunately, speak up for Alice's book, as I'm personally involved through my own novel" (13 Feb. 1976). McClelland, like Laurence, respected Munro's writing. He explained to Laurence that he "wrote to a number of non-McClelland and Stewart authors"—including Alice Munro—and "pressed them to attend" the 1978 Calgary conference he organized (6 Apr. 1978). It is understandable why McClelland came to recognize Laurence's status beyond that of author and to take her suggestions with a measure of seriousness, as that of a colleague. Indeed, in almost each instance in which she advised him about an author, he acted on her advice: he either wrote directly to the people involved or had someone at his firm follow up on her recommendations.

In one key moment, as a letter dated 31 July 1975 reveals, Laurence wrote to McClelland about Al Purdy's forthcoming sequel to *Storm Warning*, a poetry collection that had been published by McClelland & Stewart four years earlier. For the sequel, Purdy had circulated a press release asking for more poetry submissions by women because the first volume, Laurence noted, had "an overly large proportion of poetry by men." In order to include the contributions he received from women, many of whom were part of a younger generation of writers, Purdy would have been obliged to push beyond the page-length restrictions imposed by the press. Laurence urged McClelland to make this exception in order to accommodate the work of these younger female poets. It would be "an awful shame," she argued, "if the women poets could not be adequately represented." If he decided to include them, she herself would "work up ... support for the project." In this particular case, McClelland deferred. In such exchanges, it is clear that Laurence wielded some influence over the authors and titles, even the shape and length of the books he chose to publish.

The exchanges about women, if not with or about Laurence in particular, reveal why McClelland may have been sometimes regarded as a male chauvanist—and there is no denying some element of this aspect of his character. However, he was also generous towards women, as writers and as accomplished members of the publishing industry, and was significantly influenced by Laurence herself. He was as important as Laurence in terms of supporting their advancement in the industry. In one feisty exchange with Laurence, on 28 March 1973, he owned up to a suggestion she made about the nature of his character: "What you are saying is that I'm a male c. pig and you are right, of course." In this instance, Laurence had written to McClelland, lamenting the taxes she had to pay as a Canadian citizen living in England. In response, McClelland offered his help and suggested that, unlike Mordecai Richler, who seemed to have no problems with taxes, she did not know about finances. She corrected him and explained how Richler's situation was different from hers: "I may not seem too brilliant finance-wise, but I am in fact much brighter than most people realize. I really do know pretty well what I'm doing" (21 Mar. 1973). McClelland's subsequent apology and declaration that he was a "male c. pig" indicates the shifting ideologies of the period. Laurence had to explain that, as a single, divorced woman, she could be financially intelligent, a notion that was still being integrated into mainstream ideology.

Although McClelland apologized for his presumption in this case, in most situations, he allowed such accusations to take only half-flight. About Anna Porter, who had begun working with his company in 1969, he argued he had taken "a lot of flack from a lot of people during the early years about [her] because she is so beautiful." He conceded, "She may have been hired because she was beautiful, but that's not why she got promoted and moved to the top. She is a person of extraordinary dedication and ability" (18 Aug. 1980). An article that appeared in the Lifestyle section of the *Toronto Sun* on 19 September 1982 (G17), and that McClelland preserved in his papers, confirms this perception in the title "Anna Porter: Brainy Beauty." The article concerns Porter leaving McClelland & Stewart to launch Key Porter Books. In his copy, he circled what she said about him at the end of the article, "that whatever she knows about publishing ... she learned from Jack McClelland": "I will miss the contact with Jack McClelland the most." (McClelland & Stewart Ltd. Fonds, Box 114, File 18).

The letters also showcase the trajectory of her involvement in the company. McClelland first hired Porter in 1969. After a short interview, he took her to examine a boat he was considering purchasing.

There, he is said to have made the offer to hire her on the condition that she read the entirety of the New Canadian Library (the paperbacks of McClelland & Stewart) in a week. As MacSkimming asserts in *The Perilous Trade*, "McClelland didn't buy the boat, but [he] had found the employee who would be his editorial right hand for the next decade" (150). McClelland identified in Porter a truly exceptional professional and business person. After being promoted from editorial coordinator to editor-in-chief by McClelland through the 1970s, Porter became the president of Seal Books, which was co-owned by McClelland & Stewart and the American publishing house, Bantam Books. She would become one of the most successful women to work at McClelland & Stewart. By 1979, Porter co-founded her own publishing house with Michael de Pencier of Key Publishers: Key Porter Books. By the end of the 1980s, she purchased a majority stake in Doubleday Canada. It was with good reason that, upon learning of her maternity leave, McClelland expressed his fears to Laurence that she might not return: "I don't expect to find another Anna Porter in the future, but I remember very well that she turned up when I most needed her and that will happen again" (15 June 1973). He clearly valued and respected Porter's business savvy, her commitment, and her intelligence.

McClelland's assessment of Linda McKnight, an editor at McClelland & Stewart and future president of the company, was expressed in similar terms in the correspondence. When he resigned his position as president of the firm in March 1982, he handed the reins over to McKnight with approval from the board. Although he confessed to Laurence that he was not "a woman's libber by any sense of the word," he felt the timing was right for "a woman [to] take over as boss of our company." He admitted, "Quite honestly, I think she will do a better job than I have done in recent years" (11 Mar. 1982). Yet he remained concerned that Knight lacked the "promotional flair" for which he himself had become renowned. He believed she would therefore need to hire others to market the company properly. In terms of the requirements of marketing, however, he and Laurence were often at odds. In part, this difference of opinion was related to the fact that she approached books from the perspective of an author, rather than that of a publisher whose material interests might differ substantially. At moments like these, he would remind her that she had been conditioned to seeing the market as an author: "There is an essential difference between your attitude and mine. Fair enough, I'm a publisher. While you have devoted your career to writing, I have devoted mine to promoting and building up Canadian authors" (6 Apr. 1978). That difference of opinion, however, might also have been related to the fact that these interests would shape how he engaged very particularly with a female writer, if not female employees.

While women such as Porter and McKnight became high profile at McClelland & Stewart, and would become very successful individuals in the book and business world, others were more understated, although as important to the publishing house and to Laurence and McClelland's relationship. Marge Hodgeman was one such woman. She, for example, demonstrated how multifaceted their communications were and how many people were involved in implementing key decisions related to publishing. Hodgeman served as McClelland's administrative assistant at McClelland & Stewart from 1963 until 1987, when McClelland sold 75 per cent of Seal Books to Anna Porter, essentially removing himself from the company. He had already appointed Linda McKnight as president of the company in 1982. After McClelland left the publishing house in 1987—the year of Laurence's death—he started his own literary agency. Hodgeman remained with him as his assistant until her own death in 1993 (MacSkimming 165), a fact that perhaps indicates how well he worked with women and how therefore devoted they would be to the publishing company.

Hodgeman was instrumental in the company, but she also played an important role in Laurence and McClelland's relationship and communications. In his biography of McClelland, King notes that Hodgeman "became skilful at transcribing Jack's late-night (11 P.M. to 2:30 A.M.) dictation into beautifully written letters" (*Jack* 119). What King does not say, as the correspondence in this volume highlights, is that Hodgeman often enhanced his letters to Laurence by appending her own notes, or by typing or handwriting a few sentences of her own after McClelland's signature. Often these notes, many of which are included in the annotations in this edition, added pertinent information about an issue discussed in the letter. Hodgeman had at her fingertips a certain amount of power: she transcribed McClelland's letters and was the last one to see them before they were sent to Laurence, and she was the first one to see Laurence's letters before they were read by him. Numerous times throughout their correspondence, she wrote back to Laurence in lieu of McClelland; she would explain that he was away and that she would be taking care of business matters for him. Both of them clearly respected her, listened to her, and took her advice. For instance, in the spring of 1965, a Dutch woman, Juliana Allonsius, wrote to McClelland, stating she had $10,000 to invest in an author who would write her memoir on her behalf. He initially solicited Laurence, because he believed the opportunity might be of interest to her. When Allonsius sent him a detailed description of the project, however, he added, "Marge read part of it [and] didn't think much of it" (10 May 1965). Neither did Laurence: she turned down the offer.

Clearly, McClelland valued and promoted the work of many women authors and staff, but he had particular respect and reverence for Laurence's writing. Thus, he worked at cultivating her image as a Canadian author, even one on an international stage. For this reason, he suggested she secure the services of the American agent, Willis Kingsley Wing (Xiques 258). This latter point might seem to suggest that he had his author's best interests at heart—which he certainly had, not only because they affected his own. When she was working on the manuscript of *The Diviners* and expressed frustration at the sheer number of guests she had to entertain in that period, he had a poster produced for her with a "comic take-off of the Ontario coat-of-arms," which stated "no visitors allowed between Monday and Friday. An important work is going on" (Laurence, *Dance on the Earth* 199). However, he was also concerned with putting his authors in touch with agents because that would guarantee the sales of books within and outside of Canada—and, of course, the success of his own company. For example, Laurence had been working on the short stories set in Africa, *The Tomorrow-Tamer and Other Stories*, when he put her in contact with Wing, who was by this point renowned internationally and representing other Canadian authors such as Pierre Berton, Brian Moore, and Jane Rule.

Correspondence between McClelland and Wing about Laurence reveals the male-dominated publishing world that Laurence carefully navigated. Indeed, McClelland and Wing themselves discussed her in specifically gendered terms. In a letter of endorsement to Wing, McClelland wrote,

> *She is a housewife. I would guess she is in her late 30s. ... She has a somewhat unique style, powerful, virile and vigorous—when I read [*This Side Jordan*] I found it hard to believe that the novel had been written by a woman. I'm not suggesting that she is the greatest literary discovery of the last ten years, but she is a serious writer, a writer of quality, and she tells a very good story. ... She is a gal who is serious about her writing. (18 Oct. 1960, qtd. in Xiques 257)*

In this same letter, McClelland further states, "I presume you do handle women (don't we all?), even though yours seems to be a predominantly male list?" (18 Oct. 1960, qtd. in Xiques 257). His reference to Laurence's status as a "housewife" who required "handling," his implication that the "powerful, virile and vigorous" qualities of her novel make it hard to believe it was written "by a woman," and his reference to her as a "gal" are certainly telling and demonstrate how male publishers and agents viewed her not simply as a writer but also more specifically as a woman writer. It is possible he felt that he must put extra emphasis on the quality of her writing to counterbalance her gender, since Wing worked mostly with male authors.

Whatever impediment her gender may have been for the likes of Wing or others, McClelland admired her, as a writer first and foremost, but also as a growing authority on matters related to Canadian literary culture. At various turns, he quite openly expressed deep regard and awe for what Laurence wrote, especially for her final Manawaka book, *The Diviners*. "I read the manuscript in one sitting," McClelland proclaimed, "from about 9 o'clock at night until 4 in the morning." He continued:

> *It's a very moving experience. I ended up in tears during the last half hour. I don't think a man likes to admit it that he sat there like a bloody fool with tears streaming down his face, but I did and I couldn't do anything about it. You are a great writer and you have proved it once again. (12 June 1973)*

His reaction to *The Diviners* was exemplary of the way he felt about both her and the corpus of her work. He took a deep interest in her writing and that of his other authors, and passionately worked in their service and for Canadian literature as a whole.

Marketing and Censorship

If he saw her potential as a writer from the outset and actively publicized her work, how he did so was a matter of continued debate between the two and demonstrated that even the marketing features of her books would not escape Laurence's attention or influence. When *This Side Jordan* was published in 1960, he hosted a cocktail party for its release date and then encouraged her to participate in a promotional tour of western Canada. To both these marketing strategies, she balked, although she eventually, albeit reluctantly, conceded, "I am quite willing to go along with publicity matters, UP TO A POINT" (17 June 1966). She claimed in one letter that she understood "from a publicity point of view" that it was important and that the party at least seemed "to go quite well" (16 Nov. 1960). In another exchange of letters, he persuaded her to accept a complimentary Macintosh word processer as part of a promotional campaign he had arranged with the Apple computer company. She was skeptical and worried that the company would want to photograph her "receiving it from the dealer in

Peterborough." His response was characteristic: "Hell, I don't know, but it is not a bad idea. They just may and I will urge them to do it" (30 Sept. 1985). McClelland valued promotion and did not back away from any means of marketing one of his best-selling authors.

It was less a question of promotion that she abhorred than of Laurence's centrality to the events or publicity stunts of which he conceived. It was, after all, she who would suggest selling "a limited number of records" based on lyrics she devised for *The Diviners* and which were set to the tune she "whistled" to her friend, Ian Cameron (Laurence, *Dance on the Earth* 201); she believed the seven-inch records could be sold along with, and as part of, the book. On a number of occasions, she tried to convince McClelland to publish and promote the record. For instance, she wrote to Hodgeman and asked her to set up a lunch meeting with him so she could "talk to him about the record" (27 Nov. 1973). In this endeavour, she also solicited others, who then wrote to him in her support. Finally, he put an end to her manifold efforts: "Re: the record. What are you trying to do to me? We got 19 letters in today from Regina and, if you are going to be giving speeches across the country and urge people to write to me saying the record should be in the book, I'll have to get an assistant for Marge to handle the flood of material" (25 Oct. 1973). He did, however, agree to the production of the record, albeit in limited numbers. Contrary to Laurence's wishes about how to sell the record, McClelland also opted to sell it separately from the book.[2]

The correspondence shows that, at times, McClelland conceded to Laurence's ideas about marketing, about her books, about other authors—even if he needed to be persuaded to do so. Indeed, more often than not, he was especially supportive of her when it came to the public's perception of her writing, and he willingly offered his help. When it was first published, *The Diviners* was immensely popular and topped the Canadian bestseller list for over sixty consecutive weeks (Duncan). However, the novel was also harshly criticized, and there was a movement to ban the book from schools in the Peterborough County town of Lakefield, Ontario. As Mark Cohen has elsewhere examined, the dispute was first sparked by Robert Buchanan, a teacher and head of the English department at Lakefield Secondary School, who insisted upon teaching the novel after a group of conservative religious Christians demanded it be removed from the curricula. The debate extended from the beginning of February to the end of May in 1976 (89, 90). The matter resurfaced again in 1985, when Buchanan was taken to task by a municipal councillor, Helen Trotter, from Burleigh-Anstruther, Ontario, who predicated her opposition on the "profanities and sex in the novel" (Cohen 116). Although Cohen explores the public indictment of and issues of censorship in relation to this novel, his study does not draw upon the letters exchanged between Laurence and McClelland, since these were unavailable to the public at the time of his book's publication. Instead, he calls upon the brief remarks she made on the subject in letters to Ernest Buckler and Hugh MacLennan; he also refers to one of Laurence's unpublished manuscripts, a copy of which remains in the archives at McMaster University, which she drafted as a way of "transforming the events" of the period into an imaginative resolution (90). In correspondence with Buckler on the subject, she wrote, "If I'd made it all up, I couldn't have done better" (Laurence, *A Very Large Soul* 40). Cohen argues that the unpublished manuscript itself, however, reveals that she held ambivalent views on the subject. On the one hand, she espoused freedom of expression, but not at the expense of debasing others. Real pornography, of which her novel was *not* an example, did "damage not only to those who participate[d] in its making but also to women who [were] subjected to the degrading attitudes absorbed by men who watch[ed] it" (Cohen 118). On the other hand, she also saw the potential of regulating such representations without jeopardizing other forms of legitimate discourse (Cohen 118).

The manuscript, however, was not published and would never accomplish what the letters here successfully do: track Laurence's views on the subject and demonstrate how she and McClelland worked directly and cooperatively to shape the literary terrain and grapple with issues such as censorship, even as they directly affected—or impeded—Laurence's own career. Their letters thus showcase their evolving attitudes towards censorship in general. McClelland wanted to know how much Laurence expected him to intervene: "How serious is this situation? Do you want us to get into the act? How do you feel about it? Is it something we should be attempting to publicize? Or should we just play it easy for the present?" (11 Feb. 1976). She indicated there was not much McClelland could do, but his desire to step into action on behalf of the press was admirable, although not surprising, given how much he valued her writing. She began to adopt his point of view in these matters. About a misinformed and perhaps even mildly offensive interview related to *The Fire-Dwellers*, she observed, "As you say, it is probably good publicity and one must just see it in perspective, I suppose" (4 Apr. 1969).

In view of what he regarded as unsolicited publicity, McClelland was far more sanguine. He took even the protests related to *The Diviners* with a sense of equanimity. In more than one instance, they wrote to one another about those who were trying to censor that book and others, such as *A Jest of God* and *The Stone Angel*, and who called them "demeaning to human nature" (Laurence, *Dance on the Earth* 215). For example, when McClelland learned that Anita Bryant, former Miss Oklahoma beauty pageant winner and opponent of what would have been termed "gay rights" in the period, had scheduled a trip to Toronto in 1978 to support banning certain books from schools, he reassured Laurence that all publicity was indeed good publicity:

> *We must stamp out these dirty books. I am all for encouraging people [in this attitude] because this sells more books. ... These censors are so crazy. This recent censorship of the film [*Pretty Baby*] in Ontario has given this film the biggest boost it could get. (17 Apr. 1978)*

He supported Laurence wholeheartedly in her fight against the suppression of literary freedom of expression. Elsewhere, in an interview about the censorship of Laurence's books, he said, "There is a basic sickness attached to people who try to remove works of literature from the curricula" (Duncan). Still, McClelland noted the "crazy" censors could actually do her books a service by calling greater attention to them.

In another instance, Laurence wrote to him to express her concern that her children's book, *The Christmas Birthday Story*, might elicit calls for censorship. She anticipated this reaction to the book because, in it, she emphasized a female aspect to God and stated that Mary and Joseph did not object to whether their son was a boy or a girl: in other words, she was writing against the patriarchal grain of the Christian story. She wrote to McClelland, "The little book *may* be condemned by the same rednecks who condemned *The Diviners* as blasphemous," but, she added, "I hope that doesn't happen—what a hell of a way to sell books. I've had enough of being called nasty names" (8 Aug. 1980). Laurence held a strong position against the censorship of literature; she was deeply hurt by those who believed her books should be banned, a view she expressed not only privately in these letters but elsewhere. She stated, "I resent very bitterly people grouping my writing with pornographic magazines. They do not know the difference between serious writing and writing that is exploitative and sensational. But I'm fighting. I'm not going to crawl away" (Duncan).

Laurence did not like being in the spotlight, positive or negative. The various parties and tours that McClelland arranged for her thus remained points of frequent tension between them. Even though she suffered from anxiety during public events, McClelland insisted on her attendance for promotional purposes. She was, she admitted, more amenable to the launch party he organized for *The Diviners*, when "a woman in the publicity department had an inspiration" that she could not resist: a diviner was invited to the launch, located on the grounds of the Ontario Science Centre, and found "a place where two streams of water met." A divining contest was held and even "members of the media who had come to scoff were babbling with excitement" (King, *The Life of Margaret Laurence* 211).

If this event was successful, the tension that ensued as a result of McClelland's insistence about her attendance at such events reached its peak over the 1982 literary dinner he organized to raise funds for the Writers' Development Trust.[3] Their correspondence shows that McClelland had worked hard to persuade Laurence to attend the 1982 literary dinner, a "hard sell" that she claimed was the "closest thing to blackmail as I have ever encountered." She agreed to go to the "damn dinner if it kills me" (28 June 1982)—and, as she anticipated, it was a far greater ordeal than even McClelland himself could have anticipated. He had sold tickets to patrons to sit with particular authors. Among other sources of disappointment, if not outright embarrassment, the patron who had purchased tickets for the table at which Laurence was sitting as guest of honour neglected to distribute them to others, and she sat at an empty table with virtually no one to speak to for most of the evening. For Laurence, it had been an abysmal failure, although a resounding success for the trust, for which more than one hundred thousand dollars had been raised.

Yet she was initially reluctant to speak to McClelland about the matter, because he "worked so hard, not to say insanely, over this idiotic project" (2 Oct. 1982). As a letter to her agent, John Cushman, reveals, she was indignant about having to be exploited for a fund-raising event that did little to further her career or to endear herself to those in attendance. She swore to Cushman that she would "never take part in this kind of farce again, under any circumstances" (2 Oct. 1982). After some consideration, she sent McClelland a copy of the letter about the event, which she originally wrote for her agent—a letter that is included in this volume. He was deeply apologetic. She had, he declared, every right to be "embarrassed and justifiably angry at what happened": "When something of that sort happens, [there] is no way of undoing the harm and the hurt: and no degree of explanations or excuses serve[s] a useful purpose" (8 Oct. 1982). Yet Laurence assured him that "my attending the Dinner really was an expression of loyalty to you": "We don't always agree, Jack, and have had some royal disagreements, as you will recall, but you have been my publisher for 22 years, and ... I owe you a deep debt of gratitude" (9 Oct. 1982). She also confirmed that the dinner had been a resounding success, not only in terms of the money raised but also in terms of the greater visibility the trust received.

If Laurence conceded to this particular marketing and fundraising scheme, she did not always easily do so, especially if she felt that McClelland assumed a position that emphasized her gender inappropriately. About her collection of essays, *Heart of a Stranger*, for example, she balked when he spoke of the tactics he was planning on adopting for its promotion: "I think the trick here is fine design and typography. ... I think we could make it into a very fine-looking small book. It will make a great gift item and I think it will be widely read" (17 Feb. 1976). Laurence took umbrage. She registered offence at what she perceived as the gendered inflections in his remarks.

> *What a good idea about making the book a "good gift item"! Had you considered the vast possibilities of selling each copy individually wrapped in pink tissue paper, tied about with a wide pink ribbon? Or perhaps a tiny tasteful bunch of plastic forget-me-nots? ... Similarly your idea of having some competent commercial artist "dress the book up with some sketches and drawings," "mood background sketches," as you so wittily phrase it, seems to me nothing less than scintillating. (23 Feb. 1976)*

That she saw the book as being marketed along the lines of gender elicited her ire. Consistently in their interactions, she was determined to manage her career in professional terms that respected her autonomy, her intelligence, and her ability, and to represent herself publicly in terms that did not emphasize her gender.

Still, McClelland's vision for and enactment of the promotional book tour were unprecedented. Although Laurence often resisted being involved with the direct promotion of her books, there is no denying that his persistent marketing ploys, if unconventional, even radical, were advantageous for sales. They set a new standard not only in Canada but also throughout the world. Literary tours and festivals did not become popular until the 1970s and 1980s. By this time, McClelland had already been putting his heart and soul into them for years. Promotional book tours and literary festivals flourish today, a testament to his legacy. So too does Canadian literature's reputation internationally, the culmination of which was recognized by Canadian short story writer Alice Munro winning the Nobel Prize in Literature in 2013—the most prestigious literary prize in the world. Laurence and McClelland were at the roots of this widespread, even international, success.

Politics and Controversies

Laurence yet remained unflinching in her desire to be respected and heard on her own terms and to advocate for the writing community effectively, and this was nowhere more clear than when she was nominated to serve on the board of directors for McClelland & Stewart. In 1977, the board included Anna Porter, Peter Taylor, and Larry Ritchie, among others. Laurence was initially impressed and claimed to be surprised that "the publishing business was a whole lot more complex" than she had realized. As an afterthought, she noted in a letter to McClelland, "I can see you smiling sardonically and saying, 'Maybe that'll teach her not to rush in with lunatic suggestions'" (17 Mar. 1977). But, of course, the very kinds of "lunatic suggestions" of which he was apprehensive surfaced almost immediately, in March 1977, when she vehemently opposed the publishing of a book about the subject of Iran by Roloff Beny, his second one with McClelland & Stewart. After attending only one meeting as a board member, she tendered her resignation—one that was to be later revoked—and argued that publishing a book that had been "commissioned by a ruling regime" that represented a "medieval authoritarian divine-right-of-kings outlook" might prove to be embarrassing for the company (17 Mar. 1977). Laurence was overruled.

Yet her protest against this publication need not be interpreted as a "lunatic" one, despite her own representation of some of her suggestions as such. Rather, it was an ethical imperative that led her to object to a book that might present Iran as romantic or exotic. In 1977, Iran was undergoing a revolution as citizens sought to overthrow the shah, who was distributing money from the oil-wealthy country unevenly and dictating a repressive regime. The book she protested against, *Iran: Elements of Destiny*, published in 1978, included large glossy photographs and depicted Iran's beauty. It showed neither the country's diversity of peoples nor those who suffered under the contemporary political climate. The shah himself wrote an introduction to the book, which to her sense of things elided the material realities of the regime. McClelland had gone to Iran to meet with the shah before the book's publication, as Laurence notes in a letter to McClelland (23 Jan. 1977). She was wary of affiliating herself with those who supported what she believed were morally suspect regimes; moreover, as a member of the board at McClelland & Stewart, she felt it was her duty to resist any such affiliation. Although McClelland & Stewart decided to proceed with the publication of Beny's book on Iran, McClelland expressed sympathy and understanding towards Laurence's perspective: "There is no doubt about the fact that there is some validity to your point of view," he noted, and then contextualized her response by adding that "several of our international publishers have already expressed their reservations" (21 Mar. 1977).

Beyond this correspondence, Laurence consistently refused to cooperate with those involved with fossil fuel production and its profits. She stood against multinational oil companies, who she believed were exploitative. In 1974, for example, she refused to write a script for the television company, Neilson-Ferns, because Imperial Oil was sponsoring it. In addition, throughout the 1970s and 1980s, she was an active member of Energy Probe, a nongovernmental organization that opposes nuclear power and oil exploitation (Davis, "Margaret Laurence's Correspondence"). Her stance against multinational companies such as Imperial Oil was aligned with her stance on nationalism: her belief that Canada must embrace its diversity and distinguish itself from Britain and the United States. Imperial Oil "had been under the control of America generally, and the Rockefeller family specifically, since the early twentieth century" (Davis, "Margaret Laurence's Correspondence" 63). However, as Mel Hurtig explains, the company "quite successfully misled a large percentage of Canadians into believing that it [was] a Canadian company" (qtd. in Davis, "Margaret Laurence's Correspondence" 64). Neilson-Ferns and Imperial Oil wanted Laurence to write the television script—tellingly, about the history of immigration in Canada—because she supported nationalist values and exemplified them in her work. Laurence refused to accept Imperial Oil's representation of itself as Canadian and its claim that it was supportive of Canada's peoples and its environment. Therefore, her statement to McClelland that she could not support the company's publication of Beny's book on Iran was part of her larger ethical imperative that valued her conceptualization of Canadian nationalism and abhorred corporate capitalism. She believed in the diversity of the people and places of Canada and refused to "sell out" to imperialism, Big Oil, and the exploitation of peoples within and beyond her own country.

Laurence's exchange with McClelland about Beny's book is also an example of how she tried, through her publisher, to shape Canadian literature according to her strong nationalist and anti-colonialist beliefs—including the ways in which Canadian writers represented those outside of the country. As Laurence made strides as an author, gaining self-assurance with each successful novel that came into print, she also began to wade into these kinds of debates related to the publication of books—and especially with McClelland himself. The letters show not only her desire to persuade McClelland to adopt certain points of view but also her direct participation in different councils and associations in order to effect change for the publishing conditions that had an impact on both authors and publishers. Conversely, the consideration he paid to her ideas and the length of time he took to respond, often writing letters that were pages upon pages in length and that outlined the nature of the issue that had arisen and the way it might be resolved, reveals his respect for her intelligence and the degree of influence he believed she wielded as "den mother or block parent to the whole bloody writing community of Canada" (20 May 1977). Consistently, McClelland gave her suggestions and observations careful thought, sometimes agreeing, sometimes disagreeing—and not only about what authors to consider for publication or for eventual inclusion in the New Canadian Library Series, as one earlier example shows, but also about issues of equal or greater importance. On occasion in their letters, Laurence and McClelland discussed international politics, particularly colonial practices. In fact, the first time she ever met him, she discussed the topic of colonization with him because she had just read Octave Mannoni's book, *Prospero and Caliban: The Psychology of Colonization*: "I was glad indeed to meet you at last. ... I promise in future to refrain from explaining to you the more obscure points of the psychology of colonization" (16 Nov. 1960). The publishing house's readers criticized the manuscript of *This Side Jordan*, Laurence's first novel, because they thought she unfairly delineated unsympathetic British colonial characters. The latter was particularly problematic, because she had to respond to readers from publishing companies, with varying views, from three different countries—Canada, England, and the United States. To most of the readers' suggestions, she conceded, although she finally decided she could not edit further: "I cannot help wondering ... how many times this sort of pruning would be possible. I might turn the novel into a short story, if I were given a year or so" (13 May 1960).

As their letters show, there are also moments when Laurence specifically discussed with McClelland her experiences in Africa. She contemplated what she learned there and how she could represent in her writing the years she spent in Somalia and Ghana, her vision of those countries, and her anti-colonial beliefs. For instance, referring to her life in Somalia, she explained to him that, "in the final analysis, it was through acquaintance with some of the English there that I came to realize something of the common thread that runs through the lives of all Europeans who are drawn to distant lands, and, in this way, to realize my own reasons for preferring to live abroad" (1 Sept. 1962). Her books about Africa—*The Prophet's Camel Bell, This Side Jordan,* and *The Tomorrow-Tamer*—express her lack of sympathy with colonization, although not in a direct manner. She explained in a letter to Nigerian writer Chinua Achebe that, in her novels, she had been aiming to address "the sense of social injustice, an outrage that has to be communicated in fiction through the dilemmas and tragedies of human individuals and not in any didactic way" (3 June 1984). Laurence claimed that her writing sought, in part, to contest previous Westerners' accounts of "quaint tribal customs or depraved Europeans" (see "City Woman Writes Book"). McClelland's enthusiasm for Laurence's books about Africa indicated his agreement with and endorsement of Laurence's views. Her eventual shift from addressing colonialism in her writing about Africa to addressing multiculturalism in her writing about Canada demonstrated her consistency in terms of espousing more democratic value systems.

In her letters to McClelland, Laurence was attentive to international politics but, as might be expected, also to national politics: her engagement in Canadian politics contributed to her vision of and for Canadian literature. For example, she mentioned that Jack Ludwig was engaged in rewriting large sections of his 1973 novel, *A Woman of Her Age,* since "the scene had changed so much [in Montreal] because of the October crisis" (4 Apr. 1972). A significant time in Canadian history, the October Crisis comprises a series of events related to the 1970 kidnapping of two government officials by the Quebec separatist group FLQ (Front de libération du Québec). This led Prime Minister Pierre Trudeau to invoke the War Measures Act, the third time in Canadian history that a prime minister had done so but the first during a period of peace. Laurence's reference to the October Crisis in the context of Ludwig's book demonstrates how intimately interconnected federal politics and literature may be, especially during the decades in which a distinct Canadian literature emerged. Her own work is intertwined with federal politics, insofar as she takes up Métis history in the

Red River area of Manitoba in *The Diviners* and suggests the government's role in Métis oppression. They both valued historical and political aspects of literature, as is evident in Laurence's own work and the discussion of the October Crisis in relation to Ludwig's book.

The Writers' Union of Canada and the Rise of the Paperback Novel

In the realm of history and politics, the author and her publisher often agreed, but in May 1977, a conflict arose between them with respect to a different kind of politics. Their disagreement was related to Laurence's involvement with the Writers' Union of Canada (TWUC) and would have a bearing on the rights of the independent writer in Canada. The Writers' Union of Canada, an organization that continues to advocate for Canadian writers' rights and economic viability, had been founded several years earlier, in the spring of 1973. During this period, Laurence agreed to serve as interim chair, as its constitution was being formed and an agreement was being proposed that would serve as a template for a contract to be adopted in negotiations between authors and publishers, and upon which all its members would be asked to vote (Laurence, *Dance on the Earth* 206). The union's existence may be seen as part of her early efforts, even as part of her legacy in relation to advocacy: its constitution was essential, she argued, to support writers, to provide them with advice about the publication process and to create a writing community that extended across the country. Indeed, years later, on 5 November 1982, author Jane Rule, who headed up the membership committee, would write to Laurence to acknowledge her legacy and how much she had done for the union: "The tribal spirit you encouraged has not disintegrated into drunken brawls ... the general meeting is still a place of affirming our participation in the cultural life of our country. ... It is your spirit of welcome to new members and less important members which for those of us who have stayed on continues to be an inspiration" (Jane Rule Fonds).

From Laurence's perspective, an agreement or a constitution was especially needed to protect Canadian writers from less-than-scrupulous publishers, while providing aspiring writers with a proper support network. As Laurence noted in her memoir, the union addressed how writers often felt "isolated, separated from one another by vast geographical distances and differences" (*Dance on the Earth* 207). She insisted in her correspondence with McClelland that "you surely cannot claim that no writers in this country have been ripped off by their publishers." However much she appreciated his business dealings with her—and even that was not consistently the case with respect to matters of publicity—she argued she had "seen contracts offered by publishers ... that are a disgrace" (15 June 1977). She added that he was "paternalistic" in his dealings with writers when he appeared to know what was best for *all* authors. The publishing terrain was considerably wider than McClelland & Stewart, she argued, and Laurence knew the repercussions were considerably broader.

Her frustration surfaced when she realized the limitations of her influence on the board, which she hoped to use to benefit the Writers' Union of Canada, especially in her debate with McClelland about the agreement being forged to protect writers who were members of TWUC. In terms of the former, Laurence observed, "The board is only a figurehead. ... Every time I raise my voice, or write long letters to Jack, he listens attentively or replies in an equally long letter and pays not a scrap of heed" (qtd. in King, *Jack* 320). The real bone of contention between them was related to the fact that, in September 1977, Laurence decided to write a letter directly to the members of their board about the agreement being forged, without informing McClelland. Nonetheless, when she circulated the document to the board, he was singularly unimpressed: "I have, through the years, developed a standard procedure for dealing with such communications. I have a rubber stamp, which in antique English prints the word 'bullshit'" (20 May 1977). However, he noted, he had not yet found the "temerity to use it in dealing either with distinguished authors or Members of our Board of Directors"—not entirely a means of placating Laurence, for he was not always renowned for mollifying or working more cooperatively with his more prominent authors when the need arose. He claimed in interviews, at least, that the "author is the only important person": "I've fired people who forgot that" (qtd. in Friskney, *New Canadian Library* 31).

Yet, in spite of Laurence's protestations, McClelland adamantly opposed TWUC's attempt to draft a contract that its members desired all publishers to sign. The differences between publishers and writers, their competing agendas, show themselves here. Laurence was indignant.

> *You seem all along to be saying that, as a publisher, you know what is best for the writers whom you publish, and that the writer had better not lift his or her voice at all in the matter of the Agreement. I'm sure this cannot be your view, but this is how you make it sound in your letter. The union has at no time said that our Agreement should be signed in its entirety in any one case. Rather, it is a guide to our members when discussing their Agreements with their publishers. It covers a wide range of circumstances, because, in this country, as I mentioned in my previous Memo, there are many different kinds of publishing houses and many different circumstances when publishing books of various kinds. But we do assume that a publisher will be willing to discuss the matter of the Agreement, either with the writer himself or herself, or with an agent. (15 June 1977)*

As Laurence's letter makes clear, part of TWUC's complaints were also related significantly to authorial contracts. It demanded the release of authors from contracts should the publishing house with which one published be sold to another and asked that authors be permitted to retain copyright of their own work. The agreement, moreover, would guarantee greater consistency in terms of the contracts authors secured from publishers.

McClelland refused to cooperate with TWUC—and with Laurence herself. He argued that the document they were circulating was "dangerous" because it established an "adversar[ial] relationship between author and publisher" (26 May 1977). That Laurence had proposed a resignation once before signals the means by which she thought she could persuade McClelland about the error of his ways. Indeed, even he recognized the potential for the kind of tactics she might adopt, including refusing the agreement for her next book with McClelland & Stewart, or other such measures:

> *Her only possible form of retaliation here would be to insist that we sign a* T.W.U.C. *agreement for her next book. If she did, her agent would shoot himself immediately and if she did, I would say no. I wouldn't sign that agreement—as a matter of principle—with Jesus Christ if he reappeared and offered us his memoirs. (20 May 1977)*[4]

His response was clear: McClelland would not relent. Ultimately, he regarded TWUC as a "fairly useless organization except socially" and its committee as operating with "the motive of destroying the publishing industry in Canada" (26 May 1977). He rejected meeting with its representatives because, he claimed, he could not find a proper representative within his own company to grapple comprehensively with all the elements of the agreement, and because of the potential inflammatory, even adversarial, relations that such a contract implied between writers and publishers: "Does it really make sense to set up a model agreement that is going to make 95% of the authors in Canada feel they are being screwed by their publishers?" (26 May 1977). As much as McClelland wanted to protect his authors' rights, he would not take any action that compromised what he perceived as those of the publishing company.

Still, McClelland *did* circulate her letter to the board, members of which expressed support for her position, as he observed on 26 May 1977: "On balance, then, I would say that the Board tended to accept your point-of-view and feel that some sort of explanation should be sent to TWUC. Even more important in the order of priority was that some sort of olive branch be offered to you." That response indicates the place she assumed and the respect she elicited from other board members, and that she could marshal together sufficient support from various quarters to challenge him, if not to change his point of view. He was expected by the board to "tender the olive branch," a situation with which he was not altogether pleased. He observed that his branch would *not,* in fact, come from southern Italy, where the "sweetest olives" are found, but rather "from the North" (26 May 1977)—a somewhat bitter defeat for McClelland. Ultimately, this disagreement was one that was never to be completely resolved between them, notwithstanding the fact they continued to maintain a healthy respect for one another.

Laurence and McClelland were to find themselves at odds again over the forging of the New Canadian Library Series, the first paperback book series in English Canada. The significance of their disagreement is rendered clear by contextualizing it in the history behind the production of the NCL, a history that has already been thoroughly explored elsewhere by Janet Friskney. As Friskney observed, the series, which became an important part of Canadian literary culture, was launched in 1958 under the general editorship of Malcolm Ross (Friskney, *New Canadian Library* 10). However, Ross, a Canadian professor, literary critic, and author, had broached the idea of "a Canadian literary reprint series in paperback" to McClelland several years earlier, in 1952 (29). In the 1950s, it was common practice to publish books of literature in hardcover rather than in paperback. Rendering paperbacks of Canadian "classics" would make them available as "teaching texts rather than scholarly editions" and more economically affordable for university students and secondary schools (Friskney, "Case Study" 234). It therefore followed that Canadian titles would be more accessible and in greater demand. Although the series "struggled financially" at its outset, post-secondary educational institutions "showed a steady increase in courses in Canadian literature," as more and more NCL titles were adopted (234). With the NCL, McClelland & Stewart was on the leading edge of the paperback revolution in Canada. As Roy MacSkimming explains,

> *Ross's proposal [for the* NCL*] was visionary in a way scarcely comprehensible today. The paperback revolution still hadn't arrived in Canada. Even in the United States, quality paperbacks, led by Doubleday's Anchor Books, had only recently begun to emulate the success of Penguin Books by making serious literature available at affordable prices. (58)*

The shift from the production of hardcover books to paperbacks signified a vital change in the consumption of literature by the Canadian public. Inclusion in the series would, to a certain extent, determine the canon of Canadian literature in the coming years, a fact Laurence recognized. Several of her letters, therefore, focus on books she believed should be part of the series, including her own.

When McClelland assumed general editorship of the NCL, he applied the ideas he prized about Canadian nationalism and its literary life. He suggested writers such as Frederick Philip Grove, Morley Callaghan, Susanna Moodie, and W.O. Mitchell be included in the first list. When Laurence understood that the selection of the one hundred NCL titles was poised to begin, she conferred with McClelland about the process by which it would transpire. Although she was reassured that several key people would be involved in the selection process, she remained firm that the selection committee eschew "the old brigade" of "men and all academics" and instead include women, younger academics (such as John Moss), and high school teachers who taught Canadian literature. About the latter group, she noted that many had worked "to put together the educational guides in Canlit for high schools, the booklets which are not being published by the Writers' Development Trust" (24 Aug. 1977). She also expressed concern that the rights and permissions for books printed by different publishing houses would limit those books that could be published as part of the NCL and subsequently undermine the list of the "preferred" one hundred Canadian books by giving the impression that "these 100 books are *all* that are needed to teach any number of Canlit courses in schools and universities" (24 Aug. 1977).

McClelland was not to yield in this instance. Although he reassured her that the selection committee would comprise "experts," he scoffed at the notion that high school teachers could be conceived as such: "there are bloody few teachers in Canadian schools who know anything about Canadian Lit" (9 Sept. 1977). He argued that other books would remain in print, even if not part of the New Canadian Library Series, and that perhaps the list was an embarrassment to her, "because [she was] at the head of it" (6 Apr. 1978). It is no wonder that Laurence felt compelled to declare in one of her letters to him, "There isn't one of us [writers] who hasn't cursed your bloodymindedness ... your Christly ego." Yet she conceded that "there also is not one of your writers who does not, at heart, appreciate ... your admirable ability to take risks; and above all, the fact that you damn well have always *cared* about what you published" (6 Apr. 1971). McClelland was not greatly perturbed by these challenges. Indeed, when the issue about the series surfaced again in October 1980, he wrote to say that he wished to speak to her "about what we are going to do about The New Canadian Library." Moreover, he allowed her to choose the order of appearance her books were to make in the NCL. Her opinion ultimately did matter to him.

They did find common ground over the case related to Coles bookstores' "practice of selling remaindered U.S. editions of Canadian books" (King, *Jack* 277). The case specifically affected Pierre Berton and Farley Mowat, who apparently were on the "verge ... of entering one of the stores, destroying the American editions of Berton and Mowat titles from which the authors received low or no royalties, and getting themselves arrested" (277–78). The problem, as became evident when the case went before the courts, was related to the Copyright Act, which Jack Cole used to his advantage. Apparently, he claimed that bookstores should be able to offer "books at the lowest cost" rather than allow the public to assume the costs of "artificially high book prices" (278). However, as Berton's case showed in particular, lower costs translated into no royalties for him whatsoever. An American company had taken two of his books, *The National Dream* and *The*

Last Spike, and published them in a single, one-volume abridgement, titled *The Impossible Railway*—it was "a remainder (unsold stock sold at a cut-rate price), for which Berton was not entitled to a cent" (278). McClelland appealed to André Ouellet, the minister of consumer and corporate affairs (1974–1976), but the latter was not sufficiently moved to deal with the situation in any immediate sense. Upon reading a letter by Ouellet that appeared in the *Globe and Mail*, McClelland wrote to Laurence in a fury about the ineffectual measures the government was taking in relation to the issue: "As of today, I know, and Margaret you wouldn't believe it, they have set up such a wall of nonsensical bureaucratic red tape that it deserves to be in a shrine for posterity in some sort of Alice in Wonderland type locale" (11 Apr. 1975). Nonetheless, neither McClelland nor Laurence were to back down but continued to participate directly in advocating for better copyright measures.

Laurence was extremely concerned—and felt vindicated in terms of her earlier assertions of the importance of the Writers' Union of Canada agreement. Further lobbying resulted in legal changes such that the importation of American editions could be impeded if "satisfactory evidence of the legal title to the copyright" could be produced. Still, she mused, the government had been "awfully lax" and the procedure Ouellet finally provided was not clear. Too many unanswered questions remained: for example, she asked, "What action should we all be taking? Do we have to provide the gov't with one copy of each of our books?" To this she added, "I think probably the Writers' Union should circularize all members, so that individual writers can take the necessary steps, if necessary" (7 Apr. 1975). By this point, McClelland might have somewhat appreciated the existence of the union in this context, even if he was never to admit to it openly.

Whatever his concerns about the union, McClelland noted repeatedly that his authors were of utmost importance to his publishing house and that his authors secured McClelland & Stewart's success. He was loyal to his authors and supported them; he worked with them closely, not only through the writing of their early books but also throughout their writing lives. Many Canadian writers who have achieved national and international recognition were unknown before McClelland helped to build their careers. His vision for a publishing house that published solely Canadian authors was viewed by other publishers at the time as ridiculous and certain to fail: in the early 1960s, many believed there were few Canadian authors worth reading. McClelland's focus on Canadian writers turned out to be the driving force behind the publishing house and the very reason the company achieved success over many decades. By writing books that became Canadian bestsellers, Laurence helped to make McClelland's career; by promoting and marketing those books to their fullest potential, he helped to make hers. What is less known and what is revealed by this correspondence is that their work was synergistic and had a direct impact on the promulgation of Canadian writing and the publishing industry.

Changing Times in Literature and Publishing

Other aspects of Laurence's writing world and McClelland's publishing world no longer flourish in the face of globalization, free market economies, large book chains, and digitization. McClelland knew that a publisher's belief in and support for the authors of the house made its success, but that value has perhaps changed. As journalist Russell Smith puts it, "Writers find that a belief in an author, as opposed to a particular book—an author as a long term investment—tends to exist less and less" (R3). As their letters indicate, McClelland saw significant changes in the publishing industry from the 1960s through the 1980s. One of these changes involved his agreement to a partnership with the American firm Bantam Books to create Seal Books in 1977, a deal that was discussed in some detail by Laurence and McClelland. But he might not have anticipated the extent to which Canadian publishing houses would fold, as Douglas & McIntyre did in 2012, or give way to being subsumed by major American firms—as his own firm would, when it was fully acquired by Penguin Random House Canada in 2012. Nor would he have thought his fight against Coles bookstore, an attempt to protect the rights and royalties of Canadian authors, was only the beginning: that Coles and SmithBooks would merge to become Chapters Inc. in 1995, and then Chapters would merge with Indigo to become Indigo Books and Music Inc. in 2001—the largest book retailer in Canada; or that book sales would become so caught up in corporate capitalism that "the main retailers that one needs to sell one's books to the general public—Indigo, Costco and Amazon—do not even self-identify primarily as booksellers" (Smith R3). Their correspondence yet illustrates how corporate capital was already affecting the growth and direction of McClelland & Stewart: the diversification of editions (under Seal Books, for example) and McClelland's acceptance of $260,000 worth of Apple Macintosh computers for his writers provide just two pertinent instances of vast changes in the globalized publishing world.

Their legacy thus survives, in no small measure because their relationship was professional and respectful, but also a dynamic, personal, and productive one with far-reaching implications. They worked hard together to create, shape, and promote what would become known as great Canadian literature. The correspondence between them is remarkable in its broad engagement of various facets of public Canadian socio-political culture: the sales and royalties of Canadian books, both hardcover and paperback; censorship in Canadian schools; the rise of Canadian literature as a legitimate field of study in secondary schools and universities; and Canadian nation building at a time when the nation-state was reconceptualizing itself as multicultural. Laurence helped McClelland determine Canadian literature from the 1960s through the 1980s, as she rightfully argued for the inclusion of women writers, western Canadian writers, and young and emergent writers. Ultimately, Laurence and McClelland's letters—humorous, personal, intellectual—testify to the degree of influence these two figures wielded and the degree to which they contributed to the proliferation and consumption of a new body of national literature.

NOTES

1. Richler's novel is about a Jewish boy in 1940s Montreal. As Laurence and McClelland might have anticipated, over time this novel has come to receive high critical acclaim and become part of the Canadian literary canon.
2. In her memoir, *Dance on the Earth*, Laurence does not mention the disagreement with McClelland about whether or not the record should accompany *The Diviners*. Therein, she suggests McClelland agreed to its production all along.
3. The Writers' Development Trust, whose name was later changed to the Writers' Trust of Canada, was founded in 1976 by Margaret Laurence, Margaret Atwood, Graeme Gibson, Pierre Berton, and others, and is a charitable organization that celebrates the accomplishments of Canadian writers.
4. McClelland refers to Laurence here in the third person, because he is explaining to her what he would say at a McClelland & Stewart board meeting. "That could be the way it could go at the board meeting," he observed after this statement.

I | *Beginnings, 1959–1969*

West 21st, 4 March 1959

Dear Mrs. Laurence:

I have just learned from a mutual friend[1] that you have completed a novel. From the very brief description that we have received, it sounds like one we could be very interested in. Although we are essentially Canadian publishers, we are in a position to arrange simultaneous publication in the U.S.A. and the United Kingdom.

I would be delighted if you would let us have the opportunity to consider the manuscript.

Yours sincerely,
J.G. McClelland

1. The friend who introduced Laurence and McClelland was Gordon Elliott (King, *Jack* 83), a professor at Simon Fraser University. Laurence and Elliott remained friends and wrote to one another throughout their lives. On 20 April 1960, McClelland wrote to Elliott and said, "I have been intending to tell you how very much I appreciated your suggestion re: Margaret Laurence. I feel very much indebted to you" (McClelland & Stewart Ltd. Fonds, Box 26).

Hollinger, 20 March 1959

Dear Mr. McClelland:

Thank you for your letter of March 4th, and for your interest in my novel, *This Side Jordan*.[1] I am mailing the manuscript to you today.[2]

Sincerely,
Margaret Laurence [signed]
Margaret Laurence

1. Laurence's first novel, *This Side Jordan*, is a work of fiction that takes as its subject the end of British colonial rule in Africa's Gold Coast (now Ghana), where Laurence lived from 1952 to 1957. Laurence's characters include both Africans and British colonials, and she addresses how those characters handle drastic changes to government rule, changes such as the introduction of "Africanization"—the policy by which British employees of the colonial government were replaced by African ones. The book was published by St. Martin's Press in the United States.
2. Upon the manuscript's submission, between March and August 1959, there are a number of letters exchanged between Laurence and editor Claire Pratt regarding Laurence's revisions to *This Side Jordan* (McClelland & Stewart Ltd. Fonds, Box 35, File 33).

West 21st, 2 December 1959

Dear Mrs. Laurence,

You will have had the good news from Mr. Dickson.[1] It was an excellent suggestion on your part that the manuscript be sent to Macmillan's.[2] You will note from my letter to Mr. Dickson that we have no objection to direct correspondence on the editorial end, but I would appreciate it if you would send copies of any of your letters to him for our files. Meanwhile, I will ask Claire Pratt to let you have her views as to their suggestions.[3]

We shall act as your agent as agreed and will correlate publishing details with the American firm.

With all good wishes,
Yours sincerely,
J.G. McClelland

P.S. And again sincerest congratulations! We are delighted by the good word.[4]

1. Lovat Dickson, who lived from 1902 to 1987, joined the Macmillan publishing company in 1938 and was director of the company from 1941 to 1964. He was born in Australia and, at fifteen, immigrated to Canada, where he graduated with an MA in English literature from the University of Alberta in 1929. The first Canadian to establish a successful publishing career in Britain, Dickson was also an author, and published two biographies of the Canadian naturalist Grey Owl (Archibald Belaney 1888–1938) and others for English poets Radclyffe Hall (1880–1943) and Richard Hillary (1919–1943). In her exchange with Dickson on 1 December 1959, Laurence agreed to cut approximately ten thousand words from her manuscript (Jack McClelland Fonds, William Ready Division, Box 35, File 36).
2. Macmillan & Co., or Macmillan Publishers Ltd., as it is now called, was one of Britain's foremost publishing houses, and is now one of the largest publishing houses in the world. It was founded by Daniel Macmillan in 1843 and remained in the Macmillan family until 1999. During the period

in which Laurence and McClelland exchanged these letters, Canadian publishers such as McClelland & Stewart secured American and British publishers for an author's work in order to make the published work viable in Canada and to guarantee sales.

3. Claire Pratt, daughter of Canadian poet E.J. Pratt, lived from 1921 to 1995. She was the senior editor at McClelland & Stewart from 1956 to 1965. Although she retired from McClelland & Stewart in 1965 due to health reasons, she continued to do freelance work for the house after her retirement. Throughout her editing career, she also worked for Oxford University Press, Harvard University Press, Press Porcépic, and Consolidated Amethyst. Pratt was also known as a poet and graphic artist. Her published writings include *Silent Ancestors*, *Music of Oberon*, and *Black Heather* ("Biographical Sketch," E.J. Pratt Library Special Collections, University of Toronto).
4. Attached to this letter is a memo to McClelland from the editorial department about the fact that the manuscript was not yet placed with an American firm. McClelland responded by hand, "Why not?" to which Pratt replied, also by hand, "Because we had it returned from Australia and then there was a kerfuffle over getting it to England. Shall we send to St. Martin's?" (McClelland & Stewart Ltd. Fonds, Box 35, File 36).

Hollinger, 21 December 1959[1]

Dear Mr. McClelland,

I thought you might possibly like to see these issues of *Prism*,[2] containing one of my short stories[3] and comments on same from Ethel Wilson[4] and Roderick Haig-Brown.[5]

Sincerely,
Margaret Laurence[6]

1. This letter was handwritten by Laurence rather than typed.
2. *Prism*, the oldest literary magazine in western Canada, is a publication of the creative writing program at the University of British Columbia in Vancouver. When Laurence wrote this letter, the literary magazine was new. It was established in 1959 by Vancouver writers and was the only Canadian literary magazine west of Toronto. Over the years, the magazine has published many of Canada's best writers.
3. The story Laurence refers to here is "The Merchant of Heaven," published later in her collection of stories about Africa, *The Tomorrow-Tamer and Other Stories*. Like some of her other stories, this story takes up the coming together of African and Christian religions in colonial West Africa.
4. Ethel Wilson published short stories in *The New Statesman and Nation* in the late 1930s, and published her first novel, *Hetty Dorval*, in 1947. This novel was influenced by the American prairie novelist Willa Cather's novel, *My Mortal Enemy*. As William Toye explains, "Wilson's later fiction reveals an increasing interest in portraying various kinds of women at times of personal crisis, and in exploring spiritual and religious values" (673). Wilson is perhaps best known for her novel, *Swamp Angel*, which takes place in British Columbia and was published in 1954 by McClelland & Stewart (New Canadian Library). She received the Order of Canada in 1970 (Toye 673).
5. Roderick Haig-Brown (1908–1976) was born in England and moved to British Columbia in 1927. He wrote twenty-five books, including novels, essay collections, and children's books. He was an outdoorsman and was best known for his nature writing. Toye notes, "He wrote the first item in the first issue of Canadian Literature, about the writer in isolation" (266).
6. In letters dated 23 December 1959 and 29 December 1959, Laurence and McClelland work out the details of royalties and Laurence's publicity photo (McClelland & Stewart Ltd. Fonds, Box 35, File 38).

West 21st, 31 December 1959

Dear Mrs. Laurence:

When I picked up the issue of *Prism* to read the short story that you were good enough to send to me, I immediately realized that I had already read it with considerable pleasure but had, for some reason [that] now seems inexplicable, failed to connect it with you. This must indicate that I am losing my mind, at the very least. I think it's an extremely fine piece of work and its publication will help pave the way for the novel [*This Side Jordan*]. I shall make a point of sending advance copies to both Rod Haig-Brown and Ethel Wilson to get advance opinions in view of the enthusiasm they have expressed for this piece. We will keep the two issues of *Prism* on file here, but if you would like to have them back let me know.

All the best!
Sincerely,
J.G. McClelland

West 21st, 7 January 1960

Dear Margaret Laurence:

I owe you two letters, one in reply to yours of the 29th of December, and one to your letter of January 4th. I am tremendously impressed by your energy as a correspondent, I may say. What with letters to me and letters to Lovat Dickson and God knows who else, and still you have found time to revise the manuscript. It's miraculous!

... I am not wildly enthusiastic about the photograph, by the way. I suppose that is a hell of a thing to say, but what I would like to see is something showing you in a more professional attitude. This looks too much like a passport pose. I hope you won't hate me for this, but, since we would like to use a picture both on the jacket and in our advertising and promotion, I think it is important that we have a really good picture. It doesn't need to be a professional studio portrait—a picture of you gardening or hunting lions or drinking gin or tea, or wrestling with the Muse, would suffice. Will you dig around and see what you can come up with, and if you have nothing I think we should probably arrange to have one taken.

Have you done, or do you plan to do, any short stories with a Canadian background? I mention this only because it is entirely likely that Bob Weaver[1] of the C.B.C. will be writing to you shortly looking for such a story. He has an interesting project under way in which we are involved, and, if he does write you, he will offer a fairly substantial fee. Please keep this confidential and don't mention to him that I have said anything to you. I thought, however, that you might like to have this advance notice, if you have been thinking of Canadian material. I should point out, by the way, that he probably wouldn't insist on Canadian material, but I think you would have a better chance for this particular project if it were Canadian.[2]

All the best! Sincerely,
J.G. McClelland[3]

1. Robert Weaver, who lived from 1921 to 2008, worked at the CBC from 1948 to 1985, and quickly became a champion for new Canadian writers. He established many CBC radio shows and literary competitions featuring new Canadian writers. He brought to the fore writers such as Alice Munro, Margaret Laurence, Margaret Atwood, Leonard Cohen, and many others. He was also the editor of the literary magazine *Tamarack Review* from 1957 to 1982, and he anthologized Canadian writing in thirteen different volumes between 1952 and 1999 (Thacker, "*Robert Weaver*"). As Robert Thacker states in his review of Elaine Kalman Naves's book, *Robert Weaver: Godfather of Canadian Literature*, "Weaver knew all the writers, he made things happen for them, he encouraged and connected them to each other, he responded, he cared. He was 'a one-man national literary network,' as Robert Fulford once said of him" (Thacker, "Robert Weaver").
2. This statement represents the first time McClelland suggested to Laurence that she write fiction on and about Canada. The project to which McClelland refers here was a book of short stories, published by McClelland & Stewart. The book was "a selection of short stories from the special Wednesday Night short story series." Weaver aired these stories on CBC. McClelland and Weaver agreed on 17 May 1960 that stories from the following authors would be included in the collection: Woodward, Munro, Wilson, Garner, Richler, Moore, Roy, with the possibility of including stories by Callaghan, Mitchell, Ludwig, and Layton (Robert Weaver Fonds, Vol. 15, File 13, 1960, "McClelland & Stewart," Library and Archives Canada).
3. McClelland wrote again on 22 January 1960 to indicate that he enclosed the Macmillan contract and a tax form. The contract between Laurence and McClelland & Stewart for *This Side Jordan* was particularly important, since it was Laurence's first contract with a major publishing house and would set the standard for some years to come.

Hollinger, 28 January 1960

Dear Mr. McClelland:

Thank you for sending the contracts. I am returning them herewith. I enclose also the tax claim form. ...

As far as the photographs are concerned, please do not think I underestimate the value of publicity. On the contrary, I feel fortunate to be dealing with a publisher who is as well aware of its necessity as you are. My only difficulty has been in obtaining a photograph that was even reasonably decent. I have at last, however, been persuaded to call upon the services of a professional photographer, and also to take off my glasses for a picture, and I am happy to say that the results are infinitely better than anything we have had so far. I hope you will agree. I am sending the photographs to Miss Rankin.[1] I am afraid that I have caused you a good deal of inconvenience in this regard, and I do apologize.

Thank you for your patience and tact.
Sincerely,
Margaret Laurence [signed]
Margaret Laurence[2]

1. "Steve" Rankin was the nickname of Joyce Anne Rankin, later Joyce Anne Cumings. She was an employee at McClelland & Stewart who worked as an in-house editor and on the promotion of the New Canadian Library paperback series (Friskney, *New Canadian Library* 105, 140).
2. As letters exchanged between Pratt, McClelland, and the *Atlantic Monthly* indicate, *This Side Jordan* was rejected by the Atlantic in 1959, and so there was a delay in securing an American publisher for the book. As the correspondence indicates, subsequently, St. Martin's Press in the United States accepted the book for publication. (McClelland & Stewart Ltd. Fonds, Box 35, File 37). In a letter dated 6 February 1960, Laurence states, "I was under the impression that St. Martin's Press was an associate company of Macmillan of England," and that Mr. Dickson "spoke of St. Martin's Press as 'our associate company.'" She asked for clarification about the affiliation

between the two firms (McClelland & Stewart Ltd. Fonds, Box 35, File 37). The Macmillan Publishing Company in New York separated from Macmillan in England a few years prior to this correspondence. St. Martin's Press in New York, with whom Laurence published *This Side Jordan*, remained in affiliation with Macmillan in England.

•———

Hollinger, 10 February 1960

Dear Mr. McClelland:
I'm sorry that I seem to be writing you so many letters. Please don't bother to answer this one. I just want to straighten out a few points, which you raised in your letter of February 8th.

Thanks for clarifying the contract clauses about which I had enquired. Had I been more experienced in the matter of publishing, I would no doubt have realized the meaning of these clauses before. As far as Clause 13 is concerned, it is perfectly satisfactory to me as it stands—I merely wasn't sure whether it included the advance or not. I quite agree that you are entitled to 10% for all your efforts. I only hope, for your sake as well as mine, that the advance from St. Martin's Press will prove to be a reasonably substantial one.

I was not really concerned about the option clause, but I wanted to make sure I knew what was involved. Thanks for your explanation.

I am sending you, under separate cover, a fetish figure I once purchased in the ju-ju stalls of the Accra market—perhaps it will help along those astronomical 50,000 copies!

Sincerely,
Margaret Laurence [signed]
Margaret Laurence

West 21st, 25 February 1960

Dear Mrs. Laurence:

Firstly, let me thank you for the wonderful fetish carving. The magnificent creature she is! Personally, I like my women to have their breasts placed more symmetrically. But, even so, I think she is really superb. We don't hardly ever see them like that anymore (with apologies to George Gobel).[1] We should sell at least 50,000.

Macmillan's have returned the contract and it is enclosed herewith. Glad to know about the sale to *Prism*.

All the best!
Sincerely,
J.G. McClelland

1. George Gobel was an American comedian and actor best known for *The George Gobel Show*, which ran on NBC Television from 1954 to 1960.

Hollinger, 23 March 1960

Dear Mr. McClelland:

Thank you for your letter of February 25. I am glad that the fetish figure met with your approval, despite the rather odd arrangement of her upper parts. On the publication day of *This Side Jordan*, it might be as well to pour libation to this figure—a few drops to be scattered over the carving, and the rest disposed of in the customary way. A dry martini would do nicely, in the absence of palm wine.

I enclose a clipping from *The Vancouver Sun*.[1] You will probably not like the bit about the book's not being sensational enough for Hollywood. I am sorry, but it was one of those questions that are delivered without warning and which catch one unawares. All things considered, the write-up might have been much worse, although it does sound a little breathless and also makes me appear not to have written a single word in my life until the moment when Africa hit me like the spirit of God between the eyes.

I wonder if there is any word yet from St. Martin's Press, New York, about the manuscript? I have been a little anxious over the possibility that they might want extensive changes made in the manuscript at this late date.[2]

Thank you for the copy of Macmillan's contract.

Sincerely,
Margaret Laurence

1. The article Laurence refers to here, titled "City Woman Writes Book on the Birth of Ghana," appeared in the *Vancouver Sun* on 23 March 1960, p. 19. It discusses how *This Side Jordan* addresses Ghana's decolonization, which it was undergoing at this time. In this letter, Laurence

refers to the following statement in the article: "In [Laurence's] opinion, it is not the kind of book Hollywood will gobble up—not sensational enough." The article goes on to quote Laurence: "Most novels coming out of Africa tell tales of quaint tribal customs or depraved Europeans. I didn't find either theme was typical of life there. Both the Africans and the Europeans were ordinary people, involved in a historical process that was at times very difficult." Laurence differentiated her novel from other novels about Africa and challenged the myth that Africa was exotic or dangerous or destructive to Europeans.

2. Several letters that were exchanged between Pratt, who was then associate editor at McClelland & Stewart, and Laurence during the early part of 1960 and that survive in the archives suggest that St. Martin's Press would make changes when the book was in galleys. Daryn Ken, the editorial coordinator, assured Pratt on 1 April 1960 that "if there are any [changes] at that time, they will be minor [ones], easy to make in galleys" (McClelland & Stewart Ltd. Fonds, Box 35, File 37). A letter dated 15 December 1959 by Pratt to Laurence about suggested revisions to *This Side Jordan* was waylaid. Nonetheless, Laurence suggested that, even without that letter, she made changes that would conform to Pratt's suggestions: "when you look through the revised manuscript ... most of your suggestions have been carried out" (12 Jan. 1960, McClelland & Stewart Ltd. Fonds, Box 35, File 36).

Hollinger, 13 May 1960

Dear Mr. McClelland:

A few days ago I received a letter from Mr. Sherman Baker, of St. Martin's Press, together with the manuscript of *This Side Jordan*. Mr. Baker included the comments of three of his readers, and asked me to consider their criticisms and to make such changes in the manuscript as I felt might be necessary in the light of these suggestions. It is certainly unfortunate that I did not receive these changes earlier. Mr. Baker said that they intended to set the type for their own edition, and that this fact would enable me to make such changes as I wanted without affecting the English edition. I am not happy in the slightest about such a solution, however, as I definitely do not want to see two entirely different versions of the novel appear. ...

I do not think you have a copy of the manuscript, so I am not sending you a list of the detailed revisions. However, if you would like a copy, I will be glad to send it. I can tell you with reasonable accuracy which sections have been cut. In particular, Mr. Baker's readers were unhappy about the theme of Johnnie's Catholicism, and, as this was an aspect of the novel I wasn't too happy about myself, I have cut it out entirely, from chapters 3, 5, and 13. Mr. Baker's diligent readers also felt that the sections dealing with the ancient Ghana would be improved by pruning, and I have accordingly done so, in chapters 12 and 16. They felt, as well, that the reconciliation of Miranda and Aya in chapter 15 was too pat a solution, and I think they are right—I have cut it out. The scene with Nathaniel's uncle has been shortened to some extent in chapter 6. The scene with Cora at the club has been cut out of chapter 8, as being repetitive. The bedroom scene in chapter 3 (pithily described by Mr. Baker's reader as "pure corn") has been cut. Mr. Baker's chief reader, whose digestion appears to be of a fairly delicate nature, was only "reasonably nauseated" by the final chapter, but may not be restored to well being by the changes I have made there. I have cut the references to the ancient Ghana out entirely (I agree—they were repetitive) but have left the scene with Nathaniel's son. I do not believe that this is a pat ending, for Nathaniel's naive hope that Joshua will somehow, in miraculous fashion, know how to cope with the problems of a new Africa, does not seem to me to be an easy solution, or indeed a solution at all, but I think that this is how *he* would feel at the time. A number of minor criticisms were made which were not really worth considering (e.g., "these people talk too much like English in the tropics"—but after all they *are* English in the tropics). However, I have made such cuts as I felt were possible, and I honestly think that the novel will be improved. I cannot help wondering, though, how many times this sort of pruning would be possible. I might turn the novel into a short story, if I were given a year or so.

I feel most apologetic towards you and Mr. Dickson, as far as these late corrections are concerned, but I do hope you will give me your approval. If you would like a detailed list of these cuts, please let me know. The main thing I want to avoid is the appearance of two different novels in England and America, a situation [that] strikes me as absurd. I will be very anxious to hear from you and to know whether you approve in general of the changes I have outlined.

Sincerely,
Margaret Laurence [signed]
(Mrs.) Margaret Laurence

P.S. Mr. Baker, in concluding his letter, says, "We are all very enthusiastic about *This Side Jordan*. We intend to get behind this book." I do not know what he means by this. My own feeling at this moment is that I need a long holiday.

West 21st, 17 May 1960

Dear Mrs. Laurence,[1]

I can't react to your letter of May 13 in any way that will be helpful to you. The St. Martin's Press suggestions seem reasonable, but we are not able to evaluate them sensibly without a copy of the manuscript. However, since you, the author, feel that a number of the changes are worth making, we can only favour them. If I had any thought that you were being intimidated by them, I should be very much concerned, but I gather that this is far from the case and that you really feel that these suggestions have been useful.

I don't know how they will react in London. I don't know how far typesetting has proceeded—although I'm sure they have started—and how much the proposed changes will affect them. I don't think that these changes can be forced on the Macmillan Company, but I expect that, if it is at all possible, they will accept them. I don't think we at McClelland & Stewart can interfere, and we shall go along with their decision.

If it should happen that the novel appears in two versions, I don't think you should be upset about this. There [are] all sorts of precedent on record. It happens all the time. It has been our experience that American houses insist on very comprehensive editing; that English houses as a rule require little or none and are inclined to go along with the author's script almost without query. The Canadian practice is just what you would expect—a middle of the road course. We think the Americans edit too heavily and interfere with the author's rights. We think that the English publishers don't take enough editorial responsibility. Naturally, then, we consider our editing to be just about perfect. There's no doubt about it: we Canadians are a superior breed!

Because of the involvement, I am afraid that we have not taken much editorial responsibility in this case. As a result, we are faced with the disadvantages of a triumvirate. On future books, we shall be in a position to follow a better procedure. This would involve submitting the script simultaneously to the three houses, working with one editor directly (probably here), correlating the three reports at the same time, and doing a final revision for all three in the light of accumulated suggestions. You would then be in a position to say that this is the revised script, I have done all I am going to do, and this is the way it is to be published.

I think you are perfectly right in thinking that you would end up with a short story if the revision went on for too long. As a matter of fact, that's not a bad idea for a short story for *The New Yorker*. A story of the writer who had a novel accepted by three houses and tried to accommodate their editorial suggestions (which would have had to conflict like mad) and ended up [with] a short story, which was then sold to a magazine. Another publisher seeing the short story wrote to ask you if you could write a novel. You submitted the original draft. It was accepted without a change and became an international best seller. That's not a bad thought. If you don't use it, I think I will.

Well, that seems to cover the situation for the moment. I don't really anticipate that you will have any problem with Mr. Dickson. They will be fair about it and, if they can act, they will.

Sincerely,
J.G. McClelland

1. This letter appears in Solecki's *Imagining Canadian Literature*.

Hollinger, 24 May 1960

Dear Mr. McClelland:

Contrary to your expectations, your letter of May 17th was most helpful and reassuring, and my morale improved immediately upon reading it. I especially liked your short story plot.

I am very glad indeed that you are in favour of the changes I outlined. There was certainly no question about my being intimidated—Mr. Baker's request for further revision was very fair, and he made it quite clear that the final decision would be mine. Although I was reluctant at the time to go through the script once more, I had to admit that some of the criticisms made by his readers were quite correct.

I have heard both from St. Martin's Press and from Macmillan. Both, apparently, are quite satisfied with the latest revisions. It was a great relief to me to have Macmillan's acceptance of these changes. I enclose copies of these letters. I think you will want to see the one from Macmillan, and I thought you might be amused to see the ones from St. Martin's. I should say that, in my letter to Sherman Baker, I really did not make a fuss about his reader's comments—I said only that the phrase "reasonably nauseated" had interested me, as it seemed rather like saying "moderately dead." I think it was very handsome of Mr. Pope to write to me at all, as he need not have done so. I am, needless to say, very glad that Mr. Baker feels the novel has been improved. Everything now appears to be settled.

Many thanks once again for your moral support.

Sincerely,
Margaret Laurence [signed]
Margaret Laurence[1]

1. Throughout the summer and fall of 1960, there are a series of letters from McClelland to international publishers interested in the translation rights (Italian, German, Danish, and Swedish) to *This Side Jordan* (McClelland & Stewart Ltd. Fonds, Box 35, File 37).

Hollinger, 16 September 1960

Dear Mr. McClelland:

Recently, a friend told me that she had seen in your fall catalogue *This Side Jordan* listed as both a hard-cover and a soft-cover book. I wonder if this is true? I hope so, as I believe strongly in the increasing necessity for paperback books,[1] and I remember being very impressed with your publication of Sheila Watson's book *The Double Hook* in this manner.[2] I would be glad if you could let me know.

Sincerely,
Margaret Laurence [signed]
(Mrs.) Margaret Laurence

1. During this period, the "paperback revolution," paperback books were becoming popular in Britain, the United States, and Canada. Prior to this, hardcover books were the norm, although Janet Friskney points out that the origins of the "paperback revolution" are found in the 1840s, and, even prior to that, certain kinds of publications, such as those released in instalments, were produced in paperback. McClelland and Ross started a paperback series for McClelland & Stewart called the New Canadian Library in 1958 and began to expand the series significantly in 1959 (Friskney, *New Canadian Library* 7, 45, 50).
2. Published in 1959, Sheila Watson's *The Double Hook* is considered Canada's first modernist novel, signalling a turn in Canadian writing style and the beginning of contemporary Canadian writing (Besner). Watson wrote the book between 1952 and 1954, but she could not find a publisher for the book until McClelland & Stewart accepted it (Scobie 2). Watson first attempted to publish her novel with an American company, as most Canadian authors were wont to do in this period. The book's publication signalled a new age not only in Canadian writing but also in Canadian publishing.

Hollinger, 26 September 1960

Dear Mr. McClelland:

I wonder if you would mind giving me some advice. I have been working on a number of short stories set in West Africa, and have so far completed nine of these. I want to do about three more, after which I hope to begin work on a second novel. Of the completed stories, four have been or will shortly be published in Canada and one is to be in *Winter's Tales* this fall.[1] I would like to ask your advice on the following questions:

1. Do you think I would stand a better chance of selling the unpublished short stories in the U.S.A. if the matter were to be handled through an agent? I understand that stories published in Canada can be reprinted in American publications as well, and, as I have very little knowledge of the situation, I thought that an agent might be able to do something in this regard also.[2]
2. If you think an American agent might be a good idea, could you possibly give me the name of one whom you think might be interested in taking on these short stories and whom you would consider reliable?
3. If I had an American agent, would I have to let him handle the next novel? I can't see that this would be of any particular advantage to me, and, as you have acted as my agent with this first novel, I would naturally want you to do so again, if you wanted to. Or would you prefer the next novel to be handled through an outside agent?
4. Can short stories published in Canada or America be submitted to periodicals in England? I have scarcely any knowledge of possible English markets, but I have the feeling that many of my stories would stand a better chance in England than in America. The above questions apply as well to an English agent. Do you think it

would be a good idea for me to write to Macmillan and ask them to recommend an English agent?

5. I understand that publishers are not very enthusiastic about bringing out books of short stories. I have the feeling that both you and Macmillan might be more willing to consider publishing a collection of short stories if (a) most of them had been published in periodicals, and (b) if there had been a second novel before such a collection of short stories was contemplated. What is your opinion?[3]

I'd be most grateful if you could give me some assistance with these questions.

Sincerely,
Margaret Laurence

1. The short story that appeared in *Winter's Tales* is "The Perfume Sea," one of Laurence's African stories, which would eventually be enfolded into *The Tomorrow-Tamer*. Other stories by Laurence that appeared in this year or the following include "Godman's Master," "A Gourdful of Glory," and "The Tomorrow-Tamer."
2. McClelland responded to each of these beside the question. His response to number 1 was simply "Yes." To number 2, he responded, "Yes. W. Wing." To number 3, he again wrote, "Yes." To number 4, McClelland wrote, "No. Use US agent's counterpart."
3. McClelland's note at the end of this paragraph reads as follows: "Yes. Leave until after 2nd novel. 50-50 published."

West 21st, 7 October 1960

Dear Margaret:

Thanks for yours of the 26th. For what it's worth, here is my advice:

1. Yes, you would do better through an agent, and I think you should publish your short stories in the U.S.A.
2. Yes, I would recommend Willis Wing.
3. Yes, the agent should handle your next novel. We would like to do so again, but I really think it would be very much to your advantage to have an agent. I don't think it would be fair to an agent to ask him to handle only your short stories. In turn, it would not be fair to you because an agent would not give you the best attention on such a limited basis.
4. Yes, I believe you can sell to the English markets separately. Willis Wing and most of the good American agents have British associates with whom they work directly. I think it would be better to make your arrangements in New York first and then work through their English counterpart rather than asking Macmillan's to recommend an agent to you.
5. As a general principle, I would say you are right in thinking that publishers are not enthusiastic about books of short stories. However, there has been a change in this viewpoint of recent years. In the past five years, particularly a number of very successful books of short stories have been published. I think both Macmillan's and ourselves would be interested in looking at a collection of yours from this point of view. In all probability, then, we would recommend that you hold them until after a second novel has been published—this makes good sense—but a lot of considerations would have to be taken into account. It would depend on when your second novel is completed, for example. As far as a collection of

short stories is concerned, I should think it desirable that no more than half of them be published in advance elsewhere.

Willis Wing is one of the best agents in New York. He has a small, but for the most part highly successful, group of clients. As an example, two of the top-selling books in the past several years have been by his clients (*Advise and Consent* and *Exodus*).[1] He also represents Nicholas Monsarrat,[2] and he has a very strong group of Canadian writers (a particular interest of his), including Pierre Berton, Ralph Allen, Brian Moore, etc.[3] If you would like to give him a try, I think it might be better all round if I made the initial approach for you. I think I have enough of the general background to let him judge whether or not he thinks he could do a good job for you. Let me know if you want me to go ahead.

All the best!
Sincerely,
J.G. McClelland

1. Allen Drury's *Advise and Consent*, a political novel, was published in 1959 and won the Pulitzer Prize in 1960. Leon Uris's *Exodus*, a novel about the founding of Israel, was published in 1958 and was a significant commercial success.
2. Nicholas Monsarrat (1910–1979) was a British novelist. His most well known book is *The Cruel Sea*, published in 1951.
3. This brief list represents some important Canadian writers of the 1950s. Pierre Berton (1920–2004) was a noted Canadian author of nonfiction, especially Canadiana and Canadian history, and was a well-known television personality and journalist. His significant publications during the period of the letters exchanged between Laurence and McClelland include *The National Dream: The Great Railway, 1871–1881* and *The Last Spike: The Great Railway, 1881–1885*. Ralph Allen (1913–1966) was a Canadian journalist, editor, and novelist. He wrote the novel *Peace River Country* and *Ordeal by Fire: Canada, 1910–1945*. A collection of his newspaper and magazine columns was compiled by Christina McCall in a volume titled *The Man From Oxbow*. Brian Moore (1921–1999) was an Irish-born novelist, screenwriter, and journalist, who immigrated to Canada, where he won the Governor General's Award for fiction for *The Luck of Ginger Coffey* in 1960 and for *The Great Victorian Collection* in 1975. McClelland & Stewart published his novel *Catholics* in 1972. *The Emperor of Ice-Cream*, set in Belfast in 1939, was published in 1965.

West 21st, 2 November 1960

Dear Mrs. Laurence:

Willis Wing has replied enthusiastically to my suggestion that he might take on your representation for the future.[1] A letter from him to you has gone off from this office, as he did not have your address. I am sure that you will be well satisfied with him as an agent, and I hope that you can come to a satisfactory agreement with him. I make this point only to reassure you that I have made no commitment on your behalf as yet. In other words, if you like the sound of his letters, go ahead and make an arrangement with him. If you don't, then that is fair enough too. ...

I am going to be in Vancouver for a few days from the 13th to the 16th of November. I look forward to meeting you and we are endeavouring to arrange a small party in your honour at that time. I will write to you more definitely about this before the end of the week. Unfortunately, we won't have stock of our edition in the stores at that time, but we are still hoping to publish on the 19th of this month, if the ship that is carrying the shipment from England arrives on time. We just received a sample of the American edition and it looks quite handsome. They have moved quickly, and I wish now we had printed with them rather than in England.

With all good wishes,
Sincerely,
J.G. McClelland

P.S. My reference to your free choice re: Willis Wing as above is just for the record. I assume you will want to go ahead with him for, as I think I told you before, there is no better agent in New York, and I am certain that your affairs will be well handled by him.

1. On 31 October 1960, Wing confirmed that he would represent Laurence as her agent. In this letter, he states, "Everything you say adds up to an attractive picture and I would be delighted to work with her." He adds, "She certainly sounds like a fine discovery and I look forward to working with her." McClelland responds on 7 November 1960: "I think you will find her a most agreeable and most productive client" (McClelland & Stewart Ltd. Fonds, Box 35, File 38).

Hollinger, 4 November 1960

Dear Mr. McClelland:

Thanks for your letter of November 2, and thanks for approaching Willis Wing on my behalf. I am writing to Mr. Wing today to tell him I would be glad if he would act as my agent, and I am sending him a number of short stories. I think it would be as well if he would take on the foreign rights representation of *This Side Jordan*, and I am not too concerned about the double agent's fee on the enquiries already received. I would be grateful, therefore, if you would turn over the relevant correspondence to him and also send him photocopies of my three contracts.

I look forward to meeting you when you are in Vancouver. I don't suppose I could prevail upon you to have dinner quietly at our house one evening? I am sure you will be very busy and would probably not have the time to spare, but, if you felt you could make it, we would be very pleased. I should add that we have a number of excellent homemade wines of which we are extremely proud!

I suppose it is unfortunate that your edition of the novel has been delayed in publication from England, but if there are any favourable American reviews the later publication date in Canada might prove beneficial rather than otherwise. I received a phone call from St. Martin's Press yesterday, and learned that *The Saturday Review* has a good review of the book which they plan to run soon, and that they may do a cover on it.[1] This was apparently not certain, but St. Martin's asked me to send another and different photograph as soon as possible.

Thanks again for writing to Willis Wing.

Sincerely,
Margaret Laurence [signed]
Margaret Laurence

1. Mary Renault's glowing review of *This Side Jordan*, which appeared in the *Saturday Review* on 10 December 1960, referred to Laurence as "a writer of great delicacy and feeling towards human beings ... brutal to clichés, both literary and ideological" (23–24).

West 21st, 9 November 1960

Dear Mrs. Laurence:

Thanks for yours of November 4th. Glad the Wing matter is settled. We have sent all the pertinent information to him. It's a surprisingly formidable file. I begin to think these agents work for their commission.

Nothing would delight me more than to have a quiet dinner at your house one evening while I am in Vancouver. Unfortunately, for the moment at least, it looks as if it will be impossible. I have not allowed myself nearly enough time. I have an appalling number of commitments and our publicity people are working as energetically as they can arranging further commitments, because the prime purpose of this trip is publicity and more publicity for our fall list. May I thank you then for your kind invitation and say that if it is possible to leave it open until after I arrive, and, if it can then be managed at a time that would suit you, I can't think of anything that would please me more.

With all good wishes,
Yours sincerely,
J.G. McClelland

P.S. When you send another photograph to St. Martin's Press, could you let us have one as well?

Hollinger, 16 November 1960

Dear Jack:

I was very glad indeed to meet you at last, although a cocktail party is not the ideal place to talk with anyone. However, from a publicity point of view, the whole thing seemed to go quite well, and that is the main thing. Perhaps at some future point I may have the opportunity to talk with you under more calm circumstances. I promise in future to refrain from explaining to you the more obscure points of the psychology of colonization![1]

I forgot to tell you the other evening that I sent to Miss Rankin the picture you asked for—the same one I sent to St. Martin's recently. It is quite good, and I am only sorry now that I did not have it in the first place.

Speaking of pictures, I feel more and more apprehensive about the cover picture on your edition of the novel. I do hope the printers in England did not get hold of the wrong picture, but, after seeing Macmillan's edition, I am inclined to fear the worst. At least in the Macmillan book, the picture is decently small, but if that picture is blown up to relatively enormous size on its back cover, it will look ghastly. I reproach myself for ever having sent it, or for not having demanded that it be burned when I sent the subsequent photographs. However, there is no point in getting worked up about it, as there is absolutely nothing that anyone can do about it now. I would appreciate it very much, though, if you could arrange to have my copies sent as soon as possible.

We thought you did a tremendous promotion job ... here. A large number of people have phoned me to say that they heard you on radio and were most impressed. We watched you on Channel 8 TV last night, and greatly admired the way in which you managed to get in a mention of a number of your books, despite the difficulties of a panel discussion and the fact that your copies were spirited out of sight. I am sure you must have been very tired after your hectic visit.

Let us only hope that sales here will justify your efforts.

Sincerely,
Margaret Laurence [signed]
Margaret Laurence

1. Laurence admired Mannoni's *Prospero and Caliban: The Psychology of Colonization* (see Davis, *Margaret Laurence Writes Africa and Canada*), the text to which Laurence implicitly refers here. Mannoni first argued that the colonizer rather than the colonized was psychologically abnormal.

West 21st, 29 November 1960

Dear Margaret,

I am sorry that I haven't managed to get a letter off to you before this. Don't, please, apologize for your learned dissertation on colonization. It was a masterful effort and the only reason I don't suggest we put it out between hard covers immediately is the sad fact that I don't recall a word of it. Most painful in my memory is my effort as a referee between Gordon Elliott and Stephen Franklin. I wish I could remember who won the prize. Perhaps we should draw a merciful veil of silence over that whole part of the evening.

I do want to say again how much I enjoyed meeting you. You were a tremendous success at the party and I have no doubt that the book will get off to a rousing start because of the tremendous impression you made on everyone present. If we did manage to get the book off to a good start, then I am confident that the readers will carry it from there.

I have only now had a chance to examine finished copies of the book in the two editions. I am not well pleased with either, but what is done is done. I think the book looks fairly adequate[1] for our market, and I can certainly promise you that on subsequent books, whether we manufacture here, in the U.K., or in the U.S.A, we shall certainly insist on designing our own jacket. I am convinced that any slight savings we may make using the English or American jacket is usually offset, perhaps more than offset, by our disappointment in the finished product. But that's water under the bridge, and it's best forgotten as far as the present book is concerned.

I, too, am sorry that we didn't have a chance for a more sensible talk. We shall certainly do so the next time. The only useful advice I have ever given to an author, by the way, is to get back to the typewriter, so you didn't miss much.

I'll be interested in hearing your reaction to the next few weeks, which will be, I hope, "Margaret Laurence Weeks" in Vancouver. Incidentally, I told them in Winnipeg that I thought you and Pat Blondal[2] would make United College as famous as the other incident made it infamous.[3] So I assume the good burghers of Winnipeg are sitting back expectantly.

My best to you and your husband.

Sincerely,
J.G. McClelland

1. In this sentence, "fairly" has been struck through and "lovely" added in handwriting, although it is unclear whose handwriting it is.
2. Pat Blondal (1926–1959) attended United College with Laurence, although they were not close friends. In one of the letters omitted from this book, dated 6 January 1961, Laurence acknowledged that McClelland sent her a copy of Blondal's book. In his biography of Jack McClelland, James King notes that McClelland believed Blondal had even more potential as a writer than did Laurence (Jack 86). McClelland & Stewart published her novel, *A Candle to Light the Sun* in 1960. The book characterizes the small fictional town of Mouse Bluffs, set in the prairies of Canada in the 1930s. The subject matter of the novel is similar to that of Laurence's Manawaka cycle. McClelland was enthusiastic about the book, in part it seems because of its Canadian content. Blondal died of cancer, and McClelland always regretted his last conversation with her, in which he stated that he didn't want to speak about her cancer. McClelland's hypochondria—the fact that he would feel symptoms when described to him—may have, in part, caused McClelland's response to Blondal.
3. The incident to which McClelland refers here involved Harry Sherman Crowe (1922–1981), a history professor and university administrator at United College. Crowe was fired in 1958 when he wrote a letter to his colleague, William Packer, in which he expressed concern about a Conservative victory in the forthcoming federal election. The letter was publicly exposed, but his firing then became integral to the work of the Canadian Association of University Teachers, which defended academic freedom and scholarly rights (see Horn).

Hollinger, 4 December 1960

Dear Jack:

Thank you for your letter of November 29. I have not yet received my copies of *This Side Jordan,* but I have seen your edition in the Franklin's bookshop when I went there yesterday for what is known, I believe, as an "autographing party." I was so relieved to see that the Canadian edition had the right picture of me, not the bespectacled ape-woman one. I also liked your cover blurb better than either the American one or the English one. You will be glad to know that a few people actually turned up yesterday, which Jim Douglas tells me is not always the case with such ventures.[1] Personally, I would not walk across the street to get even Ernest Hemingway's signature, but one can be thankful that not everyone feels this way. I am going tomorrow to another bookshop. ...

I wonder if you saw any of the reviews from England. Most of them seemed pretty favourable. *The London Times* panned the book, on the whole, though they said it was well written. Actually, they picked out very neatly all the worst flaws in the novel. The *New Statesman* gave it a very good review, for which one can be profoundly grateful, but said the ending was suspiciously sunny. Richard Church, in *The Bookman,* felt the ending was despairing, and some of the American reviews, also, have mentioned the gloomy quality of the ending. The moral seems to be pretty clear.

I have begun to work on the next novel. It is a very good story, but I have no way of knowing at this point whether I will be able to tell it properly or not. This time I am determined to know a little more clearly where I'm going before I start.

I liked very much the comments you made in Winnipeg, re: United College!

Best regards and Merry Christmas.

Sincerely,
Margaret [signed]
Margaret Laurence

1. Jim Douglas (1924–2016) was based in Vancouver and was involved in the book business as a sales representative and editor until he started his own publishing company with Scott McIntyre, Douglas & McIntyre, in 1970. The company became the largest independent book publisher in British Columbia. It was forced into bankruptcy in 2012, around the same time that Penguin and Random House merged (see Castaldo).

Hollinger, 22 January 1961

Dear Jack:

Thanks for your letter of January 13th.[1] I am glad you liked the review. I asked Don Stainsby to run it in full if he possibly could,[2] and he did so yesterday, together with a picture of Pat.[3]

Re: your suggestion that the sale of short stories might discourage me from attempting another book, might I suggest a solution? I have ten short stories on Africa done now, and by spring I will have perhaps fifteen. I know books of short stories are supposed to be out of fashion, but Alan Maclean[4] in the introduction to *Winter's Tales* [volume] *6* says that fifty collections of short stories were published in Britain last year[5]. ...

You will recognise that this is one of my long-standing hopes, and will probably think I have a one-track mind, which is perfectly true. Perhaps I am being quite unrealistic. (Title: *The Drummer Of All The World*. It would run to 300 pages typescript if all fifteen were included.)

Sincerely,
Margaret [signed]
Margaret Laurence

1. In a letter of that date, McClelland wrote to Laurence, indicating that he was "delighted" to have a copy of her review, and also that she was publishing so many stories in the *Saturday Evening Post* (McClelland & Stewart Ltd. Fonds, Box 35, File 39).
2. Donald Stainsby wrote many literary articles and reviews for the scholarly journal *Canadian Literature*, published by the University of British Columbia. With Kuthan George, he also wrote a book entitled *Vancouver: Sights and Insights*, published in 1962 by Macmillan Canada.
3. Laurence is likely referring to a book review she wrote on Blondal's *A Candle to Light the Sun*.
4. Alan Maclean was Lovat Dickson's successor at Macmillan (MacSkimming 135). He was director of Macmillan in Britain for many years, and was the British publisher of many Canadian writers, including Mordecai Richler.

5. Two of Laurence's short stories about Africa were published in the American publication, the *Saturday Evening Post*, in 1961: "The Perfume Sea" and "The Tomorrow-Tamer." Both were subsequently published in her collection of short stories about Africa, *The Tomorrow-Tamer*.

West 21st, 26 January 1961

Dear Margaret:

My view hasn't changed—and Willis Wing concurs on this one—that it would be far better from the standpoint of your total career to leave the short story volume until after you have published at least one more novel.[1] Critically, of course, the volume would undoubtedly be a success. It's in the bookstores that it could hurt you. I don't honestly think it's worth the risk. For your sake, though, I will discuss it with Macmillan when I am in London next month, and I will also take it up with St. Martin's Press, but I am sure that their opinion will be the same as ours.

The fact that fifty collections of short stories were successfully published in Britain last year doesn't impress me. To begin with, there were probably in excess of 20,000 new book titles published there during the same period (I may be out a few thousand either way but their figure is something like that). Short stories form a very small section of this total. Also, one can't conclude that fifty collections of short stories were successfully published in Britain last year.

All the best!
Sincerely,
J.G. McClelland

1. McClelland might have been influenced by Wing's opinion not to publish a book of Laurence's short stories too early in her career. In a letter written as early as 31 October 1960, Wing stated to McClelland, "We should all consider very carefully the timing of publication of a book of her short stories" (McClelland & Stewart Ltd. Fonds, Box 35, File 38).

Hollinger, 3 July 1961

Dear Jack:

I want you to know how very much I appreciate your generous help in meeting the expenses of my trip to Toronto. I received this morning your cheque for the additional $100, and I think this was extremely kind of you, especially as the wrong information about the anticipated $250 was in no way your fault. Thanks very much indeed.

Whether the trip accomplished anything from a publicity point of view, I don't know, but I certainly had a wonderful time myself, thanks largely to you and to Steve Rankin. I was also very glad to be able to talk with you under less hectic circumstances than when we first met. In fact, I felt that my visit, if not quite an incredible journey, was at least a very pleasant one.

Best regards.
Sincerely,
Margaret Laurence [signed]
Margaret Laurence

West 21st, 5 July 1961

Dear Margaret:

Thanks for your letter. It was a delight to see you again. You are rapidly becoming my favourite author. Sorry we couldn't do more about the finances but the budget is a bit slim.

I think the whole thing was extremely worthwhile. You made a lot of friends and a good impression everywhere. How many books we sold as the result of it we will never know. That's one of the good things about this business. We don't really know what sells books, so we continue experimenting with things that obviously don't help a damn bit but are more fun than methods that might be indicated if the facts could be ascertained. That's my philosophic offering for this morning. Get back to your typewriter and let's see a new novel soon. All the best!

Sincerely,
J.G. McClelland

West 21st, 8 February 1962

Dear Margaret:

... I was very disappointed that I didn't get to Vancouver last fall. I don't know whether I got around to writing you in advance or not, but I had planned to be there in November and was forced to call off the trip. Hugh Kane[1] went out in my stead and was probably in touch. I will be going out this year though, maybe in the late spring, more probably in the fall. Meanwhile, do write and do tell me that the book that all publishers wait for is piled up in manuscript form on your desk just waiting for a few final touches.

All the best!
Cheers!
J.G. McClelland

1. Hugh Kane (1910–1984) was an important figure in Canadian publishing. He was born in Ireland and came to Canada in 1921. He worked at McClelland & Stewart from 1937 to 1969, at which point he left to work at Macmillan Canada. At McClelland & Stewart, he worked his way up from salesperson to vice-president, and he left McClelland to become vice-president at Macmillan (MacSkimming 64). King explains in his biography of McClelland that Kane and McClelland had troubled moments in their working relationship with one another, although they ultimately depended on one another. As King states, "Hugh was oriented toward the book trade and networks he fostered among booksellers, librarians and other publishers; Jack was more taken with the glamour and fun of Canadian authors and their promotion. Hugh's style of publishing was international in scope, Jack's nationalist" (Jack 50).

Hollinger, 10 February 1962

Dear Jack:

I received your letter, in which you said you needed some good news, at a point when I felt I needed some good news. Let's face it—we all need good news, and who's got any? I shouldn't complain, because I did have one piece of very good news recently—I sold another story to Macmillan's in England, for the volume of *Winter's Tales* that will come out next fall.[1] Apart from this, however, I have been working hard and have little to show for it so far. I finished the first draft of a novel a few months ago, but I have put it away for a while. It has possibilities, I think, but I haven't done with it what I wanted to do, and I think a few months away from it may give me a better perspective.[2] In the meantime, I have begun something which I naively thought would be very easy, and which has turned out to be horribly difficult—an account of our experiences in Somaliland some years ago. I kept voluminous diaries at the time, and for some years have thought I would only have to go through these diaries and select chunks of beautiful prose—but now I see that the prose was not so hot, after all, and my own perception of events has changed so much that I have had to try to re-live these years. Maybe nothing will come of it, but I hope it may be interesting when it is finished. Let me reassure you—it is not a "travel" book in the usual sense.[3] Either it will be finished by this spring, or I will be—I'm not sure which. I want to re-tackle the novel this summer.

I tried to send back some homemade wine for you and Steve Rankin last fall, but Hugh Kane (not unnaturally) wouldn't take it in his suitcase. He was afraid the plane might not be sufficiently pressurised.

All the best.
Sincerely,
Margaret Laurence [signed]
Margaret Laurence

A short story of mine that was in *Saturday Eve. Post* has been selected to go into their collection *Post Stories 1961*.[4]

1. "The Rain Child" was published in *Winter's Tales*, volume 8, in 1962, and was later published in *The Tomorrow-Tamer*.
2. This was the manuscript of *The Stone Angel*.
3. The memoir about Africa Laurence refers to here would be published as *The Prophet's Camel Bell* in 1963.
4. This statement appears in Laurence's handwriting at the bottom of the letter.

Hollinger, 28 May 1962

Dear Jack:

I have now completed the book on Somaliland, and have sent three copies of the manuscript to Willie Wing, so probably he will be sending one to you shortly. Of course, it may not be your cup of tea at all, but, in any event, it may explain to you why I once held forth at agonizing length, over innumerable cups of lukewarm saki, on the psychology of colonisation! The book is called *The Prophet's Camel Bell,* which is a more appropriate title than might appear from first glance. I have a kind of guilt complex where Willis Wing is concerned, as I have done nothing for several weeks but send him lists of corrections to be made on the manuscript, for as usual, I yielded to my impatience and sent him the scripts before I had received word from a friend who is an expert on the Somali language and who I had asked to give me the correct spellings for Somali words, and I also changed my mind a number of times regarding the use of real people's names—to identify or not to identify? However, all these things are now sorted out, and, as far as I am concerned, the matter is in the hands of Allah. Naturally, I hope that you and Macmillan and St. Martin's will like the book, but, even if you don't, I'm not sorry I wrote it.

I have just learned that a short story of mine, which appeared in *Prism* last year, has been awarded the President's Medal, University of Western Ontario. Another story of mine got the same award last year.[1] In themselves, medals have very limited value, but perhaps one of these days a publisher (no names, no pack-drill) will decide to risk a book of short stories. Or perhaps I merely delude myself. Anyway, I wrote to the C.A.A.[2] and said that much as I would like to attend the Convention in Edmonton this year, I was afraid that personal considerations unfortunately make this impossible. I haven't recovered my membership fees. Should one feel guilty, righteous or merely neutral? The latter, I think. Please burn this letter after you read it.

All the best.

Sincerely,

Margaret Laurence [signed]

Margaret Laurence

1. "A Gourdful of Glory" won the President's Medal in 1961, and "The Tomorrow-Tamer" won it in 1962.
2. Laurence is referring to the Canadian Authors Association. According to the archives of the Canadian Authors Association, held at the Fisher Library, University of Toronto, the association was founded in 1921 by Stephen Leacock, Pelham Edgar, B.K. Sandwell, and John Murray Gibbon. The association sought to establish "cultural and literary solidarity among Canadian writers." It was originally formed to oppose proposed copyright law that would discriminate against Canadian authors. The association also initiated the Governor General's medals for literature in 1937 (Canadian Authors Association, Toronto Branch, 1921–1954, Manuscript Collection 101).

West 21st, 7 June 1962

Dear Margaret:

What wonderful news! We are absolutely delighted to hear that you have finished the book on Somaliland and I can't imagine that we will be anything but delighted to publish the book, unless you have gone quite out of your mind since the last time I saw you and have written something that is completely unsuitable. Migod, do they have camels in Somaliland? What will they think of next? Willis hasn't sent the script on yet, by the way. He's probably still trying to translate the Somali words.

Congratulations on the President's Medal! I'll tell you what! If you win it three times in a row, we'll publish the short story volume. You must be driving Willis Wing out of his mind. How come you're still selling to *Prism* when you could be selling to *The Saturday Evening Post*? Migod, that's upsetting. And speaking of the volume of short stories, how's the novel coming?

I'm not going to Edmonton and I'm really pleased that you have taken the neutral stand. I fear the Canadian Authors Association is something that one must live with but better not to be part of, or some such.[1] I'll drop you a note as soon as I have seen the *Camel Bell.*

Cheers!
J.G. McClelland

1. McClelland here and elsewhere makes disparaging remarks about the Canadian Authors Association that correspond to perceptions about the association in this period, particularly about "its sentimental colonialism, its lingering Victorianism, its nationalist boosterism, [and] its feminization of literary culture" (Irvine 1). See F.R. Scott's poem, "The Canadian Authors Meet," for an example of such a critique of the association in the modern period.

Hollinger, 23 July 1962

Dear Jack:

I had a letter this morning from Lovat Dickson in London to the effect that Macmillan has accepted *The Prophet's Camel Bell,* so I am in the process of giving three rousing cheers about this. Mr. Dickson says he has written to you, asking if you would be interested in cooperating with Macmillan in the production of the book. At the moment, I do not even know if Willis Wing has submitted the manuscript to you yet, or if you have not made your mind up about it one way or another, so perhaps I should not be writing to you about it at all yet.

However, I felt you might be interested to know that Macmillan has taken it. Mr. Dickson makes a few suggestions for cuts in the manuscript—specifically, he feels that the Somali folktales and poetry are somewhat too long and could be cut without loss of effect, and also that the chapter on the British in Somaliland could benefit from cutting. I am in agreement with his suggestions, and have cabled him to return the script to me for correction and cutting. If you have seen the script and feel you might be interested in it, you could if you like return it to me for correction. I would very much like, at this time, to do only one set of cuts and corrections, but perhaps I am being overly optimistic. In any event, I would be most interested (fantastic understatement!) to hear your reaction to the book.

Thanks for your last letter. I cannot help admiring the diabolic[al] cleverness of your suggestion that when I win the President's Medal three times in a row you will consider bringing out a book of short stories. I guess I can put the African short stories away in my bottom drawer, along with the lavender and old lace.

When you have seen *The Prophet's Camel Bell* and have decided yea or nay about it, I would very much appreciate your dropping me a line to let me know—the business of dealing through an agent has undoubtedly got many advantages, but it sometimes reminds me of situations in Africa, when all communications are filtered through an interpreter.

Sincerely,
Margaret [signed]
Margaret Laurence

West 21st, 27 July 1962

Dear Margaret:

Thanks for yours of the 23rd, but the fact is we ain't seen *The Prophet's Camel Bell* yet. I suspect Willis is going to tell us either that he forgot about it because our market is so unimportant, or that he used our copy to send to a book club, to sell first serial rights, or something of that sort. The trouble is he's got us too well taped. In any case, I was nattering about this a week or ten days ago, asking where the hell the manuscript was, and I believe a letter went off to Willis then asking him to send it on.

So, Margaret, until we see it I can't really send you a sensible report. I can be certain though that we shall want to publish [it]. Even though you may not win three President's Medals in a row, I think it's unlikely that you will produce any book-length scripts that we won't want to publish. I think I've even admitted to you before that we would do your short stories now, under duress. It's just that we don't think it's wise to do them yet in terms of your total career in the book market. But, hell! Don't get me wound up on that subject again.

I would suggest that you should be absolutely intransigent on the point of conformity between British, American, and Canadian editions. If St. Martin's Press want to change to American spelling, O.K., but I don't think there should be two different versions. There was some excuse for it the first time because of the whole timing problem. But I think that you should tell Lovat Dickson that you are delighted that they will publish, but you won't complete your own final manuscript until you have reports from St. Martin's and from M&S so that you can produce one final version for everybody. We will, of course, plan to bring in sheets from England.

I promise you will have my view, plus the opinion of one of our top readers, within a week of our receipt of the manuscript.

Sincerely,
J.G. McClelland

West 21st, 30 August 1962

Dear Margaret,

Do forgive me for having taken longer to get word back to you on receipt of the script than I had predicted. What actually happened was that the script arrived about twenty-four hours before I took off on a week's holiday and I took it with me. Before writing, I decided to get a couple of checking opinions here.

My reaction—and it is confirmed by my associates—is one of tremendous enthusiasm. I think you have written another outstanding book. It is eminently readable and interesting. It's well-written. I think it will charm a great many readers and add considerably to your growing reputation as one of Canada's most distinguished authors.

Having been that nice, you will perhaps forgive me if I now voice a few mild criticisms. You are probably anticipating that anyway after reading the opening paragraphs. Let me make it very clear that these are merely suggestions. I think the book is very good, even if you make no further changes, and it is entirely possible that neither Macmillan's nor St. Martin's Press will agree with our views. But at least they are confirmed by several of our good readers here and so I shall try to express them for you in my usual inept way.

Firstly, I found myself rather disappointed in the fact that the irrigation ditches were dismissed so summarily in the latter part of the book. Initially, the building of the ditches was the reason [*sic*] d'etre. The project lent a strong unifying force to the book and I found myself looking forward very eagerly to the day when the rains filled up the first ditch and the natives reacted with orgiastic enthusiasm, or whatever. I'm sure you get the picture. Truthfully, I felt a very strong build-up towards this, and, because of it, for me, the book just didn't reach a satisfactory climax. From the standpoint of unity, it sort of falls apart, and if I may be awfully brutal, even though all the material is interesting enough, it sort of gave me the impression that you were using up tail ends of your notes with odds and ends and maybe the ditches did work and maybe they didn't, but by this point who could care less about ditches (least of all you or even Jack).[1]

I realize two things. One, you do say, specifically what happened. I hope you will realize that that isn't quite my point. Two, I also see that what actually happened after the first ditches were completed—and I really should refer back to the manuscript for I'm not sure whether I should be calling them ditches—was, in fact, anti-climactic, but I wonder if it must appear so for the purpose of the book. This may be a very difficult suggestion to accommodate but if the spirit moves you I think you would have a better book if you found some way of strengthening this aspect of it.

Secondly, and this is a bit of a sweeping generalization and I certainly don't intend to be specific about it, but I had the feeling in a number of places throughout the book that you were unnecessarily humble, or perhaps diffident, and that this didn't really fit into the overall pattern or tone of the book. What I am trying to convey here is that the reader of this book is going to get the impression inevitably that here is an extremely intelligent, capable woman, which you are. Fair enough! So it's perfectly in order for you to be upset by certain types of insects and it's perfectly in order for you to commit a few gaffes in the marketplace, but I can't help but feel that another careful reading of the manuscript would indicate that there are too many places where, through minor words and phrases and throw-aways, you go too far in appearing to be the white man's burden in Somaliland, or some sort of inept female. I realize that this is innate modesty coming to the fore and possibly in other instances you are trying to inject a bit of humour. But my overall impression, again confirmed by our other readers, was that this could be toned down to advantage. You might well ask for chapter and verse on such a criticism, but frankly, Margaret, I think you're too good a writer and this is too good a book for us to meddle in that way. So there it is. A simple suggestion that you could improve the book by a slight toning down on this aspect of it.

My third suggestion is one that is already evident in suggestion No. 1. That is that for the most part we would feel the short sketches at the end could have been better interspersed throughout the book rather than being tacked on as almost an afterthought. I can't help but feel that the form of the book does fall apart towards the end. Since I am sending a copy of this letter to Macmillan's, I will now invite a really stinging blast from them concerning our suggestions by saying we think (except as far as the form of the book is concerned) that they may have done you no great favour in suggesting the deletion of some of the sketches that have been removed. I can't help but feel that their reader was not long in the humour department, because anything that seems to reflect on English gentlemen or gentlewomen in Somaliland is now gone. Maybe there were other good and sufficient reasons for deleting this material. In any case, it doesn't matter one bit to us whether they're in or out as far as our market is concerned.

Our final suggestion is that we think you are still a bit strong in terms of the Somali poems and folktales. This is obviously a labour of love on your part and you'll probably hate me for suggesting any further cutting. But to be realistic, I wonder if this is the place to publish this material. A very small percentage of the readers of this book are going to be enthralled by this material. I think it's a question of whether or not you want to indulge yourself by including it or indulge the reader by cutting it further. Or maybe in terms of form, it may be better to put the bulk of it at the end of the book as an appendix, so that at least it doesn't intrude on the forward motion of the book.[2]

So there you have it. Three of us here think that some attention to these suggestions would improve the book. It may well be that the next three readers would think we are crazy, but who knows? It's for you to decide. Our total conclusion is that the book is a delight, that it will bring you great credit, and who knows, it may sell very well indeed. And again, re: the title, it's an absolute inspiration.

All the best!
Sincerely,
J.G. McClelland

1. Jack Laurence was Margaret's husband. An engineer, Jack was hired by the British administration in Somaliland in 1951 and 1952 to "construct *ballehs*, large structures that collect water during the rains for the long dry periods in Somaliland's Haud desert" (Davis, *Margaret Laurence Writes Africa and Canada* 24).
2. Laurence took McClelland's advice in this instance: she removed the Somali poems and folktales from the book. McClelland's statement, "This is obviously a labour of love on your part," was based on the fact that Laurence's first book was a translation of Somali poems and folktales. That book, *A Tree for Poverty*, was published by Eagle Press for the British Somaliland Protectorate in 1954. Laurence was the first person ever to translate Somali poetry and tales into English.

Hollinger, 1 September 1962

Dear Jack:

Thank you for your letter of August 30th. Needless to say, I am very glad indeed that you like *The Prophet's Camel Bell*. As far as your criticisms are concerned, I am in agreement with most, though not all, of them. I agree completely that the question of the *ballehs* (not ditches, please!) was dropped too abruptly, and I think the reason that this happened was that I was not out in camp the last few months of our tour and therefore what took place was not as real to me. However, I recognise now, as I perhaps did not when I was writing the book, that a certain amount of basically truthful fictionalizing is okay, and I think this aspect of the story can be picked up and dealt with in the last chapter. I also agree that there are too many of my own unimportant blunders. I do not think this is due to any innate modesty coming to the fore, but rather to the fact that they happened some time ago and do not bother me any more. They were, as you suggest, put in mainly for the sake of humour, but I think you are right that some should be cut. It is very difficult to strike the right tone when writing directly about oneself. At the time when we were in Somaliland, I was really very naive about many things, but I do not want to present a picture of myself as some kind of nut. I think this aspect can be dealt with by cutting out a few episodes, etc. As far as the Somali poetry and stories are concerned, I don't really care one way or another. I would rather leave this chapter where it is in the book, but I will cut out some of the material—it is not all that dear to my heart at this point, luckily.

Now we come to the point where I must disagree with you. I don't think that the general form of the book can be any different. It was not put together accidentally, nor were the parts about the English stuck on as an afterthought. In the final analysis, it was through acquaintance with some of the English there that I came to realize something of the common thread that runs through the lives of all Europeans who are drawn to distant lands, and, in this way, to realize my own reasons for preferring to live abroad. This chapter on the English, therefore, is in a sense a culmination of everything I learned, and I think it should stay where it is. As far as the sketches of the English are concerned, I cut most of the unfavourable ones, not because I hesitated to put in anything that would reflect unfavourably on English gentlemen and gentlewomen, but rather because I came to feel that this sort of thing had been done to death. The sahib-types are people we all have met so often in books that I really wonder if it is worthwhile talking about them at all, unless one is prepared to do a thorough analysis? They are archaic and in most ways quite unimportant nowadays. I came to feel that what I had done, in the first version, was only to take a few cheap swipes at a number of dead ducks. As far as I am concerned, it is a question of R.I.P. However, I do agree with you to this extent—I think it is entirely possible that when I cut this chapter I cut out too much, as is my usual tendency. I'll go back over the part, and see what can be done with it. I hope you will agree that the general layout of the book should be left as it is.

Would you please send me the copy of the manuscript you have? I will get to work on it right away. I have had Macmillan's copy for more than a month now, and I would like to get the final corrections done as soon as I can. I want to get that whole thing done before the end of September if I can, as there is a strong chance that I may be going to England then. My husband expects to take a job in Pakistan, and if all goes as planned, I will go to England for the year with our children.

Re: picture—I have managed to obtain some very good pictures, which I will send to Macmillan when I return their copy of the manuscript. The photographs we took in Somaliland are pretty terrible, but a few of them may serve to simply identify various people.

Once again, I'm very glad you are taking the book. I'll do what I can to improve the manuscript in the areas you suggest. By the way, so far from being inept, your criticisms were all expressed with considerable tact, I thought, and I appreciate this very much indeed.

Best regards.

Sincerely,

Margaret [signed]

Margaret Laurence

copies to: A.D. Maclean; Willis Wing

Hollinger, 10 September 1962

Dear Jack:

I am sending back the revised manuscript of *The Prophet's Camel Bell*. I have also returned Macmillan's copy, and have sent the photographs to them. I hope you will think the script is improved. Personally, I think it is much better. I have completely re-written the last chapter, and have picked up the thread of the *balleh* story and have finished it off in what I hope is a more satisfactory way.[1] Everything in the last chapter is quite true, except for the fact that when Jack went out to examine the *balleh* after the rains, I was not with him, and so this final part is slightly embroidered for the sake of effect, but I think it is true to the spirit of the story, anyway, and is certainly true to the character of the Somalis as we knew them—they were just not the type to dance around the completed *balleh* in a burst of gratitude and joy!

I hope you will approve of what I have done with the chapter on the English. I have put back a few of the sketches I had cut, and have added to the section on the sahib-types. I did not want to go into painful detail with the sahibs, but I did not want, either, to give the impression that I was too polite to risk offending them. I am polite, but not that polite. I tried to put down, simply and without making a major production of it, what I honestly felt about them. As far as the other changes are concerned, I have cut out a number of my own slight blunders or anxieties, while leaving in the errors I feel are pertinent to the total experience, in the sense that I learned (I think) something from them. I have cut portions from the chapter on Somali literature, and I think this chapter is now short enough not to impede the forward progress of the narrative too much. I'll be most interested, naturally, to hear what you think.

I'll be going to England around the end of October, probably, and will certainly stop off in Toronto on my way.

All the best.

Sincerely,

Margaret [signed]

Margaret Laurence

1. Laurence is referring to a letter dated 5 September 1962, in which McClelland states, "In fact, I think you will solve this difficulty in the main by putting in a little more about the *ballehs* (translated meaning ditches)."

West 21st, 19 September 1962

Dear Margaret:

You are terrific. We've now had a chance to go through the revised script and find the problems all taken care of. It strikes just the right tone and the new ending is completely satisfying.

Sorry to have to write in such haste again. It is lack of time, not enthusiasm.

Sincerely,

J.G. McClelland

Hollinger, 29 October 1962

Dear Jack:

I'm sorry not to have seen you when I was in Toronto, but I'm glad I was at least able to talk with you on the phone. I hope you're feeling very much better now. Thanks very much for offering to write to the Canada Council[1] on my behalf. I don't know whether I stand much of a chance with them or not, but I am certainly keeping my fingers crossed, especially as I realize now that the cost of living has gone up a great deal in England since I last lived here. Thanks also for mentioning to Willis Wing the possibility of submitting portions of the Somaliland book for publication in Canada. At the moment, I find it difficult to think of anything except money, but probably this phase will pass.

I have just been interrupted for an hour in the writing of this letter by the fact that my flat was suddenly total darkness—the shillings had run out in the meter box, and, when I put more in, there was a colourful blue flash that seemed to indicate that I'd blown every fuse in the house. I am having to relearn the state of mind which regards electricity as a priceless treasure which more often than not exercises a stubborn will of its own and refuses to be exploited. Rhoda Levene, the landlady's daughter, came to the rescue with thousands of fuses and tools and a cheerful running commentary—"Let's see, what was it the electrician said? Red wire over black, or was it black over red?"—At last, for no apparent reason, the lights suddenly came on again, to the accompaniment of glad shouts of "Hallelujah!" and "Mazeltov!" from Rhoda and myself. I have been fortunate in getting a flat in the area I know best and like best. It's only 5 minutes from Hampstead Heath, and my children are within walking distance of their school. Like most flats here, it is in an old house, and it is full of rather strange Victorian furniture, hat racks and such, which I prefer to the modern arborite and paper-covered monstrosities found in many rented apartments here. To me, it seems absolutely ideal, and I couldn't be happier with it if it were Windsor Castle. Now all that remains is to put into effect your old slogan—"Back to your typewriter!"

I was so pleased to see Claire Pratt and Ruth Taylor[2] for lunch when I was in Toronto, and glad that we had an opportunity to talk. Claire said she would send me a copy of Irving Layton's[3] latest book—I would really love to see it. Also, any other good Canadian books which might not be available here, and which you felt you might spare a copy.

I saw Robert Yeatman, of Macmillan, the other day, and he said they would publish *The Prophet's Camel Bell* about next May—will it be the same in Canada?

They have lost the map,[4] and, although I have other copies, I have no idea where they are, as I was very overweight on air baggage at the last minute, and sent a lot of parcels by post, including the manuscript (the only copy) of the novel I was working on, and now I could kick myself, as I am certain the parcels will all go astray and I will never see the script again.[5] You didn't have a copy of the map with your copy of the Somaliland book, did you?

All the best.
Sincerely,
Margaret [signed]
Margaret Laurence

1. The Canada Council for the Arts offers a broad range of competitive grants and financial support to professional artists and art organizations in Canada. It was initially established upon recommendation by the Massey Commission in the 1950s. Here, Laurence refers to her application for a Canada Council grant, which would allow her the time and means to write her next book.
2. Ruth Taylor was McClelland's assistant at McClelland & Stewart at this time. In a letter preceding this one, dated 27 September 1962, Taylor wrote to Laurence and stated, "Your letter to Mr. McClelland arrived after he had left the office for an absence of about a month. I know that he was hoping to meet you in October, but it is doubtful that he will have returned to Toronto before the 15th. A very warm welcome awaits you here at McClelland & Stewart, however, and all who have had the privilege of meeting you a year ago are looking forward to seeing you again" (McClelland & Stewart Ltd. Fonds, Box 35, File 39).

3. Irving Layton (1912–2006) was a writer most well known for his poetry. He "was a member of the active group of young poets in Montreal who contributed to First Statement, founded by John Sutherland in 1942" (Toye 363). He taught English at Sir George Williams College (now Concordia University) in Montreal, and was appointed writer-in-residence at Sir George in 1965 and at the University of Guelph in 1969. He published numerous books of poetry between the 1960s and the 1980s.
4. The map was published in *The Prophet's Camel Bell*, the "Somaliland book," as she calls it here. A note accompanying the map in that book reads, "This map was specifically drawn to show the area of the Haud in Somaliland where Margaret Laurence and her husband lived and which she describes in this book" (8).
5. Laurence refers here to the first draft manuscript of *The Stone Angel*. Given the success this novel achieved, it is noteworthy that Laurence mailed her only copy of the script from Canada to England, relying on the postal service for its delivery.

Hollinger, 21 November 1962

Dear Jack:

Thanks for your letter of November 7th, and also many thanks for the advance on *The Prophet's Camel Bell*, which I received the other day. With Christmas coming up, the money could not have come at a better time. In fact, I was so delighted to see it that I think I must be turning into some kind of mercenary individual.

I don't know whether this is the right time to mention this subject or not, but Alan Maclean of Macmillan has suggested to me that they might be interested in doing my West African stories as a book, so I am engaged at the moment in typing them all out. I am doing three copies, and would like to submit one to you, in the event of Macmillan's deciding they would like to do the book. Jack, I hope you do not think I have been sneaky about this question—honestly, Alan Maclean brought up the subject; I didn't. Of course, I do not know yet what his reaction will be to the manuscript. I only mention it in case you might be interested, at some future date, provided Macmillan is going to do the collection. We will see.

I am very well organized now, and completely prepared to sally forth, as it were, and so I would be extremely grateful for any contacts with people here, which you could provide. The only snag is that I cannot yet be contacted by phone. I keep ringing up the proper department and telling them I cannot live one more day without my telephone, but they remain monumentally unmoved. Six weeks is the last estimate. So perhaps it would be better for you to wait until I let you know my telephone number, before writing to people here.

Once I have finished typing out the short stories, I am going to get down to the novel I was working on. The manuscript was not lost at sea, as I feared it would be. It arrived all right, and does not read too badly, in my view.

All the best. Sincerely,
Margaret

Heath Hurst, 28 November 1962

Dear Margaret:

Thanks for your letter. I don't feel you are being sneaky about the short stories at all. I'm still inclined to think it would be a mistake to have them published before your next novel, but let's wait and see what Macmillan's has to say after the script is put together.

I'll hold off for a few weeks and then send you copies of the letters that I send to England.

All the best!

Cheers!

J.G. McClelland

Hollinger, 17 January 1963

Dear Jack:

Many thanks for your last communication. I have been waiting to reply until I got a telephone, so I could give you my number—I am happy (happy? I'm delirious with joy!) to report that yesterday a plain, ordinary man arrived at my front door, not looking at all like Sir Galahad, but nevertheless bearing in his hands the Holy Grail. I am now in communication with the world. I have been phoning everyone I know, including friends in semi-distant parts such as Glasgow, so when I get my phone bill, I will probably have a nervous breakdown. My phone number is—*Swiss Cottage*—6185.

Will you please convey to Claire Pratt my thanks for her Christmas card? I was so glad to see her when I was in Toronto, and I only wish I had been there longer—all my visits anywhere seem to be more or less hurried.[1] ...

At the moment, I am typing out a novel, which I told you about when I was in Toronto a year or so ago. I have put it away for a long time, as I was filled with terrible doubts about anything written with a Canadian setting. However, I got it out again when I arrived here, and I do not know why I was so fearful about it before. I've re-written parts of it, but the bones remain the same. For better or worse, this is the way I want to say it. I'll send copies of it to Willis Wing when I've got it finished, which will be within the next month. It has a very short and succinct title, *Hagar*.[2]

All the best.
Sincerely,
Margaret

1. In this part of the letter, Laurence indicates that Macmillan has accepted what was to become *The Tomorrow-Tamer*.
2. This manuscript later became *The Stone Angel*.

Heath Hurst, 21 January 1963

Dear Margaret:

Thanks for your letter. Delighted that you have a telephone. I shall, as soon as things ease up around here a bit, send you a list of some of the people that I have written in London. ...

I am far happier to learn that you are busily engaged reworking the novel than I am to hear that Macmillan's have accepted the short story volume. It is still my opinion that they will be doing you a disservice, but even more important that you will be hurting your own career as a writer, by allowing the volume to go ahead at this time. I just don't see much point in it.

Although the volume of short stories will be well received by the critics, it is unlikely to sell and will probably earn you less money than you can earn by selling one story to *The Saturday Evening Post*, and I just can't see any purpose. Your short story volume would have a real chance for success if it were published after another successful novel. If Willis disagrees with this point of view, all well and good, but I'm sure he doesn't.

All the best!
Sincerely,
J.G. McClelland

Hollinger, 26 January 1963

Dear Jack:

Thanks for your letter of January 21, and also for your kindness in writing to people in London—this is greatly appreciated.

I am sorry to hear that you are not keen on a collection of short stories. I can certainly appreciate your point of view in this matter, and I can also believe quite readily that such a volume is not likely to make much money. However, I would like to explain to you something of my point of view. I feel that, although these stories are not political in content—in fact, quite the contrary—they are nonetheless written about a particular country at a particular time in history, and, in this way, if they are not published within the next year or so, they will be to some extent dated.[1] I also feel, in a purely personal way, that as these stories are finished, as far as I am concerned, I would rather see them born, as it were, than have them remain a piece of unfinished business. I am therefore very glad that Macmillan wants to do them as a collection, and, although my feeling about it may be based on personal reactions to my work, and the desire to have a thing finished and completed, rather than on an assessment of the book's sales potential, nevertheless this is my firm opinion and I therefore make apologies for it. I can understand and accept your viewpoint, which I know to be based upon a knowledge of the North American market, but from where I stand, it is better to have the book done than not done, and I feel glad it will be done at least in England, even if I don't make enough on it to cover a month's cigarettes. This may not be a sensible outlook—probably it isn't—but everybody has to proceed in the way that seems right to them. I hope you can see to some extent how I feel about it—not to have the book published anywhere is like going on being pregnant indefinitely, which, let's face it, is a horrible thought.

As far as the novel is concerned, that is still an unknown quality—however, for better or worse I hope to have it completed soon, so I can get to work on something new, as I have spent most of my time here so far in completing various projects from the past and now I would like to get on with something else. One encouraging thing is that Alan Maclean has accepted a short story of mine for the next *Winter's Tales*—the good thing about this is that this will be the first non-African story I have ever had published anywhere—that seems odd, doesn't it?[2] However, to me, this has provided the greatest encouragement possible at this point.

Best wishes.
Sincerely,
Margaret

1. The collection of short stories to which Laurence here refers, *The Tomorrow-Tamer*, takes place on Africa's Gold Coast (now Ghana) during the 1950s, when Laurence was there and when the country was undergoing decolonization.
2. This story, published later in 1963, was "The Sound of the Singing," which would later be included in *A Bird in the House*.

Hollinger, 4 February 1963

Dear Jack:

I was so glad to get your letter of February 1st. It was a relief to me that you appreciated my point of view regarding the short stories and that you thought you'd want to do the book. I really am very glad about this. As far as publication date is concerned, I know you will bring it out at the time you think is best for sales there, and as long as it is coming out, the exact time does not bother me one way or another. I hope the sales will exceed expectations, although if it is true (as I once heard Farley Mowat[1] say in a radio talk) that in Canada people buy fewer books per year than in any other country except Siam, then one does not expect miracles, especially as this book is not likely to be serialised in *Ladies' Home Journal* / or purchased by Walt Disney. However, we will see. Anyway, I can't tell you how pleased I am that you are going to do this book.

Many thanks for getting in touch with various people in London. The weather here is like the Arctic at the moment, but I think the English tend to exaggerate it a little, as they are not accustomed to real winter. My grocer said to me the other day, "Well, how do you like this royal throne of kings, this sceptred isle, *now*?" As I had never had a grocer quote Shakespeare to me before, I almost said, "Thanks to you, I like it fine," but I thought it might embarrass him.

All the best.
Sincerely,
Margaret

1. Farley Mowat (1921–2014) was a Canadian author and environmentalist renowned for books on the Canadian North, such as *People of the Deer* and *Never Cry Wolf*. Over the many years during which Mowat published with McClelland & Stewart, he and McClelland became close friends. According to James King, part of their "strong bond" came from having both fought in the Second World War, "as though that event created an invisible link between them" (*Jack* 52).

Heath Hurst, 11 June 1963

Dear Margaret:

The enclosure is just to let you know that we still think of you occasionally. How are things in London? Incidentally, we're very enthusiastic about the short story volume. I haven't looked at it myself as I think I have read most of the stories, but our readers' reports are highly enthusiastic.[1] I haven't seen the novel but Willis Wing tells me it is very good indeed. I hope by now you have heard from Ted Allan or Mordecai Richler.[2] Just about everyone else I can think of over there is a publisher, and I can't believe that Macmillan's would thank me for introducing you to other publishers in London. Hope you're having fun.

All the best!
Sincerely,
J.G. McClelland

1. Pratt wrote to Laurence about her collection of short stories, *The Tomorrow-Tamer* on 20 February 1963. She stated, "One of the best things that has happened to me in a long time is your manuscript of short stories. I wish there were some way in which I could put across to you how really enthusiastic I feel about them, Margaret. Depth of compassion and insight, combined with stylistic beauty and the use of the word or phrase that is exactly right, make of each of them a pure gem, a true union of the artist and the craftsman. In short they are marvelous. I found 'The Perfume Sea' especially moving but there is little use in singling them out as I would be tempted to discuss each one in turn" (Margaret Laurence Fonds, Clara Thomas Archives and Special Collections, 1980-001/019, File 133).
2. Mordecai Richler (1931–2001) was one of Canada's most prominent writers. He was born into an Orthodox family in Montreal's old Jewish neighbourhood and wrote about that community in his fiction. He was awarded the Order of Canada, the Governor General's Award (twice, in 1968 and 1971), and the Giller Prize. Ted Allan (1916–1995) was a Montreal-born, Jewish Canadian writer. His real name was Alan Herman, but he adopted his pen name to infiltrate a fascist organization and write an exposé for the Communist Party of Canada's newspaper, the *Clarion*. He won the Stephen Leacock Medal for Humour in 1985 for *Love Is a Long Shot*. Richler was one of McClelland's most successful authors, and was loyal to McClelland & Stewart, as McClelland was to him, through his writing years.

Hollinger, 16 June 1963

Dear Jack:

Thanks so much for your letter of June 11th, and for sending me a copy of your letter to Little, Brown & Co. It was really good of you to write to them in that way, Jack, and I was quite stunned and very grateful. Even if it has no affect [*sic*], many thanks for putting in that kind of a recommendation.[1] I appreciate it very much indeed.

I am sorry there has been this difficulty over which book to publish first, the short stories or the novel. I know you have always felt it would be better to do a novel first, and, personally, I would not have any objection to this, but the way it has worked out here with Macmillan's, the short stories were accepted first and the novel later, and if they want to publish them in that order, I do not feel that I can quibble about it, considering that it seemed like some kind of miracle to me that they wanted to publish the short stories at all. Incidentally, I do not know if this will be of any interest to you or not, but I recently received a block-pull of Macmillan's cover for the short stories, and it is really a stunner, absolutely striking, guaranteed to hit anybody in the eye. I am glad to learn that Willis Wing tells you *Hagar* is very good, as this is more than he has ever told me, but not to worry. I am at last getting going at something, and have got into a five-page-per-day routine, but it is too soon to say what will come of it, if anything. For the moment, I am travelling hopefully, at least most of the time, and that is the main thing.

Things are fine in London, which is (how un-Canadian can you get?) my favourite city anywhere. Actually, I am not un-Canadian at all, and in fact feel deep sentiments towards my home and native land, especially when I am not there. This is sort of a family thing—you love people or places without necessarily liking them in an ever-present way. I feel at home here, and I really don't much care why. The weather has been marvellous; I have a Canadian university girl staying with me for the summer, and she takes my kids out on week-ends and during their holidays, thus enabling me to work without my beloved but distracting sprouts around; in general, life appears good and interesting, although not remunerative in any financial sense. I have a great talent for finding interesting projects, but none at all, it seem to me, for making money. Recently, I have done a series of scripts for the BBC African Service, which will be translated into Hausa, and, if I told you how much I was getting paid for them, you would laugh. I, however, did not laugh—I had a lengthy written battle with the BBC, which ended with their offering me half a guinea (roughly, a buck and a half) more per script.[2]

By the way, I should say how much I liked reading Irving Layton's *Balls For A One-Armed Juggler*. I'm not competent to judge poetry, but all I can say is that it said something to me, whereas Roy Daniells'[3] well-constructed efforts, no matter how beautiful the binding and the colour of the pages, did not. I liked especially Layton's "Advice to Young Poets" (or some such title), which was the only sensible thing I have ever read on this subject. No doubt I liked it because I agreed with it, but how else do you ever decide on anything? ...

Again, many thanks for writing to Little, Brown and Co.

Best regards.
Sincerely,
Margaret

1. On 11 June 1963, McClelland wrote a letter to Alan D. Williams, Little, Brown & Company, New York. In that letter, McClelland stated, "I am writing, somewhat gratuitously, to support the work of an author who Willis Wing tells me you have under consideration at the present time. I refer to Margaret Laurence." McClelland then wrote at some length about *This Side Jordan* and *The Prophet's Camel Bell*, and indicated how enthusiastic reviewers were about these books. He mentioned that she began to publish stories with *Saturday Night* as soon as Wing became her agent, and he noted that this point was significant, since, he observed, "Here is an author whose work had already been acclaimed for its literary merit by the little magazine group suddenly appearing (with the same sort of story) in the top mass media magazine in the U.S.A."

McClelland concluded this lengthy letter by asking Williams to consider Laurence's work: "We think she is a writer of quality in the Brian Moore category. We think she will write a lot of books and that she will make a steady advance into the ranks of the most important contemporary international authors. Certainly, she is one of the best that Canada has produced in a long, long time" (Margaret Laurence Fonds, Clara Thomas Archives and Special Collections, 1980-001/019, File 133).

2. As John Lennox and Ruth Panofsky explain in their annotation to a letter from Laurence to Adele Wiseman, written on 12 June 1963, "Gus Andrzejewski had introduced Margaret Laurence to the producers of the Hausa section, BBC African Service, and she had agreed to write ten scripts on worldwide folktales on some common themes. She was paid a total of forty seven pounds" (162).
3. Roy Daniells (1902–1979) was a Canadian professor who headed the English department at the University of Manitoba until 1946, after which time he left for the University of British Columbia, where he was integral to the formation of the creative writing department (see Djwa).

Hollinger, 29 June 1963

Dear Jack:

I wonder if Willis Wing has sent you the Script of *Hagar* yet? I have just received the page proofs from Macmillan's[1] and, re-reading the novel, I suddenly felt I had given you a wrong impression in my last letter when I said I liked my home and native land best when I was away from it. Actually, that is not true, as I see now when I read *Hagar*. Perhaps reading it again has made me homesick—I don't know. But when the chips are down, there is only one country in the world that I really give a damn about, and I see now how right it was to stop writing about people other than my own. I will be intensely interested to know your reaction to *Hagar,* Jack, because it seems to me the only really true thing I have ever written—this is because it is the only thing written entirely from the inside, with the kind of knowledge that one can only have of one's own people, who are, as the Muslims say about Allah, as close to you as your own neck vein. I do not know why I had so many doubts about *Hagar,* initially—possibly because I wasn't sure I could write anything in which the theme was all inner, not outer. God knows there are plenty of flaws in the novel, but I am really anxious to know what you think about Hagar herself. Personally, I think she is a hell of an old lady! Of course, I may be prejudiced. Anyway, for better or worse, the voice in which she speaks is all her own, and I think now that I can't ever again be content to write in anything except this idiom, which is of course mine.

It wasn't really necessary of me to write this letter, I suppose, but I wanted to correct what I feel was a wrong impression in my last letter.[2]

All the best.

Sincerely,
Margaret [signed]
Margaret Laurence

1. Macmillan & Co. Ltd. in London, England, had tentatively accepted the manuscript on 18 February 1963. At this time, Lovat Dickson from Macmillan wrote to Laurence: "I do congratulate you [on *Hagar*] most warmly. This is a first-class book, if I may say so, and *Hagar* is a real creation. If you go on this way I can see you becoming a very important writer, and I would not have been very far out in introducing you to the Deputy High Commissioner the other night as *the* Canadian writer. What I am giving you here is my own personal reaction. ... That we shall want to do the book there can be not the slightest doubt" (Margaret Laurence Fonds, Clara Thomas Archives and Special Collections, 1980-001/019, File 132).
2. At the top of this letter, McClelland has written, "*Hagar* not yet received. Wing wired last week."

Heath Hurst, 5 July 1963

Dear Margaret:

I was glad to have your letter and to have your views about the novel. Unfortunately, I'm still not in a position to interpret it adequately because we have not yet seen *Hagar*. This brings up several points that I think need mentioning for the record, so brace yourself. More often than not, I find myself writing to you like a Dutch uncle (is that the appropriate expression?—I'm not sure), even though that is a ludicrous position for me to assume. I do so only because, as I have said to you before, I don't want you ever to be in a position where you can come back and say, "Why in hell didn't you tell me what you thought?"

Let me review briefly what has happened since I wrote last. I enclose a copy of the reply I received from Little, Brown. In the same mail, I received a letter from Macmillan's and I enclose a copy of this as well. Yesterday, I received a letter from Alfred Knopf, as per the enclosed, and I have also enclosed a copy of my reply. All this gives me reason to think that things are not moving as smoothly as they should be. The following queries, comments, etc. occur:

1. What in hell goes on at Macmillan's? Have they gone completely berserk? They are rushing the short stories into print, and, according to the best information we have today, we won't receive copies of *The Camel Bell* until August. Are they planning to publish three of your books in one season? If they are, all I can say is please, do something about it. Even if you were the second coming of Christ, it would be foolish to publish three of your books between this fall and next spring. I have expressed my opinions gently on this subject in the past but now I say to you categorically, this is madness.
2. You will have noted the latter paragraphs in my letter to Alfred Knopf, where I suggest that *Hagar* might have some defects. I don't

know, Margaret, because I haven't seen it, but please believe, even though Macmillan is one of the great imprints in the publishing world, that editorial policy in English publishing houses is inclined to be too damn lax. We're not the greatest authorities in these matters, but I am concerned about the fact that two American houses don't like the novel. It may be that you have rushed it too much. It may be that it has flaws. I know very well that you won't make changes unless you agree entirely with the suggestions that are made and I think this is the way it should be. But surely there is time to have *Hagar* properly evaluated. This is going to be a key book in your writing career. Because I have not seen the novel, I have no right to an opinion, but my experience in this business, for what it's worth, tells me that if it is true, as Macmillan's have suggested to us, that they are going to press with this book in two weeks, that you should phone them immediately and tell them to stop. They will scream like mad, but I think you should tell them to stop.

3. If you want us to assume any sort of responsibility, I think you must make provision in the future to have enough copies of the manuscript typed so that we can receive one directly. I don't think Willis Wing can be criticised for not having sent us one. After all, we are pre-sold on your writing, and his concern is solely in selling to the major market, which is in the U.S.A. If you feel the Macmillan editorial service is sufficient, then that's fair enough. We don't need the exercise nor will we be offended. But my experience as a publisher in dealing with the English and American publishing scene inclines me to the view that for nine out of ten writers at least the major satisfactions that they seek (and I don't mean money alone) are more likely to be secured from the North American market than the U.K. So, once again, Margaret, in the final analysis it's your decision but, even though I deplore having to assume the role of wet blanket, I am not happy about the way things are developing.

Cheers!
J.G. McClelland

Hollinger, 8 July 1963

Dear Jack:

Thanks very much for your letter of July 5th. I find this reply a rather difficult matter, because I am in a sense split two ways. In the first place, I appreciate so very much the fact that you have gone to bat for me with various American publishers; I accept and trust your assessment of the Canadian situation as far as publishing and sales are concerned; I know very well that your advice to me is given not only out of a concern for business but also out of a concern for writing, as such, and I also know how many Canadian writers (Leonard Cohen[1] and Irving Layton come to mind immediately, in addition to myself) owe their first books to the fact that you thought they had something and were willing to take a chance on them and try to get these books published outside Canada as well. I know all this, Jack, and I know also that your opinion of my writing has some special significance for me, perhaps because one is always, if unconsciously, writing for one's own people, and what they think matters terribly. On the other hand, in all honesty, I cannot find myself in agreement with much of what you say, and all I can hope is that you will be able to accept my viewpoint as one that is valid for me, even though you will not agree with it, nor do I expect you to agree with it. In reply to your queries and comments, here are my own comments:

1. Re: Macmillan's decision to publish three books within one year: I think you will find that these books will not be all published in the same season, although it is certainly true that they will be all within twelve months. It is my understanding, from Alan Maclean of Macmillan's (whose judgment, incidentally, I trust in these matters) that they have at various other times, and, with other writers, published several books close together, when it happened

that a number of works had been completed, and that this policy has worked out very satisfactorily. I feel that the selection of publication dates must be the business of the publisher, not of the writer, and I feel that this is something they know, in relation to their market, a great deal better than I do. In a personal sense, the time of publication does not greatly matter to me, except that once I have finished with something, it is an enormous relief and also encouragement to get it out of my hands, so that I can begin to work on something new. This does not mean that I am content to let something go before I feel it is properly finished, nor does it mean (as I think you know, from what you say in your letter to Knopf) that I am not willing to take criticism and editorial suggestions. It does, however, mean that if I have done everything which I feel I can do with a manuscript, and if it has been accepted by a number of readers for a firm of publishers whom I trust, then I would rather see it published than not published, quite apart from both the question of money and the question of critical acceptance or rejection by reviewers or public. I don't mean that I am ever satisfied with the final product, because I am not. I only mean that it has to take its own chances, for I am not willing to remain involved with it for too long a time. I can appreciate very well your point of view about the inadvisability of publishing three books close together, as far as the Canadian (or American) market is concerned, and I wonder if it would not be possible for you to publish at different times from Macmillan, if you feel this would be best? I noticed in the contract which I recently signed with McClelland & Stewart for *The Tomorrow-Tamer* that you agreed to publish within one year of Macmillan's publication date, so I wonder if it would not be possible for you to publish *Hagar* first, if you felt this would be better (always supposing you like the novel, which you may not), and the short stories later? Honestly, Jack, I do not care when you publish any of these things, as long as they get published ultimately, but I do not feel that I want to interfere, or indeed that I ought to try to interfere, with Macmillan's policy here in England. I think you know what you are doing in your area. I think they know what they are doing in their area. Surely there can be some differences without the necessity of qualitative judgements on either side.

2. Re: *Hagar*—First of all, because this question relates very much to this novel, I would like to point out that I have not produced four books in four years. I have produced four books in eight years, which is rather a different matter. If you or anyone else thinks that I have been grinding them out like sausages, you are greatly mistaken. This fact has no significance one way or another, as far as the quality of any one book is concerned, but it does indicate, I hope, that none of these manuscripts has been done quickly or without thought. I am sorry to be nasty about this matter, but I resented your remark about the second coming of Christ so much that it was very fortunate for the both of us that you were not present at the time, otherwise I would have clobbered you with the nearest solid object available. I do not imagine that *Hagar* is without flaws, nor am I so lacking in critical perception that I delude myself about the quality of my writing. I write better than some, and a whole lot worse than many—what else can one say on this subject? Please, Jack, do not ever imagine that I am at this point over-estimating my abilities. My problem has always been the reverse—to have enough faith in my writing abilities to be able to go on, in some fashion, because the alternative—not to go on—would mean that nothing at all was any good anywhere, for me, since this kind of work appears to be a necessary condition of life. Regarding *Hagar*, I can only say this—the first draft took me only six months to write, and then I put it away for an entire year, taking it out from time to time to re-write various parts of it. When I came to England, I re-wrote parts of it again, and these revisions took about three months. In fact, if a book is good it does not matter if it was written in twenty years or two weeks, but I only mention these facts in order to show you that I did not dash it off in five minutes before breakfast. I would certainly have been prepared to consider any suggestions which Macmillan's had to offer about the manuscript,

although by the time it was actually submitted, I could not in myself see how it could have been written in any shorter or in any other form, whatever its flaws. The opinion given to me by Macmillan's was not the opinion of one man or even several, but of half a dozen readers, reporting independently. I do not say they are right—how on earth do I know who is right? All I can do at this point is to try and separate my own point of view, from the expressed opinion of various people at Macmillan's. I am only too well aware of the flaws in this novel, as I always am with anything I have written, and, although I have no intention of listing these flaws for you, I could do so in detail and have done so, to myself. However, these flaws are of a basic nature—the failure to communicate [with] enough people at enough depth—and about this kind of thing, one can only say, better luck next time. I mean, I could rewrite this script from now until Judgement Day and not get any further ahead with it. I do, however, feel that the character of Hagar herself comes across, that she speaks in her own voice and it is a true voice. If it is, as one American publisher so charmingly phrases it, "grey and lugubrious," then I am sorry but I cannot help it. You try making a musical comedy out of the Scots Presbyterians, and see how far you get. Anyway, I do not think it is in essence pessimistic, in fact quite the reverse, but this is a matter of opinion. All this boils down to only one simple fact—the novel may not be any hell, but it is written in the only way I could write it, and it was the best I could do at the time. If it is of any interest to an American publisher, that will be my good luck, but it would not surprise me in the slightest if it were not. I am very heartened and encouraged that Macmillan's in England feel that it is worth publishing, and even more heartened by the fact that a few people whose judgement I value have read it with comprehension and with an understanding of the fact that, although it is very much Canadian, it really has nothing to do with geography, but is a continuation of the same themes that appear in all my African stories, namely *Uhuru*.[2] I do not like speaking about these things because then it feels phoney. What you think of this novel matters to me a great deal, naturally, but in the long run only one thing appears quite clear—if it hits a chord with you, you will publish it; if it does not hit a chord with you, you will not publish it. All I am sorry about is that you did not receive a copy of the manuscript before all this series of complexity began, because I wanted you to look at it absolutely cold, and now this is not possible. This is the only thing I blame Willis Wing for—because I did send him two copies of *Hagar*, and asked him to send one to you immediately, and he did not do so. I have been pestering him about this matter for some time, and I certainly do not blame you for asking me in future to send a script directly to you. I will always do so in future, and, believe me, the fact that you have not yet received the manuscript is something, which annoys me very much indeed. What you must realise about me is that I have never been under the slightest misapprehension about the earning of vast sums of money from my writing, and, because I feel this way, the American market matters to me least of all. Your opinion, i.e. the opinion of a Canadian publisher therefore matters to me much more than the opinion of an American publisher. Naturally, Willis Wing does not view things this way, possibly because he believes that a few people can make a living out of writing, but this is not a belief I have ever held, in relation to myself.

3. Regarding your assuming, as you say, "any sort of responsibility"—I think I have dealt with this question in (2), above, mainly, and I completely agree that I should have sent the script of the novel directly to you, and would have done so if I had thought there would be any delay in your receiving it. Basically, however, this question goes deeper than the receiving of one particular manuscript. I don't want you, Jack, or anyone to assume responsibility for me or my writing other than that which you feel in yourself you want to assume, looking at the situation both from a business and from a literary (horrible word) point of view. If you like *Hagar*, if she says something to you, you will publish the novel. If she doesn't, you will tell me so, quite honestly, and that will be that, with no ill feeling on either side, I hope. I do not want you to feel you are committed to

my writing, if you do not want to be, and I do not want to feel that I am bound to agree with you, however much I like you and however much I am grateful to you. I don't think it is likely that I will change very much, in any important way. If anyone wants to publish the books I write, that is my good luck; if not, my bad luck—what else, in the final analysis, can anyone say?

All the best, and please write soon and tell me you are on speaking if not publishing terms with me.

Sincerely,
Margaret [signed]
Margaret Laurence

1. Leonard Cohen (1934–2016) was a highly acclaimed Canadian writer and poet, but became most famous for his work as a singer and songwriter. He was inducted into the Canadian Music Hall of Fame and the Canadian Songwriters Hall of Fame, and he was a Companion of the Order of Canada. Cohen and McClelland were close friends and had much respect for one another. However, they also had many disagreements. Cohen had an aversion to signing contracts and protested against McClelland & Stewart's design for his books. For instance, they disagreed on the marketing of Cohen's book, *Beautiful Losers* (King, *Jack* 114, 156–57).
2. The Swahili word for "freedom" or "(national) independence," *uhuru*, may also refer to the campaigns for and achievement of national independence in Africa, especially in Kenya, Uganda, and Tanzania.

Heath Hurst, 12 July 1963

Dear Margaret:

That's some letter. It makes me think you have a real writing talent. Have you ever considered writing a book? I am told it's a very interesting field of endeavour.

Seriously, Margaret, while I don't agree with everything you say, it is nevertheless a perfectly reasonable point of view, and I am not going to quarrel with it.

I sense a slight tinge of resentment in your categorical rejection of the fact that anyone "should take responsibility for you." Certainly, I assume no such responsibility. To be truthful, in this matter I think my responsibility is to myself in my professional capacity. What I mean by that is simply that I could not be satisfied with the way I perform my function unless I stated my views very definitely. Having stated them I can rest. I don't ask anyone to accept my advice—I ask only that they listen to it.

I think you do yourself a disservice, though, on the one point. There is no earthly reason why your writing cannot be successful commercially, and if your writing is to be successful commercially, there is a hell of a lot more money to be made in the American market than anywhere else. This is a simple fact of life. But if you're not concerned with it, there's no reason why I should be and certainly there's no reason why Macmillan's should be. They are an outstanding publish[er,] and it is encouraging to have such enthusiasm from them. The fact that they are inadvertently (and I say that advisedly, because they are publishing for their markets) hurting your publishing position in the U.S. should not concern them.

I don't feel that it's right for you to be annoyed at Willis Wing. His only function in life in this instance is to make money for you. This he is trying to do, and he can make far more money for you in the U.S. market than he can in the Canadian market. It's that simple, and I simply say that when he needs two copies of the manuscript, an additional one should be typed in future and sent directly to us. Were I in his position, I would still not have sent a script to McClelland & Stewart.

I could wish that we could choose our time of publication independently of Macmillan, as you suggest, but the fact of life, Margaret, is that we can't. The English and Canadian markets are tied together just as irretrievably as the American and Canadian markets. The Canadian book trade read English trade journals and many of them subscribe to the principal English book reviews. Good stores here will try and buy the book directly (when they can do so through jobbers and not through Macmillan) as soon as the book is available unless we have announced it. I don't blame them. I would do the same if I were a retailer. Thus, if we don't publish more or less simultaneously with them, the cream can be taken off our market. The same is true to a far lesser degree (because you are Canadian) in the U.S. market. In the book world there *is* no English speaking country that is isolated from the other. This is again a fact of life.

But I don't think I'll advance anything by covering old ground or attempting to answer your comments in detail. I have said that I don't agree with the position you have taken, but I certainly do respect and agree with your right to take it. And as far as your last paragraph is concerned, I have never felt that any author should feel grateful to us for publishing a book. We don't publish as a favour. We publish as a business, and we consider it a privilege to publish the work of an author whose writing we believe in. And if you should at any point write a book that either we don't want to publish or that we don't think should be published, I can assure you that I will be the first one to tell you. Meanwhile, why should we concern ourselves with that.

I have written Macmillan's re: *Hagar* and told them we cannot place a sheet order with them and will not until we have an opportunity to evaluate the manuscript. And finally, I think we can continue to be on both speaking and publishing terms for a while yet.

Cheers!
J.G. McClelland

Hollinger, 15 July 1963

Dear Jack:

I was so relieved to get your letter this morning, as I had been going through horrible agonies of doubt ever since I wrote to you, feeling that the letter must have a sounded like my last will and testament or something. The fact is that I dislike so much having a disagreement with someone I like, that when I finally do so, it usually turns out like the eruption of Vesuvius. Thank you for being so good-tempered about it.

I can now appreciate, from your last letter, your reasons for feeling so strongly about publication dates. I had not fully understood that it would be impossible for you to publish at a separate time from Macmillan, but I can see now how difficult your position would be in this respect. I'm truly sorry about this, Jack. The only thing I can suggest is that it might be possible for Macmillan's to hold publication of *Hagar* until March or April or thereabouts. It seems to me that this would be quite possible, and I'll discuss this with Alan Maclean. I wonder if such a postponement would be of any use to you? It would be a good thing if some compromise could be reached. I don't feel that I can ask Macmillan's to alter radically their plans, but I don't see why *Hagar* couldn't be put off for three months or so, if that would help your market. Let me know what you think.

Re: the financial situation, in relation to North America—it is not that I am not concerned about making money. I am, to put it mildly, extremely interested. I guess I have some pessimistic feelings about American publishers and publications, that is all.

I see what you mean about Willis Wing's reasons for not sending you the script of *Hagar*, and I am not annoyed about it now. I didn't understand before that I ought to have sent him three copies, and so I was rather puzzled and subsequently irritated that he had not sent you a copy, as I very much wanted you to see it. I agree that he's doing everything possible, and I'm afraid he has had a lot of trouble over these 3 books of mine, with very little in it for himself, at least so far.

I don't feel grateful to you because you published *This Side Jordan*, Jack—I know you would not publish anything you didn't believe worth publishing, and I trust your opinion and would not value it unless I felt this way. I meant only that I felt grateful to you for a lot of encouragement and for various things such as the letter you wrote to Little, Brown on my behalf. I didn't want you to feel that I took any of these things for granted, without noticing them, that's all.

Re: your question in paragraph (1) of your letter—"Have you ever considered writing a book?" You know, that's not a bad idea, Jack. I've often said to my friends, "some of the things that have happened to me—I swear, you could write a book about them." If I ever have time, I'm going to take a course in creative writing.

Thanks again for your letter, and for your philosophical calm, which makes me feel much calmer and better.

All the best.
Sincerely,
Margaret [signed]
Margaret Laurence

Heath Hurst, 12 August 1963

Dear Margaret:

I have finally had a chance to read *Hagar*—as a matter of fact I read it about a week ago but because we are in our sales conference period, I haven't had time to do anything about it. Let me say without hesitation, that I think it is a very fine piece of writing. It is sensitive, compassionate, moving and all in all I think a very good performance. If I were an editor (which I ain't) and under slightly different circumstances, I would be inclined to make some minor editorial suggestions, but I'm not going to, and I don't really think it would make any great difference to anything anyway.

After reading it, I have a far better understanding of your feeling about the American market, and also the reaction of the American editor. I certainly think this book should be published in the U.S.A., but I would agree that it is unlikely to have a very big sale. I think the same is true as far as Canada is concerned, although to a far lesser degree. Obviously, it has some built-in advantages for a Canadian market but, by and large, it is within our experience the type of novel that Canadians don't turn cartwheels about. I'm sure though that it will have a very fine critical reception and should sell as well as the first novel. I want to do some checking out on this with my associates, and we'll be writing Macmillan's directly in due course about a joint manufacturing deal.

In an earlier letter, you were enthused about the jacket for the short story volume. I agree with you, but I have just seen for the first time the jacket for *The Prophet's Camel Bell* and, I must say, it is just as bad as the other one is good. It makes it look like some sort of dull travel book, which is hardly what it is. I don't imagine that the jacket designer read the book, which is a pity.

All the best.
Sincerely,
J.G. McClelland

Hollinger, 17 August 1963

Dear Jack:

Thanks for your letter of July 31. I am very glad that you have settled with Macmillan on a later publishing date for *Hagar*. Being a canny Scot from way back, however, I feel it still remains to be seen whether you will want to publish the novel or not. I look forward with great interest and some trepidation to your report on it.

I heard from Willis Wing yesterday, saying that Knopf has decided to take all three of my books. Needless to say, I was overjoyed about this, and also somewhat astonished, considering that their letter to you in regard to my work was not very enthusiastic. However, mine not to question why. I am just so damn glad they are taking all three books that I can hardly believe it is true. Apparently, they will be getting in touch with you re: publication dates, but I understand they are thinking of publishing in this order—*Hagar, The Prophet's Camel Bell,* and *The Tomorrow-Tamer*. I hope, if this is what they do, that it will not complicate matters further for you. I promise never again to pull this stunt of having too many manuscripts at one time. Probably things will go to the opposite extreme, and I will spend years over the next novel.

Right now, I am only working on short stories for awhile, and was greatly encouraged and also surprised to hear in the same letter from Willis Wing that *The Saturday Evening Post* has taken a Canadian story of mine (I say "Canadian" only to show it isn't African—it is encouraging to me).[1]

By the way, thanks for writing to Knopf in the way you did.

Sincerely,
Margaret [signed]
Margaret Laurence

1. None of the stories in Laurence's Canadian collection of short stories was originally published in the *Saturday Evening Post*.

Heath Hurst, 21 August 1963

Dear Margaret:

A letter from Alfred Knopf tells me that they are to be your publishers in the U.S.A. Congratulations. I am delighted. They are fine people to be associated with. Now that vast wealth is starting to roll in, I hope that you will continue to speak to your old friend.

We plan to be quite disloyal to our Empire tie and do the novel in conjunction with Knopf rather than Macmillan's. It is not so much a question of being disloyal to the Empire really as much as it is one of being loyal to you and to ourselves. We can do a much better job with their edition and by tying in with their promotion and publicity. I don't know yet what it will mean in terms of pub. date of the novel, but they will probably do the novel in Spring, since I understand that they plan to publish the novel first and follow with the *Camel Bell* and then the stories.

They are not too enthusiastic about the title *Hagar*. I agree with them completely and wish I had thought of suggesting a change myself. They "don't think it suits the book," and I must agree. I think it is an eminently suitable name for the old lady, but as a book title—to one who hasn't read the book—it seems to evoke the wrong image. Will you give this matter your best thought and see if you can suggest some alternative?

All the best.
Sincerely,
J.G. McClelland

Hollinger, 26 August 1963

Dear Jack:

Many thanks for your letters of August 12 and August 21. As a matter of fact, I only received the August 12th one today, as it had been sent sea mail—don't tell me times are getting *that* hard! I hope the enclosed card may cheer you up, if you need cheering up.[1]

Seriously, I was very glad to have your reactions to *Hagar* at last, although when you say you think it'll at least have a fine critical reception, this sounds to me as though you suspect it may sell about six copies, probably all to members of my family. Nonetheless, I am greatly relieved that you did find something in it, and now that Knopf has taken it, the sales picture may not be so bleak as we both feared. By the way, in reference to your Aug 21st letter, I have a feeling that it will be some considerable time before the "vast wealth" starts rolling in. But you never know. If Walt Disney can make a film about animals running away from home, why not a film about an old lady running away from home? (Was that a low blow, Jack? If so, I'm sorry!)[2]

Re: the question of title—I do hope you will not feel that I am becoming awkward and difficult to deal with in editorial questions. I don't want to be difficult—quite the contrary. But the fact is that when Macmillan took the novel here, the question of title arose, as some people at Macmillan also had the feeling that *Hagar* gave the impression of a historical or a Biblical kind of novel. At that time, I knocked my brains out for about a fortnight, trying to dream up another title. Titles are not usually a problem for me, but once I've got the title, I find it difficult to change. Anyway, I suggested *Rage Against the Dying*, from the Dylan Thomas lines at the beginning of the novel. Alan Maclean wasn't keen on this title and I felt, myself, that it sounded like an imitation of an O'Hara title. Alan then made one or two suggestions, neither of which I liked at all. I then began re-reading all the Psalms, as a great deal of the spirit of

Presbyterianism and in a way of Hagar herself, is to be found there. I came up with *Sword in My Bones*—"As with a sword in my bones, mine enemies reproach me, while they say daily unto me, Where is thy God? Why art thou cast down, O my soul? And why art thou disquieted within me?" Etcetera. Alan thought this was okay, but after a few days this title seemed to me to suggest either a who-dun-it by Mickey Spillane or some kind of blood-and-thunder story, piracy on the high seas or something. At this point, it became clear to me that the title of the book was really *Hagar*, and that I couldn't think of it any other way, try as I might. And I did try, Jack, honestly. My feeling was that most people do not know who the hell Hagar in the Bible was, anyway, and that the kind of title I wanted was something exceedingly sparse, plain, un-fancy, kind of Canadian gothic, if you know what I mean. I also felt that the book was in a sense a one-character novel—I mean, she is the story. At this point, Lovat Dickson said he didn't know what all the fuss was about, as *Hagar* was obviously the right title. So it remained *Hagar*. And that is where matters stand at the present time. As far as the American and Canadian markets are concerned, it might be advisable to have another title, and I am perfectly willing to consider any suggestions, if anyone has any to make. I am very reluctant to have it brought out with different titles in N. America and England, but I don't think that it would be too late to change it, here. I must say, however, that I am not very enthusiastic about changing it, for reasons I have explained. Personally, I think the "image" of the book would depend, in this case, to a large extent upon the jacket design—i.e. if it were clear from the jacket that it was *not* a Biblical or historical tale, then people would not get the wrong idea. At least *Hagar* is simple and easy to remember. Also, I think I am getting kind of tired of these 24-word titles—"Stretch My Soul Upon A Rack Of Clouds" and that sort of nonsense. Anyway, if both you and Knopf feel very strongly about this question, do you have any good idea man who might make any worthwhile suggestions? I don't think I can. I'm really sorry, Jack, as I feel I have been so much trouble to you of late. Maybe someday it will all be seen to have been worth it—I hope so.

All the best.

Sincerely,

Margaret [signed]

Margaret Laurence

P.S. I agree with you about the jacket for *The Prophet's Camel Bell,* although it is not true that the person who designed the jacket hadn't read the book. I feel now that I should have tried to do something about this jacket, but it came to me shortly after I arrived in this country, and in my disorganized state at that time, I couldn't have cared less if the jacket had been blank—I'm sorry now about it, however. Re: your doing the novel with Knopf, I am sure this will be the best arrangement for you and for myself, as it will enable you to tie in with their publication date, etc. I had expected that you would do this, although naturally I did not say so to Macmillan, as I feel that your arrangements in this way are your business and it is not up to me to say anything to anyone about them, one way or another.[3]

1. The card says, "Be an Author, No Talent Necessary, Takes only a few minutes of your time, Amaze your Friends," and on the inside it says, "Write me a Letter." Laurence wrote, "You don't really owe me a letter, but I couldn't resist this card" (McClelland & Stewart Ltd. Fonds, Box 35, File 41).
2. Laurence refers to Sheila Burnford's novel, *The Incredible Journey*, which is about the travels of three animals trying to reunite with their masters. The manuscript was rejected by McClelland & Stewart before going on to become a huge success and getting its own Disney movie adaptation in 1963, a fact that galled McClelland greatly. Burnford (1918–1984) was a British novelist most renowned for *The Incredible Journey*.
3. Quoting this letter from Laurence, McClelland wrote to Alfred Knopf of New York, who would be publishing the American edition of this novel (which becomes *The Stone Angel*). The letter is about the as-of-yet undecided title of the novel. Knopf wrote back on 4 September 1963 to say he liked the title *Hagar*. He stated, "Many thanks for yours of August 30th, quoting that long letter from Margaret Laurence. She seems to be quite a person" (McClelland & Stewart Ltd. Fonds, Box 35, File 41).

Hollinger, 16 September 1963

Dear Jack:

... I have now heard from Knopf, via Willis Wing, about the question of the title of *Hagar*. They have made two suggestions for titles, neither of which seem suitable at all to me. These are *Mrs. Shipley*, which seems merely dull, and *Old Lady Shipley*, which seems out of character for Hagar. However, do not despair. As I was brooding about this question, another title occurred to me, and now it seems to me that it was so clearly meant to be the title of this novel that I am astonished I did not think about it before. It is *The Stone Angel*. I wonder what you think of it? I have written to Willis Wing, asking him to contact Knopf and see if they will agree to the use of this title. I have been in touch with Macmillan here, and they all agree that this is a good title. Although it will mean that they will have to have a new jacket design, and also that changes will have to be made in title page, etc., they have agreed to use this new title, provided Knopf and yourself are in agreement, for they feel, as I do, that it would be a mistake to have the novel published with two different titles, in England and in North America. I wonder if you would let me know as soon as possible your opinion about this title?

Perhaps I should explain some of my reasons for liking *The Stone Angel* as a title. The figure of the stone angel recurs throughout the novel, and Hagar associates it with her father's stern pride and devotion to outward appearances. It also has associations with her ineffectual mother and hence with Hagar's own locked-in womanhood. Only gradually does she come to see the figure of the stone angel as herself, dogmatically pointing what she feels to be the proper way to her family, without really knowing who they are at all. In the end, she sees her son Marvin as Jacob, demanding the angel's blessing. She has been a figure of rigid authority in the lives of her family. Her adherence to the conventional proprieties and her withholding of love have damaged all the people most closely associated with her. She has always wanted for herself an independence, which she has been unwilling to grant to others. The stone angel, as Hagar ultimately sees, will someday topple entirely and no one will set her upright again. But Hagar's strength and tenacity, as well as being damaging, have also been admirable. She is a fighter right to the end, and in this way she is, as Marvin says of her, "a holy terror." This, in very brief terms, is why I think *The Stone Angel* would make a good title. In strictly practical terms, also, I think it is interesting and would lend itself to a good jacket design. Please let me know what you think. I could kick myself for not having thought of this title six months ago, especially as it was there, staring me in the face all along. All this difficulty might have been avoided, but I suppose there is no use in thinking about that now.

If Knopf and yourself are not keen on this title, I would like this title to remain *Hagar*, or else to be *Hagar Shipley*, which at least relates to the title of the English edition. But if you think *The Stone Angel* is okay, I would feel happier about the book appearing under this title in all three countries. I am sorry about all this business.

All the best.
Sincerely,
Margaret [signed]
Margaret Laurence

Heath Hurst, 24 September 1963

Dear Margaret:

Thanks for your very good letter of the 16th regarding the title. I rather like *The Stone Angel*. I think it's a bit of an inspiration and I hope that Knopf will react the same way. I've sent your letter on to them. I agree with your rejection of their two titles. ...

All the best.
Sincerely,
J.G. McClelland

P.S. You will be interested to know that *Saturday Night*[1] has been revitalized in Canada and is being published again by Arnold Edinborough. He is delighted with the Somaliland book and is giving it a feature review. He wants to follow it with one of your short stories. I've given him a copy of the short story volume and he will be negotiating with Willis Wing on the purchase. There will be no money in it. They don't have any but I think it will be a very good promotion at this time and I hope it can be worked out.

1. *Saturday Night* was first published by Edmund Sheppard as a weekly in 1887, becoming a notable literary, political, and cultural journal. It came under the editorship of Arnold Edinborough in 1958, and passed to Robert Fulford, who was editor from 1968 to 1987. Its publication was suspended in 2005.

Hollinger, 27 September 1963

Dear Jack:

Thanks for your letter of September 24th. I am so glad that you like the title *The Stone Angel*, for the novel. I have recently heard from Willis Wing about this matter, and apparently Knopf [is] "delighted" with this title, so the whole thing seems to be settled, thank goodness. Macmillan are [*sic*] going to use the new title, as well, and I am very relieved that the book will be published with the same title here and in North America. ...

I was very pleased to hear that Arnold Edinborough[1] has again taken over *Saturday Night* and naturally I was delighted to hear that he likes the Somaliland book. I hope he will be able to publish one of my stories. The money doesn't matter, in this instance—I agree that it would be an excellent thing from the point of view of promotion.

I am so glad that everything seems to have been sorted out now, in regard to these three books. Thanks for bearing with me throughout all these difficulties.

All the best.
Sincerely,
Margaret [signed]
Margaret Laurence

P.S. Thanks very much for sending me a copy of Patricia Blondal's *From Heaven with a Shout*.[2] I did not like the title very much, under the circumstances, but I liked the book. I thought it didn't have the power and depth of *A Candle* ... but it was more tautly constructed. It was published in serial form in some magazine several years ago, wasn't it? I had read only parts of it there, so was glad to read the whole thing.

1. Arnold Edinborough (1922–2006) was a writer, journalist, broadcaster, and academic who worked at Queen's University, as well as the University of British Columbia. He was editor of *Saturday Night* from 1958 to 1962; in 1963, he purchased the paper and took on the offices of both president and publisher until 1970. He was also contributing editor on culture to the *Financial Post*, 1970–90.
2. Patricia Blondal (1926–1959) was a broadcaster for the CBC in Winnipeg; she wrote short stories, two posthumously published novels, and a manuscript for an unpublished mystery novel. *A Candle to Light the Sun*, which examines the prairie town of Mouse Bluffs and is set in the 1930s, was accepted for publication one month before she died of cancer at the age of thirty-two. *From Heaven with a Shout* was subsequently published by McClelland & Stewart in 1963.

Hollinger, 10 October 1963

Dear Jack:

I'll be away from London for November, as I am going that month to East Pakistan, where my husband is working. He will be taking local leave and we'll be travelling a good deal, so I don't plan to have mail forwarded. I thought I had better tell you, in case you write to me during that time, as I wouldn't want you to think I had delayed in replying, for no reason. I'll be returning to London the beginning of December, and will probably get pneumonia, coming from a hot climate to the melancholy downpour of the English winter, but if I survive, I'll write when I get back. By the way, when is *The Tomorrow-Tamer* coming out in Canada?

All the best.
Sincerely,
Margaret

P.S. Knopf sent me a list of suggested revisions for *The Stone Angel,* and I have done most of them, for the American edition. I haven't sent you a list of them, because they are minor changes and do not make any substantial difference to the book. I think you will agree with most of them, however, as they are mostly of a cleaning-up nature—knocking out some over-written phrases, etc.

Hollinger, 10 December 1963

Dear Jack:

Greetings, etc. Having spent a month in the wilds of Pakistan, I still have some feeling of unreality, although I am quickly being brought back to the realities of life by the English climate, which is pretty awful at the moment. I had a very good visit, during which my husband managed to take a week's local leave and we went to see a lot of ancient Hindu temples in India, which probably sounds rather deadly but was actually quite interesting, especially as they included the Black Pagoda at Konarak,[1] famed for its pornographic carvings. I have personally unearthed (I think) the secret of the Black Pagoda—the reason why so many of the amorous postures look so uncomfortable is that, owing to the rectangular shape of the building blocks, all the couples had to be pictured in standing positions, and let's face it, the permutations and combinations are strictly limited by the human physique. With me, a little tourism goes a long way, but I must admit I found these temples quite beautiful, although the climate was extremely warm and there were odd moments when I would have traded every ancient temple in India for one very dry martini, well iced. We went swimming in the Bay of Bengal, which was marvellous, and I acquired a wonderful tan, which I am now unable to show off, as England is too cold to expose even an arm.

I am glad to learn from Ruth Taylor that *The Tomorrow-Tamer* will be published in January. I received the contracts for *The Stone Angel* the other day, and have sent them back to Willis Wing. A Canadian story of mine is coming out in *Ladies' Home Journal*(!)[2] and Willis Wing hopes he may persuade them to publish it in June, to coincide with Knopf's publication of the books.

I liked the article about you in *Maclean's* very much, especially the parts that emphasized the pioneering aspect of many of your publishing efforts—I may say that I have said the same thing myself on many occasions, thinking of people like Irving Layton and Marie-Claire Blais,[3] etc., and also on the whole field of paperbacks. I did think that the article dwelt a little too much on your drinking habits—I could almost hear you talking ("of course, I'm probably killing myself," etc.) and it seemed to me that the interviewer might have taken you a bit too literally. Anyway, it was a good article.

I will be moving on the 30th of this month, out to the country, to a small village near High Wycombe, where I am renting a house. It is called, in the English manner, a "cottage," but in fact it has five bedrooms, which is certainly not my idea of a cottage. It is furnished, and it is old and rambling, just the kind of house I have always wanted. I can't afford to live in Hampstead, as rents are too high, and I think it will be better for my kids to be in the country, anyway, where they will have their own yard, dogs, cats, and goldfish, etc. The house will probably be cold as charity in winter, but we are greatly looking forward to having our own house. My husband [will have to leave] in April,[4] so it will be a good thing to have a place of our own then, too.

From Dec 30th, my new address will be:

Elm Cottage, Beacon Hill
Penn, Nr. High Wycombe,
Bucks., England.

The phone is Penn 2103, should you ever happen to find yourself on this side of the pond.

I hear from a friend in Vancouver that Pat Blondal's book is doing very well—I'm very glad. On second thoughts, I think the title is okay, in fact very striking.

Please write when you have time. In the meantime, best wishes and merry Christmas.

Sincerely,
Margaret

P.S. *The Tomorrow-Tamer* got some quite good reviews here, thank goodness. In fact, they were all okay, except for the *Yarmouth Mercury*, which put it enchantingly under books "For Mother."[5]

1. The Konark Sun Temple is a UNESCO World Heritage Site in Odisha (formerly Orissa), India.
2. The story published in *Ladies' Home Journal* was "To Set Our House in Order." It was later republished as part of Laurence's short story collection, *A Bird in the House*. The *Ladies' Home Journal* was an American magazine that first appeared on 16 February 1883, and, although it eventually became one of the leading women's magazines of the twentieth century and enjoyed one million subscribers by 1903, it was discontinued in 2014.
3. Marie-Claire Blais (1939–) published her first novel, *La Belle Bête* (trans. *Mad Shadows*), in 1959, when she was twenty years old. She has written over twenty novels, several plays, fiction, and collections of poetry, as well as newspaper articles.
4. The next few words are partially illegible due to tears in the paper, but the contents of later letters suggest the text is "will have to leave."
5. One such review written by William French, which appeared later in the *Globe and Mail* on 1 February 1964, was titled "Colorful Tales of Modern Africa" (A14).

Heath Hurst, 17 December 1963

Dear Margaret:

It was good to have your letter. Pakistan sounds fascinating. I don't really think you have the answer to the pornographic carvings. The fact is that, if you did a little research, you would learn that all these carvings were done by people with back problems. Slipped discs, sacroiliac, etc. This hampers the mobility and even dulls the creative imagination. It's also possible the carvings were done by elderly people with poor memories. I'm in the first of these two categories myself and am fast approaching the second, and I plan to go into semi-retirement in the future to do some pornographic carvings. Because of my background, they won't be any better than the ones you saw in Konarak but what else is there to do?

Your English cottage sounds fine and I shall certainly plan to visit you there if I ever get to England again. This seems doubtful now because we have just recently given up all our English agencies. Incidentally, I met your friend Maclean and liked him very much. We had a rush visit when he passed through Toronto, but it will make future dealings a lot easier when one knows who is at the other end of a letter. He gave me the impression that there is a fair chance that you will not be returning to Canada. Is this so? Have the long-range plans changed or have they not yet been formulated?

I'd appreciate it if you could send us copies of any of the English reviews of *The Tomorrow-Tamer*. We are publishing in January, as you know. Unfortunately, the book has been on sale in the English edition in Vancouver ever since English publication and there's not much we can do about it. This was one of the problems I referred to earlier. I don't blame the booksellers. If I were running a bookstore, I would do exactly what they did.

The Prophet's Camel Bell has done only moderately well here as yet. The reviews have been excellent and I hope copies of them have been sent off to you. If they haven't gone, this letter will [be] used as a signal for that purpose and you will get them in due course.

The Blondal book has had some extremely good reviews, but it has not sold all that well. All of which does not surprise me. I'm still convinced that it is very slight fiction in relation to *A Candle to Light the Sun* and certainly Pat thought of it as such and there just isn't a very good market for light fiction in Canada today or, as far as that goes, in North America today.

I've noted the new address. Have a good Christmas. We'll be in touch soon after the New Year.

Sincerely,
J.G. McClelland

Hollinger, 23 December 1963

Dear Jack:

I was very glad to get your letter today, and I'm replying right away because, with Christmas and the fact that I'm moving to Penn five days afterwards, I have the feeling that it may be some weeks before I settle down to correspondence again. I am fascinated by your explanation of the carvings at Konarak, but I feel you will be making a great mistake to retire and do pornographic carvings. Personally, I would advise you to become a poet instead. You could write some sensational erotic poetry, let us say, and then get Irving Layton to begin a publishing business—he could then publish your work sight unseen. You would no doubt both become fabulously wealthy within ten years, and could then establish a Home for impecunious writers and publishers, to be known as The McClelland Colony.

Re: my returning to Canada—I don't have any long-range plans at the moment, but will simply have to wait and see how things work out. I'll be back someday undoubtedly, but not yet for a while.

I'm enclosing some of the English reviews of *The Tomorrow-Tamer,* plus a couple of letters, one from Mary Renault and one from Alan Silitoe.[1] Maybe you would let me have them back some time, as they are the only copies I have—there isn't any hurry, however. I'm sorry about the book being on sale in Vancouver—I feel rather apologetic about this, as a matter of fact, and do not quite know what to say about it, so I guess I won't say anything.

Many thanks for the cheque for the first half of the advance on *The Tomorrow-Tamer,* which I received the other day.

As always, all the best.

Sincerely,
Margaret Laurence[2]

1. Mary Renault was the pen name of Eileen Mary Challans (1905–1983), an author who wrote historical novels set in ancient Greece. She was renowned for challenging societal attitudes about homosexuality in her work. Alan Silitoe (1928–2010) wrote fiction that addressed the disillusionment of 1950s post-war Britain.
2. McClelland wrote a note on this letter to Joyce Anne "Steve" Rankin: "Rankin—make copies of reviews and return to me (also be sure these are at [some text is blurred and unreadable here])" (McClelland & Stewart Ltd. Fonds, Box 35, File 42).

Elm Cottage, 8 January 1964

Dear Margaret:

Thanks for yours of the 23rd. You are quite wrong of course. I would be much better on the carvings than on erotic poetry. The English reviews are very good indeed and will be very helpful to us. By the time this letter reaches you, the book will be on sale here, although we won't get reviews for several weeks. We'll be keeping in touch. Our pub. date on the novel is June 1st to conform with Knopf promotion.

Cheers!
J.G. McClelland

Hollinger, 9 May 1964

Dear Jack:

I'm not really writing to you for any particular reason, but only because it seems to me quite some time since I last wrote to you or had a letter from you. However, I received a cheque the other day for additional royalties on *The Prophet's Camel Bell,* for which I was very grateful, so this gives me an excuse to write. I was glad to learn that the Somaliland book had been chosen as an alternative choice by the Canadian Book Club, and also that they intend to use *The Tomorrow-Tamer* as one of their selections. It should all help, I hope.

I've received Knopf's editions of the three books, and I think they look very jazzy indeed. I wonder if you will be using the same binding and cover, etc., for *The Stone Angel*? I think their cover for the novel is excellent, and the binding is so high class that all I could do at first was to stroke it in wondering admiration and astonishment. They have sent me *ten* copies of each book. I now have so many of these books around the house that I am thinking of setting up a barrow on Charing Cross Road. The odd thing, however, is that I cannot seem to get worked up about the American reviews of *The Stone Angel*—I mean, I don't feel anxious about what they will be like. What really concerns me is what the reviews will be like in Canada. Naturally, I hope they like it—I would be a terrible liar if I pretended otherwise. But what concerns me even more is what they see in it, what they think is there (if anything). However, one must not get neurotic about these things.

Have just finished reading Jack Ludwig's *Confusions,*[1] which I liked enormously, not only for its wit but also for the way in which Gillis with his inner rabbi meets the powers of sophistication with their own weapon, mockery. The whole thing is tremendously well done.

Would it be possible for me to get a list of the books you've published in the New Canadian Library series?[2] And is it possible for me to order them direct from you? If I buy books from Macmillan here, I get them at trade prices—is the same true in Canada?

Everything is reasonably okay here. I have got back to work, thank goodness, but find it just as slow and difficult as ever. I once believed that the 2nd novel was the most difficult—now I think the 3rd must be the most difficult.

I hope everything is going well with you, and that you are not working too hard.

All the best.
Margaret

1. Jack Barry Ludwig (1922–2018) was a Canadian novelist, short story writer, and sportswriter. His novel, *Confusions*, is a satirical treatment of the socio-political, moral, and sexual issues surrounding a young Jewish man's search for his identity.
2. Malcolm Ross, professor and Canadian literary critic, initially approached John Gray at Macmillan with his proposal to publish Canadian books in paperback. Gray rejected his proposal, and Ross approached Jack McClelland, his former student (King, *Jack* 96). McClelland accepted the proposal, and the new paperback series, the New Canadian Library, began in 1958 as part of McClelland & Stewart. Ross and McClelland worked on the series together. As Janet Friskney explains, "By the time Ross retired as general editor in 1978, just over 180 titles had appeared in the NCL's Main and two subsidiary lines, the NCL Original Series and the Canadian Writers Series" (New Canadian Library 14). About his vision for the series, Ross stated, "I was trying to illustrate a sort of cultural history—what was developing in the creative imagination of Canadians as they grew up here at different times and in different places" (Friskney, *New Canadian Library* 14).

Elm Cottage, 20 May 1964

Dear Margaret:

I was delighted to have your letter. As a matter of fact I was on the verge of writing to you because we are publishing *The Stone Angel* on May 23rd, and when I remember to do so—which isn't all that often—it seems an appropriate time to remind an author that we are pleased with the book—which I may say we really are in this case—and that we are delighted to be publishing it.

I, too, have received copies of the Knopf edition. I think they are extremely handsome, and I think Knopf [is] going to do an extremely good job for you in the Canadian market. ...

Our edition of *The Stone Angel* is, I think, much more attractive than the Knopf edition. It's the same binding, of course, and the same book but our jacket is, in my opinion, much more attractive. In any case, our copies are en route to you, and, if you have not had a previous opportunity, you will be able to judge this for yourself. We will, of course, send you copies of the Canadian reviews. We are sending out press releases relating to the Knopf publication of the three books on one day, and I think this will generate a lot of publicity in Canada.

I'm glad you liked Jack Ludwig's book. It's a favourite of mine. I found it tremendously intelligent and amusing. It was well reviewed here for the most part, although not everybody understood it. Despite that, it didn't sell well, either in Canada or the United States. We worked at it pretty hard. Jack made a trip across the country. He lectured at most of the leading Canadian universities and was very well received, but for some reason it didn't turn out to be the sort of book that people go out and pay $4.95 for. I have a hunch that his book should have been published originally in a paperback edition. ...

Glad to hear you are back at work, and that the next novel is proceeding. I read an extremely interesting article about you in *Smith's Trade News*.[1] I presume they sent you a copy. And incidentally, did you see the brochure that Knopf prepared for promotion? It is quite the handsomest thing of its sort that I have seen in a long time.

I expect by now you may have heard from Elsa Franklin.[2] She has been touring Europe. I'm not sure exactly when she was scheduled to reach London. She had your address and was planning on getting in touch. I came within an ace of making a trip myself, but it has now been postponed indefinitely, and I doubt that I will get over this year. Things move ahead about the same. I spent the last week or so up in Muskoka trying to get caught up on my work. In fact, I'm dictating this letter to you from my cottage. It's a beautiful night. The sun is just setting and I wish I could stay up here permanently, but I'm back to work tomorrow and off early next week for a series of sales conferences in the United States.

Every good wish for *The Stone Angel* in the U.K. and in the U.S.A., and, most of all, in Canada. We'll do our best to see that it gets the sort of reception that it richly deserves.

Sincerely,
J.G. McClelland

1. The article mentioned here is not included in Laurence's or McClelland's papers. No library in Canada holds *Smith's Trade News*, a British publication.
2. Elsa Franklin was Pierre Berton's assistant and agent, and was appointed to the McClelland & Stewart board of directors in May 1969. Berton insisted that Franklin market his books, not McClelland (King, *Jack* 236): "Franklin was described in *The Toronto Star* (December 19, 1982) as the 'organizer of the multi-million-dollar marketing of Berton's books and wide-ranging TV interests (she's full partner in the company that owns a number of his shows)'" (384).

Hollinger, 26 May 1964

Dear Jack:

Thanks very much for your letter of May 20th. I had not known that you were going to use a different jacket on *The Stone Angel*. Your copies arrived today, actually, and this letter is mainly to tell you that I think your jacket for the book is absolutely terrific, much the best of the three. Knopf's design is far better than the English edition, but I think yours is by far the most striking. Could you pass on my thanks to Frank Newfeld?[1] Everything about this jacket is just right—the colours, the jagged lines, the slightly weird figure. I'm very glad indeed that you did your own jacket for the book, and also that the cover blurb is so well keyed for Canada. We can now only hope for the best. Anyway, I'm very grateful for the job you've done on it.

I am at the moment in a state of some disorganization. I am going to Athens next week, as my husband is arriving back on leave and I'm meeting him in Greece for a week's holiday before he returns here, so I am making all sorts of complicated arrangements re: children, etc.

Ruth Taylor wrote to me a short time ago, giving me a list of titles in the New Canadian Library. I ought to reply separately to her, but have run out of air-letter forms. I wonder if you could pass on my thanks, plus the fact that I would very much like to get the following books: *As For Me and My House* by Sinclair Ross; *More Joy in Heaven*, by Morley Callaghan; *Swamp Angel*, Ethel Wilson; *They Shall Inherit the Earth*, Callaghan; *The Cashier*, Gabrielle Roy; *Under the Ribs of Death*, John Marlin [*sic*].[2] I wonder if the cost of these could be deducted from royalties? If not, I'll be glad to send the amount.

Yes, I saw the article in *Smith's Trade News*. I was very amused that they described me as a "cheerful, unflappable woman"—I thought I had missed my calling and ought to have been an actress, if anyone could think that about me! I also saw Knopf's brochure, which I thought was very handsome, too, after I had recovered from my initial reaction of pure panic.

Try to get over to England one of these days. You know you have an open invitation to come and stay here. Should you ever be able to get over with your family, remember I have lots of room and an enormous although wild garden.

All the best.
Sincerely,
Margaret

1. Frank Newfeld (1928–) is a book designer, illustrator, art director, and educator. He worked on a freelance basis for McClelland & Stewart until 1963, when he was asked to serve as the company's art director. He was then promoted to creative director and production manager, at which time he was also invited to sit on the board of directors. He became vice-president of publishing in 1969; he left a few years later to open the Frank Newfeld Studio. He designed over 650 books, including Sheila Watson's *The Double Hook*, and won multiple awards for his work, including the Canadian Centennial Medal and the Queen Elizabeth II Diamond Jubilee Medal.
2. Sinclair Ross (1908–1996) was a Canadian fiction writer, widely esteemed for his novel *As For Me and My House*. Morley Callaghan (1903–1990) was renowned as both a Canadian author and radio and TV personality; two of his more famous books include *Such Is My Beloved* and *More Joy in Heaven*. See Laurence's letter dated 21 December 1959 for information about Ethel Wilson. Gabrielle Roy (1909–1983) was a French-Canadian author whose first novel, *Bonheur d'occasion*, is often regarded as having paved the way for the Quiet Revolution in Quebec. The novel, which was translated as *The Tin Flute*, won the Governor General's Award and the Royal Society of Canada's Lorne Pierce Medal. John Marlyn (1912–2005) was an Austro-Hungarian-born Canadian. His novel, *Under the Ribs of Death*, explores the immigrant community of the North End of Winnipeg.

Hollinger, 7 November 1964

Dear Jack:

I have just received from you a cheque for quite a lot of money, further royalties on all four books, and so I thought I'd like to write and thank you very much—obviously you've been doing a very good sales job on the books, and this is certainly appreciated by me. The money, too, is appreciated, I need hardly say.

Things have been somewhat hectic for me this summer. My husband came home on leave in June, and has just departed this week for Africa, where he'll be working on an irrigation project. Most of my time was spent pretty domestically, going on holiday with the kids, and so on. I've written a number of articles this summer, but that is about all. However, I had good luck, and three of them have been taken by *Holiday*.[1] Also, a story has been taken by *Atlantic Monthly*,[2] to my intense surprise.

I'm beginning a novel, but it is too soon to know whether or not it will come to anything. I know it's there—what I don't know is whether I can do it.

Please drop me a line when possible and let me know how things are with you.

All the best.

Sincerely,
Margaret

1. The three pieces that were published in *Holiday* were "The Very Best Intentions" in November 1964, "The Epic Love of Elmii Bonderii" in November 1965, and "Sayonara, Agamemnon" in January 1966. All three were later published in Laurence's collection of essays titled *Heart of a Stranger*.
2. *The Atlantic Monthly* is an American literary magazine that was begun in 1857 in Boston, Massachusetts. It was founded by Moses Dresser Phillips and Francis H. Underwood and

brought into being in its early days by Ralph Waldo Emerson, Henry Wadsworth Longfellow, James Russell Lowell, and Oliver Wendell Holmes, among others. Its first editor was Lowell. It is considered one of America's best and most prestigious monthly magazines ("The Atlantic Monthly"). In Canada, in 1959, there were few literary magazines in which writers could publish, and so many, such as Laurence, published in American periodicals such as the *Atlantic Monthly*. The story referred to here was "A Bird in the House." It was later published in Laurence's collection of short stories of the same title.

Elm Cottage, 9 November 1964

Dear Margaret:

Just a note to congratulate you on the exceptionally fine story in the current *Atlantic*. They didn't include you in the Special Canadian Supplement, but identified you as a Canadian, which makes the treatment particularly flattering I think. In any case, I thought it was a wonderful story. The truth of the matter is that, unlike most authors, your writing continues to improve with everything you write and it staggers me to think of what the future may hold.

I don't know how up-to-date we've kept you re: *The Stone Angel*. It hasn't been a major bestseller here, but it's had a truly fine reception and we are well satisfied with the sale at least. The market for fiction is bad, and this has really done very well indeed. Although I am writing mainly to tell you my reaction to the *Atlantic* piece, I also should tell you that Sheila Burnford, author of *The Incredible Journey* and, more recently, *The Fields of Noon*[1] has just written to say that she will be in London towards the end of November and I have written suggesting to her that she contact you. If you hear from her then, you will know that it was at my urging. She is a very exceptional person and I think you might enjoy meeting each other. I'm sending a copy of her new book to you under separate cover just in case you have read *The Incredible Journey* and have formed an impression of the author as the result. ... I think this book is extremely moving and in every sense delightful. Hope all goes well. Drop me a line when you have a moment.

Sincerely,
J.G. McClelland

1. McClelland & Stewart agreed to publish the sequel to *The Incredible Journey* (published by Hodder & Stoughton), titled *The Fields of Noon*. Unfortunately, unlike *The Incredible Journey*, *The Fields of Noon* did not do well commercially.

Hollinger, 14 November 1964

Dear Jack:

Thanks for your letter of November 9th. I think I must have written to you at about the same time, and our letters crossed. I was very glad to hear how they'd done my story in *The Atlantic Monthly*, as I haven't yet seen a copy of that issue. I'm also delighted that you like the story.

I am pleased and also relieved to know that *The Stone Angel* hasn't done too badly in terms of sales.

I hope Sheila Burnford will look me up—I'd very much like to meet her. Thanks for sending *The Fields of Noon*. I look forward to reading it. It has had good reviews in this country. I haven't read *The Incredible Journey*, but I think I'll buy it (it's out in paperback here). I went to the film one afternoon in London when I had a few hours to spend, but I left after about ten minutes—I don't think this has necessarily got anything at all to do with either the book or the film. I'm just not a great animal-lover, that's all.

Thanks for your comments about my writing. I wish I could feel a similar confidence, but maybe it wouldn't be any good if I did.

Don't feel you have to reply to this letter. I know how hectic your office life must be. But please drop a line sometime when you can, and let me know how things are there.

All the best.

Sincerely,
Margaret Laurence

P.S. Could you give Claire Pratt a message from me? Please tell her that her aunt from Cheltenham dropped in last Sunday, and I thought she was really charming.

Hollinger, 2 January 1965

Dear Jack:

Thanks very much for sending me a copy of Robert Fulford's[1] article in *The Toronto Star*.[2] I don't know what kind of comment one can make on an article like that, except to say that it certainly was very nice and I'm grateful to him.

Many thanks, also, for sending me Sheila Burnford's *The Fields of Noon*. I thought it was a delightful book. I'm not an animal lover myself (I'm scared even of canaries), but I sometimes think that people who are very fond of animals tend to have rather more kindly personalities than many of us. I thought Sheila Burnford's personality came across in the writing as an exceedingly attractive one, warm without being sentimental, witty without ostentation. I enjoyed all the essays, but I liked the one on her attempts to learn pressure-flaking of spearheads almost the best, I think. I also thought the one on the pampered canary was marvellous—the personality of that absurd little bird really came across.

The novel I'm working on is going very slowly. I haven't yet found the right way to do it, but I still believe it is there. Domestic life has been rather distracting lately, as our water pipes froze, and I learned more about plumbing than I really wanted to know.

The Canadian calendar you sent for Christmas was lovely—thanks very much.

All the best for the new year.

Sincerely,
Margaret

1. Robert Fulford (1932–) is a Canadian journalist, magazine editor, and essayist, who worked as the editor of *Saturday Night* magazine, then as a columnist for the *Globe and Mail* from 1992 to 1999 and the *National Post* since 1999.
2. Fulford's rave review about Laurence, titled "A Literary Reputation Made Overnight," states, "Among Canadian writers, she was, easily, the outstanding figure of 1964." He commended the publishing of the three books all at once—*The Prophet's Camel Bell*, *The Tomorrow-Tamer*, and *The Stone Angel*—and stated, "Mrs. Laurence's North American reputation was thus made overnight" (19).

Hollinger, 26 March 1965

Dear Jack:

A line to catch you up on my progress, such as it is. As far as writing is concerned, things have come to a temporary stop owing to other difficulties. After about three years of agonizing indecision, my husband and I are finally going to separate, and this has been pretty upsetting all around, needless to say. It has been in the offing for some considerable time, but I guess it is always rather difficult to take the final step, inevitable though it may be. Anyway, there it is, and there is certainly some definite relief in taking a definite decision and also in being able to come out with the true situation, which certainly isn't anyone's fault, but just one of those changes that sometimes happen, where two people simply become too different to be able to continue together.

Anyway, I suppose this is probably the reason why I haven't been able to write very much in the past two years, as it isn't possible to get enough involved if your mind is obsessed with something else. In this period of hiatus, some ideas have been accumulating, and I feel now that they'll come in time (maybe, perhaps, and with great luck, etc.). As a matter of fact, I feel a great deal better and more hopeful than I have in a hell of a long time, so maybe that means something. I keep thinking of Muriel Spark's comment about herself when she first became an R.C. convert—her first act was to have a nervous breakdown, after which she learned to take her ideas one at a time, she said. I hope to avoid the nervous breakdown (I'm not really the type for it, I feel) but to learn after some crisis to take one's ideas relatively calmly and one at a time. I would like to write four novels, but you can't actually do that simultaneously. At the moment I'm trying to learn how to relax once more, and so I'm only writing a few articles, etc. But it will be okay, I think. I have a great many assets, compared to what I had when I came to England (when I had precisely £100 of my own money and no prospects)—mainly, I'm settled in a house which my kids feel is their home, and I'm not broke. So—we'll see.

Please write when you have a moment to spare. I hope things are all right with you.

All the best,
Margaret Laurence

Margaret Laurence in Penn, Buckinghamshire, England, ca. 1965. Margaret's son David can be seen in the background, on his bicycle. [Clara Thomas Archives and Special Collections, 1980-001 Box 10]

Elm Cottage, 4 May 1965

Dear Margaret:[1]

I have owed you a letter for a very long time. Forgive me. Actually, I wrote several weeks ago—a beautiful letter it was—and it seems my dictaphone machine had stuck on one spot and so at least a dozen great masterpieces were never recorded. I am only now beginning to recover.

I'm sorry in the one sense, but glad in the other to hear of the separation. By that I mean these things are always sad, but the real point is that since you have finally made the decision, it is undoubtedly the right one and will turn out well in the long run.

Silly though it may seem, I'm beginning to think that there may be some correlation between intelligence and marital problems. It would be too pat to conclude that intelligent and creative people don't stay married, but there seems to be some sort of pattern. Three of our most gifted authors have been involved in separations in the last twelve months, and I know at least three others who have seriously contemplated it during the same period. If misery loves company, then you've certainly got it. On the other hand, it does rather strip one of the originality of the thing. But damn it, there must be some sort of pattern in this thing. I expect someone has already investigated it at great length. Unless one is extremely fortunate, and, even if one is, I think marriage probably requires an extraordinarily unimaginative type of complacency.

I don't really know what one wants to hear when they have just recently decided to separate, but for what it is worth, let me say to you that you have something that is more important than any marriage I've ever heard about. By which I mean your career, which I say in all humility should make you one of the great international writers in the next decade or so. I don't think you can afford to concern yourself about the disillusion of a marriage, no matter how serious a jolt it may seem at the time. So forget it. It's of relatively no importance.

Although I can't imagine that it has even crossed your mind, I am mad as hell about the fact that you didn't receive the Governor-General's Award for Fiction. A number of the critics across the country have been irate about this and rightly so. It's a question of principle. As it happens, we published Douglas LePan's book, which won the Award,[2] but, even though we did, as I have no hesitation in saying, that it doesn't belong in the same category as *The Stone Angel*. I can't imagine what the committee was thinking about. It's not untypical of judgements that Governor-General's Awards committees have made in the past. It's a goddam disgrace.

So, my dear Margaret, don't have a nervous breakdown, and if you must write four novels at the same time, that could be rather fun. But in any case relax and enjoy yourself. Incidentally, did Sheila Burnford ever get in touch with you? I have never heard from either of you ... but I hope you did. She is now a great admirer of your work and has been recommending your books to other people (I've heard from them). She is still travelling somewhere in Europe. She, too, has just separated, which would mean that you would either hate each others' guts, or it would be like old-home week. I don't know which. In any case, I was hoping you would meet.

And, for God's sake, when you have time to write make your next letter more cheerful. You ask how things go here. Just dreadful. Too many books; not enough time in which to publish them. I'm beginning to despair. On my first long holiday, which I may take one of these days, I shall pay you a visit in Buckinghamshire. Wherever the hell that may be.

Cheers,
J.G. McClelland

1. This letter appears in Solecki's *Imagining Canadian Literature*.
2. Douglas LePan won the Governor General's Award in 1964 for his book of poetry, *The Deserter*.

Hollinger, 11 May 1965

Dear Jack:

Many, many thanks for your heartening letter—it was exactly the kind of thing I needed to hear, and it boosted my morale a lot. Another thing which boosted my morale recently was that I received a royalty check from you—this was marvelous on two counts: (a) money and (b) it indicated that *The Stone Angel* has sold much better than I ever thought it would.

Thanks also for your remarks re: the Governor General's Award. It wasn't any disappointment to me, naturally, as I would never expect to get it anyway. But it is nice to know that you and some others think *The Stone Angel* is worthwhile.

I haven't heard from Sheila Burnford yet, but I do hope she gets in touch with me. I'd like to meet her very much—and perhaps especially now that I know she is in similar circumstances personally. Is she going to return to Canada? I think I probably will return one day, but for the moment I don't want to move again until my kids are finished secondary school. That will be in seven years time—so I hope to get several novels written in that time. God willing. I am very superstitious about saying what one intends to do.

The present novel is coming along quite well, I think. I don't know if it will turn out to be any good or not, but I'm not especially worried at this point. All I can really do is set down what is there, and, if it doesn't work out, then write another. I feel very much more hopeful about life in general than I did. I've been doing an occasional article, etc., and one oddity I'm doing for the CBC this week is for a program called *Hermit's Choice*—what books and records would you take to a desert island? Daft question. For my records, I've chosen the bagpipes and Beethoven's Ninth, so I don't know what they are going to make of that. Still, as Hertzog says, if I'm out of my mind, it's all right with me.

Don't despair re: having too many books to publish, for heaven's sake. It's the writers who should despair at such news. Competition grows daily. Personally, I think there are too many writers about. I wish some of the others would quit.

If you do step out of character one of these days and decide to take a holiday, please try to come to England. I live only 20 miles from London, for God's sake—you don't need to speak of Buckinghamshire as though it were the mountains of the moon!

All the best.
Margaret

Elm Cottage, 20 May 1965

Dear Margaret:

A local woman has about $10,000.00 to invest in an author who will write a novel for her. It's sort of a strange situation, and I wonder if it might be of interest to you.

Specifically, the situation is this. The woman is Dutch. She is in her mid-sixties. She is now living in Canada. The story concerns an experience in her personal background and, for the moment, I won't tell you any more than that. It is set in Holland near the Belgian border. In outline, it is a fantastically good story—at least that is my evaluation—it has all the ingredients for a very good novel and a very good movie. Perhaps particularly the latter.

I would guess that the woman's interest is two-fold. Firstly, it's her personal story and she is rather proud of it. Secondly, she is interested in the movie potential. She has had all sorts of letters from Hollywood saying this is a great natural story if it were available to them in book form. It would have great film possibilities. Thus, she wants a first-rate writer to take it on and write a novel and then she will see that it is sold to Hollywood. Or so she says. Now, Margaret, I'm damned if I know if a novel can be written to order. That's something you will have to decide if it interests you at all. Certainly, it would be no great problem for you to do whatever research is needed. I think it could be done by a two-week visit to the area. If this interests you, to even a slight degree, let me know and I will send the outline on to you. I'm not really trying to talk you into it, except for the fact that it could earn a great deal of money for you.

All the best.
Sincerely,
J.G. McClelland

Hollinger, 26 May 1965

Dear Jack:

Thanks for your letter of May 20th, and many thanks for having thought of me re: writing a novel for the interesting-sounding Dutch woman. Jack, to turn down $10,000 makes me want to drop dead, or get drunk, or have my head examined, but I am very much afraid I can't do a novel like that. Please understand that I appreciate very greatly your suggesting me for the job, and also please understand that I am not turning it down through any high-flown principles or literary snob-ism. It is simply that I know my own limitations, at least to some extent, and I know that if I took a job like that I would find it impossibly difficult to do, and I would not make a good job of it. I only ever once wrote something that was not from my own ideas, and that was for a woman's magazine in this country, it was awful to write—like trying to mine a vein of ore that isn't there—and it turned out (I thought) a mess. So I could not in any reasonable honesty take on anything like a novel, in that way, because I do not really believe it would work out well. I think it would involve me in a great amount of effort and strain, which would turn out to be disappointing both to myself and the patron. So, with regrets, I have to refuse. I think maybe I am not fated to be all that well-endowed financially. At the moment this does not worry me at all, simply because I'm not broke. If I become broke at some point, I may weep bitter tears over this lost opportunity, but never mind—sufficient unto the day.

Things are going well here, I am glad to say. I have about two thirds of this novel written in rough draft, and it has just got to the point when I think I may not survive until it is finished, so that is a good sign. I am just beginning to see what it is all about, and to think that perhaps with enormous luck it may be worth re-writing, but at the moment I am trying only to take it on faith and put down whatever comes.

The summer visiting season is beginning, and friends and relatives are turning up from all over. I swear that if I stay here long enough, everyone I know in the world will drift this way, sooner or later. It is a great pleasure to see them, but I find myself uncomfortably split, as usual, between the requirements of the outer and the inner. Will I clean the house or finish chapter 7? The house is losing out, at the moment, and all I am hoping is that it will continue to do so until I've got at least the rough draft completed. I wish that either I did not have this housewifely conscience (of which I disapprove but cannot seem to get rid of) or else that I had some dear old family retainer who would not work for money but for the sheer undiluted pleasure of being with us.

Again, thanks. I really do appreciate the offer, and I hope you'll understand that I'm refusing only because I would not be able to do a job like this.[1]

All the best.
Sincerely,
Margaret

1. McClelland wrote to Juliana Allonsius on this matter on 10 May 1965. He suggested in this letter that she consider Laurence to write the book for her. It seems likely that Allonsius sent either a detailed description or a manuscript of her own. On this letter, in handwriting, McClelland wrote, "Marge will read" (in pencil). He then wrote (in pen), "Marge read part of it, then passed it to me. She didn't think much of it." McClelland wrote to Allonsius again on 18 January 1966 to turn down the said manuscript: "Our readers agreed that the material would be better suited to a film or television script than to book publication." A note by McClelland in handwriting, dated 10 January 1966 and attached to the letter in the William Ready archives, reads, "Juliana Allonsius—Unless there is some project to be developed from this (the correspondence mentions Moore and Laurence), I can see little or no possibility for the attached. ... Hold for Marge's return." A reader's report dated 6 January 1966 reads, "The author's blurb notwithstanding, Jeannot is a flop. It's a great dull bore, lacking all colour, and very much in need of imagination. It is unfortunate that Allonsius chose to narrate the story in the third person. It is quite beyond her to manufacture human beings out of her characters. They appear as nebulous ghosts in a humdrum, completely mechanical plot" (McClelland & Stewart Ltd. Fonds, Box 35, File 42).

•——

PENN HIGHWAYCOMMBE SENT JUNE 4, 8:56 PM

MASSIVE CONFUSION NOW DISCOVERED MRS ALLONSIUS WAS SENDER OF ORIGINAL CABLE HAVE PHONED TALKED WITH HER SHE IS OVERPOWERING AND NUTS AM TERRIFIED PLEASE COMMUNICATE.

•——

PENN HIGHWAYCOMMBE SENT JUNE 4, 9:38 PM RECEIVED JUNE 7TH

NEVER MIND COMMUNICATIONS HAVE SAID FINAL NO PHONE. WISE TO DUTCH LADY CORRAGIO AVANTI LOVE.
MARGARET

Hollinger, 6 June 1965
CONFIDENTIAL ETC.

Dear Jack:

Well, I guess the past few days could be described as a comedy of errors. I'd better explain what happened, so you won't think I am entirely off my rocker. On Friday morning, I received a cable which read, "Please phone me tonight 10 P.M. London time Toronto (and then the phone number was given) Jack McClelland interesting Dutch woman Mrs. Allonsius." Not unnaturally, I believed this cable to be from you. I had, however, received it one day late, owing to the dubious efficiency of the High Wycombe Telegrams Dept. I therefore cabled you, suggesting you phone me. That night, I realised you might not be in the office Saturday morning and might therefore not get the cable until Monday. I thought you would think it was pretty strange of me, not to have phoned after you sent a cable. So I phoned to Toronto on Friday evening, expecting to hear your voice. Imagine my shock when I found myself talking to Mrs. Allonsius, better known as the Flying Dutchwoman, instead. Jack, I do not know now why I became so panic-stricken. The thing was this—she was so overwhelming and so strong-minded, and somehow she terrified me, because I could see myself weak-mindedly agreeing to do her novel, and then being saddled with an impossible situation. Also, I guess until I spoke to her, the money never seemed real but then it did, and I was also, paradoxically, afraid I would *refuse* to do the novel and thus lose all that dough. The conversation was odd in the extreme. She kept telling me how much faith she had in my ability to do the story, and how it would bring me fame and fortune, and saying things like "I want to talk to you about it—I'll fly over to see you—how about next week?" and I was saying "Mrs. Allonsius, DON'T COME. WRITE." I was petrified. Then she said, "Mrs. Laurence, when were you born?" And I said, with a sinking heart, "July 18th." And she said, in a delighted voice, "CANCER!" And I said, feeling absolutely beaten-down and defeated, "Is cancer good?" She said yes, it was splendid. By this time, I was so damn nervous I didn't know what I was saying. I found myself saying yes, perhaps I could do the novel if she would send me the outline, and if I could have 3 months to finish my own novel, etc. Thus ended the first conversation. I paced the floor for about 3 minutes and then sent you the next cable, which was a bit hysterical—I apologize for that. What I really wanted was for someone to tell me what to do. I then phoned Alan Maclean (it was 1 A.M. by this time), rousing him out of a sound sleep to tell him I was going out of my mind and what should I do. He, patient and sensible man that he is, did not swear at me for waking him up—he only said very reassuringly that no doubt I would decide in due time what was the best thing to do. I paced the floor some more, and then realized that indeed only myself could decide, so I phoned Toronto again, before I could fluctuate any more, and spoke to Mrs. Allonsius again, telling her I was very sorry but I could not do her novel and I was sure she would find someone quite quickly who could do it a thousand times better, for her purposes, than I could. We parted amicably, I am glad to say. I hope she finds someone else who has a favourable zodiac sign. I thought I'd better settle the situation completely, so I sent you the next cable saying all was well.

The next day I felt absolutely limp, as though I had narrowly avoided falling off a cliff. I suppose the reason I got so worked up was that I had not fully realised how much money was involved, and, on the other hand, when I visualized Mrs. A. flying over here at frequent intervals for consultations (probably with a pentacle set up in the middle of my living room) I had only one thought—FLEE. Well, thank God (I use the phrase advisedly) that it all turned out all right, and I did the only possible thing, but man, it was touch and go for a while there! It was a very interesting experience, and I don't regret having had it—I only wish I'd been strong-minded enough to say "No" when I first talked to her, that's all.

My aunt from Victoria B.C. is here for three weeks, and my kids are on holiday and three of their friends are visiting, so when all this strange business was taking place, I had this beloved but aged relative in the house, and five kids sleeping in tents in my backyard, and one felt, as so often one does, the disparity between the two worlds of family and writing.

Anyway, I'm sorry I didn't deal with the situation more calmly and that I sent you that cable (the second), which was so emotional and disturbed, but it couldn't be helped.

Have got 1½ chapters to do in this novel I'm working on. Hope to have rough draft completed by the end of July. It is not a fashionable subject; it is not filmable. Sometimes I see how ridiculous it is to be working on something like this, which seems to bear so little relation to the outside world, but I guess in fact it bears a slight relationship to the way the outside world appears and perhaps a little more relevance to the way things *are*, according to one's own way of seeing. Hell. That sounds pompous. You can't win. The main thing is that I feel pretty cheerful about everything at this moment.

I'm sure Mrs. A. has a good story, and honestly, I do wish her luck with it. Only, it's not for me. All the best, and please write and tell me you don't think I'm off my head.

Sincerely,
Margaret

Elm Cottage, 7 June 1965

Dear Margaret:

My sincere apologies. I received your letter of May 26th and I understand fully. I was foolish enough to send a copy of it to the Dutch lady, Mrs. Allonsius, and I judge from your telegram that she has been bothering you. I've done my best to cut her off and, in fact, have cut her off permanently, so just ignore her and be as rude as you like.

I can quite understand your feeling in this matter, and I don't blame you but I felt that I should offer you the thing simply because there was a substantial sum of money involved. As I think I mentioned in my letter, I have no reason to believe that a serious writer can take on this sort of thing, and I think your view is entirely sensible.

All the best.
Sincerely,
J.G. McClelland

Hollinger, 17 August 1965

Dear Jack:

A brief note to keep you posted. I have finally managed to get a novel finished, but do not know yet if it is any good or not. I did a lot of re-writing when I was typing it out from the handwritten scribble, but I know it still needs work, mainly cutting, I think. I have the feeling that it either comes across reasonably well or it doesn't, and I don't think the extensive re-writing is really going to alter it, but I think it gets off to a slow start and needs a lot of cutting in the first chapters. It will be a very short novel, I guess. It is so far from being a topical subject that I really hate to tell you what it is about. It is about an unmarried schoolteacher in a small prairie town—please, Jack, don't faint. I'm sorry. I know it's corny. But there it is. It is called *The Jests of God*, and, in some way [that] was not intended when I started out with it, it parallels the story of Rachel, who mourned for her children because they were not. This is, by the way, though, because she either comes across as herself or she doesn't. I don't know at this point. Alan Maclean has read it, and one other reader, and they seem to think it is okay, but I know it needs a good deal of work. Anyway, at this point I am absolutely exhausted, beat, etc. I have been getting this novel finished, while at the same time the visitors from Canada and U.S.A. have been arriving weekly, and I've been terribly glad to see them but have some kind of feeling now that I'm operating a hotel. Autumn is almost here, praise God, and the visiting season will be over, and I can tell you that I really need a rest. I am going to the north of Scotland, by myself, without my kids, next week, to sit on the edge of Cromarty Firth and look at the wild swans and do absolutely nothing.

I hope to get this novel done and typed in proper shape by the end of Sept, maybe, and I think it might be a good idea if I sent you a copy direct, because of our past experience, with W. Wing not sending you a copy for some considerable time. What do you think? I would like you to see the manuscript as soon as possible, because if you think it is terrible, it would be good to know quite soon, and, if you have suggestions re: what could be done with it, I would like to know as soon as possible, also, although my feeling right now is that if it doesn't communicate more or less as it is, then the hell with it. I'm not being facetious—in a way, it is a kind of tour-de-force, and it either works the first time or it really and truly doesn't. I'll write again soon.

Sincerely,
Margaret

Elm Cottage, 3 September 1965

Dear Margaret:

Delighted to have yours of August 17th. By all means send the manuscript *The Jests of God* to us directly rather than via Willis. I look forward to reading it and if I can give you any helpful comment or suggestion, I certainly will do so.

Migod, why do you knock yourself out running a hotel—or what sounds like a hotel? As a matter of fact, I guess you can't avoid it. I almost sent a niece to impose on your hospitality this summer, but decided against it at the last minute. She had a good time in London any way. Besides, I'm thinking of coming over to spend a few weeks with you myself. Somehow, very soon, I'm going to have to get away from this damn foolish business for a period. My latest news is that I've developed a duodenal ulcer. The only good feature of an ulcer is that it's caused me to lose a lot of weight, about 25 pounds. Some people tell me I look much younger as a result. When I look in the mirror though, what I see is someone who looks like a refugee from Belsen, or possibly someone who has acquired a bad case of the rickets. Do you remember the old Charles Atlas ads, "I was a 98 pound weakling ... "? Well, I'm getting to the stage where I could pose for one of those ads. This will give you a fair picture of the situation. The bad feature is that they don't let me drink. I'm not supposed to smoke (I'm having a helluva time with that one). I can't eat anything. I have no energy, so what the hell. Perhaps reading about an unmarried schoolteacher in a small prairie town will cheer [me] up.

So that's the story. Hope you had a wonderful time in the north of Scotland and that the weather was a little better than it has been around these parts for the last month. Our summer hasn't arrived yet. We are expecting it later this month.

Love and kisses,
J.G. McClelland

Hollinger, 9 September 1965

Dear Jack:

You don't need to reply to this letter, but I'm answering yours of Sept 3 right away, in order to extend my sympathies for your grim state. I'm really sorry about the ulcer, and also about the no-booze-and-no-smoking rule, which sounds AWFUL.

It may comfort you slightly to learn that I felt some twinge of envy about your losing 25 lbs. When I was in Scotland, I spent the greater part of my time either drinking whiskey or eating hot buttered scones, and now I have to go on a diet. I was staying with Jane Duncan[1]—she writes the "Friends" novels—and she runs a teashop in Cromarty during the summers. Quite a few people come mainly to see Jane Duncan, novelist, and Jane cannot simply sit down and talk to them for hours, so, while I was there, she sort of threw me into the situation as a substitute writer (what a letdown for the clients!), and I sat and drank tea and talked and ate one scone after another. I thoroughly enjoyed it, and returned feeling that I could grapple with life once more. But now it is lettuce, lettuce all the way.

I hope you didn't take my complaints about visitors seriously. In fact, I really did enjoy having them here, if only it hadn't been so many all at once. I don't know if you really meant it about coming to England, but, if you ever can, you have an open invitation here. If you neither drink nor eat, you would certainly be an easy guest.

I'll send the novel when it is typed. Alan Maclean has seen it, and likes it—did I tell you? I've cut it considerably in the first few chapters since then, and I don't really think a great deal more can be done with it. It seems to me to be pared down to the bone, which is how it was meant to be. Anyway, either it comes across or it doesn't. I'll be very anxious to know what you think of it. I wish I could think that it might cheer you up.

All the best.

Sincerely,

Margaret

1. Jane Duncan (1910–1976) was a Scottish writer most famous for the "Reachfar" (*My Friends*) series. In 1959, she set a historic precedent by having seven novels accepted by Macmillan at once. Duncan's real name was Elizabeth Jane Cameron.

Elm Cottage, 13 October 1965

Dear Margaret:

The very last thing I did before taking off on my enforced rest cure was to read *A Jest of God.*[1] As I think you know, I have never considered myself either an editor or a critic, although I guess my opinion is of some value after twenty years in the business.

In any case, I couldn't have been more delighted by this novel.

I bow to you in awe and wonderment. I haven't the slightest doubt in my mind that the international critics will hail this as easily your outstanding achievement to date. I shall be astounded if that isn't the verdict. I shall be equally astounded if it doesn't find a far wider readership as well than anything you have done previously.

The thing that continues to amaze me about your writing, Margaret, is that you improve with everything you write. At least, that is my opinion. I'm sure this is easily the best thing you've done, but there has been a steady pattern of maturing craft and skill and insight and understanding. It has truly been one of the most rewarding publishing experiences for a number of us here at M&S who have been associated with your career, quite apart from the personal friendship that I value highly.

No, I think it is a smashing success, and I think you should have no diffidence or hesitancy about it at all. It's an intelligent and mature piece of work. The people are flesh and blood. The associations are beautifully drawn. The background, which is vividly real, and the emotional situation, have the rare distinction of singular validity and universality.

Christ, it's a fine novel! What more can I say?

On the critical side, I have almost nothing to suggest, and indeed, even if I did have, even though you have invited me to comment, the novel is so good that I would almost feel impertinent in suggesting anything. For the most part, I am sure that you and Maclean will have caught anything that I noticed. There are a number of typing errors and so on. And also, I think, one confusing time transition in the first chapter. (I didn't attempt to sort it out, but I think you mysteriously jumped to Wednesday night). And also, I suspect you should change your reference to a 222,[2] which I think is a peculiarly Canadian product, and would be obscure elsewhere.

Frankly, the only thing that bothered me at all—and I suspect it's purely personal—is Rachel's last name. For some reason, I don't feel the name Rachel Cameron is sufficiently memorable for this particular creation. I have no plausible explanation for this feeling. As I said, it may be purely personal, and I realize you would lose the value of the reference to the Cameron Highlanders over there. But you might want to consider a change.

I expect Macmillan's will want to publish in the Spring. We shall certainly favour that, and hope Knopf will go along so that it can be simultaneous in London, New York, and Toronto. I understand you are going to see Alfred Knopf on his planned trip. If the meeting hasn't yet taken place, do tell him of my reaction and give him my best.

I am sending a copy of this letter to Maclean for the record, and will also inform New York of my reaction.

I am sorry, by the way, that I won't be able to sign this letter, but it will be typed after I leave.

Again, congratulations, and warm regards.

Cheers,
J.G. McClelland

1. Laurence initially intended to title the novel *The Jests of God*, as indicated in previous letters, but the novel was published with the title noted here, *A Jest of God*.
2. A "222" (or "two-twenty-two") was an over-the-counter pain pill that contained Aspirin, codeine, and caffeine.

Hollinger, 20 October 1965

Dear Jack:

HALLELUJAH! This was my reaction to your letter. I can't tell you how glad I am that you like *A Jest of God*. Actually, everything you said in your letter meant a great deal to me, and I appreciate it very much indeed. My difficulty always seems to be that I know quite well what the characters are like, and what they mean to me, but I am in a state of terrible apprehension until I discover how they appear to a few other people whose opinion I trust. Your letter has helped enormously in that respect.

I will certainly make the corrections you suggest re: Rachel's surname—I tend to agree with you, and I think the main problem may be to find a Scottish name, which seems right. Anyway, I'll let you know about this. It's essential for various unspoken but real reasons for her to have a Scots-Canadian background. I mean, she does have that background, so the name ought to make that clear.

I have had flu and at the moment I feel as though I will never have any energy, not ever again, but I suppose this will pass. I do hope your holiday has made you feel better.

All the very best.
Sincerely,
Margaret

Hollinger, 24 March 1966

Dear Jack:

The enclosed article was in today's *Guardian*. It sounded to me so much like a book which you told me about in 1961 when I was in Toronto—at that stage, it wasn't yet a book, but I remember that you were very interested in the story and thought there was something worthwhile doing in it. I wonder if this is the same case? If it is, I thought you might be interested in the *Guardian*'s article. The case itself sounds pretty appalling.[1]

All the best.
Sincerely,
Margaret

1. The article to which Laurence refers was published in the *Guardian* on 24 March 1966, as "The Case of Steven Truscott," written by Michael Zander. In the article, Zander discusses a book written by journalist Isabel LeBourdais. Titled *The Trial of Steven Truscott*, the book argues that a fourteen-year-old boy, who was accused of murder and was serving a life sentence in Ontario's Kingston Penitentiary, was innocent. Laurence's interest in the article is significant, as her essay written at about the same time, "Open Letter to the Mother of Joe Bass," takes up similar subject matter. Laurence's essay was originally published in a collection of essays by Canadian writers on their views of America, *The New Romans*, edited by Al Purdy. It was later republished in Laurence's collection, *Heart of a Stranger*.

Elm Cottage, 4 April 1966

Dear Margaret:

Thanks for your note. It was good to hear from you. Yes, it is the same book.[1] It's had a long and chequered career. It has really taken Canada by storm. Thus far we have about 35,000 copies and it looks like we may go close to 100,000 before it is finished. The outcome depends on a decision that is to be announced shortly by the Government. It will be either a Royal Commission, a Judicial Inquiry, or no action, but if it is the latter there will be a real storm of protest from the Opposition.

How are things going? We seem to be out of touch. I judge that Knopf, Macmillan, and ourselves are publishing simultaneously. Our plan is to manufacture in Canada. I think the new novel is going to do extremely well. I hope, by the way, that you have seen the piece in the current issue of *Canadian Literature*.[2] My reaction was that it was, for the most part, a thoughtful and intelligent piece, but I'd be curious to know how you, the subject, felt about it. Do drop me a line when you have a moment.

All the best.
Sincerely,
J.G. McClelland

1. See the annotation for Laurence's letter dated 24 March 1966. The book McClelland refers to is *The Trial of Steven Truscott* by Isabel LeBourdais.
2. The article McClelland refers to, by S.E. Read, is called "The Maze of Life: The Work of Margaret Laurence." It is a very positive and extensive review of the books Laurence had published up to that point. Read states, "Today, as a result of the publication of four works, three of which appeared in a few short months in 1963 and 1964, she is recognized in many parts of the English speaking world as a serious writer who has already achieved greatly and who gives promise of even greater achievement" (5). Read further states, "It is the creation of Hagar Shipley that clearly marks—for me at least—the emergence of Mrs. Laurence as a fine novelist" (12).

Hollinger, 27 April 1966

Dear Jack:

Thanks for your letter of April 4th. Things are pretty good here, in general. I've just returned from Greece, where I took my children for a two-week holiday. We spent two days in Athens, then went by boat to Crete, where we stayed at the most beautiful beach I've ever seen. We also went to look at the ancient Minoan ruins at Knossos, which I've wanted to see for years. We had a marvellous time, and came back to find that England had had about a foot of snow in our absence, so I guess we picked the right moment to go away.

I saw the piece in *Canadian Literature*. I don't know how I feel about it. Slightly embarrassed, I guess, because, although I'm tremendously glad he likes my work, I think he overestimates it. I'm not saying this out of any false modesty, but only because there isn't any point in thinking of one's own work except in relation to everything else in a similar field being written in English everywhere in the world. I'm glad that you and Macmillan and Knopf will be publishing *A Jest of God* simultaneously. Sometimes, I hear that this will be in June and sometimes I hear it will be in July. Bill Koshland[1] is in London now and I'm with him tomorrow, so I shall ask him if he knows when they plan to publish. A very silly thing happened the day after I returned from Greece—Macmillan's phoned to say that the music publishers had denied permission for me to quote the lines of the pop song which I'd used, unless an exorbitant fee were paid. So I decided that the easiest thing would be to write some lyrics myself, thus getting around the problem of copyright and also so that I could get the right length and therefore avoid any major alterations to the type. So I did this. Probably Macmillan's have cabled you about it. The whole thing seems ludicrous, but I realize now that music publishers tend to be a little finicky about these things, so I'll take care in future. My lyrics aren't what you could call part of the Top Ten, but I simply used the method used by the popular horoscopes in women's magazines—the words could more or less mean anything you want them to mean.

By the way, how is your health these days? Okay now, I hope.

Please write when you have the time. Something very oddly like homesickness has been impinging upon my consciousness recently, and I realize that I'd really like to go back to Canada for a visit. I've always intended to go back to live, one day, and still mean to, but don't exactly know when. Don't want to move the kids again for a few years, and also, I like this house so much that I don't want to leave it. But I think I must see if I can go back next summer for a while.

I'm going to apply to the Canada Council this summer; will you write a letter for me? I've written to enquire about the right time to apply.

All the best.
Sincerely,
Margaret[2]

1. William Koshland (1907–1997) was the president of Knopf from 1966 to 1973, chairman in 1973, and chairman emeritus from that year until his death. He worked at Knopf from 1934 to 1997 (the last years primarily in an advisory capacity). He is widely considered to have been instrumental in Knopf's successes.
2. Marge Hodgeman, McClelland's personal administrative assistant, wrote back to Laurence on 2 May 1966. She stated, "Your letter of April 27th has reached the office during Mr. McClelland's absence from the city on a trip to Western Canada. It will be passed to him on his return to the office in approximately 10 days" (McClelland & Stewart Ltd. Fonds, Box 35, File 42).

Elm Cottage, 11 May 1966

Dear Margaret:

Having seen Bill Koshland in the interim, you, by now, will have a more exact idea than I have as to when *A Jest of God* is to be published. We don't really want to publish here until September. June and July are horrible months in the Canadian trade, but we will be going along with the date jointly agreed to by Macmillan and Knopf, but the longer they delay it the better as far as we are concerned. That's interesting, by the way, that you have had to write some song lyrics for the book. Perhaps this will launch you into a music career and we will have another Irving Berlin on our hands.

I'm glad you are going to apply to the Canada Council and I will, of course, be delighted to support the application. They have rather more money to spend now than they have had in the past, although I don't think they have increased the amount of the grants which seems a pity. In applying, you should ask for travel money in addition to the grant—I believe this is permissible under the rules—and use it to make a visit to Canada. I wish it could be this fall because we would certainly like to have you here in connection with the promotion of the new book. I fear, however, that we couldn't cover the cost of such a trip out of our own promotion budget. I may take this up with Knopf and see if we couldn't do it jointly.

Yes, my health is greatly improved. I seemed to have recovered, at least from the particular illness that plagued me so much last fall. I keep my fingers crossed about it though because the strain of this idiotic business never seems to ease. In fact, it gets worse. Look after yourself and hope we'll see you soon.

Sincerely,
J.G. McClelland

Hollinger, 11 May 1966

Dear Jack:

I am homesick.

I am also fed up, bored, and temporarily in need of a spell away from the role of mother. I am sick of working. I want to see some of my tribe again. So I've decided that I will go back to Canada for a visit for August and September. I don't really think I want to go anywhere except Montreal and Toronto, and maybe a short visit to New York. I thought that, if my novel is coming out in August, that might be quite a good time to pick. Also, a friend has agreed to stay here for that period of time and look after my kids, and, as this is normally the big difficulty about my going anywhere, I feel I want to take the opportunity when it presents itself. Do you think it is a good idea? Do you think it would be possible for me to find a hotel or bed-sitting room or something in Toronto for three or four weeks, which wouldn't cost me the earth?

Please write, when you have time, and let me know what you think.

All the best,

Margaret Laurence

Hollinger, 17 May 1966

Dear Jack:

Thanks for your letter of May 11th. You will have had my letter by this time, saying that I'm going to go to Canada for August and September. I've been in touch with Bob Weaver and he has discovered that there might be some possibility of my applying to the Canada Council right now, instead of later on in the summer, in order to get some financial help for the trip. I've written to find out about this, so will let you know what happens, if anything. It definitely seems worth a try, anyway.

I really want to spend most of the time in Toronto and Montreal, but if I can get some money from the Canada Council, I would like to go to Winnipeg and Vancouver as well, partly to see old friends and partly to take a look at the country and so on, before I start another novel.

If *A Jest of God* is coming out in September, maybe I should try to go west in August and be back in Toronto in September. Anyway, whatever you like in this respect, as I'd appreciate your advice in planning the trip, and if you think it can be fitted in with a certain amount of promotion of the novel, so much the better. Only please PLEASE, Jack, no TV! Do you remember my one abortive effort on TV in Toronto? I have not yet recovered from the horror of that experience.

All Knopf has said about publication date is that they "aim for" an August publication; but this does not seem to be definite. I certainly agree that June and July are bad months—not only in Canada, but also here, because all the reviewers are on holiday or else fed-up because they're not on holiday, and the fiction gets pretty bad treatment.

It will be wonderful to be home for a while—it's just beginning to seem real to me, I mean the fact that I'm actually going!

Sincerely,
Margaret

Elm Cottage, 19 May 1966

Dear Margaret:

Thanks for your letter. Yes, I think it's a marvellous idea for you to come back for August and September and we can certainly find a place for you to stay. As I think I mentioned in my last letter, I am going to talk to Knopf and see if they will join with us in putting up some money for the trip. I think this can be justified easily if you will do some TV and radio interviews because it would certainly help us get the book off to a good start. Since my last note, I have been talking to Bob Weaver, and I understand he has been in touch with you. He believes that he can more than cover your expenses by fees from the C.B.C. I don't know how far he's gone on this, but I think it can probably be worked out very quickly.

So let's make it definite. By all means come. We'd be delighted to see you. We'll get busy on the details at this end. Can you let me know what date would be suitable for you? I think early August would be desirable. I haven't yet heard a definite date from Knopf, but I think they are probably still reasonably flexible. And, yes, as far as I can tell, I will certainly be here in August and I expect for a good part of September. I think it's terrific news.

All the best.
Sincerely,
J.G. McClelland

Hollinger, 31 May 1966

Dear Jack:

... Bob Weaver has been absolutely marvellous, re: Canada Council, and has got a number of sponsors' letters on my behalf, as there was not enough time for me to do this. Even if they don't give me a cent, I feel enormously grateful to him, as he has really done a great deal.

Re: TV[1]—Okay, Jack, if you think it is advisable. I hate it, and am very nervous and so on, but will do my best. The only thing I *do* want to insist upon—I have enough time just to see people whom I want to see, etc. etc., and not every day taken up with publicity. I know you will understand this and do your best. Obviously, it is to your advantage and to mine, if we can work out some publicity, and, although I am not exactly enamoured of this kind of situation, I will try. But really, what I want and desperately need, is to talk to old friends and see people and so on. Naturally, you *know* this. I don't know why I even bother to mention it. Except that I have a kind of horror of being over-organised.

As far as both TV and things like United College are concerned, I would infinitely prefer *not* to have to SPEAK—i.e. by myself. I am not a public speaker. I don't think I know what in hell I could possibly talk about—*not* about the things which really affect my life, which are: how to write a book while a friend is having a nervous breakdown in your house and your mother-in-law is visiting at the same time, with the situation complicated by the fact that you are separated from your husband and you are trying to reassure your children's grandmother that your kids [are not] irreparably damaged,[2] and that the usual marriage isn't possible for some people, while at the same time trying to make a relatively un-upsetting situation out of the fact that psychiatrists etc. are arriving in a steady procession in an attempt to get said friend out of house and into mental hospital (and, I hope, out of *my* responsibility) and also trying to get done the standard one chapter per week. Nobody would believe it. I don't feel I have much to say, in a public-speaking way. Anything I have to say could not possibly be said, except privately!

I'll let you know definitely when I am able to know how long I'll be in Canada. I think the best thing will be for me to work out some kind of rough schedule, and book air passages accordingly, and then let you know what I've planned.

Thanks for all your help.

All the best.

Sincerely,

Margaret

1. On 25 May 1966, McClelland wrote to Laurence to encourage her to do television interviews.
2. A fold in the letter obscures a few words at this point.

Hollinger, 3 June 1966

Dear Jack:

Thanks very much for your cable.[1] I haven't yet heard from the Canada Council, but I assume you have, and needless to say I'm delighted. I feel I better not go overboard with joy until I actually hear from them—there is enough of the canny Scot in me to want to clutch the letter in my hand before I entirely believe it. Anyway, many, many thanks for your help and for all the effort you've made re: Knopf, as well, in getting in touch with them about my trip. I received the copy of Harding Lemay's letter to you, and I'm glad they would like me to go to New York for a few days. Honestly, I don't want to stop off at any other American cities. I'd like to very much if I had a longer visit, but I don't want the whole thing to be too exhausting. If I could just go to New York for a few days, that would be marvellous.

I have now worked out a sort of timetable and will book my air passage next week. I'll let you know exact times later on, if you like. Here is how I plan to spend the time:

Toronto—July 31 to August 27 (roughly 4 weeks; this to include New York)
Montreal—August 27 to September 17 (Roughly 3 weeks, mainly to visit Adele)[2]
Vancouver—September 18 to September 29
Winnipeg—September 29 to October 7

I thought I would return to London directly from Winnipeg. It seems better to me to have one visit in each place, rather than trying to return to Toronto at the end of the time, and I think this would be simpler for other people as well. I'd like to spend the longest time in Toronto, because this could include the visit to New York and also because I'd like to be there long enough, for once, to get to know people a little better.

I hope you think this schedule sounds okay. Another thing I really do realize that the publicity thing is to my advantage, Jack, but please try not to arrange too much in that way. It isn't as much of an ordeal as it used to be, but it is still a strain and I don't think I shall ever get over feeling that way. It isn't that I fall to pieces or lose my voice at the time, you understand—it's just that I am pretty depleted afterwards.

I'm looking forward tremendously to seeing everyone again.

All the best.
Margaret

P.S. As you will notice, I have managed to arrange to be away until the end of the first week in October. Also, a very odd thing has just happened—the government of the Somali Republic has invited me, along with a few others, to go out as their guests to the Independence Day celebrations on July 1st! Suddenly life contains almost too much excitement! Don't know how long I shall be in Somaliland—not more than three or four days at most, but it should be interesting.

1. The cable was not included in Laurence's or McClelland's papers.
2. Adele Wiseman (1928–1992) was Laurence's close friend and a respected Canadian writer. She moved to Montreal from Winnipeg in 1963 for family reasons (Lennox and Panofsky 23). Wiseman and Laurence met when they attended United College, since named the University of Winnipeg. They were both students in Malcolm Ross's English class, "English Thought in the Seventeenth Century" in 1947, and they remained friends in part because of their mutual interest in writing (Powers 56). Wiseman wrote novels, plays, and children's books, to high acclaim. She was of Jewish heritage, and many of her books are about Jewish characters and grounded in Biblical myths. She is most well known for her novel, *Crackpot*, published in 1974.

Hollinger, 4 June 1966

Dear Jack:

I'm writing to tell you that I'm changing my American agent. This isn't at all a sudden move, and it carries absolutely no criticism of Willie Wing. But when John Cushman[1] was with Wing, he was handling my work, and I found I could discuss writing matters very easily with him. Over a period of time, he and his wife have become friends of mine. Now that he has begun his own business, I have asked him if he will become my agent and he has agreed to do so. I have written to Willis Wing, explaining the situation, and I hope he will understand that I'm making this change not out of dissatisfaction with him, but only because I feel a sense of rapport with John where writing is concerned.

You probably have John's new address (he's in Willis Wing's old offices), but if not, it is: John Cushman Associates Inc.,[2] 24 East 38th St., New York, N.Y. 10016.

John and his wife have invited me to stay with them when I am in New York this summer, and I would like very much to do this. However, Jane[3] has not been very well, so I think we'll see, closer to the time.

All best wishes.
Sincerely,
Margaret

1. John Cushman was affiliated with the William Morris Agency until 1965, when he formed his own company as the American branch of Curtis Brown Ltd. (London). In March 1978, James Brown Associates Inc. absorbed John Cushman Associates Inc. (JCA) (from the description of John Cushman Associates Records, 1965–1978).
2. John Cushman Associates was founded by John Cushman and Jane Wilson in 1965, and was run by Jane Cushman after John's sudden death in 1984 until her own death in 1998. JCA currently continues under the leadership of Tom Cushman, John and Jane's son. The firm handles a

majority of new authors, publishing mostly literature and specific areas of genre fiction (crime, thrillers, historical romances, and so forth).

3. Jane Cushman (1930–1998) took over leadership of John Cushman Associates after her husband's death, continuing its successful run. Under her, JCA represented several critically acclaimed authors, such as Pulitzer winners Richard Rhodes and David Garrow. Her correspondence with Laurence is referred to later in the matter of Tom's education after John Cushman's death (see Laurence's letter dated 4 October 1984).

Elm Cottage, 7 June 1966

Dear Margaret:

Thanks for your letter of May 31st. I'm delighted by your reaction. I understand. I sympathize when I say, "for God's sake, don't worry about it." If you have to speak, you can speak. I can tell you what to say. On Friday, I listened to Morley Callaghan speak at a Convocation at the University of Toronto when they gave him a belated LLD. The speech was casual and didn't contribute very much, but everyone loved it. The fact of the matter is that he is a celebrity. He is a big name and they want to hear him. It doesn't matter very much what you say provided it's real. So the fact of the situation is, Margaret, that you are a celebrity. From one end of the country to the other, you are recognized by the important people in the artistic area as a writer who has accomplished a great deal already, and who will, undoubtedly, become in the next 10 years, Canada's greatest single claim to literary fame. It's an imposing burden. I envy you and I cringe with you. That's the way it is. As they say, "You have this gift, baby. There ain't much you can do about it. You've got to live with it."

I think Bob Weaver has already written you about the timing problem. It's to everyone's advantage if you can delay your trip as much as possible, although we will adjust to whatever you decide. Basically though, Margaret, you should arrive as late in August as possible and stay as late into October as is possible. Can you adjust your plans to this end? It would help in a great many ways both in Canada and in the U.S.A. We must have dates as soon as possible, and they must be firm so all these things can be scheduled, but do look at your home problems, the handling of the kids and so on, and if you can shift it so that really you are here for most of September and October, this is the ideal time.

One further thing. Because you are going to be here, and because you are going across the country, we have decided that we would like to try your book simultaneously in paper and in hard cover. This would be a $2.50 paper edition and a $5.00 hardcover edition. We can't promise results, but our guess is that the $2.50 edition will be snapped up by the campus crowd and distribution will be increased considerably and that you will end up making a great deal more money. But it's a gamble. Who knows? Fiction isn't selling well at the present time. Brian Moore's last book *The Emperor of Ice-Cream*, which I thought was a very good novel, sold only 1000 copies at $5.50. Our guess is that we might sell 10,000 of yours at $2.50 in paper, and perhaps 1,500 at the $5.00 price. But you never can tell about these things. We might end up selling 4,000 in paper, in which case we'd be out of pocket. Do you want to go along with our speculation?

Re: the planning for your trip, do make the reservations to come directly to Toronto. How long you spend here initially will depend on the departure date, so do let me know about the departure date as soon as possible and then we will project a suggested program.

Sincerely,
J.G. McClelland[1]

1. Laurence wrote back on 11 June and agreed to make arrangements to stay until the end of October.

Elm Cottage, 13 June 1966

Dear Margaret:

It was nice to hear your voice again after so long. Although I didn't manage to accomplish my specific purpose, I find that we are reasonably adaptable and I think the whole thing will work out quite well. Let me start now by trying to establish a few specifics that will make it easier at both ends to establish the ultimate details of the trip:

1. We will be paying for your travelling expenses across Canada. I make this point because you seem to be placing great stress on the necessity of having your reservations all settled before you leave. I don't think that is going to be possible. Or let me put it a different way. It may be possible before you actually leave, but we are going to need a few weeks at this end to establish the details. ...
2. Our publication date will be September 10th and ideally we would like to have you in Toronto at that time. We would plan to have a pre-publication party on the 7th or 8th. This could work out very well, because it happens that we have our annual author weekend in Muskoka from [the] 12th and I think you might enjoy it. We would certainly enjoy having you.
3. I have noted your several comments about the promotion and publicity bit. We shall plan accordingly both with a view to making certain that you have most of your time free to have a rest and enjoy a holiday, and also to see that it isn't a circus and that the whole thing is handled on a restrained basis.

   Despite that a certain amount [of] exposure is, I think, necessary and desirable, your reputation is growing with each book, but thus far the main rewards have been critical acclaim rather than financial. I think this is an opportunity to expand your Canadian market very substantially and once this has been done, Margaret, it has cumulative effect. The market, then, continues to grow with each succeeding book.

We shall plan, at the outset, to keep television to a relative minimum, although I think you will find you will begin to enjoy it after you have done a few shows. You will have a fair number of radio interviews, but we shall concentrate on relatively small receptions with the press, selected booksellers and the people from the academic and literary community who are so anxious to meet you.

4. In addition to the four principal cities on your agenda, we would like you to visit Edmonton, Calgary, Regina, Saskatoon, and possibly Ottawa. These can be very brief stopovers. We have resident people in each one of the cities, and I think they could make it interesting for you without it being too arduous.

... I realize that this schedule does not give you as long a period consecutively in each place as per your original plans. There may be a disadvantage in this, but the key to the problem is that we can't effectively publish before September 10th and we would like to have you in Toronto at that time. The only alternative to the foregoing is for you to go to Montreal, and from Montreal to New York, and from New York to Toronto, and from there to the West. As far as Ottawa is concerned, if it is felt desirably for you to spend a day there, it can be covered easily from Montreal. As far as the Western cities are concerned, if you really think this is too much, we will eliminate some of them, but I certainly think you should go to Edmonton and some of the others as well. Do let me have your reaction to the foregoing as soon as possible.

With all good wishes.
Sincerely,
J.G. McClelland[1]

1. Laurence later agreed to these arrangements by telegram.

Hollinger, 17 June 1966

Dear Jack:

Hope you received my second cable all right. When I got your letter of June 13th, I realized that the only possibility was what you suggested—to get firm dates for Atlantic flights and to leave the rest of the program open. This is therefore what I have done. ...

I am quite willing to go along with publicity matters, UP TO A POINT. I want to be in Montreal, Vancouver and Winnipeg, as well as Toronto and New York. But Jack, PLEASE don't insist on much more than that. It is all very well to make a publicity deal out of all this, but I am beginning to wish I had paid for it all myself and not told anyone I was coming home. Because, you see, the difficulty is that I REALLY DO NEED A HOLIDAY *DESPERATELY*. I am not trying to be temperamental or difficult honestly. I *do* want to go along with what you have in mind—But I really must protect myself to some extent, because, at this point, I am dead beat and I just do not think I can possibly face a trip which includes stop-offs in every major Canadian city, with all the politeness involved in each. Jack, I'm truly sorry. But please try to understand. I've gone through an awful lot of personal crisis in the past few years and have also written two books and I really am tired. If I have to go to Edmonton, Regina, Calgary and Saskatoon, I will drop dead. It isn't that I mean to be difficult. It is just that my physical reserves are limited. If you think it is essential to go somewhere else other than Toronto, Montreal, Winnipeg, and Vancouver, I would not mind going for a day to Edmonton, because I would like to meet Henry Kreisel.[1] But please, boss, have a heart. Don't press me too far or I will fold up. I do not speak in jest, believe me.

What I would prefer would be to visit Toronto, Montreal, New York, Vancouver and Winnipeg, returning to Toronto at the end of my visit. If any other place, only Edmonton, and only because of Kreisel.

Re: your paying for my travelling expenses—Jack, that won't be necessary because the Canada Council has awarded me a grant ($5000 for working on the next novel), which includes an extra travel allowance of $700, which will just about cover all my airfares. If you could help out somewhat with hotel bills, that would be marvellous, but that ought to be necessary only in Toronto, for reasons which I will explain. ...

Re: accommodation in Toronto, for August. I would really like to sublet an apartment for that month, so that I could be self-contained. I suppose this is being overly optimistic, but I like to think there might be some time when I did not have to do anything but see the people I want to see, etc. I'm sorry if I sound dejected, but this is how I feel at the moment. What started out a holiday seems to be turning into a nightmare. I KNOW publicity is necessary. I KNOW it is to my advantage. But my God, Jack, I need so much to talk to people I like. Otherwise, why bother going at all? Anyway, re: a flat in Toronto—do you think this might be a possibility? It would be better than a hotel, from my point of view, if I'm going to be there for most of August.

Re: your ideas about simultaneous hardcover and paperback editions of *A Jest of God*—I think this is a splendid idea, and I'm quite willing to go along with whatever you think best. I do hope you don't think I'm being awkward, but right now I feel lousy about the whole trip, because what I desperately need is a little relaxation and gaiety, and your description of events sounds about as gay as a session of the Ladies' Aid. Please forgive me for bitching. It makes me feel like a heel, especially in the light of what you said in your letter of June 7th, which both touched and alarmed me. Believe me, Jack, I *do* recognise that one has to accept change—and, after all these years, I see finally that I am no longer a simple country girl, etc. etc. Whatever kind of writer I am is not so important—the fact is that I know now I am a writer, and therefore committed to this. But one is essentially a private person. And sometimes you reach the limits of your endurance, and this is how I feel now—that I just need to talk to friends and shed some responsibilities, even if only for awhile.

Honestly, I *will* try to co-operate. BUT WE MUST COMPROMISE. I stand firm on that. Of course, the main trouble—as always with you and myself—is that in any crisis we both get so worked up and verbose! I appreciate you *so much*—maybe that is why from time to time I feel free to get furious at you. Anyway, don't be mad at me, please. I will do my best, but please don't expect some kind of super performance from me, because I'm not capable of that, at this point.

Re: finances once more—I'm not trying to con you out of anything, so don't even consider the air fares, as this has all been covered. If you can arrange to let me know soon re: the different places, I can stay with friends, and why pay more? Help with accommodation in Toronto would be appreciated.

Hope this is not too disorganized a letter.

All the very best.
Margaret

1. Henry Kreisel (1922–1991) was a writer and a professor and administrator at the University of Alberta from 1947 to 1975. He was "one of the first people to bring the experience of the immigrant to modern Canadian literature" (Tausky).

TO J G MCCLELLAND HOLLINGER ROAD SENT JUNE 17, 1966

YOUR JUNE 13 LETTER RECEIVED. OKAY YOU WIN. DEFINITE DATE ARRIVE TORONTO JULY 30 RETURN LONDON OCTOBER 15 FROM TORONTO. ALL ELSE IN YOUR HAND AND GODS. ANGRY LETTER FOLLOWS.

LOVE
MARGARET

Hollinger, 23 June 1966

Dear Jack:

Have just received your cable[1] and have cabled my agreement to your schedule. It sounds fine and should work out okay. I have now obtained my tickets from Air Canada, but the only definite bookings are the two trans-Atlantic flights to Toronto on July 30, and back to London from Toronto on October 15. ... I don't really mind what arrangements you make. I hope I haven't been too bloody-minded about all this. All I really want to do is to ensure that I have quite a bit of time to myself, to see friends.

I shall be staying with friends, I think, everywhere except Toronto. If some of these plans don't work out, then I can get a hotel, but it is really only Toronto [that] concerns me. For the brief stays (Sept 5 to 12 and October 10 to 15), a hotel would be best. But I think that it would be a good idea if I could rent a small flat or something for July 31 to August 21. What do you think? I love hotels because they are such a change from my normal way of life, but it seems pretty expensive for a month. Do you happen to know of anyone who might rent me a bedsitter or flat? If not, I wonder if you can make suggestions about a relatively low-cost hotel? I know you have said you will help with expenses, but in the first place, as I said before, my aim is not to become a con-woman, and secondly, my Scots soul revolts at the thought of a costly hotel for a month.

It will all work out okay. I am now quite relaxed about everything. More or less. By the way, did I tell you that Macmillan's are publishing my novel on July 4? They have done a marvellous jacket, but I am afraid all reviewers will be on holiday.

I won't write to Dr. Lockhart[2] in Winnipeg again until I hear from you.

All the best.
Sincerely,
Margaret

1. This cable was not included in Laurence's or McClelland's papers.
2. Dr. Wilfred Cornett Lockhart (1906–1991) was a notable Winnipeg citizen and a United Church of Canada minister. He served as the president of the University of Winnipeg from 1967 to 1971 and received an honorary degree from the same university in 1977.

Elm Cottage, 30 June 1966

Dear Margaret:

I am completely baffled by your cable that reached us on June 27th where you say you are mystified by my cable. The agenda that we are confirming to reiterate is the one that has now been stated in your letter of June 23rd. No further change is needed.

I have been in touch with Dr. Lockhart and their Convocation will be on October 5th, so that fits in beautifully with the program. Fortunately for you, they have already engaged a speaker for the Commencement or Convocation, or whatever it is called, so you will be spared that ordeal. However, on one of the succeeding days during the lunch hour, they do want you to speak to some of the students about the novel if you are willing. They are also arranging a reception at Government House and that sort of thing. I don't think the ordeal should be too painful.

We will organize an appropriate place in Toronto and we'll let you have the details as soon as we can make a recommendation and we shall, of course, be meeting you at the plane.

All the best.
Sincerely,
J.G. McClelland

Hollinger, 9 July 1966

Dear Jack:

Sorry about the bewilderment re: cables. I can't think what happened, but I have a suspicion that an earlier cable of yours reached me about a week after it was meant to, and after all the details of my trip had already been settled. Not realizing it was an earlier cable, I was thrown into a state of confusion. I'm sure this is what must have happened. Anyway, all is okay, if the new schedule seems okay to you. I think the hold-up in delivery of that cable happened at this end, as I now recall it was phoned through to me from High Wycombe, instead of coming to the village as they normally do, so probably someone found it in a neglected pile of papers and was a bit embarrassed about it.

I had a truly wonderful trip to Somalia, and enjoyed every minute of it. I was only there a week, but I managed to see a lot of old friends, some of whom I had not seen in 14 years. As soon as I got back, I came down with some tropical bug which I must have picked up there, and have been sick as a dog ever since—nothing serious, only the usual intestinal infection, but very unpleasant. I'm feeling a little fragile still, but on the mend. This is why I haven't written sooner.

... I've written to Dr. Lockhart. Thank goodness I won't have to do any full-scale talk there, but I don't mind doing a small amount of general nattering about the contemporary novel, if that has any value.

I'm sorry about Macmillan's publishing so early here. You have run into this problem before, and it seems to go on. I can certainly appreciate your point of view about it, and I hope you can prevent booksellers there from ordering copies here.

All the best.
Sincerely,
Margaret

Elm Cottage, 19 July 1966

Dear Margaret:

I have sent to you, under separate cover, a letter from the Winnipeg Branch of the Canadian Authors Association. They want you to speak to them while you are in Winnipeg at their monthly meeting. We have told them that we doubt your schedule will permit it. You can suit yourself on this one. They are very pleasant people. It would be an informal craft-group type of meeting. It would be our opinion, I'm afraid, that it would be a considerable waste of your time, although we can't admit that to them.

All the best.
Sincerely,
J.G. McClelland

Mayfair Mansions, 29 July 1966

Dear Margaret:

Welcome back to Canada. Sorry I can't be there to meet you, but I'm sure Tony Hawke[1] will do a noble job in my absence. As I think I warned you in advance, I'm up in North country. I shall be coming down late Monday night. I am hoping that we can have lunch or dinner on Tuesday, whichever is most convenient for you. I'll call you Tuesday morning, so we can get organized. I hope you had a good trip and that the visit turns out to be a very pleasant one. I look forward to seeing you.

Sincerely,
J.G. McClelland

1. Anthony Hawke began work as promotion director at McClelland & Stewart in 1965, and later helped start *Books in Canada* magazine. Hawke founded Hounslow Press in 1972, which published popular Canadian nonfiction, as well as quality fiction, poetry, and translations.

Dear Jack—[1]

I have to write this by hand because I can't make Marge's electric typewriter work.

I just wanted to thank you for everything. You were terrific—and I really appreciate all the help and moral support you gave me this summer. Also, everyone in the firm has been so good and considerate—Jim Douglas in Vancouver, Diane Woodman in Edmonton, Mary White in Winnipeg, and everyone here in Toronto.

I paid the $200 I owed you, as I thought I'd rather pay it now.

Once again—many thanks, boss.

All the best,
Margaret

1. This letter is handwritten and undated. It would have been written toward the end of the summer in 1966, from McClelland's office in Toronto, before Laurence left to return to England.

New York, 14 September 1966

Dear Jack—

I wanted to communicate briefly, to thank you for everything—I know I'll see you again in October, but I thought you were so damn kind when I was in Toronto that I wanted to let you know now. Thanks, boss. I hope the publicity bit was okay and that I didn't let down the side too much.

Have just learned that my novel is going to be reviewed in *Life*, and the people at Knopf's showed me the review today. It's both good and perceptive, so this is a stroke of terrific luck. I won't believe that *Life* is actually going to run it until I see it printed in the magazine, but probably they will.[1]

New York is *not* my cup of tea, but it is lovely to see people like Bill Koshland again.

All the best,
Margaret

P.S. Bill Koshland told me how much he admires you and thinks you're one of the best publishers in North America. I pass this on to you for free.[2]

1. No review of Laurence's novel appears in *Life*, and so it is possible the magazine did not run it.
2. Laurence wrote this letter by hand from New York, near the end of her tour to Canada and New York. Attached to this handwritten note is another one, addressed to Hodgeman. Laurence asked Hodgeman to forward any mail addressed to Laurence at McClelland & Stewart to Adele Wiseman, and she provided Hodgeman with Wiseman's address. She also provided details about her flights and when she was scheduled to return.

Elm Street, 30 September 1966

Dear Margaret:

As Mary will have told you I am arriving in Winnipeg about 10:30 Monday night. If you are not too tired and want to get together for a drink, leave a note at the Fort Garry [Hotel]. I'll be there Tuesday and will have to return to Toronto after the Lieutenant Governor's Reception Wednesday evening.

Hope the trip has gone well. I have had nothing but favourable reports. Hoping that you have been enjoying yourself. Incidentally, you overwhelmed Alfred Knopf. He wrote saying that you are not only an excellent writer, you are a "damn fine woman." Not many people impress him, so you should feel flattered.

All the best,
Sincerely yours,
J.G. McClelland

Hollinger, 30 October 1966

Dear Jack:

A brief note, to thank you once more for all your help and kindness this summer. The trip was slightly wearing, but I think it all went quite well. It was marvellous to see everyone again and also to meet a lot of people whom I had wanted to meet for a long time.

At the moment, I'm completely caught up in preparations for the trip to Egypt. I don't know whether the Canada Council would approve, considering that I am meant to be beginning another novel, so I am not going to say much to anyone in Canada about this trip. Actually, it will not make any difference to the novel in the long run, but it will make a lot of difference to me financially, I hope.

I was so exhausted when I arrived home that I thought it would take weeks to recover, but I am already nearly back to normal, thank goodness. In retrospect the summer seems fairly bizarre, and I don't think I would ever want to do that kind of publicity thing again, but I guess it was worthwhile simply as experience.

Willis Wing has sold a film option on *A Jest of God*.[1] Hallelujah.

All the best.
Sincerely,
Margaret

1. The film version of *A Jest of God* was released under the name *Rachel, Rachel* in 1968; it was directed by Paul Newman and starred Joanne Woodward as Rachel Cameron, James Olson as Nick Kazlik, and Kate Harrington as Mrs. Cameron. It was nominated for four Oscars (Best Picture, Best Actress, Best Adapted Screenplay, and Best Supporting Actress).

Hollinger, 18 January 1967

Dear Jack:

Happy New Year! A little belated, but we only got home from Egypt a few days ago. The whole trip went splendidly, and was one of the most terrific experiences of my life. My kids also enjoyed it thoroughly, and I was very glad I'd taken them along, as they were really good companions. We spent a few days in Cairo, then down to Luxor, where we spent 10 days looking at Karnak Temple, Luxor Temple, the temples and tombs of the pharaohs and queens and nobles (with tomb paintings that look as though they'd been done yesterday instead of 3 thousand years ago). Then took a Nile steamer to Asswan—a 2-day trip, and the most relaxing time I've spent in years, and at Asswan saw the High Dam, which is fabulous. Then back to Cairo and over to Ismailia, on the Suez Canal, where we boarded a British tanker and travelled on the canal to Port Said. That was the only really ghastly experience of the trip—disembarking with the pilot at Port Said harbour—the tanker was zooming along, and the small pilot launch had to come alongside, and we had to totter down a very narrow gangway and leap aboard the launch—I was absolutely terrified, but we all made it, thank God, with no casualties other than my shattered nerves. My kids said, "Don't be ridiculous—there was no danger at all." It must be lovely to be courageous. Spent a week in Port Said, then back to Cairo, where we dutifully crawled through the claustrophobic tunnels in the Great Pyramid in order to be able to say we'd done it (I can't think of any other reason why anyone would want to go through that kind of ordeal). All in all, the trip was great, however, and now I have to settle down and try to organise a whole mass of material into several articles—I'm praying they will turn out okay.

I have finished my book on Nigerian literature, and I think Macmillan's will publish it in due course, although it still needs some rewriting and their readers have made various suggestions about this.[1] I can't imagine that you will want to publish it, as who would buy it? However, I sent a copy to John Cushman, if you should want to have a look at it.

I heard from Bob Weaver that you had agreed to our doing a selection of Sinclair Ross' short stories, Bob to do the selecting and me to write an introduction. I'm really delighted to hear about this, and I'm looking forward to working on it.[2]

I hope everything is okay for you. Please write when you have time and let me know how things are. How has it worked out re: the fall list of novels in hardcover and paper?

All the best.
Margaret

1. *Long Drums and Cannons* was indeed published by Macmillan in 1968. Motivated by her belief that Nigerian literature was at the forefront of African literatures, and by her meetings with Chinua Achebe, Wole Soyinka, and other Nigerian authors, Laurence gathered together contemporary Nigerian drama and prose literature. The book is a compilation of Nigerian authors' biographies and analyses of their major works.
2. The book to which Laurence refers is *The Lamp at Noon and Other Stories*, which was to be published by McClelland & Stewart in 1968.

Elm Cottage, 23 January 1967

Dear Margaret:

Thanks for your letter. Egypt sounds really great; I think it was a fine idea to make the trip. I'll look forward to seeing the articles eventually. It's one of the few countries that I have always wanted to visit.

Re: the Nigerian literature book. You are right, of course, there will be no great market for it here. In a sense, we would like to do it for the case of continuity, etc., because there will be a certain demand, but it basically has to be a small market book and I really think it's much fairer to Macmillan to let them have World Rights. Otherwise, I don't see how they could do a large enough edition to work out the economics.

Yes, we are going to do the Sinclair Ross. I thought that I had written to you about that. It turned out that we had projected the idea of a Sinclair Ross collection on several occasions and he was a bit surprised when the subject was re-opened. But with you doing the intro and Bob doing the selections, we should have a good book, and we can probably get by with it very nicely. I think he's a fine writer and I think it's a good book to have on the list.

I don't know what to say about the experiment of the hardcover and paper edition being published simultaneously. We are still assessing the result and there is a tremendous variation. I'll add the exact sales figures of them just at the moment, although I know them approximately—and yours is one of the real question marks. We have found with Gabrielle Roy,[1] for example, that we would have been a lot better off, and she would have been a lot better off, if we had done the hardbound. Because of your trip, your figures turned out much better than hers. But I'm still not certain with all the publicity and with your rising reputation, that we might not have sold almost as many copies, at say $5.00 as we would of the combined edition. If this is true, it means that the experiment cost you money. I don't really know what to think about it yet. We are going to spend a few months analyzing the results, checking with booksellers etc. before we make any final determination. ... I'll let you know once we have sorted all this out.

Nothing much else to report. I am busier than ever at the moment. We have a big spring list, but I am still not able to find enough time to pay much attention to it. We are reorganizing the company. I am still going through the re-financing problems. We are buying the Centennial Library[2] and expanding it, and the whole thing is a bit of a shambles. I'll tell you more about this later.

I was tremendously impressed by your piece in *The Montreal Star* (or was it *The Gazette*) about Canadian writers and your reactions on your trip. This was a very good piece, Margaret. I have been wondering if we couldn't find some collateral use for it, by reprinting it in a different form. It was very thoughtful, very well considered and, I must say, you are amazingly well informed about what is going on in Canadian writing circles for one who has been outside the country for so long. Do keep in touch.

All the best.
Sincerely,
J.G. McClelland

1. See Laurence's letter dated 26 May 1964 for more information about Roy.
2. The Centennial Library, the public library in Toronto, built replacement edifices in the 1960s and 1970s, and it sold its original ones. Presumably, McClelland & Stewart bought one of its old buildings for the company offices.

Hollinger, 19 February 1967

Dear Jack:

Thanks for your letter of January 23rd. I'm very glad to hear that you're pleased about the idea of the Sinclair Ross book, and I'm looking forward to working on it. At the moment, I've got so much work to do that the mere thought of it is enough to induce mental paralysis, but no doubt I'll get through it eventually. I've got one of the Egypt articles still to write, and am busily lighting candles and praying like anything that the magazine likes the first one. This period of not knowing, with any manuscript—it nearly kills me. One would think it wouldn't be like that with an article, but it is. Of course, a lot hangs in balance with these articles—my bank account, mostly. ...

I am buying my house here, as I probably told you, and whenever I think of what the legal fees are going to amount to, and what a lot of responsibility I'm taking on, I go into a kind of semi-catatonic state of rigid panic. Things will be easier when I can get back to writing fiction—at least when I have an illusion of inner security, probably because involved with characters' dilemmas, not mine.

I hear from many people that the TV program on you[1] was a great success.

Congratulations.

All the best.
Sincerely,
Margaret Laurence

1. The CBC aired a one-hour documentary on Jack McClelland in 1966. The documentary focuses primarily on his work at McClelland & Stewart and includes footage of business meetings and interviews with McClelland.

•——

Elm Cottage, 6 March 1967

Dear Margaret:

I was amazed to read that you are actually going to buy the house. Perhaps you had told me this and it hadn't really registered. I think you are very brave anyway. As far as that's concerned, though, I don't think you have any problem as far as income in the future. All you have to do is keep writing. "What could be easier?" he said. "Publishing probably."

By the way, if in the course of events you should run into any bright young English book editors—male or female—who would be interested in moving to Canada, we would be more than interested in hearing from them. Things go from bad to worse. Now we have three pregnant editors on our hands, and they'll all be leaving within the next several months. I wouldn't mind so much if I had been responsible, but I can't take any credit for that. Oh well, to hell with it. Do get back to the typewriter and I'll be in touch in due course.

Cheers!
J.G. McClelland

Hollinger, 5 May 1967

Dear Jack:

I received this morning a cheque from M&S, for royalties, for over $1500. I nearly passed out in a dead faint, with surprise.[1] Most of the money is from *A Jest of God*, so it seems to me it has sold better than we thought it was going to. Anyway, I am absolutely delighted to get all this money, as you can well imagine, as I had thought I'd be doing well if I got another two hundred dollars on it. I've been laid low with a horrible throat infection, taking penicillin, which makes me feel rather disembodied and peculiar, so when this letter came with the cheque, I felt improved in health instantly.

John Cushman tells me that you aren't keen on publishing my book on Nigerian literature—Jack, please don't feel at all badly about this, as I knew from the very beginning that it was not going to be a good bet in Canada. I think I said this to you last summer. Anyway, it may have been a lunatic thing to write, but just possibly it may sell in Africa. This is up to Macmillan, as they've decided to do it here, probably in paperback with an eye to Africa.

What a stunner about the Gov. Gen. Award, eh?[2] I shall be in Ottawa June 2nd, leaving June 3rd. Am going to go to Montreal first, to see Adele and Expo.[3]

Can't stay away from home more than a week, as the Great North American Visiting Season is about to begin, and I'm happy to say I've got three lots of friends coming here this summer—this is one pleasure of having a large home: one can ask people to stay. Claire Pratt and her mother will be coming before I go to Canada, and I am really looking forward to seeing them.

Have started a novel, but all is chaos with it at the moment, so light one or two mental candles. It makes me laugh bitterly when I think that, years ago, I believed that one's second novel would be easier, and then that one's third would be easier, and so on. But no. They get more difficult all the time. This one is going to take longer than the last, I fear. The main thing, however, as I keep telling myself, is not to make a major production of it, mentally. It's only another novel, not the second coming of Christ.

Hope you are well.

All the best.
Sincerely,
Margaret

1. Comparing value, C$1,500 in 1967 would be worth C$10,765 in 2017.
2. Laurence won the Governor General's Award for *A Jest of God* in 1967.
3. The 1967 International and Universal Exposition (Expo 67 for short) was held in Montreal and was a central part of Canada's centennial celebrations. The celebrations and events continued for longer than most world Expos had, with some exhibits remaining open into the 1980s.

Elm Cottage, 16 May 1967

Dear Margaret:

Thanks for your letter. I [am] sorry that I'm going to miss you in Ottawa. Under any other circumstances, nothing would keep me away, but we have a high-school graduation that afternoon and are going to Cleveland that evening. There is not a damn thing I can do about it. It not only means that we miss seeing you, but that the Canada Council is going to think I am ducking the event deliberately. As I think they have told you, I had spoken extemporaneously from the floor at the last two Canadian council dinners. The reception has been somewhat stony to say the least and, in fact, the Chairman wrote me after the dinner last year to the effect that if I wouldn't agree not to speak without invitation, they wouldn't allow me back. It seems a pity. I expect Hugh Kane will go in my stead.

Re: the Nigerian literature, it's not really that we don't want to do the book, Margaret. It's rather more that we feel that it is to your advantage if we don't do it. Definitely, I feel that it is to Macmillan's advantage to have the Canadian market on this one. I don't know whether Cushman sent you a copy of my last letter to him but, in case he didn't, I'm enclosing a copy. I think it is self-explanatory.

Glad to hear you have started with the new novel. I can well imagine that it is tougher each time out, particularly when one becomes burden[ed] with the problem of living up to one's reputation. This bothered Gabrielle Roy a great deal, particularly after *The Tin Flute*. I think your attitude is the only possible one, though. Please don't take it any more seriously than you have to. I wish I could give you some useful thoughts, but since I know nothing about writing a novel, I'm at a loss.

I judge you will be with Adele in Montreal for three or four days. I'll try to catch up with you there. You will enjoy Expo. It's fabulous.

All the best.

Sincerely,

J.G. McClelland

P.S. Thanks very much for having Geo. Bowering's[1] novel sent to me. Haven't yet had time to read it, but it looks interesting.

1. George Bowering (1935–) is a prolific Canadian writer. In August 1961, influenced by the American Black Mountain poets Robert Duncan, Robert Creeley, and Charles Olson, he co-founded the literary magazine *Tish: a poetry newsletter* with Canadian poets Frank Davey, Fred Wah, Jamie Reid, and David Dawson. Bowering's novel, referred to here by McClelland, was *Mirror on the Floor*. The novel is about the city of Vancouver. It was published by Anvil Press in 1967 and re-released by the same publisher in 2014.

Hollinger, 23 June 1967

Dear Jack:

It was lovely to see you, even if briefly, in Montreal. The ceremony at Ottawa went off splendidly, with no hitches. M. Martineau, chairman of the Council, expressed regrets that you were not there. I was surprised at how little strain there was in the Gov't House ceremony—the great thing was that the writers didn't have to do anything but keep their mouths shut and look (if possible) decorative and not too dim-witted. Was also pleased to find lots of people there whom I knew, so it was a kind of back-home feeling.

I asked George Woodcock if I could review David Lewis Stein's[1] novel, but he said someone was already doing it for *Can. Lit.* I wrote to Stein, though, c/o your office.

Am having a dreadful time with this new novel,[2] and I feel that what I really need is a sudden stroke of inspiration [that] will solve all the problems. I don't imagine this is likely to happen. However, we soldier bravely on, pausing only to complain loudly and frequently to whoever will listen.

All the best.
Sincerely,
Margaret [signed]

1. David Lewis Stein's novel, mentioned here, is *Scratch One Dreamer*. It was reviewed by W.H. New, under the title, "Politics and Bedfellows."
2. The novel Laurence was working on was *The Fire-Dwellers*.

Elm Cottage, 5 July 1967

Dear Margaret:

Thanks for your note. Glad to hear things went well in Ottawa. I don't think Mr. Martineau was being sincere, if he deplored my absence. However that's life.

Don't worry about the new novel. I suspect the inspiration will come just as you receive this letter. In fact, I'm counting on it.

All the best.
Sincerely,
J.G. McClelland

Elm Cottage, 1 August 1967

Dear Margaret:

As you know we are planning to do *The Stone Angel* in the New Canadian Library in February. Yesterday, a letter came in from Popular Library. They are doing a paperback reprint in the United States asking for Canadian rights. We have said no to this. I hope you will approve. There could be slightly more money in it for you (no, hell, I doubt it), on the Popular Library distribution in Canada in the first year. I think the real advantages of the New Canadian Library are continuity and more long-term earnings, plus in Canada a measure of prestige.

I don't know whether or not this is something that I should be turning over to your agent, or are the earlier titles still with Willis Wing? Do let me have your views on this in any case.

All the best.
Sincerely,
J.G. McClelland

Hollinger, 10 August 1967

Dear Jack:

Thanks for your letter of August 1st. I hadn't known you were going to do *The Stone Angel* in the New Canadian Library, but I'm delighted to hear of it. You were quite right to refuse paperback rights in Canada to Popular Library. Even if I made more money on their imprint, initially (which I very much doubt I would), I would still prefer to see the book in the New Canadian Library. The NCL is a series, which I've long been enthusiastic about, and I would very much like to see one of my books there.

Re: my agent—Willis Wing still handles everything up to and including *A Jest of God*. Anything else (so far only a few articles, stories and the Nigerian literature book) is handled by John Cushman. I guess you should get in touch with Willis Wing re: the New Canadian Library edition.

I'm working on a novel, but so far don't feel very happy about it. Am determined to get it down, though, however much re-writing it may need later. I'm going in to London this evening to have dinner with Jack Ludwig and his wife. I haven't met him before, except once, briefly, a hundred years ago at college.[1]

All the best.
Sincerely,
Margaret [signed]
Margaret Laurence

Copy to Charlotte[2]

1. On 14 August 1967, Hodgeman responded to this letter to indicate that McClelland was on vacation. She noted, "We shall get in touch with Willis Wing re: the New Canadian Library edition of *Stone Angel* and a contract will be forthcoming in due course" (McClelland & Stewart Ltd. Fonds, Box 35, File 42).
2. This note is in Jack McClelland's handwriting.

Hollinger, 19 October 1967

Dear Jack:

I'm writing to ask your advice. As you know (or probably know), Paul Newman is making a film of *A Jest of God*. This, naturally, has meant a good deal of money for me. I have had long sessions with my accountant, to see how we can spread the money (*three years' spread is permitted on money from film rights*) in order to avoid paying most of it to the British Government in income tax. *My accountant has also advised me that a portion of this money could be sent to my bank account in Toronto, and that I need not pay income tax on it until such time as I bring it into this country or use it in Canada. Now, here is the situation—I received most of the film money before I knew I could have this done, but a certain amount was withheld in New York for American income tax,* and was then refunded to me after I sent the appropriate forms. I had Collins-Knowlton-Wing deposit this sum with my account in the Royal Bank of Canada, Toronto, where it now is.

Second part of this situation—I am very seriously thinking of moving back to Canada within the next year or so, although probably not for at least a year and a half. *What I would like to do, therefore, is to keep these dollars in my Toronto bank account, and pay Canadian income tax on them when I move back.* Can you ask your accountant, Jack, if this procedure would be legal? If it isn't, then of course I should have to have the money transferred here, and pay Brit. income tax on it. I should emphasize that I am not trying to evade income tax—it is just that if I can legally leave the money in Toronto, and pay Canadian tax on it when I am based in Canada, it would of course be better for me. I'd be most grateful if you could ask your accountant, and let me know the position on this. I have no wish to break the law (too scared), but I do not want to pay any more income tax than I have to, and if I can leave this money in Canada until I return, it would be helpful. My accountant seems to think this is okay, but I'd like an opinion from Canada.

All the best.
Sincerely,
Margaret [signed]
Margaret Laurence

Elm Cottage, 10 November 1967

Dear Margaret:

I am afraid the word from the experts at this end is not very encouraging. We've discussed the problem with our auditors and also without mentioning your name with the Tax Department. The opinion is that the funds you refer to are subject to U.K. tax and that having the funds directed to a Canadian bank does not in any way exempt you from personal tax on that money in the U.K. This is also confirmed by the British Government office in Toronto.

Once the U.K. tax has been paid and the money transmitted to a Canadian bank, you would be liable only for withholding tax on the interest accrued.

There should be a better way of handling the situation, but we simply have not been able to think of it. I am still inclined to think that it would be sensible to have the money transferred to a Canadian bank because, once you decide to return to Canada, you may have difficulty bringing money out of the U.K. So by all means leave the money here, but you had better report it as having been earned and be prepared to pay the tax on it.

I keep postponing my trip to London and it now looks as though I won't manage it until after the first of the year. I'll let you know as soon as my plans are definite.

All the best. Sincerely,
J.G. McClelland

Hollinger, 16 November 1967

Dear Jack:

Thanks very much for your letter with the information about my tax position regarding dollars deposited in my Toronto bank. It's as I suspected, and the best thing will be for me to declare them on this year's income tax here. What I'm trying to discover now from my accountant is whether I can pay British income tax on them and still leave them as dollars in Toronto. I have decided against moving back to Canada right now (domestic situation and kids' schools etc. make it impossible) but want to go over for the summer if I can.

Please ring me if you've got time when you do finally get to England. If you phone from London, you can dial direct—OHW 481-2105. Please copy this down, as I'm not in the phone book and I cannot seem to persuade Directory Enquiries to list my number, either. Maybe you could come out here for lunch one day—I would like you to see my place, but if you haven't enough time for that, we could probably meet for lunch in London. I expect you'll be frantically busy.

Today is a kind of semi-red-letter day for me, as I am exactly halfway through the first draft of a novel. As usual, I feel the most serious doubts about it, and the only time when I don't worry is when I'm actually writing. I don't know what it is about me, but every time I write a novel, I have the distinct feeling that I'm losing my mind. There must be some easier way both of writing a novel and of losing one's mind.

Best wishes.
Sincerely,
Margaret [signed]
Margaret

Hollinger, 12 March 1968

Dear Jack:

First draft of novel now completed, thank God. I do not know what it is like—it may be positively lousy. I have to go through and add bits [that] have been left out, and cut out all excess verbiage, then re-type. It is slightly a mess at the moment, but think it will be done, with luck, in 2 months. The tone is so different from anything I've written before that I think that anyone who liked previous novels will probably not care for this one. But can't help that, I guess. Anyway, we'll see. Will send you a copy when it's done, which ought to be before long.

All the best.

Margaret [signed]

Margaret Laurence

Elm Cottage, 21 March 1968

Dear Margaret:

Wonderful news and a typical Margaret Laurence reaction on completion of a manuscript. Some day, the historical record is going to indicate that every time you finish a script, you think it's lousy. I'm betting on the fact that historical record will also continue to show that every time you finish a script, it's actually superb.

In any case, I look forward with great excitement to seeing it, so send it along as soon as you can. Re: my trip to England, it seems now to be postponed again. Will get over in the fall, God willing, but there is no longer much chance of my making a trip before then. Someday, I'll tell you why. Meanwhile all the best.[1]

Sincerely,
J.G. McClelland

1. McClelland wrote this note on the letter: "Note—probably spring 1969."

Hollinger, 10 June 1968

Dear Jack—

At last, the novel is finished and typed out. I hope you don't mind—I gave a copy to Alan Maclean at Macmillan's before sending a copy either to you or Knopf, because I simply had to know as soon as possible how at least one other human being reacted to it. Alan was terribly kind, knowing my neurosis at this point, and rapidly had it xeroxed and sent to 2 readers. Apparently, they like it, and also he phoned a day or two ago to say that he has now read it and likes it. I realise that this means only that three people got something out of it, and does not relate to how you or Knopf are going to feel, but nonetheless it is a kind of relief for me, to say the least. This is always the worst time for me, before anyone else has seen it, when I do not know at all whether the characters are going to come across to anyone except myself. Actually, I'm very glad Macmillan's likes it, because I had been rather worried that it might be too North-American in tone. It *is* very N-A in tone, but apparently not hinderingly so.

Anyway, I will now mail you a copy direct, to save time, and anxiously await your reaction. As I have probably said before—just give it to me straight; if you hate the damn thing, don't try to soften the blow.

I think Macmillan's will have a few suggestions to make, but I guess all this can be dealt with at a later date. Alan did mention, however, several places which he thought might be clarified, and I agree with his suggestions—it's really only a matter of an addition of a couple of sentences in several places. Because I could see right away what he was driving at, I'd rather do those bits before I send you your copy, so will try to get it off to you within the next day.

Now I wonder if I should have told you that Alan liked it, or if it would not have been better for you to come to it absolutely cold. But you know my massive insecurity at this particular point. Anyway, I know you will say exactly what you think, so that is okay.

Title of novel is *The Fire-Dwellers*. Don't say it—I know. It's a damn good title. That is the only thing I ever feel sure about—the titles are good.

Was so delighted to see *The Stone Angel* in NCL. Also Sinclair Ross' stories so long overdue and now at last collected, thanks to you.

All the best. If you could let me know soon re: novel, I would greatly appreciate it, but don't feel you have to sit up all night reading manuscripts—half the night will do.

Sincerely,
Margaret [signed]
Margaret Laurence

Hollinger, 11 June 1968

Dear Jack:

Have just parcelled manuscript[1] having first made some alterations based on one or two things Alan Maclean said. There might be more alterations later, but, quite honestly, I doubt if there can be many—not because the novel is so hot, but because either it stands or it doesn't stand and, if it doesn't, there isn't much I can do about it. I am seized with the urge to try to explain to you what I intended to try to do in this novel, but I know this is pure lunacy—nothing can explain it if it doesn't explain itself.

I do apologize for the rather grubby appearance of the first and last pages of the manuscript. During the few days when I was waiting to hear what Alan thought of it—only because I needed one other human being's reaction QUICKLY—I sent this copy to Michael Horniman at A.P. Watt, who is my agent here.[2] These thin pages are hell to deal with, hence the slightly used appearance.

To think of it, a slightly used appearance doesn't suit Stacey too badly at that.[3]

If you are terribly busy, or on holiday, or making enormous deals with best-selling authors, don't feel you have to let me know how you feel about the novel instantly. Of course, I may have a nervous breakdown, but don't let it worry you.

I am trying to do a lot of gardening, painting, cleaning garage, re-tiling kitchen floor, etc. etc. etc. This is known as therapy.

Have just received Panther's cover for English paperback of *A Jest Of God*—they're printing under film title.[4] It shows Joanne Woodward topped by [an] anonymous gorgeous-shouldered guy. This cheered me more than somewhat.

All the best.
Margaret [signed]
Margaret Laurence

1. This manuscript was published as *The Fire-Dwellers*. The novel is one of Laurence's most innovative in terms of form and was deemed postmodern by many critics, which may be why she felt a need to explain to McClelland what she was trying to do with the novel, though she resisted any detailed explanation.
2. Michael Horniman and Hilary Harold Rubenstein ran the literary agency A.P. Watt from 1983 to 1992.
3. Stacey MacAindra is the main character in *The Fire-Dwellers*.
4. The film title was *Rachel, Rachel*. See Laurence's letter dated 30 October 1966 for more information about the film.

Elm Cottage, 14 June 1968

Dear Margaret:

Delighted to get your letter and the good news. I look forward to receipt of the manuscript in the very near future and promise to stay up all night and get my reaction to you without delay. If you haven't yet sent it off, do send it and make sure it comes by air. I like the title, and I haven't the slightest doubt that I'll like the novel but will certainly let you know right away.

All the best.
Sincerely,
J.G. McClelland[1]

1. McClelland thereafter sent a telegram to express his congratulations.

Elm Cottage, 24 June 1968

Dear Margaret:

As I tried to indicate in my cable, I think *The Fire-Dwellers* is superb. I have said to you several times before, and I can say it again now in all sincerity, that you are the only writer I know that improves with each successive manuscript and you are still doing it. A lot of critics didn't think that *A Jest of God* was an advance on *The Stone Angel*, but this was not an opinion I shared as you know. One was a critics' book; the other was a readers' book.

I'm confident that this one is going to satisfy both the critics and the readers. It's a gutsy novel. The intuition, insight, the incredible power that you have for allowing the reader to identify with what you are saying, it's a fantastic achievement. I read it at one sitting (and incidentally the only other person here who has had a chance to look at it is my eldest daughter who I think you have met, and who shares my enthusiasm). It's a great book.

I am not going to attempt to play editor. That's not my particular bag and to be honest about it, you obviously know so much more than anybody else about what is right and what is wrong about a novel, that it would be presumptuous of me to do much more than give a judgement, and my judgement is that you have done it again. It's a great success, and I haven't the slightest doubt that it will do very well.

Having said that, I can tell you that there is only one chunk of the novel that didn't grab me particularly and that is Luke's lengthy description of his science-fiction novel. I won't pretend to be enough of a critic to have any sense of its significance in relation to the whole, but that may be largely because I skimmed that section. It slowed the pace. It didn't interest me and no matter how relevant it may be in actual fact, I suspect its relevance may be artificial in the sense that I, at least as one reader, felt I really didn't give a goddam what his science-fiction novel was about.

Obviously, I don't think it is vital whether or not you leave that part as is; eliminate it or cut it, but I mention this one particularly, because the novel as a whole, while it is full and rich in detail, seems to be virtually devoid of relevancies or artificialities. A skilled editor might want to suggest the odd minor cut in other parts of the script, but I hope any such treatment would be fairly light.

Stacey comes through superbly (and, by the way, will be a superb character for stage and for films), but I think you have been successful with many of the others—Mac, Thor and Katie particularly—and it may be that because Luke didn't grab me quite as much as some of the others, I didn't really give too much of a damn about his novel.

But it is a fine novel, Margaret. It can do nothing but enhance your reputation ... [and] that will please everyone. I presume that Macmillan's, Knopf and ourselves will all want to do it in the early spring and I don't anticipate any difficulty in working out a simultaneous date that will please everyone. This one is going to make you wealthy, baby, and you deserve it. My advice on the film rights would be to play it very cool and wait until they are at least triple their initial offer whatever their initial offer might be.

The only news for the moment is that I expect to be taking off for London sometime this weekend. The trip may yet be postponed for a few days. I've made no reservations and have no dates, but sometime within the next two weeks I'll be there. As soon as the plans are definite, I'll send you a cable so that we can get together. It's going to be a rush visit of necessity, but my hope is that I will have the weekend through to about Tuesday night at which point I will have to go back to Verona for a day and then back to Toronto. So I look forward to seeing you and thanks again for writing another great novel. It will probably keep the bailiff away for both of us in 1969.

Cheers!
J.G. McClelland

Hollinger, 28 June 1968

Dear Jack:

First of all, MANY THANKS for sending me a cable re: the novel. You know how nervous I get, at this stage, and I think it was very good of you to let me know your reaction so quickly.

I received your letter this morning. I cannot tell you how delighted I am that you like the novel. The thing I am most pleased about is that you think that Stacey comes through, and also some of the other characters. This is always my main worry. I know how *I* feel about the characters, but will they come across to other people? I am tremendously glad that Stacey does, to you.

As far as your criticisms are concerned—I don't know why you downplay yourself as an editor, as you have put your finger on the part of the novel that worried me the most. I must have rewritten that section a hundred times. I do agree that [the] outline of the SF novel slows the action; and I think that something will have to be done about this. For various reasons, I don't want to cut out that section entirely, but I do think it can be compressed. Anyway, I think I will wait until I've got Macmillan's suggestions, and then consider them all together. No word yet from America, but I did not expect to hear for awhile yet, as John Cushman has recently been in England, and I gave him one copy of *The Fire-Dwellers* to take back and submit to Knopf. I don't really expect to hear before mid-July. If they do like it enough to want to publish it, they'll no doubt have some suggestions as well, so I'll wait until all reports are in, and then do what I can. There are, naturally, certain things, which I know are structural flaws in the novel, but I don't think I can do anything about them. But your criticism strikes me as very valid, so will try to do something.

You may at this very moment be on your way to England, but I'm writing now in case your trip is delayed. If not, then you'll get this when you return, and as I always express myself more lucidly (or so I like to think) in print than in speech, maybe it is just as well that I should put in a letter my reactions to your reactions—if you see what I mean.

I can't really go along with your optimism re: the $$$ potential of the novel, but as you know, I am very canny about these things. Not only do I not count my chickens before they are hatched; I am bloody scared to count them even after they are hatched, just in case. If the novel pays its own way and gives me something to be paying the mortgage with, I'll be happy.

I am enclosing a page with an acknowledgment to the Canada Council, and I would be glad if you would have this inserted in an appropriate place in the novel. I have also asked Macmillan to do the same with the English edition, and will ask the American publishers to include it as well, if it is published in USA. It was some kind of vast relief for me to be able to write a few days ago to the C.C. and say that the novel has been accepted by my Canadian and English publishers. I know the grants don't have strings attached, but all the same, it would have been slightly awful to have taken all that money for nothing.

Things have been rather upset here this past week, as my daughter was taken to hospital three days ago for an emergency appendix operation. She is okay now, thank goodness, but apparently it was a pretty close thing. I don't know if I told you or not, but I am now un-separated from my husband, which may be a rather odd way of phrasing it, but we think we can work out our very separate lives together, as it were. However, he has been in British Honduras for the past three months and will likely be there for another month, so the present family crisis made me feel somewhat isolated and totally responsible. Being sixteen, and healthy, she seems to be making a good recovery, and says that she is bothered only by boredom in hospital, and by the fact that her side hurts when she laughs. So I am rather limp at the moment, feeling relieved and thankful that it all turned out all right.

Once again, thanks for letting me know so quickly. And I am so damn glad you like the novel.

All the best. Sincerely,
Margaret [signed]
Margaret Laurence

Hollinger, 10 July 1968

Dear Jack:

It was lovely to see you when you were in England, extremely nice of you to come all this way out to Penn, especially with the rail strike still not entirely over. I do hope you didn't have any trouble in getting back to London that day. If so, you will probably think of Elm Cottage as being only slightly less remote than Siberia or the North Pole.

I have been doing a lot of inner battling re: the title. Of my novel, that is. I wrote a slightly conciliatory letter to John Cushman, saying that, if Knopf insisted, I might be prepared to change the title. But I was later bothered by this statement, as it did not seem to reflect my true feelings. Have just written to John again, saying that *The Fire-Dwellers* is the novel's title, for better or worse, and I really cannot change it.

My problem is that I am often torn between a desire to please all the people all the time, and the opposite—the feeling that the only thing that matters is to try not to betray one's work and the hell with trying to please anybody. The way in which this dichotomy usually works out, as you may remember from past books, is that I almost always agree to suggestions for revision which either strike me as valid or as trivial—the former because they are helpful and the latter because I can't get that worked up about an individual adjective. But from time to time I have to disagree with any or all publishers, because, in the end, the novel is my work and there are some aspects about which I have to remain firm—otherwise, I will have betrayed it.

I hope you can see this, and can accept the title. It wasn't picked out of a hat. It emerged slowly, a long time before the present novel was written, and the novel was written to it. It matters a very great deal to me.

My daughter took another (thank God, slight) turn for the worse the day you left—3 Canadian friends had just turned up for lunch, so it was pure chaos, me phoning the doctor and trying to cook the meatloaf simultaneously. The doctor and district nurses have been in every day since, and I now learn that this post-operative condition is not at all uncommon—I wish somebody had thought to tell me that simple fact when she left the hospital, but they never do. Anyway, she seems to be on the mend now, and is up today for the first time since last weekend, and I am now a real whiz at practical nursing and bandage-changing etc. But this means I can't get to London to work on Macmillan's copy of *The Fire-Dwellers*, as I had hoped, so they are mailing their copy back to me. Can't work properly on my draft copy, as pages aren't numbered right. Hope to get revisions done within the next week, while still confined to barracks, as it were, so will send you a copy same and hope they will be okay.

Alan Maclean likes the title.

All the best.
Margaret [signed]

Hollinger, 15 July 1968

Dear Jack:

I enclose a list of revisions for *The Fire-Dwellers,* and I do hope you will think the net result is an improvement. I've put together your suggestions and those of Knopf and Macmillan, and have tried to make alterations in the manuscript, which clearly seemed to need doing. ...

I do hope you will agree to keep the title. I'm sorry to have made such a fuss about it, but I can't help feeling it suits the novel.

I don't suppose you managed to get in touch with Michael Horniman at A.P. Watt & Son, when you were here? There would scarcely have been time, I think. If not, I'd like to negotiate the contract through John Cushman.

Things have been terrible here. I've had the worst bout of gastroenteritis since sixteen years ago in Somaliland, and, as my daughter is still convalescent, for a few days the meals etc. had to be done by David,[1] who is no hell of a cook, to put it mildly. Actually, I'm only angling for sympathy—I really want you to write back and tell me how brave I am to have struggled up from my bed of pain to do the damn revisions!

Bob Weaver would like a chapter for *Tamarack* and one for CBC—I think this is a good idea. What do you think? Maybe I asked you before—can't remember.

All the best.[2]
Sincerely,
Margaret [signed]
Margaret Laurence

1. David is Laurence's son, who would have been about thirteen years old at this time.
2. Hodgeman wrote back to Laurence on 14 August in response to this letter, as follows: "In Mr. McClelland's absence, I would like to acknowledge your letter of July 15th enclosing the revisions for *The Fire-Dwellers*. We are negotiating the contract for this book through John Cushman. I am sorry to learn of your illness, and do hope that you are well on the way to recovery. With all good wishes. Yours sincerely, Mrs. M. Hodgeman" (McClelland & Stewart Ltd. Fonds, Box 35, File 46).

Hollinger, 18 July 1968

Dear Jack:

I have had a letter from Judith Jones at Knopf,[1] with one final suggestion for revisions on *The Fire-Dwellers*, and her suggestion strikes me as being so simple and obvious that I am annoyed I did not think of it myself. She wonders if it might be possible to cut down on the credibility gap re: Val blackmailing Thor, simply by leaving out the conversation between Stacey and Val, and letting the matter of Thor's departure remain a speculation in Stacey's mind—perhaps Val spoke to Thor; perhaps she didn't. I think this is absolutely right, and it seems to me to be a better way of handling this scene. I have therefore written the first two pages of Chapter Ten again, and I now enclose them. I hope you'll agree that it is an improvement.

I haven't numbered these two pages, as my own draft copy hasn't got the proper page numbers. Could you see that the pages are inserted in the proper place, please? *They go at the beginning of Chapter Ten, and the old pages are to be removed.* ... Could you also number the new pages?

Sorry to keep sending in bits and pieces. I hope this will be the last.

Sincerely,
Margaret [signed]

1. Judith Jones (1924–2017) worked as a senior editor at Knopf Publishing, in New York, for more than fifty years. Early in her career, in 1950, she found a copy of Anne Frank's diary in a slush pile and insisted on its publication. Jones brought literary giants such as John Updike to the fore, but she became most famous for cookbook editing and her publications of such legendary figures as Julia Child. She published her own memoir, *The Tenth Muse: My Life in Food*, in 2007.

Hollinger, 18 July 1968

Dear Boss:

Thinking over the controversy re: the title of my novel, I now see that Alan Maclean was right. When I spoke to him about it, he said he did not think I had to write 20-page letters defending myself—I only had to keep on repeating that the title of my novel is *The Fire-Dwellers*. I am sorry I made such a fuss about it—one of these days I will learn diplomatic tactics and will be able to steer a middle course between capitulating totally and tearing into unnecessary battle with all bagpipes blazing.

I learned from Michael Horniman that you did get in touch with him while you were here—thanks a lot; it must have been an awful rush even to talk to him on the phone.

All is well here now. With my peasant constitution, I have now defeated whatever virus was quite literally bugging me, and for the first time in a month the whole family is on its feet.

With all best wishes.

Sincerely,
Margaret [signed]

P.S. John Cushman says I should wait before sending a chapter to *Tamarack*, to see if he might have any luck with serial rights in Canadian or Amer magazines.

Elm Cottage, 23 July 1968

Dear Margaret:

Firstly,[1] my apologies for not having written before. It was a wonderful visit and I enjoyed it very much. I only wish we had had more time. I may say that goddamn bus got me to the station about 2 minutes after the train had left, so I spent a full hour examining the beautiful posters. Actually, it wasn't that bad. After about 15 minutes several ravishing creatures in mini-skirts came along and I spent the remainder of my time examining them. Fortunately, the train arrived before I was arrested.

On the way back to London, I gave further thought to the title and I have capitulated. By no stretch of the imagination do I think it is a great title, but if you like it and you want it, then I think you should have it. Actually, it is not a bad title (nor is it I think particularly good), but it shouldn't do the book any harm and if it is well handled from the design point-of-view, it could after the fact become an effective title.

I think the point here as we discussed it is that authors tend to think in terms of book titles that sum up or reflect the message or meaning of the book, whereas publishers tend to think of book titles in terms of something that is going to sell the book in advance. I can understand that the author takes pleasure in thinking [of] the reader reacting to the aptness of a title after reading a novel. A publisher on the other hand is more inclined to think, "I want a title to get them to buy the book. I don't really care whether or not the title has anything to do with the book itself as long as it sells."

In any case, Margaret, as far as I'm concerned, it's the end of the argument. If you want to call it *The Fire-Dwellers* then that's what it should be and I would, as you say you intend to do, stand firm. And who knows a year from now we may be saying, "Migod that was wise of us to let Margaret choose her own title."

Sorry to hear about your daughter. I thought she looked quite well. The kids are both charming and you should be very pleased with them.

Your agents have turned out to be real pirates.[2] Michael Horniman softened me up on the phone in London and then Cushman delivered the lethal blow. I think you misunderstood my earlier letter. I was suggesting that you hold the Hollywood people up for a vast sum of money, not your poor, old, friendly publisher. However, I'll forgive you because I'm counting on the profits from the novel to keep us in business for another year.

It was wonderful to see you again. I'm in love with Elm Cottage. I can understand why you don't want to leave it.

All the best.
Sincerely,
J.G. McClelland

1. Laurence wrote the following note alongside this letter and dated it 1980: "JG. McC came out for a day to Elm Cottage, and I spent about four hours telling him why *The Fire-Dwellers* was the right title. I did *not* know at that time that he was very worried about the financial situation of McClelland & Stewart. He listened very patiently to my passionate defense of my novel's title. In fact, *all three* publishers' worries re: the title proved unnecessary."
2. Alongside this part of the letter, in the copy she placed in the Clara Thomas Archives and Special Collections at York University, Laurence wrote the following and dated it 1980: "I think the advance was about $2000 or less!"

Hollinger, 26 July 1968

Dear Poor, Old, Friendly, Publisher,

Thanks for your letter of July 23rd. Your description of your owing to the ruthlessness of my agents really made my heart bleed for you.[1] I'm glad to hear that you've forgiven me, however, re: this crass question of money. Maybe it will cheer you up if I tell you that after a year's solid work on the novel (this is not counting the previous drafts of it), I find that I may just manage to make a year's expenses—think of my joy and astonishment at discovering that I actually earned a year's salary after all! Well, I guess writers believe that writing is a mug's game; publishers feel the same about their chosen profession. Never mind, Jack, when you have to go on the dole, I feel sure that all your grateful writers will chip in to contribute a few hamburgers.

Seriously, thanks for the forthcoming advance. Much appreciated by me.

Also thanks for being understanding about the novel's title. I heard from Judith Jones today, saying that she likes the revisions, so that is a relief. It's possible that you haven't yet received the revisions, which I sent to you owing to the postal strike, but I hope you'll approve of them.

I do understand your analysis of the different ways a writer and a publisher view a title—you're quite right, of course, and the nature of both being what it is, it is hard for either side to change this basic view.

Sorry you had such a hellish time with the bus and train when you left here. Next time, I'll be better organized with taxis and British Rail may just possibly not have a strike in progress.

I'm glad you liked my house and kids—this prejudices me greatly in your favour; obviously, you are a person of reliable judgement.

All the best.
Sincerely,
Margaret

1. The wording of this letter, "your owing to the ruthlessness of my agents," seems to suggest the playful understanding they shared about the royalties owed to Laurence.

Elm Cottage, 1 April 1969

Dear Margaret:

I don't know whether anybody else has bothered to send you the story from the Canadian edition of *Time*, but I enclose a copy in case you haven't seen it.[1] I can't say that it is the greatest story I have ever seen but by and large it's good publicity. I don't really know why they brought it out at this point rather than just prior to publication. Maybe they have a deal with the *Ladies' Home Journal*. For all I know, *Time-Life* may own it now.

Nothing all that new at this end. I'm still spending all my time going from one crisis to another on the financial side, but eventually, with any luck, we'll see daylight. I'm counting on *The Fire-Dwellers* selling a lot of copies, which will help.

What is your current schedule? And when are you coming back? Everybody assures me that you are going to be in Toronto in September, but I don't really know yet whether it is so.[2] I hope it is. Does the university organize you a place to live? And, if not, do you have somebody looking or can we do anything? When you have a moment drop me a note and bring me up-to-date on your plans.

All the best,
Sincerely,
J.G. McClelland

1. This review of *The Fire-Dwellers* was published in *Time* on 28 March 1969. The article begins with a quotation from the book that focuses on the protagonist's dissatisfaction with her body and with being middle-aged. It then describes Laurence as follows: "Chunky, with short brown hair pulled into a bun behind her head, she gives the impression of being slightly mannish without being unmotherly." Finally, there is a picture of Laurence with a caption under it that states, "Margaret Laurence: Writing About What She Knows."
2. Laurence was writer-in-residence at the University of Toronto for the 1969–1970 academic year.

Hollinger, 4 April 1969

Dear Jack,

Good grief! What a dreadful write up in *Time*!! They got just about everything all screwed up. The way they try to make out that *The Fire-Dwellers* is almost bound to be autobiographical seems like a sneaky trick and is also untrue. I wouldn't have minded if they'd described me as being built similar to a Ukrainian peasant woman, but "slightly mannish without being unmotherly"—ye gods! Now I wish I had let my "short brown hair" down to where it really grows, namely my shoulders, and had posed in a black lace nightie. And I didn't tell Judson I'd never written about anything I didn't know. And I lived in Ghana five years, not two. And so on, and so on. Well, never mind. As you say, it is probably good publicity and one must just see it in perspective, I suppose. What the hell? It's not important. I'm glad they did the piece, but I wish they had waited until the book was out. They have pretty obviously timed it for the LHJ serialization.[1]

I'm sorry I haven't written before. The last few months have been like a circus here. I finished off the children's book, *Jason's Quest*—hasn't John Cushman sent it to you? I don't know whether you would want to do it or not. Both Knopf and Macmillan are going to do it, and I have been awaiting word re: M&S, but maybe you haven't seen it. I'll have to ask John about this, if you haven't. Also, just about a fortnight ago, I completed the last story in what I've always hoped would be a collection of short stories and I've sent this last story to John in case it can be sold separately somewhere. All the others have been published in various places. There are 8 stories and they are kind of based on my childhood family—maybe you've seen some of them. They are all complete in themselves, but they really do belong together, and I've always seen them as a set of stories, rather like a novel in short story form. I've been working on them, off and on, for some six years now.

Anyway, I've sent the manuscript to be typed and, when it is done, I'll send two copies to John, one of them to be submitted to you. Name of collection is *A Bird in the House,* which is the title of one of the stories. I know volumes of stories are not a publisher's dream, but we will see what you think.

I'm sorry to hear about your problems and hope things are less complicated by now. Lines of encouragement follow in another letter. I'll be taking my kids to Canada in July, mainly B.C., and will be proceeding to Toronto the beginning of September, where I will work in residence at the U of T for the academic year, i.e. until May. God knows what I'm getting myself into. I hope I don't make a hash of it. I don't really know what a w-in-r *does*. But I thought it would be a good idea to accept the offer, as I do not want to write ANYTHING for about a year, having spent the last 2 years slogging away most of the time. I am getting a young Canadian writer and his wife to come and live here and be company for my kids while I'm away, and I hope my husband will be in England most of that time, too, and therefore home on weekends. Actually, I'm nervous as hell about the w-in-r job, but perhaps it will be okay. I am no academic, though, as you know.

Al Purdy[2] and his wife have been staying with me for the past few weeks, while she recuperates from an illness, which struck while they were in Greece. It's been lovely for me to have them here. Al has done a radio adaptation of my last story, so we'll see what comes of that. Got *Wild Grape Wine* a few days ago, and think it is his best book of poems yet.

I'm taking the kids to Scotland after Easter for a week, and soon after that I will have to start getting organized for our Canadian trip. Thanks for your offer of help re: house in Toronto—actually, I've already rented one from a couple who teach at the U of T and who will be in S. America for that year. All I am looking for now is some agreeable female to share the rent with me—some agreeable male would be even nicer, but I don't suppose the university would go for that.

All the best.
Margaret

LINES OF ENCOURAGEMENT TO J.G. MCCLELLAND

Roses are red
Violets are blue
One of your authors
Has faith in McStew.

Violets are blue
Roses are red
I don't believe
You've got rocks in your head

Violets are blue
Roses are pink
Let nobody say
As a bookman you stink

Violets are mauve
Or purple or worse
In two hundred years
Who'll give you a curse?

Roses are crimson
And green is the chive
Whatever your troubles
I know you'll survive

Roses are red
Violets are blue
Be heartened old buddy
I'm betting on you

With love from your slightly mannish but not unmotherly,
Aunt Margaret

1. *The Fire-Dwellers* was serialized in *Ladies' Home Journal*.
2. Al Purdy (1918–2000) was one of Canada's finest poets. He published over thirty volumes of poetry. His poetry has been regularly anthologized and his work continues to be read and studied in Canadian literature courses. Purdy began to publish with McClelland & Stewart in 1965, with his book of poetry, *The Cariboo Horses*.

Elm Cottage, 11 April 1969

Dear Margaret:[1]

Firstly, how does one reply to a poem? It's great. It's much appreciated and I'll also promise not to publish it.

I enjoyed your letter. I ran into the local *Time Magazine* rep a week or so ago and I told him that I wasn't overly delighted with their piece, and I didn't think you would be and he was quite upset. They have their own particular problems at *Time Magazine*, but as I have said, it does no harm.

Before your letter arrived, I talked to Cushman and he brought me up-to-date on *Jason's Quest* and, indeed, on the short story collection. I congratulate you in advance on both. *Jason's Quest* has now arrived in script form. I haven't had a chance to look at it because I am so bloody busy but will do so soon. Certainly, we will want to publish it as we will publish the short stories.

Glad you've got a house and we are going to look forward to having you here. If Ludwig's experience is any criterion you'll have a marvellous time. No duties, obligations, or anything of that sort. He has actually completed a novel since his arrival and since he's taken at least six years for each of his previous novels, it's some real indication of the demands they have made on his time. Actually, that's not fair. His reason for writing so feverishly is that he is sick as hell and I think basically suspects he won't be around too much longer or be able to write much longer. I may be overdramatizing the situation, but he has fantastic physical problems.[2]

So you'll love it at the U. of T. and actually I understand that you are going to be the first woman with an office or apartment or whatever the hell you call it in Massey College. This has great possibilities. If I do actually ever solve all my problems and can become a book publisher again, I'll revert to my real character and arrange a series of wine festivals with you in your digs at Massey, so that you will be thrown out of the University in great disgrace, which will sell hundreds of thousands of copies of your books which is, after all, what publishers are supposed to do.

As you know, we are using the Knopf edition of *The Fire-Dwellers* with, of course, our imprint. It looks great. I think they have done a marvellous job. I don't know whether you have seen it yet, but you will be pleased. Meanwhile, I'll try to find an agreeable female or male to share your house. Will write as soon as I have had the chance to look at *Jason's Quest*.

Cheers!
J.G. McClelland

1. This letter appears in Solecki's *Imagining Canadian Literature*.
2. These comments are particularly ironic, since Jack Ludwig, who was born in 1922, far outlived both Laurence and McClelland. Ludwig died in February 2018.

Hollinger, 16 April 1969

Dear Jack—

Thanks for your letter of April 11th. I am sure you are right about the *Time* piece—it can only do good, in terms of book sales. Also, I think that if the *Time* man who interviewed me knew that I objected to some of the article, he would be surprised; genuinely. Well, life is too short to think about such things for more than half an hour.

I am delighted to hear that you feel pretty certain about publishing *Jason's Quest* and also the short stories. However, Jack, with my old Scots canniness, I will wait until I hear *definitely* before I begin cheering too loudly. Alan Maclean says he feels certain about the stories, too, but as neither of you have yet seen them in their final collected state, I am not taking anything for granted. It would be lovely (from my point of view) to see the stories all published together, but as I said before, I realize that short story collections are not calculated to support publishers in style. As far as the kids' book is concerned, you still may want to publish it. I'm only thinking that you are probably not a well-known admirer of little animals. I'm not, either, if it comes to that, but this book sort of took me by surprise.

Received *The Fire-Dwellers* in your (and Knopf's) edition—it looks splendid, I think. The orange binding is perfect. The typesetting I'd seen before, in galley proof, and I think it catches the form of the novel in just the right way. I couldn't be more pleased. Now let us wait and see how the Canadian reviewers will say, "Yes, all very well, but what a pity she didn't write *The Stone Angel* all over again." I understand very well why *The Stone Angel* hit home in Canada, but in a way it saddens me to see that people would like a repeat performance, or some people, anyway. One can't do the same thing twice—that would be death. Also, although Hagar was a natural, as a fictional character, the novel itself was in form and even outlook more traditional than either *A Jest of*

God or *The Fire-Dwellers*, by which I mean that I've changed and I can't be sorry about that.

Interested in your comments re: Ludwig as Writer-In-Residence—he wrote to me not long ago, and I gathered from his letter that he had nearly completed a new novel. I'm very glad indeed about that. He must have been working very hard this past year. I know he's got terrible physical problems. One cannot even sympathise openly because he is not that kind of guy. But I admire him a hell of a lot, for having worked so long at other jobs and still got some of the essential writing done, under such circumstances.

I think the idea about getting me thrown out of Massey is a lovely fantasy. But let us remember I am 45 and, in another 5 or 6 years, I may well have grandchildren. Am I willing, I ask myself, to alienate my kids in order to sell hundreds of thousands of copies of my books? Ah, the dichotomy of life.

I received Clara Thomas' book on me[1]—I think she has done a very good job, generally, and I appreciate deeply her sympathetic approach to my work, and I also (from letters) like her very much. But my God, Jack, how embarrassing to read a book about oneself and one's own work. I think it ought to have been done after I was decently dead. The memories of my old college buddies make me squirm. The awful thing is that I know they meant well. However, none of this matters, really.

I'll send off the manuscript of the short stories as soon as it is finished. I'm getting a typist to do it this time.

All the best,
Margaret

1. Clara Thomas (1919–2013) was a professor in the Department of English at York University. She wrote two biographical and critical books about Laurence and her work, published by McClelland & Stewart: *Margaret Laurence* and *The Manawaka World of Margaret Laurence*.

Elm Cottage, 22 April 1969

Dear Margaret:

Migod, you are right. I do hate animals and animal stories. I'm remembered as the publisher who achieved his greatest fame by turning down *The Incredible Journey,* but I'll be very surprised if we don't enthuse about *Jason's Quest.* Kids' books are the life of many publishing houses. We need more of them.

As to the short stories you are quite right. They are usually tough but funnily enough the market is beginning to develop for good books of short stories. It depends on the author. I don't have the slightest doubt that your collection will do well.

Jack Ludwig's new novel sounds very good. He's had a couple of readings—both of which I have attended for God's sake—and it sounds very impressive, although I would rather read a novel than have it read to me by the author. I still think you will shake them up at Massey even more than he did—and that takes some doing—even though you are an incipient grandmother.

I had a meeting with Cushman in New York last week. I haven't seen him for a long time. It looks to me like we are actually going to get a contract signed for *Fire-Dwellers* one of these days and we have also, thanks to his good offices, got a direct contract from Doubleday's Book Club for Canada, which is a first. Like it's bringing them into the Twentieth Century. He's a good agent.

Cheers!
J.G. McClelland

Hollinger, 25 April 1969

Dear Jack—

Thanks for your letter of April 22nd. I was actually thinking of *The Incredible Journey* when I said you didn't strike me as a great lover of little animals. Remember—I was there at that peculiar Awards Dinner of the Can. Authors Association, and when Sheila Burnford appeared, you turned to me with an expression of deep anguish and wondered if you should commit suicide now or later. Nevertheless, that whole unfortunate episode endears you to me.

Well, maybe you'll want *Jason's Quest*—we'll see. I hope so.

I will also be anxious to know what you think of the short stories. I've sent two copies to Michael Horniman in London, and, when he's looked at them, he'll forward them to John Cushman, who will send a copy to you. It seems a rather lengthy way of doing things, but unavoidable.

I am delighted to hear that Ludwig's new novel sounds good. But we have one problem—Jack, I am NOT going to read aloud from any work in progress. It isn't that I am modest; I am not. It's just that I agree 200% with your point of view—I'd rather read a novel than have an author read it to me. Anyway, maybe I won't have anything in progress then. But even if I do, I'm afraid I have to play it very close to the chest while the thing is being written. I don't really believe excerpts from novels are very effective, anyway—if the thing is anything, it's a whole. So where does that leave me? I guess I will be reduced to whomping up little talks on the CREATIVE PROCESS ("I Was A Middle Aged Madwoman" and like that). I think poets are lucky—they can read their poems in public and it sounds okay. But prose isn't like that. Not mine, anyway.

It appears that the business about your deal with Doubleday is pretty good, or at least hopeful. I don't really understand all the details, but for all this I trust John.

All the best. Sincerely,
Margaret

Hollinger, 10 June 1969

Dear Jack,

May I ask a favour of you? Norman Campbell, the CBC director and composer,[1] is in this country at the moment (partly for the launching of *Anne of Green Gables*, the musical for which he did the music and many of the lyrics), and I've talked with him recently, and he has expressed interest in seeing both *Jason's Quest* and *A Bird in the House*, with a view to considering how the former would make into an animated cartoon film and the latter into a film. Unfortunately, I do not have any spare copies of the manuscripts—he's glanced through both, at my house, but I've only got my own original copies, which I can't part with until I'm sure about revisions for both. Norman will be returning soon to Toronto—do you think you could lend him your copies of these two manuscripts, just for about a week, so he can read them? I don't even know if you've got *A Bird in the House* yet, but if not, you certainly ought to have it shortly. Anyway, I'd be most grateful if you could do this, when Norman gets in touch with you.

I'm delighted that you're taking *Jason's Quest*, and delighted also that you express confidence in taking the short stories. I am having a hell of a time about the stories because Knopf would like to see me make a more unified narrative of them—i.e., to "de-story" them, and I just feel I cannot do that. I don't think it would improve the book, and because so many of the stories have been published, some in Canadian anthologies, I feel that to tamper with them a lot would be to make myself very vulnerable to the charge of trying to do a kind of "made up" book or of trying to palm off stories as a quasi-novel. Anyway, I'll keep you posted on the situation. I've written to John Cushman asking his advice. I really don't know what to do, Jack. I feel I can't mess these stories about. It would be awful for me if the book weren't published in America, but to tell you the truth, it is really Canada I am thinking of most when I say I cannot change the natural form of these stories. They may not be known very much in America, but many of them are known fairly well in Canada, and I just do not feel they ought to be altered now from the form in which they were written. I'd be glad of your opinion. It isn't that I mind going back and working on a manuscript. But my instinct tells me loud and clear that this would be a mistake in this case, and would lay both of us wide open to nasty charges of trumping up a book. I hate to argue with Judith Jones and Knopf, as she is such a good editor and I have worked so amicably with her, but I cannot see that I can do otherwise now.

Well, *The Fire-Dwellers* has certainly got mixed reviews, eh? They seem to be absolutely split—those who are very enthusiastic and those who hate the book. I was much heartened by Bill French's review in *The Globe Magazine*.[2] Also, got a very good one from Edward Weeks in *Atlantic Monthly*.[3]

All the best.
Sincerely,
Margaret Laurence

P.S. Macmillan here agrees with me re: the stories.

1. Norman Campbell (1924–2004) was a notable CBC employee who produced some of its first television broadcasts. He received many awards, including the Order of Canada in 1978.
2. William French's review of *The Fire-Dwellers* appeared in the Globe and Mail on 3 May 1969 and is combined with his review of Clara Thomas's *Margaret Laurence*. The review itself was glowing: it argued that Laurence had "succeeded admirably" with Stacey MacAindra, the protagonist, and that "her grasp of the rhythms of dialogue is perfect" (A17).
3. Edward Weeks's positive review of *The Fire-Dwellers* appeared in the *Atlantic Monthly* in June 1969.

Hollinger, 11 June 1969

Dear Jack—

A hasty note, further to my letter yesterday. I shall need your copy of *A Bird in the House* back again, to make revisions—could you bring yourself to send it to me airmail? I'll return it as soon as possible, with my comments on revisions, for your opinion. And Norman Campbell can pick it up from your office after that, if you will be good enough to lend it to him.

Am having a session with Alan Maclean this week about it. Also, Jane Cushman is coming over for lunch tomorrow, as she is visiting her parents in Oxford, so I may talk to her about it. This awful business of having to disagree with Judith Jones of Knopf is really just what I do not need at this point when trying to prepare for Canada and also surrounded by multitudinous personal difficulties of one kind and another, so I am becoming almost paranoid. For God's sake reassure me—you *do* think they ought to remain as stories, which they ARE, don't you? I feel I may possibly [be] losing my mind.

Cheers—
Margaret

Elm Cottage, 17 June 1969

Dear Margaret:

Thanks for your two letters. Our copy of *A Bird in the House* went off to you today by air and we will be delighted to lend it to Norman after we get back.

I have had several discussions with John Cushman about the problem and was glad to hear from him on Friday that the matter had been resolved with Knopf and that they have decided to go ahead with the material as a collection of short stories.

The conclusion here after several of us had looked at the material was very close to your own. From the strictly commercial point of view, we had to agree with the Knopf position. We felt, however, that it could lead to confusion and, indeed, to specific criticism in Canada where the stories are better known. In short, Margaret, I think your judgment has prevailed as usual, and certainly you have our full support in the conclusion that you reached.

It's my understanding then that we will be doing *A Bird in the House* in the Spring of 1970 and *Jason's Quest* in the Fall. It's a delightful book by the way, and I congratulate you. John hasn't yet been able to get a publication date from Virginia Fowler at Knopf—he tells me she always takes far too long to bring books out, although it's probably worth it because they are so beautifully produced—but in any case it looks like it will be in the early Fall of next year.

It should be a big Margaret Laurence year here then because we are also hoping to bring out *The Tomorrow-Tamer* in the New Canadian Library in January or February. The reviews of *The Fire-Dwellers* have been mixed, and on the whole disappointing to me. I think most of these reviewers are raving idiots, but there have been enough good reviews to compensate.

I'm looking forward to meeting you before too long.

All the best. Sincerely,
J.G. McClelland

Hollinger, 26 June 1969

Dear Jack—

Many thanks for your two letters. I am pleased and relieved to hear that you agree in general with my viewpoint about the stories. I think you are right about the commercial angle—I could see Judith Jones' point of view very well in this regard. But I'm glad that you feel, as I do, that to alter the stories basically would be to invite criticism in Canada. Anyway, the whole issue is now settled, and I have returned Knopf's copy to Judith with the revisions—actually, many of her suggestions I have accepted, especially those dealing with parts which were repetitious, statements which did not need to be made in more than one story now that they are to be published as a collection.

I'm also glad to hear that you like *Jason's Quest*. I have just received Virginia Fowler's suggestions for revisions—most of these are concerned with making the text more clear for North American readers, and she has also spotted one or two of the discrepancies which I had missed. I wonder if I need to send you a list of these revisions, Jack? Will you be buying papers from Knopf? If so, I don't think I need send you the revisions, most of which are pretty minor in any event. But if you would like a list of them, would you let me know, please?

I'm delighted that you are doing *The Tomorrow-Tamer* in the New Canadian Library. Should I give you my Toronto address? After September 7th, I will be at 9 West Grove Crescent, Toronto 305. Phone 483-2656. But I'll likely phone you before then, as I'll arrive in Toronto about 1st September and will be staying with my friends for the first week until I can get into my house.[1]

All the best.
Sincerely,
Margaret

1. Hodgeman wrote back to Laurence in response to this letter to state that McClelland was out of the city on vacation for three weeks. She added that it was not necessary for Laurence to send McClelland & Stewart a list of revisions, since it would be buying directly from Knopf. She noted Laurence's Toronto address to pass on to McClelland closer to Laurence's arrival.

Hollinger, 7 October 1969

Dear Jack:

I have recently been talking on the phone to John Cushman and he has suggested that it might be possible for you to send the advance payment for *A Bird in the House* and *Jason's Quest* to me here minus the fifteen percent agent's fee.

I would like this to be done if possible because I am trying to build up a reserve of dollars in this country with a view to my ultimately coming back to live in Canada. I have to pay Canadian income tax this year anyway, so it seems to me that anything I earn in Canada apart from my salary at the University should be left in this country and I will pay taxes on it here. I don't think that anything I earn here this year needs to concern the British Government at all. If you can arrange to have the money sent to me here I would be most grateful.[1]

All the best,
Margaret [signed][2]

1. On 9 October 1969, Hodgeman wrote to Laurence in response to this letter: "Thank you for your letter of October 7th to Mr. McClelland. We are arranging for the advances due on *A Bird in the House* and *Jason's Quest* to be sent to you as quickly as possible."
2. At the bottom of this letter, McClelland wrote, "Marge, Say yes to arrange for this to be done. Jack."

Hollinger, 16 October 1969

Dear Jack:

I'm terribly sorry I didn't make it to the party but, as well as having a sprained ankle, I had just spent some three hours in talking to some of the girls in one of the residences here where I was invited to dinner. At the time when I accepted the invitation I didn't realise it would turn into a three-hour quiz. It was enjoyable, though. ...

I have been sent an application from the Guggenheim Foundation suggesting that I apply. Do you happen to know anything about this sort of thing, Jack? What I would like is to apply and, if by any chance I get the grant, to have them send the money here to Canada with a view to using some of it to buy a cottage on a Canadian lake. Do you think that if I am in residence in England they would do this? Also, do you happen to know anything about the income tax aspects of a grant like this? Most importantly, would you be willing to put your name down as a reference?

Love,
Margaret [signed]
Margaret Laurence

Massey College, 20 October 1969

Dear Margaret:

Thanks for yours of the 16th. We all missed you, but it couldn't be helped. It turned out to be a moderately good party. I hope your ankle is fully recovered. ...

Re: the Guggenheim Foundation, yes, I would be more than willing to have my name used as a reference. On the tax side, it is my impression—although I am not certain—that such grants are tax-free. I will try to find out for certain. As for sending the money to Canada, I can think of absolutely no reason why they wouldn't do so. I don't think the Guggenheim people concern themselves with what you do with the money, and they will send it to any address that you give them. As a matter of fact, I presume that they would prefer to send it to Canada because I am assuming that yours would be one of the Canadian quota grants. My basic opinion, Margaret, is that I would not tell them any more than they ask. In other words, I certainly wouldn't tell them that you are planning to use the money to buy a cottage and I wouldn't even tell them that you will be residing in England unless there is something in the application form that requires you to do so. Your future plans are hardly their business. What they are interested in is your writing ability.

Cheers!
J.G. McClelland

Massey College, 6 November 1969

Dear Margaret:

Yes, I'll certainly be there on November 20th, God willing. How could I resist? I hope we will see you at the Harold Town[1] opening on Saturday.

Cheers!
J.G. McClelland

1. Harold Town (1924–1990) was a Canadian painter, printmaker, and illustrator, and a member of Painters Eleven, a group of abstract artists who worked out of Toronto from 1954 to 1960.

Hollinger, 24 November 1969

Dear Jack:

Will Ready of McMaster University has recently gone into publishing, in a very modest way and would like to re-issue the small book of translations of Somali poetry and prose, which I did many years ago and which was published by the Somalian government in 1954. Mr. Ready would like to do a limited edition, by the offset method, for the use of universities. I know you don't have any claim on this book, and I assume it is nothing you yourself would ever want to publish but I thought I had better check with you to be sure.

It was a good party last week and I'm sorry that I couldn't stay longer. It could hardly have failed to be more entertaining than the group, which I went on to meet and give a talk. The latter part of the evening was unbelievable and the group reminded me of that poem of F.R. Scott's, "Canadian Authors Meet."[1]

Hope to see you soon.

All the best,
Margaret

Tell her ok[2]
—Jack

1. F.R. Scott (1899–1985) was a modernist Canadian poet and constitutional expert. His poem, "The Canadian Authors Meet," first published in *McGill Fortnightly Review* in 1927, is a satirical portrait of the Canadian literary scene, particularly of the Canadian Authors Association (see McClelland's letter dated 7 June 1962) and its lack of genuine creativity, which was poorly counterbalanced by patriotism and religious belief. One stanza, for example, reads as follows:

The air is heavy with Canadian topics,
And Carman, Lampman, Roberts, Campbell, Scott,
Are measured for their faith and philanthropics,
Their zeal for God and King, their earnest thought.

2. This comment is handwritten by McClelland at the bottom of the letter.

II | *Challenges and Successes, 1970–1979*

•——

Hollinger, 9 April 1970

Dear Boss—

Had lunch with Pamela Frye[1] today and received your various tender messages re: Booksellers' meeting in Wpg (will go if they pay my fare) and the fact that I owe you a dinner. Jack—my life has been a three-ring circus, I jest not! Of course, I assume your life is the same. I find myself doing all kinds of things, like giving talks and being a kind of low-grade performer, and some of it is okay and some of it isn't, but it sure cuts into the time. Actually, it's been a marvellous year for me, total change of atmosphere, etc. etc., but now I feel it is time to go back home (and I don't mean Eng or Canada, I just mean my own house) and connect with the typewriter again ... Anyway, have not really seen you at all, this year, so could you and Elizabeth come for dinner either Friday, April 24th, or Sat April 25 or Sunday April 26th? All you will get is a tired old tuna fish casserole and my charming company, but brace yourselves. Let me know, eh?

Am off to Peterborough this coming week. Want to get things done in my cottage there. Will be staying with W.L. Morton[2] and wife, really good people. I have many offers of help to find good 2nd-hand furniture, but I am more interested in finding good 1st-hand plumber. I have already had a well dug by a lunatic water diviner who has taken to phoning me up when he is three-sheets-in-the-wind of a Saturday night, and asking me how much I weigh, and, as I've never met him, I cannot help but feel that some of the Peterboro' Irish may well be descended from Jack the Ripper—however, let it pass. My main entertainment of late has been Eaton's Catalogue and now I'm sorry I did not attend that party at J.D. Eaton's, so I could tell the present incumbent that the Catalogue is probably one of my favourite books—wow! what reading![3] I have ordered everything for my cottage from it, and get home every night to find lovely parcels to open, like Christmas, and now I'm going to have to rent a small truck to get all this stuff from Toronto to my shack. It is really MARVELLOUS what you can buy with $500! Lamps, brooms, stainless steel cutlery, wastepaper baskets, blankets, etc. etc. It has been one of the great experiences of my life!

Workwise, I have been going like a bomb, but I'm getting paid for it—I never knew how secure the academic tenure really is; it must be nice to have it forever, or—well, no, I guess it would be a comfortable coffin.

Phone, write, or telegraph!

Love,
Margaret [signed]

1. Pamela Frye was the McClelland & Stewart editor of the title, *The French Kiss*. Written by Eric Koch, the book is a political satire about French President Charles de Gaulle and Quebec. However, three thousand books were recalled and "small slips pasted over the offending passages and copies returned to retailers" when it was understood that "some of the family members of the later Quebec premier Daniel Johnson might have been libeled" (King, *Jack* 204).
2. William Lewis Morton (1908–1980) was a renowned Canadian historian who specialized in nineteenth-century political history and the Canadian west and was a friend of Laurence. He taught at Brandon College, at the University of Manitoba and, finally, at Trent University. He was the master of Champlain College at Trent in 1970. As Manitobans, he and his wife were in a good position to host Laurence in her early visits to Peterborough and Trent.
3. Founded in 1869 and closed in 1999, Eaton's was once Canada's largest department store, and its mail order catalogue was commonly found in the homes of most Canadians.

Hollinger, 20 July 1970

Dear Boss,

I am now back in England, and très sorry I did not phone you before I left Canada. Last weeks in Can were lovely, out in shack on Otonabee river, but also more filled with events than one would have imagined possible. I always think I am about to lead the quiet country life, which always turns out about as quiet as a three-ring circus. However, I did have some time alone, to sit on my riverside dock and to contemplate the wildlife, so that was good. Hope to be back next summer, God willing.

All is fine here, more or less. Kids are doing splendidly, but house needs many repairs, so am immersed in passionate conversations with builders, painters and Rising-Damp Specialists. You don't know about Rising Damp and Dry Rot? Lucky you. Lots of things now being done to the old dump, so we can keep in business a while longer. At the moment, seem also to be running some kind of hotel, my usual fate in summers, everyone in N. Amer turns up here. I love it, actually, but am finding it slightly odd to be getting back into pattern of cook-housekeeper, not that I ever really do ... whoever happens to be here at mealtimes gets something nourishing like stew and *they* do the dishes.

Can't think of novel yet—makes me want to throw up. But probably the time will come, I hope. I love the reviews (Can) of *Jason's Quest* ... the *Van Sun* says it is a candidate for classic kids' books; the Tor *Globe and Mail* says seldom has a kid's book seemed so long (I hope Dr. Goldborough breaks her leg on the subway).

Got a letter (fan) from an old lady (I assume) in Ohio the other day, saying *Cleveland Plain Dealer* assured her *A Bird in the House* was clean family reading, but she read it and found a four-letter word. "Why oh why did you do it?" she cried. "It spoiled the book for me." Nice balancing review came from *The Canadian Mennonite*, which said book was "frankly conservative" (I guess because deals with past?). My only comment is SCREW ALL REVIEWERS.

Well, Jack, to tell you the truth, it is nice to be here, where I am a totally private person. No one in this area knows me from a hole in the ground, and, in fact, among my Country neighbours, I am thought to be a pretty low-class N. Amer gypsy or something, which is just great. Last yr was fine and I really thought it was good because of the kids I talked to, but it is nice to be back in anonymity for the moment, where yr neighbours look down on you because you ain't got their kind of cash. I love this house; don't love England much ... really want to live back in Canada, but maybe can work here for next 3 years.

Love,

M

Elm Cottage, 19 January 1971

Dear Margaret:

That's a great story in *Chatelaine*. Hope you approve. I thought it was very good. In fact, I really think she did an intelligent job, and you came through as the real Margaret Laurence.[1]

Glad to read in the article (from Anna Szigethy)[2] that the novel is proceeding well. We could certainly use it. Last year was a great one, but the problem with this business is that there is always the next year. It doesn't really get easier.

Am busy these days trying to save Canada from the American aggressor (see enclosed form that I am sure you will want to sign).[3] Little time for publishing as the result—but am hooked on the problem.

In haste.

Love,
JG McC

1. McClelland appears to be referring to an interview that appeared in the February 1971 issue of *Chatelaine*, titled "Margaret Laurence: The Woman Behind the Writing" (Wigmore).
2. Anna Szigethy (1943–); later Anna Porter, is the editor Jack McClelland hired to work at McClelland & Stewart in 1969 when she was twenty-six years old. She married lawyer Julian Porter in 1971.
3. This form is not included in Laurence's or McClelland's papers. However, as James King explains, after Ryerson Press's sale to the American firm McGraw-Hill in 1969, a "big blow to Canadian-owned publishing" (*Jack* 219), McClelland "became co-chairman of the Committee for an Independent Canada" (221). This group began a petition in September 1970 to "limit foreign investment and ownership" and, to this end, had attained 170,000 signatures by April 1971 (221). It is quite likely that the form mentioned here is a copy of this petition.

TELEX

J G MCCLELLAND AND STEWART LTD
25 HOLLINGER ROAD

STAND FAST COMMA CRAIGELLACHIE LOVE MARGARET LAURENCE

TORONTO ONTARIO
MARCH 3, 1971

CABLE TO: MRS MARGARET LAURENCE
ELM COTTAGE,
BEACON HILL,
PENN, BUCKS, ENGLAND

FULL RATE

IT'S NOT ALL BAD AND WILL PROBABLY WORK OUT WILL WRITE SOON THANKS FOR YOUR CABLE

JACK
MCCLELLAND AND STEWART

Hollinger, 6 April 1971

Dear Boss—

Well, having followed your upheavals with some difficulty owing to the British postal strike, and having spent more hours on the telephone to Mordecai and to M. Atwood[1] than ever before, and having worried myself sick about you—hell, not just you as a publisher but you as you—I have now gotten myself together enough to write.[2]

First and foremost, Jack, as I implied in my cable (hope you did not mind that I quoted that great phrase re: the survival of the CPR ... thought it was relevant under the circumstances)—I am very relieved that you won't in fact be selling the old house. I have complex feelings about this, and they are not all related to "selling out to the Americans." I know this would be the last thing you would want to do. If you do have to, at some point, then my feeling about the situation is quite clear—if McClelland & Stewart is ever owned by an Amer firm, I won't want to be published by them; and if J.G. McC is not there, whether the firm is Amer-owned or not, I also won't want to be published by them. You and I have had our ups and downs, Jack, as you have had with all your writers, but there is not one of us who does not feel this way, when the chips are down. There isn't one of us who hasn't cursed your bloodymindedness, your incredible ability to take umbrage, your christly ego, and all the rest. But there also is not one of your writers who does not, at heart, appreciate the fact that for about 2 decades you were the only original and interesting publisher in Canada; your admirable ability to take risks; and above all, the fact that you damn well have always *cared* about what you published. You have always read my manuscripts yourself—don't you think I know that?

I hope it'll be okay, and that the firm will continue, with you there.

But, of course, I see something else as well, which is that you feel kind of trapped and would like to get out, having spent many years of your life doing one kind of work, and (even tho' I believe you do not fully realize it) making the only good publishing house in Canada, and establishing yrself as one of the few good publishers in North America (this is the reputation you have in N.Y.). I kind of feel that you really *do* want to do something different, Jack, and I really feel for you in that dilemma. You know something? I think I want to write one more novel, and maybe one more kids' book (not so important) and then I want to quit being a writer. I really feel that I want to quit being a fighter, Jack, and become a coach. Not that I can tell kids how to write—it isn't like that. It's just that maybe I can do reviews, and publishers' readers reports, and the like. But the time is rapidly approaching when I cannot any longer endure the almost impossible stresses of novel writing. Also, I feel that after I've done this one more novel, it is now really the turn of the younger writers. I am not going to be like Sarah Berndhart [*sic*], who played Juliet, with a wooden leg, in her advancing years. There is something else I can do, and I hope I will do it. I feel somewhat the same about you. I think you probably really *do* want to get out of publishing and do another kind of something. And I think you will be right, to quit that work while you're ahead. But all I hope is that you will quit it, if you do, while you *are* ahead, on your own terms.

Whatever you do, God bless and good luck.

I really wanted to express a kind of loyalty, which I deeply feel, but without making you feel that I think you'd be selling out if you quit publishing. You won't be. But it would be good if you could do it in your own time, on your own terms, that's all.

Love,
Margaret [signed]
Margaret Laurence

1. Margaret Atwood (1939–) is most renowned as a Canadian novelist, poet, and essayist. She has published approximately fifteen novels and fifteen collections of poetry, which have garnered a number of awards or award nominations, including the Governor General's Award, the Booker Prize (now the Man Booker Prize), the Arthur C. Clarke Award, and the Prince of Asturias Award (now the Princess of Asturias Award since 2014).

2. Facing bankruptcy and increasing competition from the United States market due to lack of protection of Canadian arts and culture by the federal government, McClelland reluctantly put McClelland & Stewart up for sale in 1971. He stated he did not wish to sell to an American buyer (King, *Jack* 221–26). In mid-April 1971, shortly after this letter was written, the Ontario government agreed to provide the firm with a loan, and so the company was not sold at this time (230).

Elm Cottage, 14 April 1971

Dear Margaret,

My God, that's a nice letter! I feel very badly that I have really been ignoring you and other good friends lately, but the fact is that I just haven't had time to write letters. But I shall treasure yours, even though I'm gonna have to talk to you one of these days about my "bloodymindedness, incredible ability to take umbridge [*sic*], christly ego, etc." I was not aware that I had such impressive qualities.

As far as the firm is concerned, there's nothing very new. I am still struggling to try and solve the problem. I imagine it will be solved either one way or another, but as of this point in time I don't know just how. Needless to say things are a bit tense.

I understand one of the Canadian universities—I guess it's Windsor—wants you as a Writer-in-Residence. I told them that I thought you might be interested but not for several years. In any case, you will by now have heard from them directly. I did get the impression that, although they would like to have you for the next year, they would be quite happy to make a deal for a subsequent period.

Meanwhile, how goes the new novel? Anna indicated after her meeting with you that there was some chance you might have it ready for publication this year. I judge that this is not the case, but I hope it's progressing well.

When the smoke clears, I'll write a proper letter.

All the best.
Sincerely,
J.G. McClelland

Hollinger, 3 May 1971

Dear Jack—

Thanks for your letter. All the unseemly comments I made about you, in my previous letter, were of course aimed only at gaining your trust. You don't want to say anything really loyal and supportful [*sic*] about a person unless you let them know first that they've got feet of clay. So what you say in a loyal way, then, becomes genuine because not sentimental, flattering or all of that. Or something. Let it pass.

Have had a terrible bloody year here, with many problems re: my young, and also have had to throw out 8 months work and thought, re: the novel I was trying to do. No dice. But have begun writing again, just last week, something quite different, probably unpublishable, but I do not care one damn. I want to write it; I couldn't care less if no one else is interested. I will earn my living by—ahem—book reviews, publishers' reading, and I'm a pretty good cook/cum/charlady. If need be.

I arrive in Tor on May 25. McMaster giving me Honorary Degree. Doc Letters. Heavens. Will attend their convocation May 28 and then take off for shack, where I will be incommunicado from 7 June to 15 Sept. Address: R.R. 11, Peterborough, Ontario. Phone: Area 705-745-8053.

Love,
Margaret [signed]
Margaret Laurence

•——

Elm Cottage, 11 May 1971

Dear Margaret:

Great to have your letter and to hear that you are going to be in Canada this summer. You maybe [*sic*] incommunicado from June 7th to mid-September, but this time I am sure as hell going to visit you.

It just happens, by the way, that we shall be having a party at the house on the night of May 25th for Mordecai Richler to launch his new book. You'll have to have another broken leg or something of that sort to be forgiven for not attending. It will be a relatively small party, but it will give you a chance to see a few people in a hurry and get that over quickly so you can relax, so do count on coming. I'll send more specific details to reach you before you take off. Where will you be staying in Toronto so we can track you down before you take off?

That's a pity about the novel. You sound depressed. Don't be. Remember that I depend on you for my livelihood, and I need a few more books from Margaret Laurence to justify the massive loan that the Ontario Government keeps telling us that they are going to give us. See you soon.

Cheers!
J.G. McClelland

Margaret:[1]
I know where you will be staying. It's just that I haven't been giving JGM any more details or information on various matters than is absolutely necessary. He has been under such pressure during the past while, that only absolute essential information has been passed on to him.

I will have a few books waiting for you. Some will be M&S and some from our American publishers. Any you don't want, just return them to me, and I'll see that a credit is issued.

Hope to see you while you are here.

1. This note after McClelland's signature is from Hodgeman. There are a number of letters exchanged between Laurence and Hodgeman from May 1971 to August 1971. In these letters, Laurence asked to buy some books published by McClelland & Stewart and to have the expenses taken off her royalties. The books she ordered include Mordecai Richler's *St. Urbain's Horseman*, Jack Higgins's *Storm Warning*, and James Stevens and Carl Ray's *Sacred Legends of the Sandy Lake Cree*. Laurence also mentioned the novel she had been working on, which would eventually be called *The Diviners*: "I am writing like hell, but think it is going to turn out to be 8000 pages of first draft, 7900 of which will be worthless. Never mind. We will see" (7 July 1971); "I think I have the equivalent of about 150 pp of typescript written, so you can see my alarm re: length, as I am only about a third of the way through the first draft" (3 Aug. 1971). Laurence also consulted with Hodgeman about whether or not Jack would be interested in a book of travel articles and essays, which she had written over the past few years; she referred to the book that would eventually become *Heart of a Stranger*. To this, Jack wrote "yes" on the letter, which is dated 28 July 1971 (McClelland & Stewart Ltd. Fonds, Box 35, File 46).

Hollinger, 3 August 1971

Dear Jack—

How goes the battle? This is an interim report from the wilds of the Otonabee. The novel proceeds at a terrific rate but promises to be 800 pages long. I hate long novels unless they are as entertaining as *St. Urbain's Horseman*,[1] so am trying to figure out a way of keeping it shorter. Yesterday had brainwave, which I think may possibly work. Technical problems are terrible, as the novel covers nearly half a century but echoes go from 1811 to 1973 (and yes, I do know we have not yet reached 1973!). Sometimes, it seems a lunatic project, but it feels good when I am writing, altho' [it] will take countless amounts of rewriting and revision.

Partly, I am writing now to ask if you might be willing to interview a young friend of mine, if you think there might be any chance of your being interested in taking her on staff as an editor, junior ed, or whatever. Maybe you know her. Her name is Phyllis Bruce, and she edited that recent book of contemporary Can poets, with Gary Geddes.[2] I don't know much about her ability as an editor, but my guess would be that she is a first-rate one. She also has had considerable experience. I have talked with her a lot, when she was in Engl, about Can writing, and she is extremely well informed. She will, I think, shortly be doing some poetry reviewing for *Can Forum* but can't eat on that, as you know. Anyway, her address is: 62 Summerhill Gardens, Toronto, and her phone is 921-9423. I pass this on, because I know you are sometimes looking for good editors, and I think she is one.

I think I have the equivalent of 150 pp typescript written, so you can see my alarm re: length, as I am only about a third through the first draft.

Love to all,
Margaret Laurence[3]

1. This novel by Mordecai Richler was published in 1971.
2. With Gary Geddes, Bruce edited *15 Canadian Poets*, which was published in 1970. She went on to become one of Canada's most distinguished editors and publishers.
3. Hodgeman replied to this letter on 11 August 1971. She thanked Laurence for her letter of 3 August to "Mr. McClelland," and stated that he had not had time to read it. She also provided details about his interview, which took "place at 2 p.m. at CHEX," and stated that afterward he would drive to Laurence's place for dinner. She added that she was unsure whether or not he would have his wife Elizabeth or his daughters with him (McClelland & Stewart Ltd. Fonds, Box 35, File 46).

Hollinger, 16 August 1971

Dear Boss—

Got the posters today.[1] They are much too jazzy to put up on my back fence, so have put them up in my living room—a terrible warning to One and All. They are great, and much appreciated, and—let us hope—effective.

Work proceeds. This is going to be the longest and most boring novel in Can history. I really hate long novels. Used to wonder why anyone wrote them. Now I know.

Anyway, many thanks for posters, which now share place of honour with the only other pic in my living room, i.e., Louis Riel.

See you Sept. 1st.[2]

Best,

Margaret Laurence

1. McClelland had sent a "comic take-off of the Ontario coat-of-arms," which stated, "No visitors allowed between Monday and Friday. An important work is going on" (Laurence, *Dance on the Earth* 199).
2. Attached to this letter is a typewritten page of explicit directions to Laurence's cottage on the Otonabee River. At the bottom of the letter, Laurence typed a note to Hodgeman: "Dear Marge—Sept. 1st would be great. I will expect J.G. McC sometime during afternoon, and for dinner. If he wants to stay over until next day, there is plenty of room—altho I call it a shack, it has 3 bedrooms. Will Elizabeth be coming, so I know how many to prepare dinner for? If not, don't bother replying; just let me know if there will be anyone except JGMcC. These instructions are better than the map I drew once of the area. A cartographer I ain't, but I'm pretty good on the verbal description. M" (McClelland & Stewart Ltd. Fonds, Box 35, File 46).

Hollinger, 12 September 1971

Dear Jack—

First, many thanks for having the various books sent to me. I read Farley's *The Boat Who Wouldn't Float* the day the books arrived, and loved it. I had known it would be funny (and it certainly was) but had not known how much of the Newfoundland background he had put in. He is a wonderful storyteller, and I really connected with the book. Also, I liked the bits about you, and felt he really did present you très lovingly, altho' you may have felt otherwise.

Am only halfway through Sheila Burnford's book, so do not know yet what I think of it.[1] I have to read Berton's book before I leave,[2] a week from today, and also have a huge novel to review for *Books in Canada*[3], so have closed my own writing shop for the moment. Pierre's book looks great ... this kind of closely-researched book, written with dramatic impact, is what he does best, I believe.

Jack, I am enclosing a short comment on a novel, which will reach you soon, by a young Can writer.[4] I think it is a good book, and I hope you do not mind my writing to you about it. We all know that this kind of comment makes no difference in the long run, but when I feel this way about a young writer I seem to have to say so.

Hope to see you in Toronto. I leave here a week from today and will be at Adele's for a few days. For your information, phone 247-9806, from Sunday until Thursday, at which time I will be at Clara Thomas'. Marge knows how to reach me there if necessary.

All the best,
Margaret Laurence

1. Laurence is likely referring to Burnford's, *Without Reserve: Life with the Northern Forest Indians.*
2. Laurence is probably referring to Berton's *The National Dream: The Great Railway, 1871–1881.*
3. *Books in Canada* was a monthly magazine that reviewed Canadian books. It was one of the country's most prominent literary magazines in the 1980s and 1990s. it ran from 1971 to 2006.
4. No such "short comment" survives in the archive.

R.R. 11, 14 September 1971

Dear Margaret:

Thanks for your note re: the books. etc. and Toronto. I hope to see you while you are here. Sylvia Fraser,[1] Anna Szigethy, and Suzanne McClelland[2] are all hoping to catch you on the 25th.

Will watch for the novel you refer to. The comment is very helpful.

Cheers!
J.G. McClelland

1. Sylvia Fraser (1935–) is a Canadian novelist, journalist, and travel writer. She won two Canadian Women's Press Club Awards and, in 1969, the University of Western Ontario President's Medal for journalism. She published *The Candy Factory* with McClelland & Stewart in 1975. Her first novel, *Pandora*, focused on wartime Ontario childhood.
2. Suzanne McClelland (Drinkwater) is Jack McClelland's eldest daughter.

Hollinger, 13 March 1972

Dear Boss—

A word to let you know I am still in the land of the living. Life as usual is circus-like here, but okay. I have finished the rough draft of Part III of novel. There are V parts, but part V will be (God willing) short and snappy. It is a total MESS, and far too long, and sometimes I despair, but can only try to see it through and then try to make some kind of shape out of this amorphous mess. If I could do it as 3 novels, I would, but no way. It is all one. I know exactly what I'm trying to do—it's just *doing* it that is difficult.

Switch to single space, as I have more to say to you than I thought at first.[1] One thing—what has happened re: Jack Ludwig's novel that he was working on when he was W-in-R in Toronto? I thought it was to be called *A Woman of Her Time* or some such thing, and it was an expansion of a very fine story he once wrote. Where and how *is* he, and what's going on with his writing?[2]

Secondly, if you ever need a v. excellent editor, Jack, there is someone here who might be interested, namely Alice Frick, who worked for years as a CBC editor and then with the BBC and who is now teaching in this country but thinking (as all of us expatriate Canadians do) of returning home.[3] She worked with Andrew Allan on the famous radio play series some yea-many yrs ago but has certainly not lost the touch. Also, is très conversant with contemporary fiction, Canadian and otherwise, plus theatre etc. Don't know how you stand, editor-wise, at the moment, but thought it worth mentioning.

Am going to Can on May 10, unless I have a heart attack or get run over by a bus. Have to get 3 honorary degrees, which is kind of embarrassing—wish there were some $$$ attached, but no dice. Dalhousie, Trent, U of T. This, plus the meeting of Assoc of Can Univ Teachers of Eng (ACUTE[4] ... how I hate these smart abbreviations; who thinks them up?) in Montreal. By about June 2nd, however, I will move back to shack in P'borough[5] and spend summer—friends on weekends ONLY. Otherwise—RIVER BIRDS WORDS PEACE WORK. I hope. God willing, first draft will be done end of August. Then another year's re-write. Anyway, will be in Tor about May 15 for about 5 or so days, and will phone. I can't wait to get to shack and settle into work and no formalities.

Am reviewing (when I get the book) Sylvia Fraser's *Pandora* for my old buddy Dave Billington, now Book Ed of *Montreal Gazette*. He phoned from Montreal the other day and I said I'd be absolutely delighted to review it, but could he please try to get from M&S my report on it (maybe Sylvia has it; dunno). Will have to re-read book, I think, but maybe not every page; we'll see. Was going to write you, anyway, and suggest you send me free copy! Got a good letter from Sylvia some time ago, which was nice of her, and I was glad she'd cut some of the novel and felt okay about it. I never get the 100 pp novels to review; mine is the fate [that] gets the 673 pp novels. Such is life. My sympathy with LONG novels is growing by leaps and bounds, now that I'm writing one.

See you soon. Best to all,
Margaret

1. The rest of the letter is single-spaced, since Laurence wanted to complete her letter on a single sheet of paper.
2. Ludwig was the writer-in-residence at the University of Toronto between 1968 and 1969. The novel was actually titled *A Woman of Her Age* and eventually appeared in 1973.
3. Alice Frick, a friend of Laurence's in London, was a journalist "associated with the CBC" (King, *The Life of Margaret Laurence* 192).
4. The acronym used to be ACUTE, as McClelland and Laurence state, with an extra C for "College" added by the association in 1991 (now ACCUTE). The president of the association at that time, Shirley Neuman, initiated the change, which was supported by 92 per cent of the membership ("President's Remarks").
5. This is Laurence's abbreviation for Peterborough, Ontario.

Elm Cottage, 20 March 1972

Dear Margaret:

It was good to have your letter. When I think of all the work that you have put into this novel and still have to put into it, it makes me less unhappy with my lot as a publisher and I regret less that I am not a writer leading the easy life. If you can't do it as three novels, we'll do it as a three-volume work. I'm very high on multi-volume works at the moment. My new theory being that they are much more profitable.

That's really good news about the three honorary degrees. I realize that it is a chore and there ain't any dollars attached, but I think it is a good thing for you, a very good thing for Canadian writing generally. Canadian universities have been far too slow to recognize the importance and significance of our great writers. In the past, the odd writer has got the occasional degree and I think it is really great that Canadian universities are doing it for you. They should because God knows most of them are using your books.

Sad news about the dates, because we are going to miss each other initially at least. As luck would have it when you are coming to Canada on the 10th, I am leaving for Europe on the 9th. I'll be back for the ACUTE Conference and will see you there, but I have got a fair trip lined up. I'm going to Cannes, spend a few days at the Film Festival with Mordecai, and then on to a Publishers' Congress in Paris, London foraweek [*sic*] and then to Rome. So I'll be back the last weekend in May. Still, I figure you are very anxious to have me visit you in the shack again. If I remember correctly your estimate was that my last visit only cost you one week's work while you recovered from the hangover. So that's not too bad. Perhaps we can organize things so that we travel to the ACUTE thing together. Will you call Marge when you are in Toronto and she can work out a plan that makes sense for our mutual schedules.

Re: Jack Ludwig, I can't honestly tell you. I have seen him several times over the last few months. He tells me he is making progress, but the manuscripts are slow to materialize. I suspect that he is doing too many other things. The last time I saw him, for example, he was travelling with the Boston Bruins hockey team doing a story about them, and I think he has been doing a lot of things of that sort. Articles, reviews, and so on and generally keeping busy in the usual Ludwig way but not being very productive as far as his own major work is concerned. You probably saw his piece in the recent *Maclean's*, which I must say I felt was only fair.[1]

We could be interested in Alice Frick. I used to know her moderately well but haven't seen her for a long time. I have a notably bad memory and I should remember much more about her than I do. My initial concern would be that she must be about a contemporary of mine in age, which would make her far too old for publishing. It's not just that we put people under so much pressure that they can hardly survive, it is also that I really do believe that publishing (perhaps not so much with editing) is a young person's game. In any case, if she is just thinking about returning and unlikely to make any fast decisions, if you could let me have her address, I would arrange to see her when I am in London and talk it over with her. Or if she is more anxious to reach a decision than that, perhaps you could send me more information about her.

I was delighted to hear that you are doing *Pandora* for the *Gazette*. Marge did send a copy of the book to you (with a note in it from Sylvia). It is just hot off the press and I believe a copy of your previous report was sent along to you. It took us much longer to get Sylvia's book out than I had anticipated and we are a bit late in the season, but I think it should stand up well. She really did a fair amount of work after meeting with you, and I think it was very helpful.

I look forward to seeing you reasonably soon.

Cheers!
J.G. McClelland

1. In the April 1972 issue of *Maclean's*, Ludwig wrote two pieces about Derek Sanderson, "The Unreal Derek Is Unreal" and "Doting on Derek: Judy Martin Loves Derek Sanderson." In these articles, Ludwig argued that Sanderson, a NHL hockey player who played for the Boston Bruins, was not a great hockey player but rather a media-savvy individual who created an image of himself in order to win contracts and money: "He [Sanderson] and the image junkies depend on each other. They exploit him and he, by letting himself be exploited, exploits their exploitation" ("The Unreal Derek" 37). Ludwig added that Sanderson "neatly converts the phony image into an offer from the World Hockey Association—$2.5 million for 10 years, or $250,000 per annum" (37). Ludwig then stated, "Almost any follower of hockey will agree that Bobby Orr is the greatest hockey player ever. Derek Sanderson's name would never come up in that kind of discussion. Yet it's his name flying from the balconies, not Orr's" (37).

•——

Hollinger, 27 March 1972

Dear Boss—

A brief note, to thank you for your good and newsy letter, much appreciated. Sorry I'll miss you at Can and Eng initially, but look forward to meeting you at ACUTE meeting in Montreal end May. Will make my own arrangements re: getting to Montreal—absolutely NO WAY I'm going to travel on plane with you, because you zing into airport 2 seconds before plane departs, whereas I have to get there 2 hours in advance, and, after weighing in baggage, do the following: (a) have 3 cups of coffee; (b) go to john; (c) look at airport bookshop, to see if they have a decent selection of Can books; (d) take decision not to read the novel I've brought along with me for flight reading, and buy latest *Maclean's* or *New Yorker* instead. And so on.

Actually, I hate travelling with other people, even my own kids, and am much happier on my own. But it was a nice thought, so thanks.

I don't think Alice Frick is thinking of returning instantly, so maybe you could see her in London. Her address:

Miss Alice Frick,
18 Beauchamp Road,
London, S.W. 11.
(phone — 228-0562) (if phoning from some place other than London, add 01 at the beginning, area code.)

I don't quite get your distinction between "publishers" and "editors"—I think she *is* an editor. However, will pass on yr message, and maybe she'll write to you. Of course, she is your contemporary and mine, age-wise. But très sharp and reliable.

In a way, sorry to hear about Ludwig's delays. I think he needs someone to lock him up in his study and say, "Get on with it." It is so damn easy to do so many other things. They pay; they're interesting; and they are also evasions of the real thing. Or at least, in my opinion. I guess he's too good a PR man for himself. Wish it were not so, because he's such a good writer. Yeh, I saw the *Maclean's* article. It wasn't bad, but was—well, just another article. I've done some 30 articles, I now realize, over the years. There isn't one which I would really wish to come out in a book. It's bread, but more than bread it isn't.

I am no one to talk, tho, re: slowness. Have gone through 2 weeks now of trying to get started on Section IV, without success. I am really sick of making meals, cleaning house, listening to various problems of the many young who come here—that's unfair, I know, and I'm not really fed up with it, but I do feel the need to get away on my own, to the shack. Will be there about June 3, I hope, and yes, you will be welcome to come and visit—would love to have you visit there, and no, it *didn't* take a week to recover from hangover. Only about three days!

Got Sylvia's book[1] about 2 days after I'd sent off my review to *Montreal Gazette*—I'd only had the galleys, and hadn't seen Town's illustrations, so could only mention them in the review. I thought, naively, that I'd be able to write a review from my publisher's report, but of course could not, and had to re-read the entire novel, as she really did do a lot on it—cut out some 60 pp, I think. It's really a very fine piece of work, and her re-writes on it made a lot of real difference, I thought. I've written to thank her for the copy. Also, Town's drawings are lovely—just right, I thought. A beautiful production job, if I may say so. I have long been a believer in having drawings to accompany novels, but was somewhat scared off this concept when once talking to Bruno Bobek[2] (sp?), who said "Why should I illustrate a novel—why shouldn't *you* write a novel to illustrate *my* paintings?" For this, I found no reply but silence. But the drawings of Town do add a lot, I thought. Hope the book does well. It deserves to.

All for now. See you soon.

Best,
Margaret

1. Laurence is referring to Sylvia Fraser's first novel, *Pandora*.
2. Bruno Bobak (1923–2012) was a Polish-Canadian artist and instructor who worked primarily in watercolours. He was named an official war artist by Canada's Second World War art program, which was called the Canadian War Records (Canadian War Museum). He eventually became artist-in-residence at the University of New Brunswick and would have held that post at the time of this conversation.

Elm Cottage, 4 April 1972

Dear Margaret:

Thanks for your letter. Okay. We won't go together to Montreal. It is clear that you would make me far too nervous.

I'll write to Alice directly and try to see her when I am in London. I saw Jack Ludwig again after I wrote. He tells me that he has had to revise the novel—which as you recall was set in Montreal—almost completely because the scene had changed so much there because of the October crisis,[1] etc. so he is working at it. At least so he says.

Thanks for your good note about Sylvia's book and the Town drawings. I think it turned out very well. We'll keep our fingers crossed. Publication is on Saturday. That's all for now. I don't want to keep you away from your type-writer. You have a long way to go and we do need the novel next year.

See you in Montreal.

Cheers!
J.G. McClelland

1. During October 1970 in Montreal, the FLQ (Front de libération du Québec) kidnapped British trade commissioner Richard Cross and Quebec minister of labour Pierre Laporte. The FLQ wanted an independent Quebec, and threatened to kill both government officials unless FLQ prisoners were released. To gain control over the situation, Prime Minister Pierre Trudeau invoked the only peacetime use of the War Measures Act. The next day, Laporte was killed by his captors, while Cross was eventually released. The October Crisis was eventually resolved in December 1970, through a series of negotiations.

Hollinger, 11 September 1972

Dear Jack:

Thanks very much for sending me Farley's book, which I think is absolutely splendid on all counts. I have written to him, c/o M&S, as I am not sure where he is at present. It really is a fine book, maybe the best he's written, although I don't like to make these comparisons, which are slightly unreal.

Anna will probably have conveyed the happy news that I am now finished the first draft of my novel. Jack, to be frank with you, it is a MESS. It is fifteen thousand pages too long, and is repetitive, etc. But I do not care. The rewrite will begin when I get back to Eng and start putting the 28 notebooks of handwriting into the first typescript, and (hopefully) cutting out quite a bit of the garbage. But I have at least got through it for the first time, so feel both depleted and euphoric about that.

Good to see you, even if briefly. I'll be going to Trona[1] the end of Sept, so maybe will see you then. Will be based at Clara Thomas'.[2]

Best,
Margaret

1. Laurence here spells "Toronto" according to the colloquial pronunciation among locals.
2. Hodgeman responded to this letter on 13 September 1972. She stated, "Thank you for your letter of September 11th to Mr. McClelland. Anna [Porter] did let him know that the manuscript was finished and he is, of course, delighted." She added that Laurence's letter for Farley Mowat "has been forwarded on to him." She asked to be informed when Laurence was next in Toronto (McClelland & Stewart Ltd. Fonds, Box 35, File 46).

Hollinger, 10 November 1972

Dear Jack—

Have just heard from Anna re: the *Wpg FP Weekly*[1] doing a serial on *The Stone Angel*, and have written back agreeing to the deal, ludicrous as the money certainly is. But I think all of you are right—it might do the book some good. How come the *Wpg FP* can only *afford* to pay $150? Where is all their bread? Don't tell me it doesn't exist. Anyway, it doesn't matter. I think this will be a good thing, even without any money.

I am now working very hard and getting quite a lot done. Got back to the novel a week and a half ago, and now have some 80 pp typed, rewriting as I went along. Naturally, much will remain to be re-written, even after I have the whole 500 or so pp typed out, but I am just tentatively beginning to feel that maybe perhaps with luck,[2] if God is good, I may have a novel here. Have quit seeing anybody; will lose all my friends because I am not writing any letters, or hardly any; have become totally involved with this goddamn thing. It is a surprise, you know, to read what one has written some 12 months ago, and to find that the instincts in some ways *did* work, that the parts written that long ago do fit in with the parts written only last summer. Well, Jack, the whole thing will take a lot of work, and it may be quite likely that only myself will ever be all that grabbed by it, but, at this moment, I just don't care. I'm so happy to be working on it, and could not care less about anything else. My next letter may be all Black Celt.[3] But for now, things seem reasonably okay.

Thanks much for sending me Brian Moore's *Catholics*. So incredibly short, for all the things it says. He really is stupendous. I don't agree with you that it is his best novel, but I think it is stunningly good all the same.

God bless,
Margaret

1. An influential daily paper, with a circulation that "extended well beyond the province," the *Winnipeg Free Press* had a weekly Young Authors section that was "directed primarily to advanced amateur writers" and offered advice and writing contests to encourage their efforts. According to Laurence's biographer, Xiques, the newspaper had an "enormous impact" on her "literary apprenticeship" during her teenage years when she submitted writing to it (64).
2. Laurence deliberately includes these spaces, probably for emphasis.
3. Laurence's reference to "Black Celt" means a dark or angry mood, but it also has significance when one considers that she was immersed in writing her novel *The Diviners* at this time. The protagonist of that novel, Morag Gunn, says to her husband, Brooke, "I will never let him see the Black Celt in me" (Laurence, *The Diviners* 246). In the novel, the phrase carries various nuances of meaning in relation to Morag's identity.

Elm Cottage, 23 November 1972

Dear Margaret:

Great to have your letter and to know that the novel is going well. I'm always intrigued by your doubts and reservations. I certainly don't share them. You are one of only a small handful of authors to whom I have never had to say, "this script doesn't measure up." In your case, I don't think I'll ever have to say it. Go to work. Have faith. In fact, it will undoubtedly be your greatest job.

I agree with you about the *Winnipeg Free Press* price, but newspapers will simply not pay national magazines like *Maclean's*, or *Weekend* or *The Canadian* and compare their circulation, etc., one begins to understand why specific newspapers pay very poorly. Like for a syndicated column the *Winnipeg Free Press* probably pays about two dollars and a half per column. It's depressing, but it is the secret of why newspaper publishers are invariably wealthy people.

Things go along reasonably well here. Busy as usual. I begin to despair of ever changing that one, but I keep hoping.

Love,
J.G. McClelland

CABLE TO: ELM COTTAGE

CONGRATULATIONS ON ORDER OF CANADA AND A VERY MERRY CHRISTMAS[1]

JACK

1. In 1972, Laurence was made a Companion of the Order of Canada.

Elm Cottage, 28 February 1973

Dear Margaret:[1]

You will by now, I think, have had a letter from Jack Ludwig about the possibility of your doing an introduction to a Ludwig volume in the New Canadian Library Series.[2] The first point to be settled is whether you have the time and are willing to do it. The second is whether or not you and Jack can reach an agreement on which of the three alternative books is [*sic*] should be. We are fairly easy on that and would go along with your mutual decision, although, of the three, *Confusions* is the one that appeals to us least because it has been readily available in paperback already.

The real purpose of my letter is to say that we would be absolutely delighted if you can undertake this, but also to say please don't start right away (which I am sure you can't do anyway), because there are a couple of points of procedure that have to be cleared first. The first is that Malcolm Ross must be brought into the act as General Editor of the Series if you agree to proceed and when one specific book has been determined.[3] To a degree this is protocol, but Malcolm will work out the terms with you and also, of course, act as editor of the Introduction which, of course, would go to him rather than to Jack. The second point is that we will have to reach a publishing agreement with Jack himself before we can proceed and that hasn't yet been achieved, but you won't hear from Malcolm until we have a contract with Jack.

I was delighted to hear that the novel is completed. I judge that to mean that you won't actually deliver it until sometime later in the year but migod that's great progress and I'm really pleased that it moved so well. I am still trying to get back into book publishing and finding it extremely difficult. I'm just back from a 5-day trip to Frobisher Bay (only an idiot would go there in February they tell me) with Farley Mowat and Max Braithwaite.[4] In point of fact, it was a most exciting experience and I recommend an Arctic tour if you have never made one. At least I am now in the position to give the lie to all those people who claim that Farley has never been North. He even managed to dig out a few Eskimos who remembered him, so I was quite impressed.

Love and kisses,
J.G. McClelland

1. On 5 February 1973, Laurence wrote to Hodgeman to thank her for sending the New Canadian Library edition of *The Fire-Dwellers*. She stated, "It's a really nice production job, and I'm delighted with it. What an improvement the new NCL cover format is from the old ones, in my opinion. My only quibble, this time, is that I wish the quote had not been used on the back jacket, from that lady on the *Cleveland Plain-Dealer* who loves me almost to excess—'There is no better novelist writing in English today' ... embarrassing because untrue, and believe me, that is not false modesty! However, let it pass" (McClelland & Stewart Ltd. Fonds, Box 67, File 42).
2. *Above Ground*, which was published as part of the New Canadian Library Series in 1968, is, in fact, introduced by Laurence, who remarks upon his "finest talent" as his ability to capture character.
3. Malcolm Ross was made general editor of the series in 1958 (see Friskney, *New Canadian Library*).
4. Max Braithwaite (1911–1995) was a Canadian writer from Saskatchewan.

Hollinger, 9 March 1973

Dear Jack—

Thanks for your letter of February 28th. I have not yet heard from Jack Ludwig, but I would be delighted to write the Intro for one of his books for the NCL. We do have one slight problem—I have not yet read the third novel. Not, I may say in passing, for lack of trying. I wrote to you and also to Marge, several times, enquiring about the book and each time you said it wasn't out yet. Now that I think of it, this may have been not last year but the year before, because during the time I've been writing this novel of mine, I've sort of lost track of time and things which I think happened about 2 years ago, as I've only surfaced briefly for about 3 years during the goddamn book. Anyway, no one's fault, but I have not read Jack Ludwig's last novel. Please rush me a copy AIRMAIL. I've read *Confusions* and *Above Ground* and would certainly prefer to write an Intro for *Above Ground*—I agree re: not putting out a book which is already available in paperback, and also, there are some marvellous scenes in *Above Ground* I'd like to comment on. This is not to say that I don't admire *Confusions*, because I do, but I found *Above Ground* a more wholly satisfying novel, quite frankly. Anyway, I'd like to read the third novel, naturally, before I express an opinion.

How come Ludwig gets to have a say in which of his books is to appear in the NCL? No one ever asked me which [one] of mine I'd like to see—you just wrote and said various ones were coming out in the NCL and I said "hurrah." Well, let it pass, Boss—I can't complain. I never did think you'd bring out *A Jest of God* in NCL, or not yet, as it is readily available both in your paperback and under the title *Rachel, Rachel*, with that gorgeous pic of Joanne Woodward being topped by James Olson.

My personal domestic life is CHAOS. Well, not really, but I have just learned from my accountant that if I go to Can in May and return following year in Spring 74 and sell Elmcot,[1] because of that absence the Brit govt will stick me for 30% Capital Gains Tax on sale of house. Furthermore, unless I go to Can (which I will be doing this year) with A CANADIAN EMPLOYER WAITING WITH OPEN ARMS for me, that is, if I return permanently in 74 instead of now, I will be liable to pay Brit income tax for 3 years on all earnings, during which period the Bank of Eng will probably not release my assets here, which would mean I'd be in Can with no money and couldn't get a house. Furthermore, unless I transfer all my assets at one time, and return permanently as a "repatriated" Canadian, the Brit govt will put upon me the regular Brit emigrant's tax. ... namely, I get to take only £200 tax free out of this country and everything else I pay 25% to the Brit govt. HORRORS AND WOE. Needless to say, I do not intend any of this to happen. I think I can avoid all (or most) of it by selling Elmcot now, with vacant possession mid-August (my son does not finish school until mid-July, so can't move until a few weeks after that) and moving back permanently in August, just in time to zing out to Western U for mid-Sept as writer-in-res,[2] pausing briefly to wave a wan hello to friends in Trona and to zap out to Peterborough to check on my shack there. How simple life without money matters would be. But I am damned if I am going to hand over my hard-earned wherewithal to the British government, especially Ted Heath.[3] It may, actually, turn out all for the best, as at least when I do go to Can in Aug, I will have (pray God) got things all sorted out here and will at last be back in my home & native land for keeps. The thought of cleaning this house of ten million tons of old rubbish, which has built up over 10 years, is almost too much to imagine, but it wouldn't be any easier a year from now. I will therefore have lots of time to work on Ludwig's Intro and also on final revisions of my own novel, as really it won't take me 4 months to get things organized here, providing I can sell house quickly. I already have one possibility—this past week has been hectic in the extreme. Will keep you posted. I am surviving, true to M. Atwood's theories,[4] and all will be well, I trust.

Your trip to Frobisher Bay sounds wonderful. I had hoped to go to Churchill in N. Manitoba this summer but that will have to wait.

My daughter is making progress with typing novel, but it is very long. Hope to have final Xeroxed copies by end April. Am going to Rome beginning April, to visit a cousin there, as I think I need a holiday.

Please send J.L.'s last novel *soonest.*

Kind regard to one and all,
Margaret

1. Laurence means Elm Cottage, a "ramshackle labourer's cottage" that Laurence rented in Penn, Buckinghamshire, from her Macmillan editor, Alan Maclean, and later bought—as is referenced in these letters. So many Canadians visited there that it became an "unofficial Canada house" (Stovel, "Introduction" xx). She wrote prolifically there and subsequently dedicated *The Diviners* to "The Elmcot people, past, present and future, and for the house itself, with love and gratitude" (qtd. in Stovel, "Introduction" xxi).
2. In the autumn of 1973, Laurence was writer-in-residence at the University of Western Ontario, and, in the winter of 1974, she was writer-in-residence at Trent University, in Peterborough, Ontario.
3. Sir Edward Richard George Heath, or Ted Heath (1916–2005), was the Conservative prime minister of Britain from 1970 to 1974.
4. Laurence is referring to Margaret Atwood's book, *Survival: A Thematic Guide to Canadian Literature*, in which she argued that a consistent theme in Canadian literature is the will to survive, and that this theme might be seen as parallel to the theme of the frontier in American literature. Influential at the time of publication, the book was criticized by academics in later years for homogenizing Canadian literature and failing to take into account Canada's multicultural character and contributions to Canadian literature by ethnic minorities.

Elm Cottage, 15 March 1973

Dear Margaret:

It was great to have your letter and I am delighted that you will undertake the Ludwig. There is, by the way, one very good reason why you haven't received a copy of his latest book. It simply hasn't been published, so apart from the book that he did on the Canada/ Russia hockey series, his latest book is *Above Ground*.[1] The short novel set in Montreal—which I am sure is the one you are thinking of—is still in the word. He is rewriting it completely at the moment, because the background became dated too quickly, so it is either *Confusions*, the first second of *Above Ground* (the Winnipeg part which Jack feels is a complete novel in itself) or a collection of short stories. I expect you will hear from him in the near future.

I don't know why he has any opportunity to have any say in this matter. I guess largely because he asked. If you have any preference about the order in which your books appear in the NCL, please say so. You are quite right that *A Jest of God* has been available in other editions, but the fact of the matter is that the NCL now seems to operate out of a momentum of his [*sic*] own. There was a considerable demand for *A Jest of God*, even though it was available elsewhere and so we did it. Seriously, I would like to know which book you think we should do next. There is a real possibility that we will want to do another one in January, because we have some thought that we might proceed at a faster rate than we have in the past.

You have confused the hell out of me with the tax and moving situation. Is there anything that we can do to help? Mordecai Richler doesn't seem to have encountered this particular difficulty. I am wondering if he has a gimmick that you don't know about. He still owns his house in London and, in fact, I think plans to keep it permanently if he can. His long-term plan is to live half the year in Montreal and half in London, which makes it rather different, but I am really wondering about the tax situation. If you want to ask him his address is 28 Edgehill Road, Westmount, Montreal, but is there anything we can do at all by adjusting income, advancing you money, offering you a job, fake or otherwise. Seriously, if there is any way that we can help, you have only to let me know.

Glad to hear the typing of the novel is proceeding. A holiday in Rome seems like an excellent idea. Migod, I may see you there. I am expecting to go to Tehran sometime in the next three or four weeks, either via London or Rome but specifics are still very indefinite. I'll let you know if it seems we might connect in either place.

All the best.
Sincerely,
Jack (signed)
J.G. McClelland

1. McClelland and Laurence spell the title of Ludwig's book incorrectly, as "Aboveground" in some of the original letters.

Hollinger, 21 March 1973

Dear Boss—

Thanks much for your letter of March 15th. I hate to bring this up right away, Boss, but I am afraid you have goofed slightly—you say, rightly, that the NCL seems to have taken on its own entity, but you go on to say that there was a considerable demand for *A Jest of God* "even though it was available elsewhere and so we did it." Boss, you *didn't*. *A Jest of God* ain't out in the NCL as yet. What is out in the NCL, of my books, is: *The Stone Angel*, *The Tomorrow-Tamer*, and *The Fire-Dwellers*, which was just done recently and which I have only recently received.

So, okay. ... If Jack Ludwig can ask, so can I. What I would like is this: that you should, first, bring out *A Bird in the House* in the NCL, because the book is *not* readily available in paperback elsewhere. Secondly, that you should then bring out *A Jest of God* in the NCL, because, although it is now available both in your paperback and in Panther paperback in Canada, it would be nice to see it in the NCL. When these two books are out in the NCL, it will mean that the following of my (if you will excuse the expression) Manawaka books are out in the NCL: *The Stone Angel*; *A Jest of God*; *The Fire-Dwellers*; *A Bird in the House*. There remains only one more Manawaka (so-called) book, namely the one I am sweating over at the moment, and I would like to hope that someday that might come out in the NCL as well, making five books of fiction which really are all of a piece. We will see.

Re: taxes in Eng—well, Mordecai's situation is not quite the same as mine. For one thing, he has, I would have thought, considerably more assets than I have, so he could likely afford to keep his house in England, while at the same time buying a house in Canada. I can't. If I'm gonna move over, I'm gonna move over, and burn bridges, because I can't buy a house over there, unless I sell this one. It's as simple as that. Which is okay. I would guess that Mordecai is still "a British resident," which means he pays income tax in Engl, and, if he doesn't sell his house here, then obviously Capital Gains Tax does not affect him. I think in his position he is quite right to be doing what he's doing—he can afford to, and also, some of his kids are much younger than mine, so he is not at the moment thinking of moving *away* from his kids, as I am. I can quite well see why he is keeping his house in England. But he *hasn't* got hold of a gimmick which I ain't, Boss. I may seem not too brilliant, finance-wise, but I am in fact much brighter than most people realize. I really do know pretty well what I'm doing. In fact, I've already sold Elm Cottage—the shortest time to sell a house in Eng in history, probably. To a private buyer, a neighbour, who will give me what I want for it, and no estate agent's fees. Will also buy it furnished. May even rent it, when I've left, to a young Can couple, friends of mine. So it is all kind of exciting at the moment. I may be able to get to Can sooner than expected; we'll see. I am the lady who gets to the airport, not one but two hours before required, if you will recall. I think I am selling my house the same way. And I don't need advice—it's all going on fine.

Re: Ludwig's books—I would be happy to do an Intro for *Above Ground*. But what does Jack mean about the Winnipeg bit being a novel in itself? I have not read any of the short stories, except possibly the really fine one about the junk dealer in Wpg, which was published in *Atlantic Monthly* some years ago, and which was one of his best things. I can't quite see, however, how you could consider publishing a collection of his stories in NCL, if they weren't already quite well-known stories, which I think most of them aren't.[1] *Above Ground* would seem the best bet to me, but I would be very reluctant to see it published *in part*. That is, the way it was first published should, I think, remain. I agree that the Wpg part probably is the best part, but for heaven's sake—it was *all* part of what Ludwig had to say, then, and it should remain so, in my opinion; I mistrust deeply the efforts of writers to re-shape later their earlier works, which may be truer than they think. I would like to think that Ludwig would just keep his hands off *Above Ground*, which is just fine as it stands, and I wouldn't like to see him mess it about at this point, quite truthfully. You can communicate this to him, if you like. Only my opinion, of course, but a true one.

Boss, dear, you *know* I won't see you in Rome. You would be too busy, and I too taken up with coming to a foreign city. Hope to God my daughter comes along with me; she speaks some Italian. My cousin (with whom I'll be staying) has a husband who works for the Can Diplomatic; I have promised to talk to the Can wives (will give a plug for Can ... [2]

1. Jack Ludwig never published a collection of short stories, although he wrote several of them and published them in literary magazines, including the *Atlantic Monthly*.
2. This letter ends abruptly here, and the rest does not seem to be available in either Laurence's or McClelland's papers.

Elm Cottage, 28 March 1973

Dear Margaret:

You are perfectly right, of course, that I'm ahead of myself. *A Jest of God* is tentatively scheduled for January '74 and that's really what I was thinking about. It has been the subject of a lot of discussion here and there has been pressure to have it in the NCL Series as soon as possible. However, I stand corrected.

Okay, the letter is very timely. We will do *A Bird in the House* in January '74. There is a real possibility, Margaret, that we will do *A Jest of God* as well. I won't go into a lengthy explanation of this at the moment because I don't know whether this will come about or not. I'll know in about a month, but I certainly accept your wishes in the matter and we will do *A Bird in the House* first but, if for reasons that I will explain later, we want to do the two, then that's the way we'll proceed.

Okay re: the tax situation and Mordecai. What you are really saying is that I'm a male c. pig and you are right of course. In fact, Mordecai doesn't know a damn thing about taxes, renting or selling houses, or any of those things, but he keeps getting free information from high finance people. I suspected that he had a gimmick. In any case, I'm delighted and sad that Elm Cottage is sold, but it sounds like a fine deal.

Re: Ludwig, you may be right. I simply don't know. The idea of doing only the Winnipeg part of *Above Ground* was his. Naturally, I latched on to it quickly, because it is a nice length and because *Above Ground* in *toto* was a minor publishing disaster both here and in the U.S.A. I think perhaps you found a lot more in it than some other critics. A lot of people seemed to feel that it was a self-indulgent novel that needed more blue pencil or that Jack needed more self-discipline, but that level of criticism is not my bag, although I must say I do think personally that *Above Ground* might survive a lot longer in the shortened version.

So, we will wait to hear from Jack and we'll see you soon, but not in Rome because I didn't make it.

Cheers!
J.G. McClelland

Hollinger, 19 April 1973

Dear Jack—

The novel is at last typed, and a copy should reach you fairly soon. I'm sending it to Michael Horniman first, as he wants to look through it, and then I've asked him to airmail it to John Cushman, who'll send it to you. So fret not if you don't get it for a little while—it seems a kind of circuitous route, but this way it saves me the airmail postage on it! It's called *The Diviners*. I'm afraid it's long—578 pp in typescript. I could probably cut some, but it does all hang together, I think, so massive cutting wouldn't be possible. I'm afraid there are a lot of typographical errors in the manuscript—my daughter typed it as quickly as possible, and seems to have an odd quirk of transposing letters. I should have corrected all these, but, in the interests of time, I didn't. I hope you don't find this aspect too off-putting.

Re: NCL—if you could do both *A Bird in the House* and *A Jest of God*, that would be marvellous. However, whatever you decide is okay with me.

I've heard from Jack Ludwig but haven't replied yet. Things incredibly hectic here. I shall ask him to let me know exactly what pages of *Above Ground* will be used, as he didn't specify. Maybe you know—if so, could you let me know, please?

My daughter is being married May 13; friends from Can are coming to stay for 2 weeks; I've got a zillion things to do re: clearing house; honestly, if I can survive this summer, I can survive anything. Morale is high, but I sometimes panic and think I won't get everything completed by the time I have to get out of the house.

Love to all,
Margaret [signed]
Margaret Laurence

Elm Cottage, 26 April 1973

Dear Margaret:

That's great news and I'll look forward to getting the script in due course from John Cushman. The length, by the way, doesn't concern me at all. In fact, I think it's probably plus value in today's marketplace. It really shouldn't affect the retail price all that much because, if necessary, plant costs can be shared between London, New York and Toronto. I am really looking forward to the opportunity to read the script.

Re: NCL's, okay. We will definitely do *A Bird in the House* and, in all probability, will do *A Jest of God* too. We should have the answer to this within a month, but you can take it for certain that *A Bird in the House* will be published in paper in January.

Malcolm wants to write you about the Ludwig project. I have just come from Halifax and a meeting with him. In my recent meeting with Jack, I told him of your feeling about *Above Ground* and he is now inclined to agree with you, but Malcolm Ross really doesn't, so I am sending Malcolm a copy of your letter and it might be well if you wait until you hear from him before you write further to Jack Ludwig.

Don't bother replying to this letter. Migod, you have enough to do with the wedding coming up, etc. My best to the bride. I think she is a very charming gal and I think it is just great, even though I basically disapprove of marriage.

Cheers!

J.G. McClelland

Hollinger, 16 May 1973

Dear Jack—

I hope to heavens you've received your copy of *The Diviners* by now. I assumed that John Cushman would take the copy I sent him to Knopf, and the other (third) copy I gave to Michael Horniman, so he could read it—he phoned about a week ago to say he'd airmailed it to John, who will send it to you. I should've asked him to send it to you directly. Anyway, I hope you've got it by now. I have heard from Macmillan that they like it, and have just now received a letter from Judith Jones at Knopf that she is very enthusiastic about it, so I feel pretty cheered. She really must have read it quickly, as she could only have received it late last week. If you haven't yet received your copy, maybe you could phone John. I'm very very anxious to know what you think of it. Maybe I shouldn't have told you about the Macmillan and Knopf before you had read it.

All the best,
Margaret Laurence

P.S. My daughter's wedding went off beautifully.[1]

1. On 22 May 1973, Hodgeman responded to this letter in McClelland's absence. She wrote, "Thank you for your letter of May 14th [*sic*] to Mr. McClelland. It has reached the office during his absence from the country on an enforced vacation (his doctor ordered him away before he had a nervous breakdown, but don't tell him I told you). He is off in Bermuda where no one can get at him and won't return to the office until the first week in June." Hodgeman also noted that the manuscript for *The Diviners* was on its way to McClelland & Stewart from John Cushman and that she would send it directly to Anna Porter when it arrived. Hodgeman wrote again to Laurence on 31 May 1973. She observed that McClelland would return to the office the following week. She added, "I have talked to him several times since he has been away and he certainly sounds 100% better than he has done in a long, long time, so I certainly think the vacation has done him a great deal of good" (McClelland & Stewart Ltd. Fonds, Box 67, File 21).

Hollinger, 23 May 1973

Dear Jack—

Two things. First, I've heard from Malcolm Ross and also again from Jack Ludwig, re: selection of material for Ludwig's NCL volume. I've written back to both, saying I am quite willing to write an Intro for whatever material is decided upon among the three of you, and, although I did feel that perhaps *Above Ground* should be left as it is, and not published in part, I didn't really want to participate in the selection of material, especially at this point with trying to get moved out of here etc. etc. and revise my own novel, all by July 22nd. So whatever you, Jack, and Malcolm decide is okay with me. Just let me know what I'm supposed to be writing the Intro on.

I am sending you a tape of the songs for *The Diviners*. All the necessary information is written on the tape box. Judith Jones will be in Eng sometime this week and hopes to come out and discuss novel with me—she has some suggestions, and in general I think her criticisms are right. So we will see.

All the best,
Margaret Laurence

Elm Cottage, 12 June 1973

Dear Margaret:[1]

I am hoping that I will have reached you by telephone or failing that at least by cable before this letter arrives. That being the case, the content is or will be a substantial confirmation, although hopefully I will have been able to go into rather more detail in the letter.

Let me start by saying that the manuscript contains some of the greatest writing that you have ever done. I have told you before that you are the only author that has improved every time out and I think you have kept your record intact. I read the manuscript in one sitting from about 9 o'clock at night until 4 in the morning. It's a very moving experience. I ended up in tears during the last half hour. I don't think a man likes to admit it that he sat there like a bloody fool with tears streaming down his face, but I did and I couldn't do anything about it. You are a great writer and you have proved it once again.

This is not to say that I think everything is right about the novel. I don't. I have your letter. I am totally in accord with its contents and most particularly the plan to work directly and solely with Judith Jones in bringing the script to its final form. One of my great regrets in publishing is that I have never managed to get to know Judith Jones more than casually, but even on the basis of the limited contact I've had with her, I am satisfied that she is one of the better book editors in the world and I'm more than happy to go along with the decision to work with her. In the best sense, it is a very Canadian novel and there could be the odd point of idiom or spelling where we might have a minor disagreement, but, where we would have one, I am sure you would have one too, so there is no problem. Since I am going to be sending a copy of this letter to Judith, I will note here that we will ultimately make a deal with Knopf for repro proofs and a sharing of plant cost, at which point we'll be more than happy to absorb our share of her time and costs.

You have said in your letter that Judith has referred to it as an ambitious novel and that you agree. It sure as hell is. All your novels, of course, have been ambitious. This is more ambitious than its predecessors, I think, only in the sense that you have confronted yourself with the formidable problem of relating the two streams or heritages. You achieve it and it is totally credible, hence the tears I think—but it is in this area where the fundamental problem exists as I see it.

In principle—and ultimately I am certain in totality of detail (detail not being my bag)—I'm in agreement with your own functional criticism and that of Knopf and Macmillan. As I see it, the problem with the novel is essentially that you have not been confident enough in your own achievement and as [a] result have larded the script with material that impedes the flow and that really is unnecessary in terms of what you are trying to do. I read every page, but I can be honest and tell you that it bugged me as a reader to have to do so, because too often I was taken away from your beautiful characterization and forced to read background material that I really didn't want or need.

In fact, Margaret, having said that, I think I have said everything that I need to say. That's what is wrong. You know how to correct it a helluva lot better than I do and I leave that to you with Judith as your sounding board. I don't think we have any concern about the length of a Margaret Laurence novel in real terms any more than Macmillan or Knopf would have, but this one needs artistic paring and once you have done that, we'll have a great book.

Having said that I should probably stop. I didn't make any notes while I was reading and, in any case, very detailed comments from me would be gratuitous. You have your own judgement and a damn good editor. For what it is worth, though, without any attempt at being comprehensive, let me jot down a few thoughts not in chronological order or in order of importance.

- morag, jewels, pique, christie, prim [*sic*][2] are superb—I am old-fashioned enough to believe that you should grab the reader at the outset. You don't really grab this reader until page 14.[3]

- the infactuality section—unquestionably an impediment.[4]
- one character that really didn't come alive for me was A-Okay. This may be that I simply didn't identify with his name or him, but I think he may need some thought.[5]
- I liked the [C]atharine Parr Traill material but wondered if there may be a bit much of it for a non-Canadian reader.[6]
- the insert plot bothered me for the most part except in the early stages of the book.[7]
- I thought there might be some paring [down] at the University stage of musings re: John Donne, etc. It may be necessary. I'm just not sure.[8]
- I wondered a bit at the fictional credibility of the visit of Brooke and his new wife in Vancouver.[9]
- I wondered, too, about the meeting with the young undertaker. You have done this area so well before that I just raise a question here.[10]
- I could see a minor cutting of the Piper Gunn and Ryder Tonnerre episodes.[11]
- Milward Crispin and the communications with him maybe a bit "in" and not the best thing you have ever done.[12]
- for some reason the expression "go like 60" stands out in my mind. It appears anachronistic. I have no idea where the expression comes from.[13]
- I had made a note about being enthusiastic about some of the English material, but you have covered that in your letter and I can only say that I agree, both that some of it should go but that some should be retained.[14]
- the only other note—mental note—that I made was that I was not totally sold on the heading technique. I'm not referring here to "writes of passage," which I am inclined to think is an obvious horror, but rather that I mean that I am not sure about using terms like "memory bank movie" or "inner film." This[15] is probably personal prejudice, because I have never really liked this type of thing, so making allowances for that personal prejudice, I would say that I am unsure about it and maybe a typographic distinction is a workable alternative.[16]

In putting together a list of comments like that, any good or competent editor would have been certain to achieve some appropriate balance between positive and negative comment. I haven't bothered to do that. I've stuck with the negative, because I don't want to waste your time. If any of the negative comments are useful, fine. But whatever you do, don't take time to reply to the comments. Where you and Judith agree with what I have said, you'll have a further reassurance; where you don't, I wouldn't lose too much sleep.

I think we come back to the main point of the agreement, which is that it is going to make a fine novel once you delete the extraneous, which for the most part tends to be artificially inserted. Anna Porter will be reading the manuscript here in the near future, as will others in due course. If they have any specific points that they want to bring to your attention, they will be sent on to you for consideration, but the only fixed point that I want to make is that we are pleased by the content of your letter and more than delighted to go without equivocation with whatever you decide in consultation with Judith.

I just hope you don't find the burden of completion in the context of your move and everything else too much. If you do, I would suggest that you don't drive yourself to completion by the end of August (and I guess you would like to do it earlier). It would be great if you could manage it, but I say again that I wouldn't drive yourself. This one is really worth the time that you have spent on it. And if more time is needed, you should take it. I may say I look forward to your return to Canada and, if there is anything we can do to assist before your departure or after your arrival, you only have to let me know but do phone me when you get here in any case.

Re: Jack McClelland personally, I can report that I had a great three-week holiday. I've returned to the job not only somewhat renewed physically, but almost totally renewed mentally and philosophically. I now know what I am going to do in the future and what I am not going to do and there is no way that I am ever going to get back on the treadmill that I operated for so many years. I even go to bed early most nights (for some reason this doesn't incline me to get up any earlier, which is a phenomenon that I haven't been able to understand), except when I stay up most of the night reading a new manuscript by Margaret Laurence. That, I need not tell you, however, comes under the heading of pleasure, not business, and it is one of the pleasures that I hope to be indulging in from time to time for many years to come.

So there it is, Margaret. Again, my congratulations. I hope this letter is helpful.

Sincerely,

Jack

1. This letter appears in Solecki's *Imagining Canadian Literature*.
2. In this list of characters, both "Jules" and "Prin" are spelled incorrectly.
3. Laurence wrote in red marker and blue pen next to all of these points. The comment on this point says, "I always get off to a slow start—it isn't too bad."
4. This point has a check mark in red marker next to it, indicating a cut.
5. Laurence wrote, "This has been dealt with as much as possible."
6. Laurence noted, "Much has been cut."
7. Laurence wrote, "All this has been done."
8. Laurence wrote, "Ditto" next to this.
9. Laurence wrote, "I disagree. This is okay."
10. Laurence noted, "Ditto."
11. Laurence noted, "This done."
12. Laurence first ticked this in red and wrote "TO DO" on the other side of the paper, before crossing out the "TO DO" and writing "NO" next to it in capitals in blue marker.
13. Laurence wrote, "It comes from when 60 mph was like raising hell." There is also a blue "NO" on the other side of the paper.
14. Laurence wrote, "But this could be explained."
15. Laurence circled the word "This" and wrote in the margin, "Give thought to this." She then crossed out "Give thought to this" and wrote "NO."
16. Laurence wrote, "No, I disagree—these will have to stand—'writes of passage' being an ironical ref to rites of passage, and possibly not too successful but I think this must remain. (Explain M. Movie)."

55

McCLELLAND AND STEWART LIMITED

Publishers 25 Hollinger Road Toronto Ontario Canada M4B 3G2
CABLES: *Emandess* TELEX: *06-219745* TELEPHONE: *(416) 751-4520*

June 12th, 1973

Mrs. Margaret Laurence,
Elm Cottage, Beacon Hill,
Penn, Nr. Bucks,
England.

Dear Margaret:

I am hoping that I will have reached you by telephone or failing that at least by cable before this letter arrives. That being the case, the content is or will be a substantial confirmation although hopefully I will have been able to go into rather more detail in the letter.

Let me start by saying that the manuscript contains some of the greatest writing that you have ever done. I have told you before that you are the only author that has improved every time out and I think you have kept your record intact. I read the manuscript in one sitting from about 9 o'clock at night until 4 in the morning. It's a very moving experience. I ended up in tears during the last half hour. I don't think a man likes to admit it that he sat there like a bloody fool with tears streaming down his face, but I did and I couldn't do anything about it. You are a great writer and you have proved it once again.

This is not to say that I think everything is right about the novel. I don't. I have your letter. I am totally in accord with its contents and most particularly the plan to work directly and solely with Judith Jones in bringing the script to its final form. One of my great regrets in publishing is that I have never managed to get to know Judith Jones more than casually, but even on the basis of the limited contact

Pages 281–86: Letter from Jack McClelland to Margaret Laurence upon his first reading of The Diviners. *Laurence's handwritten notes indicate her reactions to his comments.* [Private collection]

I've had with her, I am satisfied that she is one of the better book editors in the world and I'm more than happy to go along with the decision to work with her. In the best sense it is a very Canadian novel and there could be the odd point of idiom or spelling where we might have a minor disagreement, but where we would have one, I am sure you would have one too so there is no problem. Since I am going to be sending a copy of this letter to Judith, I will note here that we will ultimately make a deal with Knopf for repro proofs and a sharing of plant cost at which point we'll be more than happy to absorb our share of her time and costs.

You have said in your letter that Judith has referred to it as an ambitious novel and that you agree. It sure as hell is. All your novels, of course, have been ambitious. This is more ambitious than its predecessors I think only in the sense that you have confronted yourself with the formidable problem of relating the two streams or heritages. You achieve it and it is totally credible - hence the tears I think - but it is in this area where the fundamental problem exists as I see it.

In principle - and ultimately I am certain in totality of detail (detail not being my bag) - I'm in agreement with your own functional criticism and that of Knopf and Macmillan. As I see it, the problem with the novel is essentially that you have not been confident enough in your own achievement and as the result have larded the script with material that impedes the flow and that really is unnecessary in terms of what you are trying to do. I read every page but I can be honest and tell you that it bugged

me as a reader to have to do so because too often I was taken away from the narrative from your own beautiful writing and characterization and forced to read background material that I really didn't want or need.

In fact, Margaret, having said that I think I have said everything that I need to say. That's what is wrong. You know how to correct it a helluva lot better than I do and I leave that to you with Judith as your sounding board. I don't think we have any concern about the length of a Margaret Laurence novel in real terms anymore than Macmillan or Knopf would have, but this one needs artistic paring and once you have done that, we'll have a great book.

Having said that I should probably stop. I didn't make notes while I was reading and in case any very detailed comments from me would be gratuitous. You have your own judgement and a damn good editor. For what it is worth though, without any attempt at being comprehensive, let me jot down a few random thoughts not in chronological order or inorder of importance:

- morag, jewels, pique, christie, prim are superb - I am old-fashioned enough to believe that you should grab the reader at the outset. You don't really grab this reader until page 14.

  I always get off to a slow start - 14pp isn't too bad

- the infactuality section - unquestionably an impediment ✓

- one character that didn't come alive for me really was A-Okay. This maybe that I simply didn't identify with his name or him but I think he may need some thought.

  this has been dealt with as much as possible

McCLELLAND AND STEWART LIMITED

Publishers *25 Hollinger Road Toronto Ontario Canada M4B 3G2*
CABLES: *Emandess* TELEX: *06-219745* TELEPHONE: *(416) 751-4520*

-4-

- I liked the Katherine Parr Traill material but wondered if there may be a bit much of it for a non-Canadian reader — much has been cut

- the insert plots bothered me for the most part except in the early stages of the book — all this has been done

- I thought there might be some paring at the University stage of musings re John Donne, etc. It may be necessary. I'm just not sure — ditto

- I wondered a bit about the fictional credibility of the visit of Brooke and his new wife in Vancouver — I disagree. this is okay

- I wondered, too, about the meeting with the young undertaker. You have done this area so well before that I just raise a question here — ditto

- I could see minor cutting of the Piper Gunn and Ryder Tonnerre episodes — This done

- Milward Crispin and the communications with him maybe a bit "in" and not the best thing you have ever done — ~~TO DO~~

- for some reason the expression "go like 60" stands out in my mind. It appears several times and I wondered if it was anachronistic. I have no idea where the expression comes from. — ~~TO DO~~ ~~will check~~ NO — it comes from when 60 mph was like raising hell

- I had made a note about being less than enthusiastic about some of theEnglish material, but you have covered that in yourletter and I can only say that I agree, both that some of it should go but that some should be retained — but this could be explained

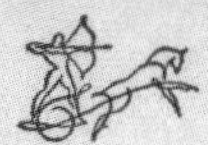

McCLELLAND AND STEWART LIMITED

Publishers 25 *Hollinger Road Toronto Ontario Canada M4B 3G2*
CABLES: *Emandess* TELEX: *06-219745* TELEPHONE: *(416) 751-4520*

- the only other note - mental note - that I made was that I was not totally sold on the heading technique. I'm not referring here to "writes of passage" which I am inclined to think is an obvious horror, but rather that I mean that I ~~am not~~ sure about using terms like "memory bank movie" or "inner film". This is probably personal prejudice because I have never really liked this type of thing so making allowances for that personal prejudice I would say that I am unsure about it and maybe a typographic distinction is a workable alternative.

? Give No thought to this

No — I disagree — these will have to stand — "writes of passage" being an ironical ref to rites de passage, + possibly not too successful but I think this must remain. [Explain M. movie]

In putting together a list of comments like that, any good or competent editor would have been certain to achieve some appropriate balance between positive and negative comment. I haven't bothered to do that. I've stuck with the negative because I don't want to waste your time. If any of the negative comments are useful, fine. But whatever you do don't take the time to reply to the comments. Where you and Judith agree with what I have said, you'll have a further reassurance; where you don't, I wouldn't lose too much sleep.

I think we come back to the main point of agreement which is that it is going to make a fine novel once you delete the extraneous which for the most part tends to be artificially inserted. Anna Porter will be reading the manuscript here in the near future as will others in due course. If they have any specific points that they want to bring to your attention, they will be sent on to you for consideration but the only fixed point that I want to make is that we are pleased with the content of your letter and more than delighted to go without

McCLELLAND AND STEWART LIMITED

Publishers 25 Hollinger Road Toronto Ontario Canada M4B 3G2
CABLES: *Emandess* TELEX: *06-219745* TELEPHONE: *(416) 751-4520*

equivocation with whatever you decide in consultation with Judith.

I just hope you don't find the burden of completion in the context of your move and everything else too much. If you do, I would suggest that you don't drive yourself to completion by the end of August (and I guess you would like to do it earlier). It would be great if you could manage it, but I say again that I wouldn't drive yourself. This one is really worth the time that you have spent on it. And if more time is needed, you should take it. I may say I look forward to your return to Canada and if there is anything we can do to assist before your departure or after your arrival, you only have to let me know but do phone me when you get here in any case.

Re Jack McClelland personally, I can report that I had a great three week holiday. I've returned to the job not only somewhat renewed physically, but almost totally renewed mentally and philosophically. I now know what I am going to do in the future and what I am not going to do and there is no way that I am ever going to get back on the treadmill that I operated for so many years. I even go to bed early most nights (for some reason this doesn't incline me to get up any earlier which is a phenomenon that I haven't been able to understand) except when I stay up most of the night reading a new manuscript by Margaret Laurence. That I need not tell you however comes under the heading of pleasure, not business and it is one of the pleasures that I hope to be indulging in from time to time for many years to come.

So there it is, Margaret. I hope this letter is helpful. Again my congratulations.

Sincerely,

Jack

JGMcC/m

J.G. McClelland. per m

Hollinger, 4 July 1973

Dear Boss—

I am enclosing a list of the revisions I've now made on *The Diviners*. Yes, I think I have them all done—please do not shriek in horror; I can explain everything! I don't think I've rushed them. The truth is, Jack, that my well-known punctuality neurosis has become really bad, just lately. About three months ago, when I was fuming and carrying on about how difficult it would be for me to get the fourteen million tons of rubbish cleared out of this house, and actually get moved to Canada, my daughter said with admirable calm, "Ma, we all know what will really happen—you will have your suitcase packed and the house cleared and be ready to move on July 1st, and will be pacing the floor until July 22." And so it has proved. After my 6-hour session with Judith Jones, I spent the next day or so clearing the rest of the cupboards in this house. Then suddenly realized I could do nothing more until the movers came on July 6th, to take my books etc. for shipping. So I have spent about 3 ½ weeks working non-stop on the novel. My daughter and her husband visited for a week, during which time she made all the meals; now a Can friend is here, and she is making all the meals. The house is indescribably FILTHY, but what the hell—I'll have to clean it before I go, so why worry? Result—I've worked about 10 hrs a day on novel and I think I have done as much as I can with it.

I feel kind of apologetic about getting it done now, because it may seem that I've rushed it. But I haven't. When Judith was here, I became strongly motivated to get back inside the novel, and when I'd talked to her, and also received her list of minor details, and your list of criticisms, and Caroline Hobhouse's crits (Macmillan), I really wanted to do only one thing—get all the things done with the manuscript that I now could see needed doing. The England-Scotland sequence are [*sic*] totally rewritten and is still not the best part of the novel, but it is necessary, and I have tried to do it at least to get in the essentials, with some tenderness and (hopefully) without sentimentality. I know it is much better than it was before, anyway.

Your comments dovetailed very much with Judith Jones', which was not surprising, as all three publishers' comments pretty much confirmed what I knew myself about the areas of weakness. Thanks a lot for your enormously long and detailed letter, which was a great help. Also for the comments, which pointed out flaws no one else had pointed out.

I'm going to try to get the final manuscript to Judith before I leave here, and then will be in touch with her when I arrive in Toronto. I will phone you then. I'll be there on July 22 and will be staying with Clara Thomas for a while. Will then go to shack and briefly collapse before beginning writer-in-res job. The Ludwig introduction I'll do in August at shack. Malcolm Ross wants it by the end of August, which shouldn't be too difficult.

All the best,
Margaret [signed]
Margaret Laurence[1]

1. There are some surviving letters exchanged between Laurence and Hodgeman during the summer of 1973. For instance, Laurence wrote to Hodgeman on 6 September 1973: "Margaret Atwood is doing an article on me, for *Maclean's*, and hopes to have it coincide with publication of *The Diviners*, so this could be a very good thing, but of course she'd like to read the novel. Do you think when you receive the new revised copy you could let her borrow it briefly, or have another Xerox made for her?" (McClelland & Stewart Ltd. Fonds, Box 67, File 21).

Hollinger, 7 October 1973

Dear Boss—

It was great to see you the other day. I'm writing now for several reasons. First, re: *The Diviners*—I talked with Diane Woodman and Peter Taylor about 45-records, and Diane told me that M&S had included one in each copy of a recent book (of a somewhat different nature than mine—the name enchants me, *The Pelvic Tilt*).[1] She said she'd find out approximately how much each of those records cost to produce. I've heard from her now, and the cost was 28 cents per record. I've got a pretty good—in fact, very good, tape of my songs, with Ian Cameron singing 3 of them, and playing lead guitar and another friend playing backup guitar. The fourth song, by Pique, is sung by a girl with an English accent, and altho' her voice is lovely, the accent is all wrong, so this one song might have to be recorded again, with a Canadian girl singing it. The tape of Ian singing seems to me good, altho' I dunno how it would reproduce on a record. The recording is not Nashville, of course, but after all it is supposed to be Skinner Tonnerre and Billy Joe doing it, under far-from-Nashville conditions. Also, the record isn't likely to be top of the Hit Parade—it just belongs with the novel, that's all. What I am getting at, of course is—how do you feel about the possibility of producing a record to go with the book? Would this add very much to cost of book? Could M&S do it if Knopf and Macmillan weren't willing to go along with the deal, or would you have to ensure their co-operation first? Would it be a good publicity thing—I don't think it's ever been done with a novel before?

Could you give a little earnest thought to this, Jack, and let me know your views? Also, are we ensuring that the musical notation is being copyrighted along with the novel, the music to be copyrighted in Ian Cameron's name? Do I have to do anything about this, or will M&S?

Boss, I'm sorry to bug you about all these things, but I think a record would be a great publicity thing and I also think the songs belong as another dimension to the novel. Anyway, let me know your reaction. If favourable, should I write to Judith Jones? Incidentally, Malcolm Ross has been here in London this week, and came over one evening for dinner—I played the songs for him, and he thinks it would be a great idea to have the performed music included with the book, if financially feasible.

Okay—Point Two. I've recently been talking with Adele Wiseman, about her novel, *Crackpot*. It had been accepted by Anansi and was to come out in the spring. Jack, all this is in strict confidence. But she has encountered some incredibly ignorant editorial comments and has now withdrawn the novel from Anansi. Originally, when M. Atwood[2] was still there, Adele discussed changes and revisions, and I gather went along with much of what Peggy Atwood had to say. Adele then spent quite a long while doing substantial cutting (which the novel really did need; I read the original version) and a certain amount of re-shaping and re-writing. At this point, she feels very definitely that she has done most of whatever revisions she is willing to do. She is very sensitive about editorial criticism and has never really had a first-rate editor whom she trusted. (Same problems as Scott Symons,[3] until Scott got Dennis Lee[4] this time around). I think she'd like to submit the novel to you, but is a bit shy owing to your not having published *The Sacrifice*.[5] I told her (no extra charge, Boss) that you might be a nut in some ways, but you most definitely were not of an ungenerous spirit and would certainly not hold a grudge against her on account of her first novel. However, I think she'd rather you wrote to her about it, if you feel so inclined. The thing is this—as I understand the situation, she would *not* be willing to do major structural changes, but would be willing to consider minor points if challenged intelligently (and, I add, tactfully) by a good editor. But I think it really would have to be on this basis—if she submits the novel to you, your response is either a clear Yes or a quick clear No, and if it is Yes, M&S has to be prepared to accept exactly as many new changes as she is willing to make, and not to press for changes she isn't willing to make, and this should be made abundantly clear both to Adele and to whatever editor might handle the book. In other words, if you're willing to publish, you might have to publish without all the changes you'd like to see, and simply take a chance of it and let the book out into the world. Already more revisions have been done that have been done on many Can novels published in the last few years especially by some of the new young publishers. (BURN THIS LETTER, BOSS). I read *Crackpot* a couple of years ago, when it was newly finished, and before much revision had been done. So did Malcolm Ross, and I think (from talking with him the other night) that our reactions were very close—we both felt it had splendid and brilliant scenes and that the protagonist, Hoda, was an unforgettable character, but that in the second half of the book, the narrative flagged and got confused with a sub-plot. It is this second part that Adele has now re-worked, and altho' I have not seen the new version, I would guess that it is now a much tighter and more effective piece of work. But, as I say, the essential thing to remember, if you ask her to submit it, is this: you have to be prepared to give a definite Yes or No, and if it is Yes, to make it quite plain both to Adele and to your editor that she is not bound to do all or any of the suggested changes which an editor might bring up. That's not, in this particular case, such tough terms from your point of view. And it is the only terms she could now accept. The alternative, which is that the book won't be published, seems to me to be nothing less than tragic—and I say this as a writer, not as her friend.

The other thing re: Adele—she has a play, completed some years ago, which has never been performed. It is, quite simply, a brilliant piece of work [that] may, in my opinion, be totally unperformable in its present length. ... it is very long for a play. But it *is* in fact a NOVEL IN PLAY FORM. It is called *The Lovebound* and takes place on a ship, which before World War II was turned back from Palestine and took its load of Jews back to Europe, to a fate we know. It is one of the deepest and most perceptive pieces of writing I've ever read, not just about the Jews, but about the human condition, about loyalty and betrayal, etc. etc. etc. Some years ago, I tried to convince John Gray[6] (BOSS, FOR

GOD'S SAKE EITHER BURN THIS LETTER OR PUT IT IN YOUR PRIVATE FILES) that it should be published as a Novel in Play Form, which it is. John kept saying "What the hell is a novel in play form? Whoever heard of it?" It was at that time that Adele broke with Macmillan's. It should be published; it's a crime that it is not published. One reads it like a novel. If you took *Crackpot,* the play might be an immediate follow-up.

More. Adele now wants to write a non-fiction book dealing—wait for it—with the dolls her mother makes.[7] Her mother, a lifetime seamstress, a Jew from the Ukraine, for years has made the most beautiful and bizarre dolls you have ever seen. From scraps of material; from plastic lemons; from a million unlikely bits and pieces, transformed into grotesque and lovely creatures, which express her inner life as well as memories of her early life in Russia. Adele has applied to the Can Council, and I've just been talking to her (she's in Winnipeg and I phoned because of something else I wanted to talk to her about) and she tells me she's just heard that she does have a grant—not a huge one, but probably enough to be getting on with. She wants first-rate colour photos of the dolls (or some of them—there are huge numbers of them, which Mrs. Wiseman will never sell—she gives them away). Anyway, all this is a part of our heritage [that] should not get lost. So, if you did the novel, then the play, the doll book might come along as well. If you want to discuss this with anyone, Malcolm Ross would be very willing to do so.

So if you want to contact Adele, her address is:

Mrs. D. Stone,
P.O. Box 193
Kleinburg, Ontario. Phone: 893-1847

Am reading Rudy Wiebe's *The Temptations of Big Bear,* and think it is the best book he has ever written. He knows quite a lot about that period of history, and he recreates it beautifully. In the character of Big Bear, he has recreated a very complex man and managed to get across the difference in basic concepts of the Indian culture from our own in what to me is a totally convincing manner.

Have decided not to run for President of the Writers' Union for the forthcoming year. I've liked being interim Pres, but don't think my psychic energy will run to being President for the next year. I operate better in private situations, as you know, and am not very good at politicking—the strain is too great, and I absolutely hate hassles. I think it is all I can do to make myself do battle in my own life, when it has become necessary, I'll support the union, of course, but not in an executive position. There are people who are younger and more energetic (and, at this point, more radical!) than I, who ought to be doing it. I can be of more use to younger writers (a) in a private capacity, and (b) as a kind of Cassandra figure, probably, occasionally uttering warnings from the floor (I speak meeting-wise, of course, not literally!). I've had another Freudian accident—this time I think I've busted a toe bone, opening a door sharply right onto a foot. The wrenched back happened largely due to tension, as well, I believe. These things are warnings to me to cut down on the areas of strain. It's a psychic drain in odd ways that writing a novel is not—it is because I don't like being a public person, of course. So I'm taking steps to ensure my own self-protection. The Writers' Union will survive without ML as Pres, but I may not survive if I take on anything else at this point. The long haul of writing the novel, plus the strain of selling Emcot and moving back here, have just begun to be felt. I'm okay, but must take some reasonable care. Also, my son is on a charge of possessing marijuana, in Eng, and I'm pretty sick with worry about the kid. It's simple possession, and we've got a good solicitor, and Alan Maclean has offered to speak for him in court if the solicitor thinks that would be a good idea. Still, it is one more area of mental strain.

My thanks to Marge and others for sending me the posters—my office looks splendid, walls covered with M&S posters!

All the best,
Margaret

1. Willy Blok Hanson wrote *The Pelvic Tilt: Master Your Body in 7 Days*, a book published by McClelland & Stewart in 1973. It is a health book about how to maintain good posture and a healthy weight.
2. Atwood worked on the editorial board of House of Anansi Press during the late 1960s and early 1970s.
3. Scott Symons (1933–2009) was a Canadian writer known for his novels *Place d'Armes* and *Civic Square*. He wrote a "series of 25 articles that predicted the emergence of the Quiet Revolution," a period of rapid change in Quebec during the 1960s, and he "later claimed to have coined the term" (Lewis).
4. Dennis Beynon Lee (1939–) is a Canadian poet, editor, and critic perhaps most renowned for his award-winning book of children's rhymes, *Alligator Pie*. He also edited *The New Canadian Poets, 1970–1985*, published by McClelland & Stewart in 1985.
5. *The Sacrifice* was Adele Wiseman's first novel, published by Macmillan in 1956, which went on to win the Governor General's Award. It's a story of an Orthodox Jewish man, Abraham, whose traditional values conflict and cause discontent in the New World. McClelland & Stewart published *Crackpot* in 1974, in the New Canadian Library Series.
6. John Gray (1907–1978) was "one of Canada's most revered publishers." He served as general manager of Macmillan and became president of the company in 1955 (Panofsky, *The Literary Legacy of the Macmillan Company of Canada* 149).
7. This book would eventually be published by Clarke, Irwin in 1978, under the title *Old Woman at Play*.

Regent, 12 October 1973

Dear Margaret:

Great to have your letter. Sad news about your accident. You really are becoming accident-prone and are probably right that it is tension. I am convinced that that is my total problem: tension. I am thinking of having my nervous system disconnected one of these days.

Re: the record, it poses some very tough technical problems, not the least of them being size. It is true that we do have a record in *The Pelvic Tilt* and we are not opposed to record attachments as such except for two problems. *The Pelvic Tilt* is a large-size package or carton into which the record fits. This would not happen with the book. In other words, the record would presumably be an awkward size to be attached to the book. However we can look into that. The other problem is, of course, cost and yet you feel so strongly about the matter that we will certainly explore it as thoroughly as we can and as quickly as we can, and I'll get back to you. It would be very good for publicity without any doubt and it may be that we should do it in a promotional sense quite separately from the book. However, leave it with me and we'll get back to you on this.

Re: copyright, there is no problem. We will look after that and also will take it up with Judith Jones as soon as we have enough information to talk sensibly.

Re: Adele Wiseman, I'll certainly get in touch. We would be delighted to have her on our list. God knows I harbor no grudge or ill-feeling about the *Sacrifice*. I was disappointed that it didn't come to us, but was more than able to understand the pressures that were imposed on Adele at that time and so, as I say, I have no ill-feeling about it except regret that we didn't publish the book. We would certainly like to publish her next. I have no objection to a novel in play form and I also like the sound of the book about dolls, so yes, I'll get in touch with her right away and I certainly would accept the conditions that you impose.

I was pleased to have your comments re: Rudy Wiebe's book. Could we use them by the way? They might be helpful because it is not an easy book to sell.

Re: the Writers' Union, I can't tell you how delighted I am. I don't know whether she told you or not, but I had a long talk with Clara about it and found that we both feel the same way about your involvement. I think it has been a good thing for them that you have been the President for a period, but I really think you have already done your part and I really feel for you to stick with it would be a terrible drain and one that you don't need. Truly, Margaret, you have much more important uses for your time, and I feel that you can accomplish much more if you are not officially part of an organization that is not going to be able to avoid difficulty and dissention. I know, too—despite the fact that I still don't have the package I promised you from the Canadian Authors Association—that the purpose, motives, objectives of the Writers' Union are damn well confused and probably not all that purposeful. I know you don't share my views there and will probably convince you that you should change your mind and stand for President again, but I urge you not to. To give you some idea of how I really feel on the subject, I am enclosing a rough draft—and it is a very rough and unpolished first draft—of a letter I put together for fun that I was going to circulate at the next meeting of the Writers' Union.[1] I won't do that, of course, and the letter isn't nearly good enough, but it will make a few points very effectively.

Finally, I am really sorry to hear about your son. If I can be of any help at all, do let me know. I have some good contacts in London but I am not sure that I have any that could help you in this respect.

Cheers!

Jack McClelland

1. No such copy of this letter exists in Laurence's or McClelland's archives.

Hollinger, 17 October 1973

Dear Boss—

You are a clever devil, aren't you? I got your letter yesterday and tried to phone but, of course, couldn't get you. I wanted to convey my admiration for the draft letter and to say that I think it is very funny but I don't think my assessment would be shared by all my fellow tribes folk. Please do not circulate it among too many of my clan or you will find your house and office being picketed. Don't worry—I am not going to change my mind re: running, or rather not running. I do feel guilty and rather badly about it, but I have got to try to survive personally, and with a one-track mind, all I can handle now is this job here. The job, incidentally, gets busier and busier—as well as seeing young writers 9 hrs a week, I've been doing a lot more seminar discussion type of things with Can Lit classes, and have done several readings ... with more readings to come, from *The Diviners*: advance publicity!

Re: record—yeh, I can see problems. Don't worry; I don't think Knopf would buy the idea anyhow. Maybe a limited number for publicity could be issued, I don't know. It was just a thought.

Re: Adele—she has been away in Winnipeg etc., but I think she will be back the end of this week. I'm very glad you're interested.

Re: what I said about Rudy Wiebe's novel—please feel free to use it. Was it phrased well enough?

A friend who recently returned from England tells me that Books Canada[1] is only handling books published in Canada ... i.e. if Can novels are published also in Eng, they don't handle them. Why not? This means none of mine or Mordecai's, etc. Couldn't they get them from the Eng publishers in the same way other bookshops do? Do you happen to know anything, or could you ask Susie[2] when you write her? I understand she's working there.

Must go. Another million letters await. I go west end of week for 3 readings—wish me luck! I'm very nervous, but probably all will be not too terrible.

All the best,
Margaret

1. Books Canada was an independent Ottawa retailer specializing in Canadian titles.
2. Laurence likely refers to Jack McClelland's daughter, Suzanne.

Regent, 25 October 1973

Dear Margaret:

Thanks for your letter. There is no way that I am going to distribute any further copies of that letter. I am pleased, however, that there is no possibility of you changing your mind or being talked into continuing. Re: the record. What are you trying to do to me? We got 19 letters in today from Regina and, if you are going to be giving speeches across the country and urge people to write to me saying the record should be in the book, I'll have to get an assistant for Marge to handle the flood of material.

Adele's manuscript has just been received. I'll be reading it over the weekend.

Re: Books Canada, in their retail store, it is my understanding that they are handling books of all Canadian authors whether published in England or Canada, so unless there has been a change in policy—and I am certain that there hasn't—your books and all the books in the English editions will be in Books Canada retail. They will not, of course, handle them on a wholesale basis (they can't), and I think that is possibly where the misunderstanding arose. In any case, I'll write to Susie and just satisfy myself that there had been no change.

Cheers!
Jack McClelland

Hollinger, 6 November 1973

Dear Boss—

Thanks for your letter. The conference of the Writers' Union of Canada went really well over the weekend. I was there nearly 4 days, as I went in advance to help get things in order. We had 2 extremely intensive days, getting the constitution, electing officers, setting up areas of action. I thought it was really great. Also, there was a very strong sense of solidarity and a kind of tribal feeling—it was good to see everyone again. I'm on the Membership committee, which is okay, but otherwise no office. I feel optimistic about the union—I think it can really do some things.

I was talking to Pierre Berton at lunch one day about another of the horror stories with which writers regale one another. He advised to get in touch with you, as something may be done about the problem. Thing is, about a year or so ago, two of my novels came out in American paperback (can't remember the firm)—*A Jest of God* (naturally, title *Rachel, Rachel*) and *The Fire-Dwellers*. Arranged through Knopf and Cushman, of course, I didn't see proofs, and I don't think Knopf did either. They sent me copies and I remarked on the lurid covers but otherwise didn't pay much attention. I have recently discovered two awful things: (1) in both paperbacks, which were re-set for that edition, there are a whole lot of errors, and, in *The Fire-Dwellers*, the chief error is horrifying—they've left out the long dash which indicated Stacey's thoughts, so the reader has no way of knowing what the character is saying outwardly or thinking inwardly; (2) these Amer editions are being sold all over Can in Canadian bookshops. Now, Jack, two things strike me: (a) both novels are being used in courses in this country, and kids who buy the Amer edition of paperback are getting a mutilated version; (b) Canadian—i.e. your—paperback editions are available, so the cheaper Amer edition is cutting into your market. SURELY THIS IS

NOT RIGHT!!! I am very upset, and wonder what can be done to keep the Amer paperbacks out. Don't you hold the Can rights here? I don't know what the legal position is, but I am alarmed about the whole thing.

Another point—it's none of my damn business, Jack, but is there (pause of about 4 hours whilst ML saw 3 young writers and discussed their work; made many phone calls; went home; had a drink, and now is resuming this letter on another typewriter). Boss, is there any way you can put out some more $$$$$ for advertising and pushing Rudy Wiebe's novel *The Temptations of Big Bear*?[1] I have a terrible and sinking thought that maybe you Upper Canadians[2] feel this novel will chiefly be of interest in the West (i.e. the Prairies). But I do so profoundly feel that it says such meaningful things to all Canadians, and indeed that it reaches beyond geographical boundaries and ought to be published elsewhere in the Eng-reading world. I've seldom see[n] the contrast in concepts between two cultures (in this case Indian and white) handled so well and so convincingly, with such sympathy and understanding o[n] both sides. This really is a remarkable novel, Jack. If it does not get the Gov-Gen for this year, justice will not have been done, and I say that knowing that Bob Kroetsch's *Gone Indian* (good good novel, but not as good as *Studhorse Man*)[3] and Jack Ludwig's *A Woman of Her Age* (also, altho I've read only half of it so far, a splendid job, and I think Jack was right to hold it back and take account of Oct 70, because he's done so in a beautifully specific and individual sense, in the beginning, with Doba's incredible talk with the young Amer radical ... just right in tone and everything; the work is really fine). ... anyway, knowing that these two, amongst some other very good novels have been published in Can this year. But Rudy's novel is something else ... that kind of thing that happens very rarely. Anyway, them's my sentiments.

While we're on the subject of writers like me horning in and giving you their opinions (Boss, forgive me; I mean well!), I heard from Adele about your letter, which seems to me (and, I gather, to her) really good good news. I think she'd be willing to consider editorial comments and suggestions as long as she didn't feel bound by them—in other words, I don't think she minds a few tactful suggestions being made at this point, but would want to feel that as an article of faith, you'd already accepted the book—which, from your letter, I gather you have, and hallelujah! I can't really agree about your comments re: her title, tho. *Hoda* would be a name title, much as *Hagar* (my original title for *The Stone Angel,* if you recall) would have been, and I don't personally feel that in the bookshops this type of title would grab me very much, if I [k]new nothing about the book. *Crackpot* seems to me not only to be related in very essential ways to the novel, but also, on a more superficial level, to be more curiosity-making re: potential readers. It is a title [that] has interesting ambiguities; it would, I think, make me want to find out what the book was all about.

Again, Jack, the above is really none of my goddamn business, but I can't help giving voice. Probably what will happen, ultimately, is that you will either cut me off without a penny or in desperation (when I've quit writing novels) hire me as an amateur editor.

I laughed like hell over the 19 letters from Regina. Honest, Boss, I didn't solicit them! A young high school teacher came up to me and said, "Is there any way a record is going to be made?" And I said, "I dunno." (I guess I said a bit more than that). So she said, "Would it help if all my class wrote to Mr. McClelland?" And in a moment of euphoria and relief that the reading was over, I said, "Sure!"

I can see that a record to go with the book might not be the right size. All of us writers cannot guarantee a book will be manufactured the size of the female pelvis, or with a similar circular shape.[4] But what about putting out a limited number of records to be sold in bookshops along with the novel??? We wouldn't look to making a lot of money on them; just covering costs, etc. Please at least discuss with Diane Woodman.

News from New York seems good. Galleys should be in by beginning Dec. Talked about dust-jacket (among other matters) with Anna Porter today, and she has some doubts about pictorial representation of a character as I have, but we will see. Judith has been so great over editorial matters that I would hate to bother her re: jacket, but Anna's point about the possibility of the book falsely[5] appearing to be a "woman's" book seems to me to be CRUCIAL, and I agree so much, so we'll see.

Best to you all,
Margaret [signed]
Margaret Laurence[6]

1. Rudy Henry Wiebe (1934–) is a Canadian author and professor emeritus in the Department of English at the University of Alberta. Wiebe's novel, *The Temptations of Big Bear*, won the Governor General's Award for fiction in 1973. It is noteworthy that *The Temptations of Big Bear* historicizes and fictionalizes the story of the Cree Chief Big Bear on the Canadian prairies during the years leading up to the Riel Resistance and the eventual hanging of the Métis leader, Louis Riel. In the 1990s, Yvonne Johnson wrote to Wiebe from Kingston Penitentiary to state that she was in awe of how articulately Wiebe spoke of her people, and that Big Bear was her great-great-grandfather. That letter led to the eventual (and controversial) publication of Johnson's autobiography, *Stolen Life*, co-authored with Wiebe.
2. Upper Canada, named in 1791, well before Canada's Confederation, comprised part of what is currently Ontario. Lower Canada was the area that is currently Quebec. Laurence uses the term "Upper Canadians" to refer to those from Ontario, rather than those from the prairies of western Canada.
3. Robert Kroetsch's novel, *The Studhorse Man*, won the Governor General's Award in 1969. *Gone Indian* was published in 1973.
4. A possible reference to the book, *The Pelvic Tilt* (see Laurence's letter dated 7 October 1973).
5. The word "falsely" is inserted in handwriting, over the typed letter.
6. Prior to her next letter to McClelland, Laurence wrote a letter to Hodgeman, dated 27 November 1973. Therein she stated, "I'll be in Toronto on the 14th Dec, and will be staying at Clara Thomas's place for a week. I'll phone when I get there. Could Jack have lunch with me one day? I really want to talk to him about the record and also several other things, including the sale of the absolutely incorrect and mutilated American paperback versions of *The Fire-Dwellers* and *A Jest of God* in this country" (McClelland & Stewart Ltd. Fonds, Box 67, File 21).

Regent, 28 November 1973

Dear Margaret:

I haven't got around to answering your letter before this and I apologize. I had very good reports on the Writers' Union meeting from others as well and I am delighted that it went so well. I am particularly delighted that you didn't get involved in any further heavy duties in connection with it.

I was aware that copies of *Rachel, Rachel* had been sold here and, in fact, I have some feeling that we agreed to this via John Cushman. *The Fire-Dwellers* are certainly in the country illegally.[1] I will talk to John Cushman about it and then see what we can do. It's not an easy matter to handle. We are in the midst of legal action at the moment, which we hope will put an end to the problem, but it is going to take probably at least six months and probably longer to clear it up. It's very difficult to do anything about copyright infringement in Canada at the moment. The government's position, the Department of Justice's position, the RCMP position is very weak. They don't really seem to feel that copyright is important. We are doing what we can, but it's slow. Incidentally, [what] I do hope and I haven't really talked to you about this—is that we are going to back into the mass-market paperback field (as contrasted with the New Canadian Library) and that we will do *A Jest of God* and *The Fire-Dwellers* in mass-market editions in May of next year (with possibly one more of your books) to coincide with publication of *The Diviners*. Nothing final about this yet. We are still looking at costs and looking at the whole proposition, but we do think that this is an undertaking we should make. Incidentally, I have a copy of the Panther edition of *The Fire-Dwellers*. How did you react to the cover on it?

Incidentally, I hope you don't think that I am taking this matter of the American copyright infringement too lightly. I'm not. We will do what we can, but for practical purposes it is a difficult situation.

Thanks for your very good word about Rudy Wiebe's novel. We are going to settle our pre-Christmas promotion within the next few days and I'll bear in mind what you say. I must feel that it is a more significant book than *A Woman of Her Age* in many respects. Whether it will appeal to as many people is another matter. At the moment, though, it seems to be selling very well indeed.

Yes, we are going to publish Adele's book and I am really grateful for your help in this matter. I really liked the book and think it is a fine piece of writing. As to the title, I don't know. I have a letter from Adele explaining its significance. It may be a prejudice of mine, but I still don't like the title *Crackpot*. I've known too many titles of that sort that have ended up on the remainder table. I just don't think it is a good title, even though it is relevant to the subject, but I'll discuss in detail, your views, her views with our people and see if we can't find a solution or maybe, as I say, we'll agree that the aversion to *Crackpot* is my own personal bias. As to your being an amateur, I would love to hire you as a professional editor and, as a matter of fact, once you get settled in Peterborough, I really want to talk to you about this. I have some thought that you should become Chairman of an Editorial Committee or Publications Committee or something of that sort for McClelland and Stewart, which would be an advisor function, but let's not go into that for the moment. We will talk about it when we have time, but the matter has been discussed at length by our Board, and it is something that they are very enthusiastic about if it can be worked out with you. So we are serious.

What do you mean the letters from Regina? Now we are getting them from Quebec. As a matter of fact, one of my daughters reports that, at her school in Lennoxville, they are organizing a whole group of letters that are going to arrive here in the near future. If many more come in, I am arranging for Marge to prepare a form letter, which will say, "Thank you very much for your letter about the record. On receipt of the order, we will take your letter seriously," or something to that effect. In fact, I will make the undertaking that we will have one edition of the book available with the record, but I don't think we will have a record in every copy of the book, because I don't really think it is practical.

By the time this letter gets to you, you will have heard from Marge about Judith Jones' trip, the Pellan party and so on. Even if you don't make the Pellan party, hopefully we will see you in Toronto while she is here.

All the best.
Sincerely,
Jack McClelland

1. *Rachel, Rachel* was the title given to the American edition of *A Jest of God*. McClelland was extremely concerned about American versions of the book being sold in Canadian bookstores. These were sold at a lower price than the Canadian editions, undermining business for McClelland & Stewart and threatening Canadian literary production as a whole—a significant problem at that moment in Canadian literary history.

Hollinger, 30 December 1973

Dear Jack—

Am writing this at Adele's, on an unfamiliar typewriter, so it may read rather oddly. When you reply, please reply to me at Champlain College Trent University, Peterborough, Ont.

I've given a lot of thought to the de Visser[1] book, Jack, and I don't think I can do it. It occurs to me that you might give thought to having a selection from various Can prose and poetry to go with the pics, instead of having one person write the text. I think I could make a lot of suggestions re: selections, but perhaps the problem would be (damn this typewriter) obtaining the rights for various pieces. I don't think I could write the text because I don't easily work to order ... So, with much regret, I have to tell you I would not be the right person for the job. However, if you do decide to have bits from various writers, I'd be glad unofficially to make a few suggestions.

Damn this typewriter triply! This is a very n.b. letter and the typing is the worst I've ever done. Oh, for my own dear typewriter!

NOW, ABOUT THE RECORD, HERE IS ALL THE INFORMATION:

1. On the enclosed sheet you will find the copy [that] will have to go on the record label. I don't imagine you will want a printed sleeve, in order to keep costs down.
2. The fourth song, Pique's song, has now been taped in a very fine and well-recorded version, in Boston, by friends, with Joan Minkoff singing and Peter MacLachlan on guitar. We now have 2 tapes, the one with the first three songs being sung by Ian Cameron (which also includes some versions of the 4th song which are NOT to be used, as the girl who sings these has an English accent), and the tape of the 4th song being properly sung with the right accent (American Midwest, actually, but near enough). A RECORD PRESSING CAN

BE MADE FROM THESE MASTERTAPES. NO RECORDING OF THE SONGS IS NECESSARY. THE RECORD MUST BE FROM THESE TAPES.

3. THE TAPES ARE NOW IN THE POSSESSION OF A YOUNG FRIEND, PETER MACLACHLAN, WHO WILL DELIVER THEM TO YOU. GUARD THESE WITH YOUR LIFE!

Peter has recently set up a music publishing business, but for the purposes of this record, he has agreed to act as Ian Cameron's agent—he is an old friend of Ian's and is also one of my Elm Cottage people, and is totally trustworthy. Ian is in England, so it is good to have Peter acting on his behalf ...

—Interjection—damn this typewriter!!

If you put out the record on these terms, Ian should really get about $200 advance, on sales, for 5,000 copies, but if you are not prepared to put this up, I am. I just want the record to come out. At the same time, should it become a runaway bestseller in the record world (highly unlikely), I must protect both Ian's rights and my own. So I suggest that you hand over all this (this letter, enclosed sheet, and, ultimately, the tapes) to whoever will be handling it at the Old Firm, probably Diane Woodman, and let her get in touch with Peter MacLachlan or with me, and BASH ON WITH THE RECORD. Also, that you let me know whether or not you are prepared to put out some $200 to Ian as advance on sales of records. ... if you aren't, that's not really a problem. At the moment, I'm willing to do quite a lot just to get the record out, but I want to do it professionally, and also to protect Ian's and my rights if by any chance one of these songs catches on.

I will be reporting all this to John Cushman, but I don't think any U.S.A. thing will be a problem, as the copyright obtained in Canada seems to be pretty well world-wide.

4. The timing of the tapes seems to be pretty well okay, but there may be a slight problem with the long first ballad, in which case some of the guitar interludes can be cut out—this is partly why I want Peter

MacLachlan to be in the recording studio when the record is made—he will not be obtrusive, but he DOES know the songs very well and knows which bits can be cut out, time wise, the non-vocal bits, if necessary.

5. PLEASE HAND OVER THIS MATERIAL TO DIANE WOODMAN OR WHOEVER WILL BE DEALING WITH THE RECORD. I WILL BE IN TOUCH BY PHONE AND ARRANGE FOR PETER TO DELIVER TAPES TO YOU.
6. The galleys were completed by me, as no doubt you know re: proof-reading them, and sent back to Ye Olde Firm, and Marge was going to ship them to N.Y. Let us pray they get there, with the uncertain mails we now have.

Boss, please excuse this awful typing—I can't use Adele's typewriter, which is attuned to her, nor Dmitry's which is attuned to him, so am working on Dmitry's ancient Remington, which is an antique. They seem to have 3 typewriters in this beloved house, and oh hell, none of them work by me!

All the best, and will phone next week,
Margaret [signed]
Margaret Laurence

1. John de Visser (1930–) is a Canadian photographer. He has been the sole photographic author of over fifty books and has won many awards for his work. He was born in the Netherlands and moved to Canada in 1952. In the foreword to de Visser's book, *This Rock Within the Sea*, published by McClelland & Stewart in 1976, Farley Mowat writes, "When John de Visser and I resolved on the making of this book, we had in mind a mutual endeavour in which one art would complement the other in tenderly portraying the lineaments of a world we loved."

Trent University, 3 January 1974

Dear Margaret:

Thanks for your letter. Quite apart from the typewriter, I think you must have been quite smashed when you wrote it. It's a strange letter, but I guess everything comes through intact and no problems.

John Newlove[1] will be the one here who is responsible for handling the record, and I will turn it over to him for the handling of the detail. As far as the advance is concerned, I don't really think we want to pay $200.00 to Ian. God knows I don't want to be niggardly about it. Two hundred dollars is not very much money. The problem here is that at the rate of 4c a record, we would have to sell 5,000 copies to earn back the $200.00. The one thing we don't like to have around here is unearned advances. It's too goddamn messy for our Accounting Department and, honestly, Margaret, although I'm really pleased to put out the record and do what we can with it, I don't think there is a peanut's chance in hell of our selling 5,000 copies of it. I don't know anything about selling records to be truthful. If we had distribution, proper distribution, through record shops, we might sell a helluva lot of copies, but we don't have that sort of distribution. Through bookstores it would seem to me that 5,000 copies would be a helluva lot of records. We will probably give away 500 or perhaps 1,000 but, even at that, I don't expect us to sell very many records. It's a promotion stunt. ...

We will have a contract drawn up. If you really want Ian Cameron to get a certain $200.00, I think you should pay it to him and we'll pay the royalties to you instead, which would make the whole agreement much simpler and then we can split the royalties between you two after 5,000 copies are sold.[2]

I'm really sorry about the de Visser project, but I understand how you feel about it. I don't know what we will do. I would like to avoid an anthology. As I said to you at the time, I thought an essay could be well laced with poetry, but I really think we need an essay or a text, and I even have the feeling that confining it to poetry or even a mixture of poetry and prose would confine the market and we really want to get a big market for this book. I presume you won't reconsider, so we will give it some further thought on this end.

Cheers!
Jack

1. John Newlove (1938–2003) was senior editor at McClelland & Stewart from 1970 to 1974. Originally from Saskatchewan, Newlove was also a poet who became known for his poems about the prairies and the Canadian west. He won the Governor General's Award for his collection of poetry, *Lies*, published in 1972.
2. For some time, Laurence had been trying to convince McClelland to sell an album of songs, with lyrics by Laurence and music by Ian Cameron, to accompany *The Diviners*. In a letter Laurence wrote to McClelland & Stewart editor Anna Porter on 12 November 1973, Laurence asked, "What is your opinion about simply putting out a rather limited number of 45-records to sell in bookshops along with *The Diviners*? I think myself this would be a great publicity thing, and would also be good for some readers who might want to hear the songs. No doubt you have talked about this with the Boss. If you can do anything to persuade that stubborn Upper-Canadian mind of his that a record pertaining to the West would be relevant to all Canadians, please do so. (It's okay—you can show him this letter!) I have not yet ceased to do battle in this area—as I have warned him. I hope he's enjoying this fight as much as I am" (McClelland & Stewart Ltd. Fonds, Box 67, File 21).

SONGS FROM THE DIVINERS
QCS 1091
Side 2
1. LAZARUS
McClelland and Stewart Limited,
in association with Heorte Music, presents
The Diviners
songs from the novel by Margaret Laurence
These are the songs in the life of Morag Gunn–the songs sung by her Métis lover and their child, an accompaniment to Morag's search for a birthright.
Morag Gunn is the main character in The Diviners, a major new Canadian novel by Margaret Laurence, a novel which weaves together the strands of history and the personal dilemma of a person seeking her roots. Her search, and the songs specially written for The Diviners, rove back through the heritage of the vast Canadian prairies.
Side One
Ballad of Jules Tonnerre (3:40)
Song for Piquette (2:55)
vocals, Ian Cameron;
guitars, Ian Cameron, Bob Berry
Side Two
Lazarus (5:45)
vocal, Ian Cameron;
guitars, Ian Cameron, Bob Berry
Pique's Song (2:20)
vocal, Joan Minkoff;
guitar, Peter MacLachlan
Lyrics © Copyright 1973 Margaret Laurence
Music © Copyright 1973 Ian Cameron;
Heorte Music; C.A.P.A.C.
Recording remastered and produced by
Quality Records

The "album" of four songs from The Diviners*, produced to promote the book's release in 1974.*

[Image courtesy of John H. Meier, Jr. collection. www.ggawards.ca]

Trent University, 3 January 1974

Dear Margaret:

Just a note to let you know that the Book-of-the-Month Club[1] will use *The Diviners* as a full selection in Canada. The conditions you want will be applied (i.e. they will use our edition, printed in Canada, and we'll have first option on any remainders they may have). They haven't made a decision as yet about the U.S.A., but there is a real possibility that it will be an alternate selection. You will hear about that eventually from Knopf because, as I say, they have not as yet made a decision.

It's not a bad New Year's present in a sense, because they will pay an advance of $7000.00 for the use of the book. Hope you had a good New Year.

All the best.
Sincerely,
Jack

1. At its height of popularity in the 1960s and 1970s, the Book-of-the-Month Club was a mail order book club that sent subscribed and paid members a new book each month.

Hollinger, 4 January 1974

Dear Boss—

Well, my luck in typewriters is improving, but there is still some room for improvement—this fancy machine, which carries all kinds of unusual signs such as $ ... and so on, HAS NO QUESTION MARK! This will be a challenge to my style in writing letters—how can you phrase a question without a question mark (obviously not *this* way). Well, at least it is legible.

I do think (at the moment, anyway!) that you are one of the most splendid persons around these days. Boss, I am certain you are doing the right thing in putting out that record—I talked with John Newlove on the phone today, and he says you are going to do a record sleeve—an excellent idea and I#m (the apostrophe on this machine is not where I expect it to be) really delighted. In fact, I#m (that means I'm) overjoyed about the whole thing.

Could you read the bezaz,[1] which is to go on the record, and the record sleeve[2] (ques mark). It is Heorte Music—old Anglo Saxon word meaning Heart, according to Peter, and I#ll take his word on that, as I wouldn't know. (Hurrah, I#m ... oops, I was about to say I'm mastering that damn apostrophe!) ...

I discussed the question of a contract briefly with John. He said he would be drawing one up. I asked him to suggest to you that it would be nice if you could see your way clear to giving me 2 cents per record AFTER 5,000 copies and leaving Cameron with the 4 cents per—not much is likely to be made, but I#d be sorry and would feel mean to ask him to cut *his* royalties in half, should the thing sell more than 5,000 copies. I would also feel damn mad if by any weird chance it sold a zillion copies, if I didn#t make a cent on it. Anyway, give it thought, please.

Also, I would like to buy 100 copies for myself, to give away etc., preferably paying the rate which you#ll be selling them to bookshops, if you would agree to that. But anyway, I'd like 100 reserved for me.

All is well here. Haven't begun term yet, but am flying around getting my program set up, phone installed, and other things, plus making complex arrangements re: the Lakefield house and getting a bank account transferred to village etc. etc. etc. I have about two hundred letters, which have been marked "Urgent" for 3 months. If I survive the term and the publication of the novel, I plan to move into the house and for one whole year do NOTHING. I can see it all now, can't you (ques mark).

All the best, and thanks for being so *intelligent* about the record,

Margaret [signed]

... P.S. nearly forgot the most n.b. thing—I phoned Judith Jones yesterday, and she had just that moment received the second instalment of the galleys! Thank God they got there okay. I was very anxious, owing to the chaotic state of the mail today. We also talked about the dust-jacket—she does agree that we must at all costs avoid the women#s mag look, and says they will do something based on your art dept#s use of the lettering, and possibly get some good colours. She says "It will probably stand out from the flossy commercial jobs" ... my feelings exactly, and I would think, yours. She's not going to send me page proofs, as neither of us think this will be necessary—I went over those damn galleys with a fine-tooth comb. Also, time is of the essence.

So now I am beginning to feel impatient to see the novel in print. Well, three months or a little more, Godwilling. ...

Incidentally, I'm reviewing Ludwig's *A Woman of Her Age* (did I mention) for *Dalhousie Review*. I think it is a splendid book.

Best,

M

P.S. 2. have just worked out a formula in which one can ask a question without using a question mark:

Instead of saying, "How are things?"[3]

You simply say: "I am wondering if you might let me know how things are with you."

The Henry James style, possibly.

1. Laurence seems to spell the word "pizazz" phonetically here.
2. The words "and the record sleeve" are handwritten in red.
3. The question mark is inserted in red pen.

•———

Hollinger, 7 January 1974

Dear Jack—

Thanks for your two letters of January 3rd. What terrific news about the Book-of-the-Month Club. Also, I am extremely glad that you have managed to get all the conditions we wanted. I had no idea that they pay such a sizable amount—wow! What happens re: the timing of all this, I wonder. (No question mark on this machine, as I mentioned in my last letter.) I mean, will they wait a set number of months after your first edition comes out (query). I assume this will have to be the case. Anyway, I'm delighted about the news.

Re: record—no problem. I think the best thing will be for John Newlove to draw up a contract assigning the royalties to me, and half and half to myself and Ian after 5,000 copies. I will then advance the $200 to Ian. I thought it was likely that you would feel this way, and it is quite all right. Anyway, it will be easier to have them come to me. If it were only myself involved, I would not worry about anything like royalties on the record, but I feel I must be fair to Ian. The contract can be a very simple one, I think.

I'm really sorry about the de Visser book, too. It was just that when I saw the pictures, I realized that the text would have to be awfully damn good, and to write that sort of thing to order would, I believe, not be possible for me.

I'm settling in okay here—very nice apartment with office attached. Owing to the design of the buildings (which are, of course, very beautiful), the wind howls like a banshee outside my office door, giving me some slight sense of being at the North Pole, but apart from that, all is well.

All the best,
Margaret [signed]
Margaret Laurence

Trent University, 18 January 1974

Dear Margaret:

I'm enclosing with this letter a copy of the new jacket from Knopf. I don't know whether you have seen it or not. Personally, I think it is absolutely great. I think it's strong, attractive and just what is needed and that opinion is shared by our marketing people.

There is a problem, however. I am enclosing with it a copy of Margaret Atwood's *Surfacing* jacket. There is a marked similarity. This is purely accident, as you know, because your jacket was designed in the U.S. However, in Canada, they are not going to be aware of that particularly and they are going to be aware of the similarity perhaps. I must say I like the Knopf jacket much better than our Atwood jacket and it was a pretty successful jacket. The question is will the similarity be of any embarrassment to you. If it doesn't embarrass you, it certainly won't embarrass us.[1]

All the best.
Sincerely,
Jack

1. A small typewritten note from Hodgeman is attached to this letter. It reads, "Margaret: We have just learned that you too are delighted with the Knopf jacket, so that's what we will use. I am not enclosing either jacket, since Anna [Porter] tells me that you are aware of the similarity between your jacket and the Atwood one. If you have any concerns at all, do give Jack a call."

Trent University, 24 January 1974

Dear Margaret:

Just a note to acknowledge your two letters and tell you everything is under control as far as the record is concerned. John is looking after all the detail. We are going to produce a very handsome job, I think. Your friend, Peter, wants to do the record company distribution, and this is okay with us. It will also enlarge the first printing (or whatever you call it in the record field), which will keep the unit cost in line, and I have noted that you want 100 copies personally. John will look after this in due course.

I have already written about the jacket. I am really pleased with the Knopf jacket. I think it is a very good one indeed.

I like your idea about wanting to go into hibernation. What a hope. You can dream about it, but that's as close as you will get as far as I can see with the promotion we hope to generate with the new book.

Love and kisses,
Jack

P.S. For the record, in case you haven't seen it (and, if you haven't, don't admit that you got it from me), I enclose a copy of the Atwood piece for *Maclean's*.[1]

1. In this article, Atwood discusses her interview with Laurence, and addresses Laurence as a person and as a writer. She speaks about Laurence's connection with the Winnipeg Old Left, and feminism, or, as it was then called, "women's liberation." When Atwood asks Laurence how she feels about the fact that her works are said to represent women's liberation, Laurence says she did not realize how widespread such feelings were until she began writing and witnessing the reactions to her work. Atwood also discusses Laurence's new book, *The Diviners*, praising it for its "worm's eye view" of the small prairie town. In a letter dated 28 January 1974, Jack McClelland admits to

Atwood, "I've just finished reading your piece on Margaret Laurence for *Maclean's*. It's a fine piece of writing. As an old friend of Margaret's, I'm really pleased to be able to tell you that I think you have captured her on paper much more successfully than anyone has ever managed before. It's a really outstanding piece. Hope all goes well with you" (Margaret Laurence Fonds, Clara Thomas Archives and Special Collections, 1980-001/008).

Hollinger, 24 March 1974

Dear Jack—

A brief note. I've been thinking lately of an idea for the NCL, namely a selection of Ernest Buckler's stories. These are all unavailable right now, and I think some of them should be in print. I was discussing this with Dr. Rob Chambers, of the English Dept. here, who has just finished a book on Buckler[1] and Ross.[2] He says he managed to discover all the stories, and he will get them zeroxed [*sic*] for me during the summer. There are about 47, which obviously would not be possible, but Bob says they are of uneven quality, and about 12 are first-rate, which would be about the right number for a selection in the NCL. If Malcolm Ross is enthusiastic, and, if you are, and if Buckler agrees, I'd be willing with Bob, to do a selection, and he would be willing to write an Intro. Let me know what you think, when you have time. We can discuss this, perhaps, when I'm in Toronto in May.

All the best,
Margaret

P.S. I've written to Malcolm Ross about this.

P.S. Please *don't* send a copy of this letter to Buckler. (You probably wouldn't anyway.) If M. Ross and yourself agree, I think Buckler should be approached personally by you, Malcolm and perhaps myself.

1. Ernest Buckler (1908–1984) was a novelist and short story writer. McClelland & Stewart Ltd. published *The Rebellion of Young David and Other Stories*, a series of short stories that appeared in periodicals between 1941 and 1959, in 1975. He published his first novel, *The Mountain and the Valley*, in 1952 with Henry Holt. This novel treats a young boy's attachment to Nova Scotia and the means by which his creativity, as a result, is curtailed.

2. Malcolm Ross (1911–2002) was a pre-eminent Canadian literary critic and professor of English at Queen's University until 1962. He then served as dean of arts at the University of Toronto from 1962 to 1968. From 1968 to 1982, he was a professor at Dalhousie University. He founded and served as the general editor for the New Canadian Library imprint through McClelland & Stewart.

Trent University, 28 March 1974

Dear Margaret:

Thanks for your note about Ernest Buckler. It's an interesting idea and it may, in fact, be the solution to a problem that we are struggling with at the moment. We have a Buckler manuscript of articles and short stories that we are committed to publish. This commitment resulted from a misunderstanding. The problem with the material is that it just isn't very good. We sought an opinion from Claude Bissell,[1] who is a great Buckler supporter and, unfortunately, he is such a Buckler supporter that he failed to recognize our problem.

It seems to me that we might be able to substitute one for the other. In other words, do a book of short stories if there are 12 really good ones. Do it originally as a hardbound and then eventually put it in the New Canadian Library. That's a reaction off the top of my head. In any case, I like the idea. I know that Malcolm Ross will like the idea, so by all means proceed and I'll get back to you about our problem and whether we can solve it in this way.

All the best.
Sincerely,
Jack

1. Claude Bissell (1916–2000), an educator and author, was the eighth president of the University of Toronto from 1958 to 1971. His books include *The Strength of the University*, *Halfway up Parnassus*, *The Humanities in the University*, and a two-volume biography of *Vincent Massey: A Brief Biography: Vincent Massey, 1887–1967* and *The Imperial Canadian: Vincent Massey in Office* ("Claude Bissell").

Regent, 27 May 1974

Dear Margaret:

I'm sorry that I didn't get to see you again before you went back to Lakefield. This is just a note to thank you for bearing up with the promotion nonsense[1] and doing such an extremely good job. From all the reports I have had, everything worked with great effectiveness. The book is off to an extremely good start. It is selling well everywhere, getting a lot of attention, and I think will achieve the success that it deserves.

So, I mean, thanks sincerely. I know that you hate that whole business of promotion, but it does help and it has helped a great deal in this case. I'll see you at the CR[I]A[2] Convention. I really think it is good of you to come in for that promotion particularly. I think it will be worthwhile. See you then if not before.

All the best.
Sincerely,
Jack

1. McClelland here refers to promotional events for *The Diviners*. These events were important to him and for the firm, but Laurence did not enjoy attending them.
2. McClelland likely refers to CRIA, the Canadian Recording Industry Association. It was important for Laurence to attend, McClelland implies, to promote the record that accompanied some of the copies of *The Diviners*.

Hollinger, 17 August 1974

Dear Jack—

I'm wondering if anything has happened re: Bantam's offer, and whether they have accepted our terms of 2 years exclusive rights plus another 3 years to sell their edition in Canada? I would think these terms are pretty reasonable, as surely a mass-paperback market would tend to concentrate on quite a lot of sales over a relatively short period of time, and then to replace titles fairly quickly. Anyway, I'll be anxious to know.

Also, what has happened re: Book-of-the-Month Club? Do you happen to know when they plan to offer *The Diviners* in Canada, and also, what is usual re: a contract and an advance? I was told they'd pay $7,000 advance, but haven't heard any more about this. I'll be writing to John Cushman re: this, but thought you might know something.[1]

My quiet summer has been a three-ring circus, but pretty good. I still have a billion letters to answer, which I feel slightly defeated about from time to time. Otherwise, all is okay.

Best,
Margaret

1. Following up on Laurence's query, Hodgeman wrote to "Dave" on 19 August 1974 and stated, "Could you let me know what is happening on both the Bantam deal and the Book-of-the-Month Club as per Margaret's letter attached. JGM has written to her and I have to append a note. Thanks." On the bottom of the letter, McClelland wrote the following: "Bantam is still reconsidering our last set of terms: 5 years only, 2 inclusive, last 3 our option for an NCL: $12000 advance against 8%; publication with [blurred] in U.S; .75 differentiated between Bantam list price and N.C.L." He added, "We have just received their advance of $7000. Author's portion is going out" (Margaret Laurence Fonds, Clara Thomas Archives and Special Collections, 1980-001/008).

Regent, 19 August 1974

Dear Margaret:

Thanks for your letter. The Bantam situation is not finally settled. They countered with a proposal for seven years plus a dollar difference between their edition and the New Canadian Library edition. I felt, frankly, that they were asking too much and said "no." My understanding is that they are still actively interested and the matter will probably be resolved favourably, but it is not yet settled.

As I dictate this letter away from the office, I don't have the answer re: the Book-of-the-Month Club. I'll ask Marge to append the information as soon as she can.

Cheers!
Jack

No firm decision yet re: Bantam. Advance received from Book-of-the-Month Club and your share is being sent to you right away.[1]

1. This postscript was written by Marge Hodgeman.

Hollinger, 24 August 1974

Dear Jack—

Thanks for your letter of August 19th. Marge added a note saying that BOMC[1] advance had been received and my share was being sent to me—good news! As far as Bantam is concerned, I'm not really surprised that they countered with their own proposal, but I do agree that their terms aren't really very good. If they had a seven-year period in which to sell their edition, it would virtually kill the NCL edition, if their price was a dollar less. I still think your suggestion—that they should have 2 years exclusive rights in paperback and a further three years non-exclusive—is the best arrangement. But I do think that it is likely they will be unwilling to agree for the sum of $10,000. Maybe you should suggest $8,000. Anyway, I leave it totally up to you to make the best deal you can, which I know you will do. It seems to me that, in this case, my interests and those of M&S are very closely related—i.e. to get as good a price from Bantam as possible, while still leaving the possibility for the book to come out in the NCL and to *sell* in that edition.

I have also received a copy of your letter of August 21st to Clara Thomas.[2] I had a long conversation with Clara on the phone yesterday, and explained to her all about which editions come out when, and all these things will be corrected. You're absolutely right, of course, about the fact that M&S were my first publishers, and also that you (you personally, actually) had a lot to do with Knopf accepting those three books, which they published simultaneously. I'm sure all this will be corrected in the text of Clara's book and also in the bibliography (which I have to admit I didn't actually read with care, as I was concentrating on the text, which I felt was excellent). I think that part of the problem re: *This Side Jordan* and *The Tomorrow-Tamer*, in the hardcover editions (both of which you bought from Macmillan, if you recall, with your imprint, of course) has been that apparently the M&S editions aren't much in evidence any more, whereas there seem to be quite a few of the Macmillan ones still around—probably because Macmillan had a lot left over, which found their way to this country one way or another; I just don't know. Anyway, I think all this is now straightened out, and the bibliography will be correct. I'm really pleased that you will be doing Clara's book first of all in a hardcover edition.

Hope the summer has been good for you. I'm at my shack at the moment, and will be here most of September and October, I hope, although with weekly trips back to Lakefield. Should you have to phone for any reason, if I'm not at Lakefield, I'll be here. I think you've got both phone numbers.

All the best,
Margaret

1. BOMC stands for the Book-of-the-Month Club.
2. In this letter, McClelland praises Thomas's manuscript, *The Manawaka World of Margaret Laurence*, which McClelland & Stewart would publish. It was the first published study of Laurence's writing. He extended his congratulations and observed, "We will publish it with great pride." Of significance is McClelland's point about Thomas's recounting of Laurence's history of publishing her novels. He adds, "A reference on page 46 on page 57 and in the bibliography seem to give the impression that Macmillan's in London were Margaret's original publishers. It is my recollection that this is not so. I don't really care all that much about a credit being given to McClelland & Stewart, but as a Canadian publisher I am aware of the fact that in the history of Canadian writing, a great many of our fine writers have had their first start either in the U.K. or in the U.S.A. This brings no great credit to indigenous Canadian publishing, although in the majority of cases it is understandable how this happens." Responding to the letter on 31 August 1974, Thomas stated she would make the change and expressed her gratitude to McClelland & Stewart for publishing her book (McClelland & Stewart Ltd. Fonds, Box 67, File 22).

Regent, 21 September 1974

Dear Margaret:

I am sorry I haven't replied to your letter before this. I've just got sadly behind in all my correspondence. I think you have probably heard from other sources here that it is our understanding that Bantam are going to confirm a slightly modified deal—I think it is for five years. If you haven't heard anything official, then official record will be forthcoming shortly. I think we are having dinner with one of the Bantam editors next week.

Things are all sorted out re: Clara's book. It is difficult and complex, I think, but worth having the total record straight.

You may be relieved to know that my grand author tour is off. At least for the present. It is just too bloody costly. I am still determined to do it, but obviously it won't be in the early spring of next year.

Nothing new. I'm having a great time up at the cottage at the moment getting caught up on my backlog. The weather is great. For every hour I spend dictating, I spend about an hour out in the boat or on the golf course, so I am really enjoying it.

All the best.
Sincerely,
Jack

Hollinger, 3 October 1974

Dear Jack—

Thanks for your recent letter. I'm sorry to keep deluging you with letters—no need to reply to this one. I just wanted to say that I've just finished reading Bob Chambers' selection of Ernest Buckler's stories, and I think it's a fine selection and collection. I'd never read any of Buckler's stories before, and was fascinated by them—the ways in which one can see, in a few of them, the beginnings of themes of *The Mountain and the Valley, The Cruelest Month,* etc. Also, the way he has of catching the sound of human speech—the local idiom, without ever overdoing it. I like the way Bob has arranged the stories, thematically—I think that works well.

I wonder if you have any idea when the book might be published? In confidence, Jack, I'm kind of worried about Buckler. I've been corresponding with him recently, and I think he is not a well man—not only pretty depressed, but physically ill. It would be wonderful if the book could come out early next year ... it might cheer him up somewhat.

Just thought I'd like to give you my response to the collection.

All the best,
Margaret[1]

1. Hodgeman responded on 9 October 1974 to this letter as follows: "Thank you for your letter of October 3rd to Jack. It has reached the office during his absence from the country on a trip to Rome, the Frankfurt Book Fair and Iran. It will be passed to him on his return and I know he will be delighted to have your comments on the Buckler selection. Your daughter is a delight" (McClelland & Stewart Ltd. Fonds, Box 67, File 22).

Regent, 4 November 1974

Dear Margaret:

I am sorry that I have been away from the office for so long—it seems like months—that I am only now able to respond to your letter re: Buckler and the Bob Chambers selection. I'm delighted that you are pleased with it. We think it is excellent and Buckler himself reacted very favourably. The book will be published in the spring and we are rushing it through to publication as quickly as we can.

You are quite right about Buckler. He is not well. He is in good spirits when you see him, but he has had some fairly serious stomach operations and he persists in drinking. I haven't any doubt that he is going to kill himself, but I don't think there is any solution to the problem. I don't think anybody can do anything about it. I think it is the way he has to go. He is a thoroughly charming man. I enjoy him very much and I wish I knew of a way to help him, but I just don't think there is one.

Hope we will see you soon. All the best,

Sincerely,
Jack McClelland

Regent, 20 November 1974

Dear Margaret:

Thanks for your letter. I don't really know what has been happening about the money. We seem to get bound up in so much red tape at this end in the subject area that I hate to even think about it.

I can, of course, be more helpful than that. Marge has investigated on my behalf and the report seems to indicate the following: First, the Book-of-the-Month Club money is here. It should have been sent to you long before this. It will be sent this week. Second, the Bantam money has not yet been received. Apparently, the Bantam contract was sent to you and John Cushman for approval. It has been mailed back but has not yet been received. Bantam seems to feel that we are stalling and we are not. We will get it to them as soon as possible and, as soon as they get the contract, I presume some money will be forthcoming. So it should all be settled before the end of the year.

That's good news about England. Hope the book will do very well there. Meanwhile, as you have seen from *The* [*Toronto*] *Star*—if you do see *The Star*—it continues on the bestseller list here.[1] It will probably be pushed aside before Christmas, because so many new books are coming out from almost every conceivable source, but it has held up very well. If you had started on a new book, you might keep us in business a little while longer. I don't really mean that, dear. Take a holiday. At least try to take a holiday. I hope we will see you very soon.

All the best.
Sincerely,
Jack

1. *The Toronto Star's* bestseller list indicates *The Diviners* held the fifth-place position for the period 16–30 November 1974.

Hollinger, 1 February 1975

Dear Jack:

This may seem like an odd suggestion, but here goes. I've been judging a high school short story contest, which the Canada Permanent Trust sponsors every year. They print in a small booklet the First prize winners from each province, but it seems to me that many of the Second and Third prize winners this year should be published as well. If you could get Canada Council funding, I wonder if you'd be at all interested in putting out a collection of these stories in paperback? Something like Al Purdy is doing with *Storm Warning II*,[1] in poetry. I'm not especially interested in advertising a Trust Co., but a line of acknowledgment would probably suffice. I'd like to see some of these kids get a wider audience than the Permanent's booklet, and also, as I say, only the Firsts are printed in the booklet. If you're at all interested, could you drop me a line?

All the best,
Margaret Laurence

P.S. Joyce Marshall did the initial sifting[2]—there were 1800 entries!—and I judged from among 5 stories for each province. Joyce, of course, also did the final judging of the French stories, of which there are 2 winners. The Top Prize is going to a 13-year-old Newfoundland girl, who is a natural.

1. *Storm Warning 2: The New Canadian Poets*, a book edited by Al Purdy, was a companion piece to *Storm Warning: The New Canadian Poets*, both published by McClelland & Stewart.
2. Joyce Marshall (1913–2005) was a Canadian translator and writer who produced two novels, *Presently Tomorrow* and *Lovers and Strangers*, and a short story collection, *A Private Place*.

Regent, 6 February 1975

Dear Margaret:

Yes, in many ways I think it is an odd suggestion. I haven't any doubt there would be some real interest in such a book—at least from parents, relatives and friends—but it is sort of beyond our practical range of interest in the sense that it is neither commercial nor literary in the proper sense of the word. I have no doubt that some of the stories are good, but such a book would be more of a curiosity than a serious contribution to Canadian letters.

The problem with the Canada Council idea, Margaret, is that they no longer fund projects. They give the established publishers what they call block grants, and this money has to be spread over the literary works in our regular publishing program like *Storm Warning*, for example. I don't really think I would want to cut off a chunk of that money to devote to this project.

A better idea, it seems to me, rather than involve the Canada Council would be to suggest to Canada Permanent[1] that they fund such a book. It wouldn't cost them a helluva lot of money. They would get credit for it and, if it were done on that basis, we would be prepared to do it. I think it could be done easily for $6–$7,000 and I think you are in a good position to take it up with them. Why don't you see what they say?

Cheers!
Jack McClelland

1. Canada Permanent was a bank that merged with Canada Trust in 1989.

Hollinger, 6 February 1975

Dear Jack—

Have you not ever heard of the tactic of the United Front? All the newly formed Book and Periodical Development Council[1] wants to do, as I understand it, is to present such a united front to the government, not for the kind of band-aid treatment announced in Hugh Faulkner's recent speech,[2] but to try to get legislation which will, among other things, revise and clarify our Copyright Act, so that American editions of Canadian books (which are available here in Canadian editions) may not be imported into this country. I thought that was what your recent case against Coles[3] was all about. What the hell am *I* doing, writing letters to *The Globe and Mail* re: the copyright act and greatly in support of *you*, when you turn around and refuse (the only one!) to join such a council???? I simply do not understand your point of view at all, and, believe me, this is the last time I write a letter to a newspaper saying anything at all in support of you. I am very disappointed in you, to say the absolute least.

Margaret

See my letter in *The Globe* today,[4] plus Bill French's column.[5]

P.S. Have you recently been inside Melzack's bookshop in the National Arts Centre, Ottawa?[6] They have a few Can paperbacks and virtually NO Canadian hardcovers.

1. The Book and Periodical Development Council was formed in 1975 to "provide a venue for members to discuss industry issues, address mutual concerns and undertake projects for the benefit of Canadian writing and publishing" ("About the BPC").

2. James Hugh Faulkner was appointed to the cabinet of Prime Minister Pierre Trudeau as secretary of state following the 1972 election. He increased Canada Council money distributed to publishers from $4 million to $5.5 million annually. Canadian publishers were incensed by what they considered an insufficient surplus because they needed the resources to compete with American publishing companies that produced editions of books that were considerably less expensive (*Montreal Gazette*, 10 February 1975, Association of Canadian Publishers Fonds).
3. In January 1975, McClelland "staged a protest against Coles Bookstores' practice of selling remaindered U.S. editions of Canadian books" (King, *Jack* 277). Coles was a bookstore that opened in 1940 by Carl and Jack Cole on Bloor Street in Toronto. By the mid-1980s, the chain, Coles the Book People!, was purchased by K-Mart and became Waldenbooks. In November 1995, the latter merged with W.H. Smith and opened Canada's first two Chapters stores.
4. Laurence's letter, published in the *Globe and Mail* (7 Feb. 1975), is titled "Novelist Wants Copyright Changed Now to Combat US Books." In the letter, Laurence expresses her concern that Canadian bookstores were importing and selling American editions of her and other authors' books at cheaper prices. She wrote, "My contract with my Canadian publisher states that McClelland & Stewart have sole distribution rights of the paperback editions in this country. But McClelland & Stewart cannot bring court cases against every bookshop which buys the American paperback edition from American jobbers. ... Those sections of our Copyright Act which deal with the importation of books should be revised *now*. American editions of Canadian books, in cases where the Canadian edition is available here, should not be allowed into this country" (7).
5. William French (1926–2012) was a highly influential literary editor and book reviewer at the *Globe and Mail* for over forty-two years. He received two National Newspaper Awards for his columns about censorship. On 24 November 1978, he published an article titled "Heated response to problem of censorship in high schools" about the problem of censorship vis-à-vis *The Diviners*.
6. Louis Melzack (1914–2002) and his wife, Rose, were the founders of Classics Books, a bookshop that began in 1930 in Montreal and expanded to over one hundred stores across Canada. In 1985, the business was sold to the Canadian branch of the British bookstore W.H. Smith. In 1995, Coles and W.H. Smith joined to become Chapters Inc. In 2001, Chapters and Indigo merged to become Canada's largest bookstore chain, Indigo Books and Music Inc. James King characterizes Louis Melzack as "the only major retailer who shared Jack's enthusiasms and vision" (*Jack* 170) and as instrumental to introducing Jack McClelland to Leo Kolber, who "managed the Bronfman-owned Cemp Investments." King adds that Melzack "facilitated ... a whole new direction in the relationship between M&S and the House of Seagram" (166).

Hollinger, 7 February 1975

Dear Jack—

I may have been a little hasty when I wrote to you yesterday, owing to my rage, anger, and fury. I still think you are *wrong* about the new Council. But I have to admit that my 16-years' feelings of loyalty to you and the Old Firm were again brought to the surface this morning when I read your letter in *The Globe*, which I thought was excellent.[1]

Best,
Margaret

1. The letter Jack McClelland wrote and to which Laurence refers was published in the *Globe and Mail* on 7 February 1975. Titled "Book Invasion," the letter explains that the Canadian government, led by Prime Minister Pierre Trudeau, needed to revise the Copyright Act, so that Canadian authors and their works would be protected from the infiltration of cheap American editions of their works. McClelland argued, "We are not U.S. publishers. Our function, as we see it, is to maximize our authors' income in a small market."

Regent, 11 February 1975

Dear Margaret:

Yes, I have heard about the tactic of the United Front. I have also heard about committees on committees. For a long time now, Margaret, I have remained silent and observed the idiotic nonsense that has been going on in the book industry in this country. I have taken that position, largely because I have neither the time nor the energy to argue personally with all the instant experts who have emerged. I have now reached the point where I am going to make one effort to try and make people see reason. If this puts me out of step with everybody else, then so be it. It won't be the first time.

If I thought for a minute that the formation of the proposed Book and Periodical Development Council would change anything for the better, I would be in favour of it. As it happens, I don't believe it can or will accomplish anything useful. Because I believe that, I have to conclude that it could, in fact, be a backward step because it will, in fact, give the government continuing excuse for doing nothing.

Do you really think that anything can be accomplished by forming a council of official representatives of pressure groups with widely varying positions and widely varying objectives? If it is motherhood recommendations you are looking for, you will get them. What else can they possibly agree? Each representative is bound to go back to his association or chaos will result. So what is the net result? In my view, nothing that is very useful to the book industry.

Let's start with the IPA for God's sake.[1] It really doesn't know what it stands for. Its official recommendation to Faulkner before the Peterborough Conference was for the most part garbage. I enclose a copy of a letter that I sent to Paul Audley after he asked me to review their proposal.[2] Who needs this sort of thing? Do you seriously think anything useful will emerge if Paul were to sit down at a meeting with the Book Publishers' Council? Well, you may think so. I don't. I happen to believe the whole thing is a bad idea and I believe that sincerely.

I was rather pleased by Melzack's reaction to the Council. Melzack is far from being the perfect bookseller. I am mad at him about half the time, but, historically speaking, I would say he has done these things: (1) He has opened a chain of fairly good bookstores across the country, (2) he has always paid his bills promptly, which helps the book industry as a whole, (3) he has done a fair to good job of supporting Canadian books. All these things are important. I know some individual stores do a much more effective job of supporting Canadian books and I applaud them, but honest to God, Margaret, we do need some bookstores in this country that do a moderately good job and that do pay their bills. One of the reasons we can't pay ours is because we can't bloody well collect.

I enclose a copy of a letter I sent to Louis [Melzack] after the Bill French article appeared.[3] I think it is self-explanatory. I have sent copies of it to a handful of other people in the book trade. Regrettably, I couldn't think of very many. After reviewing in my mind all the people in the publishing industry and the retail bookselling industry, I came up with the following categories:

1. Those whose position is coloured by British or American ownership.
2. Those who are crazy.
3. Those who are totally motivated by self-interest.
4. Those who are too busy with their own problems to give a damn.
5. Those who I consider to be responsible.

I would hate to tell you how few people I could place in the last category, but when I tell you I didn't need any extra fingers, you will have some idea.

Margaret, do you really have any idea how many committees [there] are in this Goddamn book industry? Are you aware, for example, that there are three separate Boards or committees administering the disaster known as Books Canada? Are you aware that the Book Publishers' Council has a liaison committee with the Booksellers'

Association, the Library Association, presumably with the Writers' Union, and with any other group that wants to have an association with them? Are you aware that the I.P.A. has similar committees and that is only the tip of the iceberg. All these people are pursuing their own specialized interests and nobody—and I really mean nobody—is worrying about the overall picture. You have Hugh Faulkner at the top—poor lamb—who has far too many things to look after and really doesn't know enough about the book business. He means well. Unfortunately, he is surrounded by one of the most inept group of Civil Servants ever gathered in one department. I imagine he inherited most of them, but there is a real disaster area. These inept and totally irresponsible Civil Servants are accepting advice and recommendations from what must surely be the most diverse, inexperienced block of incompetent business leaders ever assembled by one industry. It's a chaos film. For that reason, I think an entirely different type of leadership is needed. About half of that leadership should come from people in the industry; the other half should come from the public sector or people who just care about books and writing generally.

I hope this cheers you up. All the best.

Sincerely,
Jack McClelland

1. The Independent Publishers' Association (IPA) was supported by funding from the Canada Council and the Ontario Arts Council. It operated its business through the Book Society and House of Anansi Press until it acquired its own office in Toronto in 1972. McClelland refused to join the IPA. The 10 February 1975 issue of the *Montreal Gazette* quotes his refusing to do so on the grounds that he thought it was "being run by idiots" (Association of Canadian Publishers Fonds). The IPA was incorporated as the Association of Canadian Publishers (ACP) in 1976.
2. Paul Audley at one time worked with McClelland & Stewart and the Association of Canadian Publishers before becoming an independent publishing consultant. He served as the IPA's first executive director in January 1974.
3. The enclosed letter to which McClelland refers is not included in Laurence's or McClelland's papers.

Hollinger, 14 February 1975

Dear Jack—

As it is Valentine's Day, it seems as good a time as any to respond to your long letter of Feb 11th, for which many thanks. I am the first to admit that you know about 1000 times more than I do about the publishing business, and I'm grateful for all the information that you put across in your letter. I also can see that your idea for a council has a great deal to be said for it.

My own feeling about the newly formed Book and Periodical Development Council (what a name) is that it may prove to be a short-run measure. That is, I believe that, if all branches of the industry could unite in pressuring the government to take legislative action on, let us say, two simple points (not simple, but plain, I guess), then it would have justified its existence, however brief. First, naturally, I'm thinking of the Copyright Act. By the way, your press release on that question was included in the recent Writers' Union newsletter, I am glad to say. I would think that your point of view on that matter corresponds exactly with my own, and with the union's—that is, the sections relevant to the importation of Canadian books in American editions should be revised immediately to prevent the remaindered and paperback editions being brought into this country. The other issue, in my mind, would be the strict limitation of new American branch-plants here. I'm not suggesting we should say Doubleday, go home—that has never been the union's stand, as you know, and many of our writers are getting very good treatment from branch-plant firms. Our stand (and I am not speaking for the Union, but just my understanding of the WUC stand) is that there are enough branch-plants here—we don't need any more. But quite frankly, if this new Council could even achieve a quick revision of the relevant terms of the Copyright Act, I'd be happy. I don't imagine it *will* have a very long life as a Council, for the reasons you point out—the diversity of views and interests.[1]

I would see your plan as a more long-range one, a body [that] might continue in the functions you describe. It just seems to me that to wait for such a body to get going would be to delay the whole thing on Copyright, and I'm concerned that the damn law is changed now and enforced. I've suffered from it, too, and although I haven't had the remaindering experience, I soon will have. Knopf's hardcover edition of *The Fire-Dwellers* is going out of print in America—I would bet money that it appears very shortly in Coles for 99 cents, thus undercutting even the NCL paperback edition. It just seems to me that if all branches of the industry are truly united, even if *only* on this one issue, the government can hardly fail to act.

And incidentally, I'm not blaming Faulkner and never have. Sure, I was disappointed in his statement at Trent. But he is not the government—he's got to deal with a lot of people inside the house and the cabinet, as well as receiving conflicting advice from outside government, as you rightly point out. But, as I have said all along (and remember, I voted for the man in the last election and would do so again), he is intelligent and sympathetic and we could have many a person in that post who would be neither. I think he is open to reasonable suggestions, and, because this copyright issue has had a lot of exposure recently, I think this is the time, that's all. Which is why I would personally support the new council at this time. In the long run, I can see that your plan might be the better one.

I'd like to send your letter, plus all the enclosures, to Graeme Gibson, chairman of the union.[2] I think the union should be informed about the points you've made. I hope that's okay with you.

Pat Bowles[3] and I were talking on the phone the other day, and she mentioned that you're about to go on a nationwide tour for the 3-for-the-price-of-2 deal. You may not receive this letter until you return. I hope the tour won't be too exhausting, but I suspect it will. My advice to you is to take 2 weeks off after you return and go up to Muskoka. Don't know if your place there is winterized, but go anyway!

All the best,
Margaret [signed]
(see p. 3 for cheery story)

A VALENTINE'S DAY PRESENT FOR J.G. MCC.

Three days ago, I was awakened at 8 A.M. by the phone. I shot out of bed and groped my way into my study. "Is that Margaret Laurence?" a lady's voice said. I allowed grumpily as ... it was. "Well, I'm living in Milbrook [*sic*], Ontario," she said, "and I'd like to have a little chat with you." Not now, I implored her—I was very very busy. Could she phone back tomorrow? (I never have the guts to say, "Drop dead"). Next morning, I left the phone off the hook all morning. I replaced it around noon. An hour later the bloody thing rang. It was the lady from Milbrook [*sic*], who said she had a whole lot of terrific stories, enough to make a couple of books, and would I read them? No, I said, I don't do that kind of thing. "Well," she said, "I took a Creative Writing class at Sandford Fleming Community College,[4] and the instructor told me my stories were just terrific, but my syntax was just terrible." Oh, I said. "So I was wondering," she said, "if you'd just rewrite them for me." No, I said, I didn't do *that* sort of thing, either. "I thought they had people who would go through and put the stories, like, into the right language," she said. I said, No, actually, I wrote all my books by my own self, and what she needed was just to get some publisher's opinion. Then, Jack, seized with desperation and the need to get away from the woman, I did a dire thing. I gave her the address and suggested she send it to—Macmillan's.

I hope that makes your day, as it did mine.

Of course, you may have lost the Canadian *Gone with the Wind*.

Don't tell Hugh Kane. He and I have always been on good terms.

1. Contrary to Laurence's belief, the council did survive as the Book and Periodical Council.
2. Graeme Gibson (1934–) is a Canadian novelist perhaps best known for his nonfiction book *Eleven Canadian Novelists Interviewed by Graeme Gibson*. He was one of the organizers of the Writers' Union of Canada between 1974 and 1975, and a founding member of the Book and Periodical Development Council and its chair in 1975. Gibson has been in a long-term relationship with Margaret Atwood since the early 1970s.
3. Pat Bowles was a book publicist at this time. She is currently a communications and public affairs professional in West Vancouver, British Columbia.
4. Fleming College is a college of applied arts and technology in Peterborough, Ontario.

Regent, 11 March 1975

Dear Margaret:

That was a great Valentine's Day present, even if it arrived a bit late. I am beginning to wish that all unsolicited manuscripts could be referred to Macmillan's or somewhere. We are processing about 5,000 of them a year at the present, and, on balance, it is a major waste of time. Out of that 5,000, we seem to get a lot less than 10 publishable books a year and would be better off without most of those 10. However, it's one of the joys of this business. We can hardly claim to be a serious publishing house if we didn't go through the procedure.

I was glad to have your comments on the Book and Periodical Development Council. My own attitude now is to sit back and wait to see what happens, which will probably be nothing. I had a talk with Jim Douglas while I was in Vancouver—one of the few sensible people in the IPA and their new President,[1] which is a step in the right direction—and he tells me that the first recommendation of the B&PDC is the formation of the sort of council that I have described. Fair enough. Unfortunately, the subsequent list of recommendations starts immediately to take the shape and form that has worried me, i.e. horse trading between lobby groups. If you endorse my proposal, I'll endorse yours sort of attitude. The problem is that that is inevitable. The council formed from lobby groups will probably lead to the whole thing being pigeon-holed, but I have agreed to shut up and sit back and wait.

When I say shut up, I mean it. I have done enough talking on this tour to last for several years. Funnily enough, the tour itself was not all that exhausting. It was such a relieve [*sic*] to get away from the office that I really felt in better shape when I returned than I would have been if had I been at 25 Hollinger all that time. But I enjoyed the trip. It was promoting the paperback sale from coast to coast and attacking Andre Oulette [*sic*] and Mr. Trudeau and Cabinet apathy at every turn.[2]

I was fairly kind to Faulkner for the most part because he did, at that stage, at least have my sympathy.

I am now less certain that he deserved it. I was heading back to Toronto when the first press notice of his announcement hit the CP [Canadian Press] wire. It was only a couple of days ago that I finally got a chance to study the full text of his statement. So I am going to wait another few days before I get mad. It is my suspicion that he has done nothing but introduce another delaying ploy. The press release says Oulette [*sic*], Faulkner and Basford held discussions and concluded that the Copyright Act can be enforced. It may be, but the fact of the matter is that the courts have already indicated otherwise and the Department of Justice, through the R.C.M.P., have already written us to that effect. In other words, pending clarification, it appears that this most recent announcement of Faulkner's is saying no more than "we don't plan to amend the Act. Protection exists. Take the matter to court and you will win." I say "bullshit." Coles have already said, "it's a laugh." However, I am going to wait and see what they come up with before going after Mr. Faulkner's jugular.

By all means, feel free to send my comments on the Council off to Graeme Gibson. I suspect they already know how I feel to a degree, but it can do no harm.

The Diviners still seems to be doing well, although obviously at this time of year, its continued presence at the top of the bestseller list doesn't mean all that many copies. The paperback will be taking over very shortly. I don't know whether we are going to be in a position to stop *Rachel, Rachel* or even the Knopf hardbound of *The Fire-Dwellers*. I am going to check into that one.

Meanwhile, apart from working too hard, what are you up to? I have always assumed that, by now, the new novel would have started to formulate in your mind, even though you don't intend to write it. Incidentally, Margaret, a book that I think you could and should write when time permits if it appeals is a very simple, relatively short book on what it means to be Canadian. I am not talking about a nationalist manifesto or anything like that—there has been too much already—

instead I am thinking of something dealing simply and directly with the heritage roots, etc. This is what you have been dealing with essentially in your fiction, but in a very short [piece]—maybe 100 pages.

The feelings of this country—I now call it Canadianism—are still out there from coast to coast. Funnily enough, I find it more among taxi-drivers than anyone else. This is probably a good sign. Increase in sales of Canadian books is another evidence. The sad truth is that leadership is disappearing. Politicians are backing off quickly for reasons of expediency. And also from lack of understanding. My sense of the situation is that we could very well, because of external pressure, fall into a state of considerable relapse in this whole subject area.

The other point that came home to me very forcibly on this trip was that there were very few Canadians whose names are as highly respected as yours. It came as no surprise, of course, but I had a new awareness of how real it is. If you could find the right form, the right tone for a simple, sane message for Canadians—and, strangely enough, I think our teachers need it more than anybody else—I think it would be not only a spectacularly successful book, but a very valuable one for the country. Sorry to lay that one on you. Don't respond to the idea for a while. Think about it.

All the best.
Sincerely,
Jack McClelland

1. Jim Douglas served as the president of the Independent Publishers' Association between 1975 and 1977.
2. André Ouellet (1939–) was a former chairman of Canada Post and a long-serving Liberal politician. In 1975, when Laurence and McClelland were exchanging these letters, Ouellet was the federal minister of consumer and corporate affairs.

Hollinger, 7 April 1975

Dear Jack—

I have just received Buckler's *The Rebellion of Young David.* I think you've done a fine production job on it—it really looks good. Also, you get the medal for having brought it out so quickly. I am sure that Buckler will be pleased. I'm really glad that you moved at [that] speed. I wanted to review it for *The Globe*, but Ed O'Dacre says he thinks Bill French is going to do it.[1] Anyway, if you bring it out in the NCL in a year's time, I'd really like to do the Intro.

Thanks for your long letter. Did you see Ouellet's letter in *The Globe* the other day? I do not know what to make of it. He says that importation of American editions can be stopped now, but that "this action would require satisfactory evidence of the legal title to the copyright, but, once such evidence was provided, the Minister of National Revenue would place [on] the foreign edition the prohibitory schedule of the customs tariff."[2] Well, Jack, why were we all not told this years ago, eh? Why did you have to go through an expensive case against Coles, if all you needed to do was establish the Can copyright of Berton's and Mowat's books? I really think the government has been awfully lax. Anyway, where do we go from here? Should all writers whose books are published in both American and Canadian editions register this fact with the National Revenue? Ouellet doesn't make the procedure very clear. And also, do you know what we have to do to establish the fact that, for example, I hold the Canadian copyright on my books? It would seem to be to be pretty obvious that I do, and that I have signed a contract with M&S for sole Canadian rights. What action should we all be taking? Do we have to provide the gov't with one copy of each of our books? Sorry to ask all these questions, but if you know the answers, I think we should all get busy and take the necessary steps. I'd be grateful if you could let me know whatever you happen to know about this, and also what other writers published by M&S are doing. Seems to me we have to discover 2 things: 1) how to provide proof of copyright; and 2) what address and dept. to send such notification to, in order to have them take the appropriate steps. Once we've discovered this, I think probably the Writers' Union should circularize all members, so that individual writers can take the necessary steps, if necessary. Or will it be done by their publishers?

I don't know if I can write the kind of book on Canada that you mention, but it's a thought. What I am doing now is [trying] to get about 12 articles typed out so you can have a look at them, if you want to. Over the years I've written about 40 articles, most of which are not worth reprinting. But there are about 12, which are mostly articles—in a sense, all are travel articles—Somaliland, Ghana, Egypt, Nigeria, Greece, Scotland, Canada. Some haven't been published (the articles I did on Egypt, just before the Israeli war wiped out American tourism in that country). I don't know whether you would be interested at all or not, but I thought I'd type the things out, anyway. After that, when I can get out to my summer cottage and firmly lock the door and take the damn phone off the hook, I want to try to write a kids' book. Incidentally, did I mention before that I'm reviewing Mordecai's kids' book for *The Globe*?[3] I think it's a hilarious book.

Any information you can give me re: the copyright thing would be greatly appreciated. I think we must act quickly. I wonder how we can be sure, once we've registered the books with the appropriate dept., that no more copies are being brought in?

All the best,
Margaret [signed]

1. Ed O'Dacre, the reviews editor for the *Globe and Mail*, became the director of magazine publishing with the same newspaper. French did indeed review Buckler's book, in an article titled "Just Blame Enthusiasm for Flaws."
2. In this letter by André Ouellet, titled "Book Dumping," he stated that despite protests by Canadian writers and publishers about American editions of Canadian books being sold in

Canadian bookstores, Ottawa would not change the copyright law. He claimed that in the Copyright Act "it is possible to stop the importation of books from the United States." He also argued that his "responsibility is to achieve a reasonable balance among the varying interests which have a stake in copyright, including the interest of the consumer" (6).

3. Laurence reviewed *Jacob Two-Two Meets the Hooded Fang*, published in 1975. In her review, "Richler's Tender, Two's Magic, and So's Fang," she observed "that Richler has all the qualifications" for a children's literature writer: "wit, an ability to carry through a fast-paced narrative, an appreciation of fantasy and the fantastic, and an implacable refusal ever to talk down to anyone" (37).

•——

Regent, 11 April 1975

Dear Margaret:

Glad to have your note about the Buckler and I am sorry that you are not going to review it. I think it has turned out well and I hope it will do as well in the marketplace.

Ouellet's letter in *The Globe* infuriated me. Mind you, I had already seen it, because it was published in *The Toronto Star* on April 1st. I dictated an instant reply—which naturally I didn't mail—which described it as the best April Fool's joke I had seen in a long time. Because the government has been promising to do something, I have ignored all these nonsensible letters and have held my peace waiting to see exactly what they propose.

As of today, I know, and Margaret you wouldn't believe it, they have set up such a wall of nonsensical bureaucratic red tape that it deserves to be in a shrine for posterity in some sort of Alice in Wonderland type locale. I will send you a copy as soon as I receive it. A girl from the C.B.C. in Ottawa read it to me on the phone today. It is just bloody well unbelievable. The follow-up that Faulkner referred to on March 3rd turned out to be a letter dated April 8th from Basford, which reiterated pretty well what Ouellet says in his letters to the newspapers. It goes on to say that any publisher or author wanting further information should then write to the Department. Well, I have written to the Department, but they haven't replied as yet. However, I did hear that the reply will be from this gal at the C.B.C. As I say, it is just bloody unbelievable.

Frankly, Margaret, we have grave doubts as to whether this thing will work. You can judge for yourself. I will send you the material as soon as I receive it. I am just gathering strength to make another attack on the government. I have learned, unofficially, from friends in Faulkner's department, that the real truth of the matter is that there is a Cabinet split on this subject. There are members of the cabinet who are not certain that Canadian authors and publishers deserve this sort of protection. Don't be surprised at that. I don't know whether you saw the government draft of the Envision of the Competition Act. The basic White Paper from government virtually proposed the abolition of copyright in total on the grounds that copyright tends to be monopolistic and interferes with the rights of consumers. Apparently, there are quite a few people in our Federal Cabinet who believe this. People from the Secretary of State's Department gave me this information and they also said to me that the reading of public response—even in the Secretary of [State's] Department—was that the public in Canada were not all that favourable to the position of publishers and authors in the Coles controversy. Or, to state it differently, we haven't won the battle yet. But don't worry about it for the moment. I'll send you further information as it comes along, although I suspect you are going to receive it directly in any case.

Okay re: writing—the article book and the juvenile. That's great but do think about the Canada thing in your spare time. Instinct tells me that it is not a bad idea. Hope we will see you soon—indeed we will—I had almost forgotten. I'll be with you in New York.

Cheers!
Jack McClelland

Hollinger, 22 April 1975

Dear Boss—

Thanks for your letter. I await news from you before I try to write to THE GOVERNMENT etc. Re: establishing my copyright on my own books. You are absolutely right—they make these statements, but when it comes down to the real practical details, one is still left not knowing what to do, or how to get them to implement the law, which they maintain is adequate. We will see.

I thought the old firm did a very fine production job on Clara Thomas' book on me.[1] It really looks nice, Jack, and I think that means a lot. Also, of course, it has to be one of the finest Can books to do a study on an individual writer, which is *not* one of the "series" ones, written to length, but a full-scale study. I like it a whole lot, because Clara has a serious critical outlook; is a knowledgeable reader (which some academics and critics are not, in my view); and she does not write in jargon or gibberish, which so many academic writers do. I thought Marian Engel's review in *The Globe* was right on.[2]

You may like to know that, although I missed out on reviewing the Buckler book for *The Globe,* I am reviewing it for the *Montreal Gazette*. French's review in *The Globe* was meant to be favourable, but he did seem to miss quite a lot. He seemed to think that Buckler equates Country with Good, and City with Evil. It is never that kind of simplistic thing in Buckler's writing. If you put it out in the NCL next year, I really would love to write the Intro.

When June rolls around, and I am at last freed from all these crazy commitments I seem to have, I am moving out to the shack and enforcing the poster you had made for me some years ago—NO VISITORS EXCEPT ON WEEKENDS.

Have just begun Sylvia Fraser's *The Candy Factory,* and it seems awfully good to me. There again, I would suspect that the pretty favourable review it got in *The Globe* (French) was not serious or deep enough. Goddamn it, can't these reviewers *read*?[3]

Best,
Margaret [signed]

1. Laurence refers to Clara Thomas's book, *The Manawaka World of Margaret Laurence*, as distinct from Thomas's earlier book on Laurence, titled *Margaret Laurence*.
2. Marian Engel (1933–1985) was an award-winning Canadian novelist. Her most controversial and highly acclaimed book was *Bear*, which won the Governor General's Award for fiction in 1976. In her review, titled "It's the Grit: Laurence is Unforgettable because She is Us," she lauded Laurence for showcasing "gritty women" who inhabit "gritty little towns." Laurence refers to Engel's review of Thomas's book on Laurence.
3. The review by French, titled "If People Were Nourishing Nougats...," essentially characterized Fraser's book, *The Candy Factory*, as a "peanut brittle novel" (32).

Regent, 28 April 1975

Dear Margaret:

Apart from congratulating you on the Molson and on the G.G.A.,[1] let me also congratulate you on the review of the Richler juvenile. It is really a fine, sensitive, and outstanding review. He should be very grateful to you.

Cheers!
Jack McClelland

1. On 25 April 1975, Peter Taylor wrote a memo to McClelland in which he observed, "Margaret Laurence received word yesterday that she has won both the Molson Award—$15,000.00 tax free—and the Governor-General's Award for fiction. I presume both items remain confidential until officially announced by the Canada Council. Incidentally, as I think you know, publication of the Bantam edition has been postponed (*The Diviners*) until the fall. I think it is now scheduled for September." There is also a handwritten note in the McClelland archives signed "L." It states, "Margaret Laurence called re: Bantam launching in May (you and she were going). Anyway 'tis off 'cause the cover is going to be redone. Sept. pub now. Margaret says the cover was awful and a Canadian artist did it. Victorian figures and English village in the background" (McClelland & Stewart Ltd. Fonds, Box 87, File 22).

Hollinger, 30 April 1975

Dear Jack—

Thanks for your letter. I'm glad you liked my review of Mordecai's book. I did sort of want to put the kids' book into some kind of perspective with the rest of his work, and also to quell any thoughts that people might have that Richler's writing a children's book might [not] seem a good thing. I hope he writes more kids' books.

I hope to write one myself, if the sound and fury of my life ever subsides, which it ought to do by mid-June.

Boss, may I ask you a small favour? Thing is, I believe that I have overpaid my 1973 income tax by about a thousand bucks, and my accountant is working on this now. The Income Tax people have disallowed my request to have the advances on *The Diviners* spread back over three years (I would naturally still have to pay in one year, and have already done so, but I think I should be paying at a lower rate). My accountant has appealed this decision. I got a dim-witted phone call yesterday from some idiot lady in Belleville, in the tax dept., saying she wanted to know what all that advance money was *for*, exactly. I patiently explained that it was the normal thing with books [that] have been accepted for publication, and what it was *for* was permission to print the book and sell the bloody thing. Yes, she said, but she would really have to see my contracts. Well, this is just lunacy, Jack, but I only have 1 copy of my contract with you for *The Diviners*, and, if I send it, I am damn sure I will never see it again. Do you think you could get a xerox copy made of your copy of this contract, and send it to me?

Favour number two, still tax-related. This dumb broad also said she would need proof that, in fact, I had worked on *The Diviners* over a three-year period. I said, "What kind of proof do you suppose I could possibly have?" (I've no doubt lost the appeal by now, as I was getting really annoyed.) I mean to say, how stupid can they get? Do I need to go to my lawyer on the day I start a novel and get a sworn statement? Honestly. Anyway, I said I could get a statement from my publishers, and she seemed to think that would be okay. Like, they'll believe you, Boss, but not me—and who in hell should know better than the writer about when a novel was begun? Could you therefore please write a short note ... [and] *send it to me*, so I can forward it to her with the copy of the contract and also to get Knopf's contract. Just say something like this: This is to confirm that Margaret Laurence spent the three-year period from January 1971 to December 1973 writing the novel *The Diviners*. I'd be most grateful. Every time I have anything to do with the income tax, I can feel my blood pressure rising. Ye gods—I thought England was the depths as far as taxes are concerned, but Can is just as bad.

My accounting firm, by the way, is the same as yours, Gardner Macdonald. I like them. Yearly, they save me from a nervous breakdown.

Thanks a lot, and all the best,
Margaret [signed]

P.S. Boss, I don't know if you will want to attend, and if you don't, please don't worry, but I have asked the Can Council to have an invitation sent to you for the Gov Gen's on May 22 and for the Molson on June 16th.

P.S. To Marge—do you think you could send 4 copies of Clara's book on to me?

Ordered May 6.[1]

1. This note is handwritten by Hodgeman.

Regent, 6 May 1975

Dear Margaret:

These income tax people are not only difficult, but almost totally inflexible. I have had nothing but grief from them through the years. I am satisfied that one should face them with every possible determination and press every possible advantage.

I am sending to you today a copy of *The Diviners* contract, plus a copy of the letter that I have sent in the same mail [for taxation purposes]. I hope it will do the trick.[1]

You will be interested to know that I met a translator of the Italian edition of *Jest of God*. A strange woman who lives by herself somewhere in the Italian Alps with a large German shepherd dog. Frankly, I was not impressed by her English, but since naturally we were both very drunk, it is probably nothing to be disturbed about. The translation will be carefully checked by Amleto Lorenzini,[2] and I think he has a suspicion that it may have to be substantially edited. We will have to wait and see. She is due to submit the finished translation on May 15th and is apparently on schedule. Naturally, they want you to go to Italy for a promotion trip. If you would like to [go], it is yours for the asking, although I have warned them that you are not keen about this type of thing and may not be enthusiastic. Before you make up your mind about that, I'll see you and we can discuss what takes place. Leonard [Cohen] and I ended up one night with this lady somewhere in the middle of Milan. We were all quite drunk. She was apparently having some difficulty making up her mind whether she wanted to go to bed with me or with Leonard. I can't remember now whether it was because of her indecision that caused it, or whether Leonard and I sobered up sufficiently to realize simultaneously that we weren't in this sort of competition—whatever it was. The last I can recall of your translator is the sight of her staggering across the cobblestones in some huge city square. She may never be seen again. I have, however, undertaken to send her copies of *The Manawaka World*,[3] the CWS, etc. It is possible that you will become very famous in Italy.

Yes, thanks for the Canada Council invitation, which has been received. At the moment, I think I will probably skip that one and let Anna Porter go in my stead. Because of a rather spotty record, [I] am not all that well received at these G.G. Award functions. I will, however, go to the Molson thing. It appeals to me much more, because of the money involved and also because I have much more respect for the Molsons than for the office of the Governor-General (unless, of course, they decided to make me Governor-General).

Marge is sending the books. All else is under control.

Cheers!
Jack McClelland

1. A copy of the letter was included with it and sent to Laurence, and it reads as follows: "I am the publisher of Margaret Laurence's books in Canada. I would like to confirm that she spent the period from January 1971 to December 1973 writing her recent novel *The Diviners*. For the record, I think it is fair to say that in fact she spent a much longer time than that. The outline for a serious work of fiction germinates in the mind of an author for many months, often for many years, before actual work starts. Mrs. Laurence, who I am sure you recognize as one of Canada's great creative artists (she has just won her second Governor General's Award and also the Molson Award), writes very slowly and very carefully. She is one of Canada's most valued and respected citizens and is certainly entitled to every possible consideration that our taxation laws permit. Yours very truly, Jack McClelland" (McClelland & Stewart Ltd. Fonds, Box 87, File 22).
2. Amleto Lorenzini is a photographer, editor, and translator.
3. McClelland refers to Clara Thomas's *The Manawaka World of Margaret Laurence*.

Hollinger, 14 May 1975

Dear Jack—

Thanks much for your letter to the tax people—I really appreciate it. They are probably illiterate, so your mention of my work will probably fall on closed ears, but thanks all the same. I try to think about the tax thing as little as possible, because, when I brood about it, I get so angry I feel like doing something really rash, like writing them a poison-pen letter. However, let's face it—if you have to pay income tax, at least it means you have some income, so things could be worse. I just think they are too tough on writers, who lead very insecure lives. I guess the same thing could be said of publishers as well.

Your description of my Italian translator is intriguing, to put it mildly! My own memories of Milan are hardly less bizarre. Went there with the kids and my husband (on one of those attempts at reconciliation which are always so unsuccessful) and had colitis, partly because of emotional situation and partly because *The Fire-Dweller*[*s*] was just about completed, and sometimes an almost-completed book hits me that way, in the guts. I can vouch for the fact that to find a lavatory in Milan is about as difficult for the amateur as scaling Everest. I hope the translator lady did not have the same difficulty I did, but being a native, maybe she knew where to look, even in her somewhat uncertain condition!

I *can't* go to Italy, Jack. Like, I've *been* there! No, it isn't that—it is just that I am firmly trying to say "No" to everything from now on, or else I will simply turn into a performer, not a writer. I want to get out to the shack and get started on the kids' book I have in mind, and if you will believe it, there is no way I can do that until the end of June. May and June are going to be like a 13-ring circus for me.

I didn't think you would go to the Gov-Gen's, but I wanted them to send you an invitation just the same. By the way, there is no big Can Council dinner this year (thank goodness)—just the ceremony at Gov house. They've already sent me a cheque for the crass monetary part of the award, which is just splendid as far as I'm concerned. I do hope you can be there for the Molson, tho'. I think it, too, is not a dinner but a reception. Much better. I'd rather go out for dinner with a few dear friends. My daughter and her man will be here for the Gov-Gen's, and my son and his lady for the Molson, so that will be good. I also have 3 honourary degrees in May-June, and my schedule is so complex that I fear I will turn up in Brandon when I'm supposed to be in Ottawa, or vice versa. Roll on, the end of June!

... I'm so glad that the Ludwigs are back in Canada. They are splendid people. How about putting *A Woman of Her Age* into the NCL?[1] I think it is a terrific book.

Guess who phoned me re: the Gov-Gen's and the Molson? Ernie Buckler! I was so delighted. Had [n]ever actually spoken with him before, altho' have been corresponding with him a lot this past year. Pat Bowles was a tower of strength for me, at Canada Day. Came with me to the first seminar (which proved to be an auditorium, packed, and you know how I love that kind of mass situation, like the plague), and managed to steer me out at the end of it, very firmly and yet courteously, without offending anyone—I was so grateful.

Thanks again for help with the tax dept.

All the best,
Margaret Laurence

P.S. I guess you've probably heard—Adele's just got the Can Bookseller Award for *Crackpot*.[2] What a good piece of news! Beth Appledorn(?)[3] phoned to tell her, while I was there, as it happened. The book Adele is working on now is going to be, I suspect, a real winner. I've only seen one short section of it, but she's told me some things about it, and I've known about the subject matter for years. It'll be quite short, I suspect, in text, but visually as well as intellectually exciting, and also humourous [*sic*] and an incredible character portrayal.[4] This is in confidence. I will say no more. But just wanted to indicate that something very fascinating is in the works, with her.

P.S. To Marge—received the copies of Clara Thomas' book. Many thanks.

1. See Laurence's letter dated 13 March 1972 for information about Ludwig's novel, *A Woman of Her Age*.
2. See Laurence's letters dated 3 June 1966 and 7 October 1973 for information about Wiseman and her novels *Crackpot* and *The Sacrifice*.
3. Beth Appledorn and her partner Susan Sandler owned Longhouse Books on Yonge Street in Toronto, a well-known bookstore in the 1970s that favoured Canadian writers.
4. The book by Adele Wiseman would become *Old Woman at Play*, published in 1978 by Clarke, Irwin. It was Wiseman's most autobiographical book and the one in which she writes about her mother's doll making.

Regent, 29 May 1975

Dear Margaret:

This won't get to you in time but, for the record, I will be seeing you in Ottawa after all and just maybe we will end up having dinner. Who knows? That is amazing that Ernie Buckler called. It must have taken all his courage. In fact he must have been smashed. Incidentally, your review of *Young David* appeared in the *Gazette*[1] in the middle of the Montreal Book Fair, which was good for them, good for the Fair and good for us. It's a fine review, by the way, and I really enjoyed reading it.

I was also delighted by Adele's good news. It is a book that I really like and I am just delighted that she made a little extra money and prestige out of it.

June sounds awful, but just remember how good you will feel when it is all over. No, you won't have to go to Italy. I warned the Italian publisher that you wouldn't want to go.

Incidentally, publication is going to be delayed. They had just received the translation prior to coming to Montreal for the Book Fair and a fast assessment of it in Montreal indicates that it is lousy and it is going to have to be translated. I would guess it may mean putting off publication until next year. I learned that Peggy Atwood had the same problem with the French edition, which was badly translated and which is going to have to be redone. Too bad these problems occur, but what the hell. The fact that you and others are being translated is a very important step for Canada. I think the Montreal Fair was a great success, exhausting but really a fantastic success.

This letter is largely for the record because I will be seeing you, I think, before you get it.

Cheers!
Jack McClelland

1. This review appeared on 17 May 1975, in the *Montreal Gazette*, under the title "Buckler's People Possess Strength and Dignity." Buckler's volume is a collection of short stories. Laurence calls attention to themes of father-son relationships, connections to the land—"the beloved place"—and escape from the hometown; she observes that Buckler's "portrayal of David Canaan and his family ... not only have the ring of truth in terms of their community, but in terms of the older community which includes all humankind," and that he "writes very specifically and very profoundly out of his own time and place."

Hollinger, 11 July 1975

Dear Jack—

Sorry to burst into your summer with a few problems. Nothing serious. But I have received a certain amount of flack from Dave Godfrey re: *The Diviners* coming out with Bantam.[1] Apparently (and I guess he must have got this from Stoddard), he heard that General[2] asked if there were any use in making an offer, and you said No. Then (thus goes Godfrey's version) when Bantam said no dice in the USA unless they get the Can rights, you said, Fine. He said in a rather short sharp letter to me that he wanted the facts, because he didn't like to stab a friend without the facts. Well. I was, of course, initially furious. However, I calmed down and wrote him a long letter ... [3]

Finally, I pointed out to him my sense of loyalty to you and to the firm of M&S, and said that it should not be forgotten how much you have done for *Canadian* publishing, much of it at a time when no one else gave a damn.

Now, Jack, the thing is this—I wrote this letter to Godfrey a couple of weeks ago, and did not say anything to you, because I thought it might be sufficient to clear things up with Dave, for whom I have the greatest respect and who has been (or so I thought) my friend for a long time. However, the union contract committee had a meeting with Paul Audley yesterday in the IPA offices, and, as we were leaving, Dave came in. We discussed the matter briefly. He said, "Well, there's still something fishy about it." I asked him if he had done as I had advised to do—namely, to contact you if he wanted further details. He said he had not. He then said, "Well, the book looks pretty bad there, pretty bad." I then said, rather coldly, "I expect it will be in the NCL in two years time, and in the meantime, I have 2 children to put through university." I then walked out.

Now, Boss, here is the thing—did in fact General make any offer on or show interest in that novel? If they did (and if indeed it was prior to Bantam's offer), I can only think you turned it down because General wanted (as I have heard is their custom) rights forever and ever on it, and you knew I wanted and Malcolm Ross wanted and I believe you also want to see the novel in the NCL in a couple of years, along with the rest of my fiction. Could you just let me know, in case Godfrey or anyone else starts any further hassle? (By the way, Audley came out to the elevator with me, and was quick to assure me that he personally did not see anything wrong in our sale of it to Bantam, so I don't think Dave's attitude to me is shared totally by all the IPA.)

I personally do not want to have this made an issue, so I will not say anything further to Godfrey unless he forces me to do so, and I hope you will act in the same manner, as I'm sure you will. But I think at this point you should know about this, so we can present, if necessary, a united front.

Also, you *do* want the novel in the NCL, don't you? I am sorry to go on about this, but it means a great deal to me, in terms quite other than financial, to see it there, as, by that time, I think virtually all my fiction will be in that series. I've also been wondering how you might feel about putting Clara Thomas' *The Manawaka World* into the NCL. We would then have a very neat little package deal, should anyone want to use the books on a course, with the fiction and a critical survey of the same. Anyway, I'd like to know your response to the idea. The NCL, granted, is mainly fiction, but it does have some critical works in it as well.

I hope you are able to get away to the cottage for a good length of time this summer. I'm at my shack now, and beginning to unwind after all the excitement of May and June.

All the best,
Margaret[4]

1. Dave Godfrey (1938–2015) was a Canadian writer and publisher, whose novel, *The New Ancestors*, won the Governor General's Award for fiction in 1970. He was one of the founders of House of Anansi Press and New Press.
2. General began as a book publisher in Toronto in the 1930s. It was sold in the 1950s and went out of business in 2002, but it was revived as General Publishing Inc. and continues to produce trade books and e-books (General Publishing Inc.).
3. Laurence proceeds to elaborate on the facts as she understood them in relation to this situation, one of these being that no paperback offer prior to Bantam's had been made.
4. Hodgeman responded to this letter on 7 July 1975: "Thank you for your letter of July 11th to Mr. McClelland. It has reached the office during his absence from the city on a trip to Western Canada but will be passed to him on his return to the office early next week" (McClelland & Stewart Ltd. Fonds, Box 87, File 22).

Regent, 21 July 1975

Dear Margaret:

Migod, you are a nice person. To think that you have been shielding me from the problem with Dave Godfrey is really nice. The fact that I think Godfrey and Lorimer[1] have done more harm to Canadian publishing than anybody else I can think of—leaving their professional abilities aside—must have seeped through in May of 1974. At that time, they were told simply that, since we were contemplating the re-entry into the mass-market paperback field, we were not considering offers seriously at that point. They did not submit a proposal, nor were they invited to.

It is true, unfortunately, that when Bantam approached us, we had forgotten about this earlier expression of interest. Bantam [was] told precisely the same thing as General, but they decided to submit a bid anyway. They submitted a low one, as you know, and we told them to forget it. We then laid down what were almost impossible conditions for them, including the combination of high advance and a short, exclusive selling period, and they agreed to all terms.

So I can confirm the following points: (a) the deal was made before the moratorium, (b) the offer, not only in terms of the advance, but in terms of royalty rate and short term, was irresistible—and one General would not have met, and (c) the book will appear in the New Canadian Library as soon as their two-year period is up, as will *The Manawaka World.*

Much as I like to be shielded from Godfrey, Audley etc., I really think, Margaret, that the shielding should be the other way around. I think you should take the position that if they want to quarrel with anybody, they can quarrel with me. You happen to publish with me and it is from me that you take your publishing advice. ... I am very much in favour of any measure that will assist Canadian publishing interests, help to develop more Canadian publishing, Canadian-owned publishing houses, and generally stimulate that area provided that any such measures are not inimical to the interests of Canadian authors themselves.

So if you hear any more flack on the subject, refer the buggers to me. Incidentally, *The Diviners* seems to have tremendous distribution. I have just returned from a fast trip through the West and found it everywhere, even in the smallest cigar stores. I presume it is selling well. I must say I am not wild about the cover, even though it was revised, but that's life.

Hope you are having a good summer. I still don't know about holidays, but I seem to be surviving very well at the moment.

Cheers!
Jack McClelland[2]

1. James Lorimer is the founder of James Lorimer and Company Ltd., a publishing company in Toronto that primarily publishes educational materials and children's books.
2. Laurence wrote to acknowledge this letter on 24 July 1975.

Hollinger, 31 July 1975

Dear Jack—

I've only recently received my copies of Bantam's Canadian edition of *The Diviners,* and was stunned and delighted to see that it has already gone into two printings! I would certainly be interested to know when their first print run was. Would you, by any chance, know? Or could you find out? As we both have a considerable financial interest in the paperback, it would be kind of nice to know. Not essential, but interesting.

I've just returned from a visit with the Purdys in Ameliasburgh, and Al was showing me some of the poems by women which he's received in response to a press release asking for same, as *Storm Warning Two* [*sic*] had thus far an overly large proportion of poetry by men, which was certainly not Al's fault, but only due to the fact that that was what he received.[1] Well, as you no doubt know, he has recently been inundated by poems from women writers, and, of course, many of them (most) aren't very good, but there are quite a large number which are absolutely excellent. In fact, Al tells me that if he included all or most of the really good ones, the book would be almost equally by men and women poets. The snag here, of course, is that he'd need about 50 more pages. Jack, I realize this is none of my damn business, but I'm writing all the same about it, partly because I believe so strongly, as you do, that young writers must be encouraged *if* they have real talent, and partly as a woman writer. If the poems exist, and they *do,* it would seem to me to be an awful shame if the women poets could not be adequately represented. Some of the poems Al showed me were really terrific. I didn't have time to read all the good ones, but the ones I saw were very impressive.
I have the feeling that to add the extra pages would make this into a very important collection of young poets. I also think with the support of a few older poets and prose writers (of whom I'd be happy to be one),

a sizeable amount of pre-publication publicity could be whomped up. I'm thinking of things like articles in, for example, *Chatelaine* and/or *Maclean's* and/or *Saturday Night*. Anyway, I'm really writing to say that, if you do decide to do the longer book, with the women poets really represented as they should be, I'd be glad to try my best to work up this kind of support for the project.

Al certainly did not ask me to write this letter, but I am going to send a copy of it to him.[2] Thinking of the whole thing on the bus coming home, it just seemed to me that it was a very important project.

All the best,
Margaret

1. See Laurence's letters dated 4 April 1969 and 1 February 1975 for information about Al Purdy.
2. On 2 August 1975, Purdy responded to McClelland. He had just received a copy of this letter from Laurence. Purdy was open to including more women poets in the collection and observed that an extra twenty-four pages would be necessary to do so (McClelland & Stewart Ltd. Fonds, Box 87, File 22).

Regent, 5 August 1975

Dear Margaret:

Thanks for your letter. By coincidence, one of my spies was in the office on Friday and told me that Bantam now have 25,000 in print for Canada. The book is selling very well. He thinks that their first printing was 75,000 copies and the next printing 50,000. Because this spy has his own network system of sorts that does a regular stock check, he is able to report that the book is selling very well indeed. I may say that from personal observation, I am impressed by the distribution; I have seen copies in lots of out-of-the-way places where very few paperbacks are available—small smoke shops, etc.—and I would think the results are going to be impressive.

I am, of course, familiar with the Al Purdy problem and I agree with your concern. I had already written Al that we should find a solution to it in one way or another. There is a problem with enlarging the book—it is the simple problem of pricing it out of the market. This type of anthology will, as a rule, sell well only if it is a fairly low-ticket item. Once we know the final shape of the book—assuming it may run an extra 50 pages or so—we are going to try and get help from Ron Evans at the Ontario Arts Council. It is impossible to anticipate whether or not they will co-operate. It is a problem of setting a precedent and until we try—with the specifics laid out—we can't really anticipate the answer.

If the answer is no, we will consider doing two books, i.e. *Storm Warning II* [*sic*] and *Storm Warning III* a year later. Obviously, the male poets will be annoyed as hell if they are kicked out because of the women. But the women, too, have a fair complaint, because I think it is probably fair to say that Al did not research the field as thoroughly as he should have. We can't win in either direction there. It amounts to McClelland's Choice (this is the Canadian version of a Hobson's choice.[1] As nationalists we have to drop that expression and substitute McClelland's Choice. I think I deserve to be remembered in this way and I expect the term to become part of your vocabulary. I can't think of anybody who is faced with a lousier selection of options than I am in the normal course of the day). ...

So one way or another, the problem will be solved. I do appreciate your interest and Pat Bowles may, in fact, bug you later for help with the promotion.

Cheers!
Jack McClelland

1. A Hobson's choice is a "free choice" in which only one option is offered.

Regent, 27 January 1976

Dear Margaret:

We are sitting here waiting expectantly for your manuscript and here we don't even have a progress report. If you can find time to drop me a note, it would be extremely helpful. We are trying to put together our fall program. I am expecting your book to keep the wolf away from the door here during that period. Do send us some cheerful word about its progress.

Cheers!
Jack McClelland

Hollinger, 4 February 1976

Dear Boss—

Thanks for your letter of January 27th. I'm sorry I haven't got the manuscript to you by now. I spent 2 weeks in Toronto over Christmas, and arrived back home to find that over the holidays I'd conveniently forgotten a whole lot of things I had committed myself to do—3 book reviews, an article, judging a short story contest, etc. etc. So I have spent all that time in meeting deadlines. I guess, also, I have been procrastinating about the manuscript because copy typing is so boring and I hate it. But alas, I can only type these articles—some were published in American mags and have been re-paragraphed and American spellings inserted, so now I have to put them back into their original form, and some I only have my original working copy, with lots of scribbling, so only I can read them. I have decided that the only way I can get them done is to do three hours typing per day, no excuses. So I will promise to get the manuscript to you in the middle of March. There is also a final article, which I think should be included but which I have not as yet written. I will keep on saying to myself what you always used to say to me whenever I'd finished a book. ... "Back to your typewriter, slob."

I don't think that either Macmillan's in Eng or Knopf in NY will be interested. This is a very Canadian-oriented book, and the short Introductions to each article presuppose a certain familiarity on the part of the reader with my work. I don't know how that may affect your response to the manuscript, but I think you ought to know.

So—I'll have it to you by mid-March, at the latest. By the way, it is titled so far:

Road from the Isles[1]—travels, entertainments & politics.

All the best,

Margaret[2]

1. This collection of travel essays was eventually published under the title *Heart of a Stranger* in 1976.
2. On 6 February 1976, Hodgeman responded, "Thank you for your letter of February 4th to Jack. It has reached the office during his absence this week on a trip to New York. He is expected back this weekend and your letter will be passed to him at that time. Hope all goes well with you" (McClelland & Stewart Ltd. Fonds, Box 87, File 23).

Regent, 11 February 1976

Dear Margaret:

We saw the bit about the censorship of *The Diviners* in *The Globe*.[1] How serious is this situation? Do you want us to get into the act? How do you feel about it? Is it something we should be attempting to publicize? Or should we just play it easy for the present? I wish you would let us know.

Cheers!
Jack McClelland

1. The editorial, "Cannonballs from the Educators," to which McClelland here refers appeared on 10 February 1976, and was related to censorship of *The Diviners*. It elicited a slew of letters, including one on 13 February 1976, which appeared in the *Globe and Mail*. Written by Donald F. Sim, it declared that censorship was not the issue, as the headline to his letter indicates: "Compulsion, Not Censorship, Seen Issue on Laurence Book" (7).

Hollinger, 13 February 1976

Dear Jack—

I don't know whether I should be writing this on Friday the 13th or not, but here goes. I'm sending you today the manuscript of *Road from the Isles*, the collection of essays and articles. I didn't know whether to send it to you or to Anna [Porter], but I thought probably you would like to have a look at it and pass it on to her. I'd also be grateful if you'd hand this letter on to her as well.

There are a couple of comments I'd like to make. First, if you decide to publish the collection, I wonder if it would be possible to get a xerox copy and send it to John Cushman? I am getting a xerox copy for myself today, but it will cost me about $25, so I'm not keen on getting two. If you could have a copy made for John, I'd be very grateful.

Second, I don't think that either Knopf or Macmillan London probably want[s] the book. It is pretty Canadian-oriented. The travel articles from Egypt etc. are kind of interesting, so they might want the book, but I'd be rather surprised. Some of the articles give a Canadian's views on such subjects as imperialism (Brit) and neo-imperialism (USA), and, in a sense, they *should* be interested in these views, but whether they are or not is a different matter.

Third, the two articles on Egypt were done on commission for *Holiday* magazine, nearly 9 years ago, and never published because of the Seven Day Israeli War, after which tourism in Egypt came to an end for a long time. Do first serial rights run out after a period of time, if not taken up? Or would we have to get permission from *Holiday* to use the articles? I imagine John Cushman will know, and I will write to him about it. The only other permission would be to use a few lines from a poem by George Woodcock,[1] "On Completing A Life Of Gabriel Dumont."

I'm afraid my typing in these articles is not so hot and the manuscript is full of x's. I apologize for this. It was because I was trying to get them done quickly, so tried to go too fast.

I'd be very grateful if you or Anna could let me know your response as soon as possible.

All the best,
Margaret

February 14th

P.S.[2] I didn't get this posted yesterday, and perhaps Valentine's Day is a better time to mail the manuscript to you.

Have just realized that, as far as permissions are concerned, I've also quoted some Somali poetry, and probably we'd need permission to use that. However, it's a minor point.

I have just received your letter, re: the banning of *The Diviners*. There's a good write-up in today's *Globe and Mail*, which just about covers the situation. I don't think anything much can be done until the book comes up to the review committee, and thank goodness, the High School teachers of English in P'borough County are prepared to do battle for the book. So we will see. I feel that personally I can't do much, as it is my book. I also can't, unfortunately, speak up for Alice's book,[3] as I'm personally involved through my own novel.

HOWEVER. There have been several very nasty letters in *The Globe*, saying, in effect, that *The Diviners* is "loaded with vulgar language" and "disgusting" sex scenes. It would be awfully nice if someone could write a few letters simply in support of some of the merits of the novel itself. Maybe not necessarily you, Jack, as obviously you, like myself, cannot be deemed impartial. But perhaps you could suggest to a few people that a letter to *The Globe* would be much appreciated. It'll be kind of ironic if *The Globe* only prints anti-*Diviners* letters.

All this damn (oops, sorry ... darn ... er ... *blank* is what I meant to say) business has virtually occupied a week of my life. My phone has never stopped ringing. All phone calls have been supportive, so far.

I got one anonymous nasty letter from someone in Peterborough, grouping me with Jacqueline Susann and Xaviera Hollander.[4] All this is very unpleasant. I feel sorry for Bob Buchanan, head of the Eng Dept at Lakefield High School—he feels badly on my account, altho god knows it isn't his fault. He has been marvellous. But it's a bit odd to have this happen in my own Village. I'd feel worse if it were Neepawa, Man., tho'.

1. George Woodcock (1912–1995) was a Canadian literary critic and essayist. In *Heart of a Stranger,* the collection of travel essays that Laurence and McClelland discuss in these letters, Laurence included an essay called "Man of Our People." The essay is a discussion of Woodcock's biography of the Métis leader, Gabriel Dumont, who Laurence long believed should be as well-known and as celebrated as Louis Riel.
2. This postscript is handwritten.
3. Alice Munro's book, *Lives of Girls and Women*, like Laurence's *The Diviners*, was under scrutiny by some members of the public, who believed her books should be banned.
4. Jacqueline Susann (1918–1974) was an American writer most renowned for her novel, *Valley of the Dolls*, which sold thirty million copies. Xaviera Hollander (1943–) is a former call girl and madam, who published a bestselling memoir, *The Happy Hooker: My Own Story*.

Regent, 16 February 1976

Dear Margaret:

You will have had my interim note about the censorship matter. As I indicated, we are prepared to do anything that needs doing under the circumstances.

Now I am responding to yours of February 4th re: the manuscript. That sounds fine. The schedule is good and there are no problems. I have known from the start that U.S. or U.K. publication[s] are probably not in the cards. That will have no bearing on the Canadian situation at all. After we have read it, however, we may want to suggest to you that you at least give them the opportunity to look at it and make their own decisions.

And don't let the fact that they consider you a dirty old lady in the Peterborough area bug you. I think you are very nice.

Cheers!
Jack McClelland

Regent, 17 February 1976

Dear Margaret:

Letter and manuscript just received today, which proves that there is some hope for the postal service after all. I think that is really damn efficient. I am dictating this letter before leaving the office on Monday and will hope to add a P.S. tomorrow, because I will take the manuscript home and read it before passing it on to Anna.

Yes, we will send a Xerox off to John right away and I will withhold any comment re: Knopf or Macmillan's until tomorrow and until after I have read it. John, by the way, is the person to sort out the *Holiday* thing. I can't imagine it is a problem and the other permissions seem easy.

Yes, we will get a few letters in re: *The Diviners*. I think it is probably right that they shouldn't come from me. I'll see what we can do. It is funny that I was speaking to a group of English teachers in Ottawa on their Professional Development Day last week, and I suggested to them that it would be a useful thing to do on their Professional Development Day to send a telegram of support to you (they were all extremely supportive and appalled by the situation). Whether they did it or not is another matter. I took up their full morning and had the impression that they all intended to go out and get drunk at lunch, and I doubt that there was much professional developing going on in the afternoon.

One curious thing did arise. I was on to one of my favourite themes complaining about standards and the use of a book called *Ice Station Erebus* (or some such) by Alistair MacLean[1] as required reading in an English course in Calgary, Grade Eleven. I do myself proud on this subject. It is not a nationalistic pitch. I point out simply that Alistair MacLean is one of the worst writers in the world—which he is—and that I find the use of his book in English courses in Canada or anywhere else totally inexcusable, even for slow learners. Okay, so I gave them the full pitch on that. When we came to the question period at the end of the session, one idiot actually got up and said, "here you have been complaining about censorship of *The Diviners* and, at the same time, you are attempting to censor Alistair MacLean." It's a crazy fucking world.

The only sensible conclusion that I can reach, Margaret, is that you have simply got to stop writing these dirty, vulgar books. It offends my sensibilities. Speaking of sensibilities, I haven't yet told you about the new corporation I have just formed. It has occurred to me that, since you have been earning so much money lately, you might like to invest. It is a highly specialized operation, although I have to admit that I haven't had much direct experience in the field, I am inclined to think that it is going to make money. It is called "Rent A Bear Unlimited." I plan to make a deal with the Minister of Tourism to take an option at Provincial Parks on the services of all bears (no, don't phone Marge to find out if I am serious. I don't actually proceed with all my great promotion ideas).

Nothing else for the moment. I will add a postscript tomorrow.

Cheers!
Jack McClelland

Margaret, the manuscript is great.[2] I think I would describe it as a feast of good reading. You come through as a warm and interesting person, which you are. It's varied. There is a lot of colour and for the good general reader and the Margaret Laurence fan as well, it is going to be a book that will be very much enjoyed.

That is not to say, I don't have a few quibbles. These I would point out are all strictly from the publishing point-of-view. I'm recording them now, while they are fresh in my mind. I am, of course, passing the manuscript to Anna Porter and, after she and several of our senior editors have looked at it, we may find that they don't agree with me on all points or even on any. They may, of course, have other items they want to raise. Incidentally, as far as the stage of the script is concerned, there are a fair number of typos and word omissions—your typing—but that is, of course, an absolutely minor matter. Okay, on to my quibbles:

1. The title is horrid and will have to go. Okay, I understand the rationale for it, etc. but the title should do two things. It should be memorable and it should sell books. This one is anything but memorable and it won't sell books.
2. There are two pieces in the book that I think should be dropped. This has nothing to do with their merit or quality. It has directly to do with their nature and tone in relation to the rest of the manuscript. I am referring here to the review of the Woodcock book and the piece based on your lecture in London re: Nigeria. I understand their thematic relevance—no, I don't really understand that. I understand their relevance thematically, but it seems to me that they have sort of been dragged in by their heels. Relevance to you and your views, yes, I understand.

The problem I see is two-fold. First, I think the Nigerian piece will be a bore to many of the readers of this book. The book isn't aimed at Margaret Laurence students (even though they will of course use it), but this one just doesn't seem to relate to the nature of the rest of the book. The Woodcock piece is a little different in that it is certainly easy enough in a sense, but, Margaret, it is a book review. It is the only book review, and its inclusion to me in a short book seems to imply by its inclusion that it is the only book review that you have done that is worthy of inclusion and that simply isn't true. It is a good piece, but its effect on me was akin to that of someone wearing very good brown shoes with tails or a dinner jacket. It just doesn't seem to belong in this book.

This, in turn, raises the question of length. It does seem to me that the inclusion of these two pieces draws attention to the relative shortness of the manuscript instead of actually adding to its length. In other words, it could give those who want [to] carp the opportunity to say, "well it appears that Margaret—almost by her own admission in the Introduction—has reprinted everything she has done that is worth reprinting and it doesn't add up to a helluva lot. In fact, she has had to include a lecture and a book review to reach the respectable length." I am not suggesting that that is a fair comment. I am suggesting that it is the sort of comment [that] might be made.

And, frankly, Margaret, I am not all that worried about length *per se*. The material is good; it is rich; it's good reading; it's fine reading. We could chop those two pieces or, alternatively, you could substitute other material if you want to and still have a pretty good book. I think the trick here is fine design and typography anything illustrative here so much as ground sketches. I think we could make it into a very fine-looking small book. It will make a great gift item and I think it will be widely read.

Having referred to the introduction, I would like to see you do some further work on this. I think it is too short for one thing. For another, you can really stick your neck out on the chopping block by sounding your view of what should not be preserved. It is an open invitation to some of the slobbish reviewers in this country. The truth is, Margaret, they can't resist that sort of thing. It is so easy and it adds to the fame of the critic. I can see the headings now: "Pity Laurence doesn't follow her own rules."

Some editors might want to quibble with you about the explanatory intros for each piece. They are good and interesting and useful, but what I don't like, I think, is the inclusion of the date and the magazine. That should be included elsewhere. I think it is off-putting here. I think you should simply explain the circumstances, the reasons for writing it—other than the magazines commissioned you to do it—and put the dates and publications in a listing at the back of the book. Call it artistic deception if you like, but I really find that hard information intrusive.

One other argument about the dropping of the two pieces I have referred to. These could be done in another book at a later date, Margaret. I think they are part of the essential academic apparatus re: Margaret Laurence. Your reputation, obviously, is going to grow and grow and grow. The students *are going to demand this* sort of thing, but not in this book. I think this book is for the general reader. It will come into wide general readership, and I think we should do everything in our power to remove any even very minor flaws that might limit that possibility.

These are all the comments I have. I congratulate you. I think it is fine and I think it will do very well.

Oh, I almost forgot. It is my guess that they will want to do this book in London. I am less sure about New York: even there it wouldn't surprise me. It's pretty damn good stuff.

Cheers!

Jack McClelland

1. Alistair MacLean (1922–1987) wrote *Ice Station Zebra*, a thriller novel set in the Arctic.
2. McClelland refers to Laurence's collection of essays that would be published as *Heart of a Stranger*.

Hollinger, 23 February 1976

Dear Jack:

Thanks for your letter re: my manuscript. My first reaction to it, not unnaturally, was one of incredulity and rage. However, my normally calm and indeed incredibly patient personality has once more reasserted itself, and I am able to look at the situation with my usual tolerance and cool assessment. What a good idea about making the book a "good gift item"! Had you considered the vast possibilities of selling each copy individually wrapped in pink tissue paper, tied about with a wide pink ribbon? Or perhaps a tiny tasteful bunch of plastic forget-me-nots? This village, you know, has numerous gift shops—perhaps I might start one myself, handling only two items ... this book plus *The Diviners*. I would, of course, call the shop (oops ... I mean shoppe) PORN 'N CORN. Similarly, your idea of having some competent commercial artist "dress the book up with some sketches and drawings," "mood background sketches," as you so wittily phrase it, seems to me nothing less than scintillating. How about a group of tourists, couchant, against a background of pyramids, rampant? Or a couple of tartan dollies? Or a dear old man, such as Norman Rockwell might have drawn, holding a fishing rod and looking adorably homespun? The possibilities are endless. Or why don't we just scrap the whole thing?

I had in mind a modest collection of essays, such as Mordecai's *Hunting Tigers Under Glass*.[1] I see I was naive. Again.

Seriously, however, some of your criticisms are justified. Perhaps I should outline the things, after much thought, I find I am able and willing to do. We can then see if these are acceptable to Anna and the others. If they are not, then I really think I would rather not have the manuscript published. ... [2]

I'm not sure when you'll be back from your world travels, so I'll send this letter to Anna.

I'll be interested in your reactions and Anna's to my suggestions. I'd like the manuscript back as soon as possible, please.

All the best,
Margaret

P.S. Thanks again for your offer of aid and assistance re: *The Diviners* being banned. I don't think anything is necessary right now, but it will be interesting to see what happens when the book goes to the Textbook Review Committee. Naturally, I'm hoping they'll okay it. If they don't, it would be nice to have a few letters in support of the book, in the papers. The file grows—today, in *The Peterborough Examiner*, there was a letter from someone in Cultus, B.C. saying perhaps at last the perfect way to increase sales on Can books had been found!

1. Richler's book of essays, *Hunting Tigers Under Glass*, won the Governor General's Award for nonfiction in 1968.
2. Laurence elaborates on the changes she was prepared to make.

Regent, 10 March 1976

Dear Margaret:

That's some letter! I am glad they banned your book in Peterborough. I am writing to *The Examiner* today suggesting that they are on the right track; that all your books should be banned forthwith; that all your awards should be withdrawn because you are corrupting our children.

The fact is, my dear Margaret, that I was paying you a great compliment. A modest collection like *Hunting Tigers Under Glass*! Do you know how many copies of that modest book sold in the original edition? At a guess 1,823. We could publish *Road to the Isles* (ugh! It *is* a horrid title) in a simple, unassuming little edition, which will sell 3–4,000 copies. No problem. However, because you are Margaret Laurence, if we dress the book up a little physically (the price will seem outrageous today whether we do or whether we don't), the fact is that I believe we can sell at least 10,000 and perhaps many more if we make it look like a book and not like a modest collection of essays. What it is, in fact, is a collection of really outstanding writing. It is very interesting and it will appeal. If we dress the book up and make it look like what it is, it will appeal to a market far beyond the academic or the in-group.

And what is wrong with trying to dress a book up a little bit? Alfred Knopf did this for years and I don't remember anybody complaining about it. All I want to do is make it look like something that somebody wants to own. Books, as I have indicated, are very expensive today and, if we turn it out looking like a modest book of essays, then there is just no market for it. Does it need illustration to carry it? No, of course it doesn't. But it will do better in my view with a little decorative work throughout than it will if it is just a simple little book.

Okay, you have responded fairly and well to all my other points. Anna is now in direct touch and I think it is probably better, since I have had my say for me to stay entirely out of any further involvement on that side of the book. The only point that still bothers me is the title. I don't like your new suggestion any better than *Road to the Isles*.[1] I think this book deserves a good title. We really ought to give this one its best possible opportunity, Margaret, and you really should stop thinking about it as a modest collection of essays. It's good and it will sell, but let's give it a chance.

So that's all. I am writing as usual in haste.

Love and kisses,
[Jack McClelland]

1. Laurence's "new suggestion" for the title of this book is not known and not referenced in this correspondence.

Hollinger, 13 March 1976

Dear Jack—

Thanks for your letter. As you will have seen, if you've seen my recent correspondence with Anna, I have now simmered down and revised the manuscript. Actually, I posted it to Anna yesterday, so I hope you'll have the chance to look at it fairly soon, as I'll be anxiously awaiting your response.

What I've done, in brief, is this: 1) changed the title to *Where the World Began*—I think this is a good title; it does express the collection, in ways which I mention in the Foreword; what do you think of it? 2) Totally re-written the Foreword—it is now longer and more personal; I came to see you were quite right about this. 3) Re-written some of the individual introductions; removed refs to original places of publication. 4) Put Acknowledgments at the end. 5) Expanded Dumont article somewhat; removed ref to its being a review. 6) Taken out article on Nigerian literature. 7) Added seven more articles, most of them on a fairly light and humourous [*sic*] nature—after all, what the hell, why not? It makes a longer book, and the humourous [*sic*] ones will add variety of tone, or so I believe.

So—that's about it. I'll be interested to hear what both you and Anna think.

Re: dressing it up a bit—okay, you've convinced me. I can see your argument, and I concede that you are probably right. I'd like it, however, if you could see your way clear at least to consulting me about what type of illustrations, or whatever, you plan to use. I don't mean that I should have power of veto ... obviously, you aren't going to agree to that. But I'd like to be consulted. I might even have some ideas. I recall now that Knopf did that sort of thing with Buckler's *Oxbells & Fireflies*,[1] and it looked good. So you've made your point. (You must admit, however, that if I didn't bash out a furious letter to you from time to time, something of the—shall I say zest—of our professional relationship would be gone.)

Of course, as usual, now that I have mailed the manuscript back to you, I begin gloomily imagining all the rotten reviews [that] could be written about it. I always think it would be fun to review one of my own books—to do two reviews, rather, one favourable and one unfavourable. As a matter of fact, it would be awfully easy to do both—the writer usually knows both the strengths and weaknesses [better] than any reviewer.

Someone has just sent me Coles Notes on *The Stone Angel*.[2] If you haven't seen it, don't. It is *vile*. Chapter summaries, for God's sake—no need to read the book! To see a novel mushed down into miniature, in somebody's crass prose—it nearly made me throw up. You'd think they'd have to get permission to do that sort of thing, but I guess not. The twit who did it says that the novel's main theme is the futility of escape. Oh? That's news to me. I feel enraged, but, of course, can do nothing. Such things are best forgotten, I suppose.

All the best,
Margaret

1. Ernest Buckler's *Ox Bells and Fireflies: A Memoir* was published by McClelland & Stewart in 1968.
2. Coles Notes, which provide plot and chapter summaries and analyses of major literary works, were initially published in Canada in 1948 by Coles bookstore. Ian Brockie notes that Coles "made use of both reprinted and original titles to keep pace with developments in the secondary and post-secondary student markets," and that the guides for Canadian works thus "first appeared in the 1970s and burgeoned during the 1980s with the addition of notes for novels by Morley Callaghan, Margaret Atwood, Hugh MacLennan, and Mordecai Richler" (233).

Regent, 18 March 1976

Dear Margaret:

Glad to have your letter. I haven't seen the manuscript, but will try to get my hands on it as quickly as possible. I very much like the sound of what you have done, and I will be surprised if we are not totally pleased with the way it stands now.

As to the furious letter—you are right. I was pleased to get it. I think it confirms our mutual love. I imagine it scared the hell out of some people in our Editorial Department, though, because I was away when it came in.

Re: the title, I think *Where the World Began* is an improvement, but honestly, Margaret, I don't think it is good enough yet. By this I don't mean at all that it is not significant in terms of the book. What I really mean by it is that I think it is a difficult title to remember. The titles of all your books have been memorable, but I can't see people remembering *Where the World Began*. They [are] going to say that book of Margaret Laurence's about the world or something, wasn't it? You know what I mean. It's a book of essays. Although I don't think it is going to be easy to come up with the right title, but we will think about it and see what we can do, but I don't think this one is the right one yet.

Re: dressing up the book, I am glad you now agree and, yes, we will certainly let you know well in advance what we work out and you will be able to approve it. We are better without decoration unless we can do it well, but I am more and more convinced that the book should be a good-looking physical object.

That's terrible about Coles Notes. No, I won't look at them. I would rather sue them. Unfortunately, we can't. Incidentally, that reminds me that the I.P.A. has finally got an opinion from a very expensive firm of lawyers in Toronto (I hope the government is paying for the opinion) and, to my no great surprise, it is totally in support of the stand that I have been taking and the stand that our own lawyers have been taking, i.e. it is not Coles that is at fault on this whole thing (except morally). It's our bloody government. Or, to put it differently, the Writers' Union should have been picketing the House of Commons, not Coles, when they were in Ottawa. Oh, well, to hell with it. I'll be back to you as soon as I've had a chance to look at the revised script.

Cheers!
Jack McClelland

Regent, 31 March 1976

Dear Margaret:

Sorry it has taken me so long to get back to you. I finally had an opportunity to review the new material and the changes that you have made. I am really pleased. I think it strengthens the book and I think it hangs together very, very well indeed. I am inclined to agree with Anna that "The Catalogue Dream" could perhaps be dropped on the grounds that it is not as strong as the rest of the material, but I don't have very strong convictions about it.[1] Some people will like it. I think perhaps what Anna has in mind is that a lot has been written on the subject recently, since the demise of Eaton's [catalogue].[2] I suppose it could be argued that it is all the more reason to include it.

I am still hung up on the title problem and I really wish we could solve this one. It occurs to me, Margaret, that the title for the first piece in the book is sort of confusing in context. In other words, when I came to it right at the start of the manuscript—"Sources"—I thought it was an explanatory note about the sources of the material in the book and, for a minute or two, I was somewhat confused. I think that is going to happen in the finished book. I would suggest here that you come up with a better title for that introductory piece—and it really is a damn good piece—and, if you can find the right title for that piece, you may well have the title for the book. I fiddled around with the word *Souvenirs* for awhile and you might try the same, even though I didn't come up with the right title from the word, but I, of course, picked this up from your reference to the travel pieces being your souvenirs of the trips and I thought the point was well made. Somehow if the right inspiration occurs, that reference could be expanded slightly to suit the title. Well, hell, I am hoping we will be lucky on this. I realize the reference is in the introduction rather than in the *Sources* piece, but maybe somewhere between the two the answer is going to be found. It is true that all your titles have been good and I personally think that

The Prophet's Camel Bell was one of the great ones. We are all doing our best to come up with the right title for the new book at this end, but it is my guess that you are the one that will ultimately have the inspiration.

All the best.
Sincerely,
Jack McClelland

1. Laurence's essay, "The Catalogue Dream," was not published in *Heart of a Stranger*.
2. Founded in 1869 in Toronto, Eaton's department store was the first Canadian store to introduce mail order shopping through its catalogue, to great success. The spring-summer catalogue in 1976, however, was its last, although the store itself remained with locations throughout the country until its bankruptcy in 1999.

Regent, 6 December 1976

Dear Margaret:

I tried to get you on the phone without any luck and, because my schedule is so hectic at the moment, I probably won't be able to call for a few days. The members of our Board were delighted that you had agreed to join them and you were duly elected at our meeting today. I told them what you had said to me—that your main interest would be in getting us to publish more books by young authors. Everybody said great. As I say, you were unanimously elected a member of the Board.

Not much more I can tell you for the moment. The next meeting will be February 28th. You will receive a detailed notice about it well before then. The meetings usually run from 12.30 through to about 4 P.M. with lunch served during the meeting. You get a nominal fee—$75.00—which may just about cover your expenses. The meetings should normally be held only once a quarter. The last Monday in every three-month period, unless otherwise needed.

At the meeting today, things were rather cheerful. We are having an extremely good year. Naturally, there are a few trouble spots like impending lawsuits, etc. but generally the picture was good. Just for the record, the other directors include: Anna Porter, Peter Taylor, Larry Ritchie[1] and myself, all of whom, of course, are employees, Frank Newfeld, and then a group of three from the outside who you won't know, Dan Casey, a retired former Vice-President of the Bank of Montreal, Sam Orenstein, a chartered accountant, Don Early, a broker, and then, elected at our current meeting, you and Hugh Kane. That's it.

Again, I am delighted to report that the new book has done damn well.[2] Our printing was 10,000 copies. We have only about 1,200 left at the moment, and they will probably all be gone before Christmas, so it really has been well received.

Love and kisses,
Jack McClelland

1. Peter Taylor was an author who published *Watcha Gonna Do Boy ... Watcha Gonna Be?* with McClelland & Stewart in 1967. He also worked for McClelland & Stewart as a vice-president and marketing director, and as co-chair of the editorial committee. He resigned in 1982 to commit to writing books full time. Larry Ritchie worked there during the 1970s, as vice-president and general manager.
2. McClelland here refers to Laurence's collection of essays, *Heart of a Stranger*.

Hollinger, 23 January 1977

Dear Jack—

You won't receive this letter for a while, as I understand from my spies that you are at present in Iran, with Roloff and the Shah.[1] My spy in this case is your daughter Anne! I was so delighted to see her—I was at Trent University last Friday, and in a Common Room coffee session at which I and a Trent professor were chatting with students about prairie literature.[2] She came up afterwards and introduced herself. I do hope she will phone me and come for lunch soon—I've asked her to, and I think she will. She seems to be liking Trent. It *is* a good place, I think—small enough so that students can get to know their profs, and yet (at least in the faculties I know best. ... i.e. English, History, Can Studies, Native Studies) with an excellent faculty. Anne apparently knows Bill Dickson, the young editor who handled *The Lakefield Leader*—he has really made a good little paper out of *The Leader*,[3] and I sometimes review books for them; I am very much in favour of independent local papers. So she hopes that maybe Bill and his wife may be able to drive her to my place and all come one day for lunch or whatever. ...[4]

Several other of my spies tell me that the McClelland-Bantam press party was lively and that lots of other publishers' reps were there. I'm delighted that I did not attend, as you know how much I love big parties of that nature, like the plague. However, Jack, I think you will probably be criticized in some quarters for this Bantam deal, but in my opinion it can only be A VERY GOOD THING, both for Can writers and for M&S, and potentially for some of the smaller publishers as well. I can visualize a time when a number of good Can novels originally published under the imprint of some of the smaller publishers could come out in Seal edition and hit a mass paperback market—fairly obviously, under those conditions, the original hardcover publisher would get 50% of the advance and the royalties, this being the usual arrangement with paperback editions put out by a publisher other than the original one. Financially, and in distribution, this could benefit both writers and other publishers a lot. Of course, as far as M&S writers are concerned, the new mass paperback thing seems to me to be just great. I realize, of course, that I am in a kind of privileged situation. ... i.e. the NCL editions of my fiction mean that the books will be kept in print and available for courses, etc., and the mass paperback editions, of whichever books may mean a brief but wide distribution. So—hurrah all around!

Best,
Margaret

P.S. As "McClelland-Bantam" is kind of a mouthful, I think everyone should be encouraged to say "Seal" edition.[5]

1. Photographer Roloff Beny (1924–1984) published *Iran: Elements of Destiny* with McClelland & Stewart in 1978, the foreword to which was written by the shah. Its companion volume was *Persia: Bridge of Sighs*. The shah funded the publication of the book, hence Beny and McClelland's visit to Iran.
2. Laurence alludes to Professor John Wadland's course, "Canada and the Land" (Canadian Studies 200), in which she attended a lecture on prairie literature by Professor Michael Peterman and then engaged in a discussion with him and the students in the Champlain College Senior Common Room (Peterman).
3. The *Lakefield Leader* was a small, independent, local newspaper, as distinct from the *Lakefield Herald*. Ray Collins started the *Leader* in 1961. When the *Leader* ceased publication, Collins continued to run the print shop affiliated with it, Economy Printers, until its closure in 2010 (Steel).
4. Laurence proceeds to discuss details of the contract.
5. In January 1977, Seal Books was founded as a partnership between the American publishing company, Bantam, and McClelland & Stewart. Laurence's suggestion to refer to the "Seal edition" rather than "McClelland-Bantam" was employed by McClelland. With regard to the emergence of Seal as a partnership between Bantam and McClelland & Stewart, Laurence wrote to Anna Porter, then editor at McClelland & Stewart, on 20 May 1977. She stated, "I would like some reassurance that any books of mine going into Seal editions, and which are also out in the NCL, will be kept in print in the NCL. I extend this hope, obviously, to others' books as well.

I don't think the two markets will conflict, and many of the NCL books are standard works now on Canlit courses in high schools and universities. ... Also, in regard to possible changes within the NCL, I do think it is important that all the present titles be kept in print, even if some of them do not sell very well. The titles from the long-ago past in Canlit may not sell all that many per year, but they really are essential for students doing thesis work in the field, and these are increasing in number" (Margaret Laurence Fonds, William Ready Division, Box 12, File 11).

•———

Regent, 7 February 1977

Dear Margaret:

It was good to have your letter. Your information was absolutely correct. I was in Iran but visiting the Empress, not the Shah. Somehow she appeals to me more.

Daughter Anne was home this weekend. She is thrilled at the prospect of going to visit you and I think you will hear from her before too long. And yes, she will probably arrange to come up with the Dixons. He is a very bright kid and I am glad he is doing well with the paper. I agree with you totally about the value of Independent papers. They serve a very useful purpose and some of them can be surprisingly good.

Re: *The Prophet's Camel Bell,* the first printing was strangely enough 7,541 copies. It is my guess that we will order a reprint sometime in May. While it is true that it doesn't have the same impact as your fiction, it is a good book and I would guess that in paper it will find a good, continuing market.

Re: the Seal edition of *A Jest of God,* Henriette Neatrour's figures are, of course, correct—i.e. $5,000.00 as an advance. I don't know how the $8,900.00 figure got into the act. Larry may have misunderstood, but, Margaret, it will go to 10% (that is the 100,000 copy figure), and I think very quickly. *The Diviners,* according to Bantam, has passed the 220,000 mark in Canada alone already and while *Jest* will not do quite that well so quickly because it has been available, we are counting on their distribution to open up a new market. I can tell you that I will be very disappointed in Seal Books and the new operation if *Jest* doesn't reach 150,000 before the end of the year.

If you were or are in urgent need of money, I would certainly be willing to push the advance up to $8,000.00 but it is one part of the financing that we are involved in directly and as usual I am trying to curtail immediate capital outlay as much as possible. In fact, the Seal edition will earn you $15,000.00 and hopefully double that before the end of the year.

You are right in assessing that the Seal arrangement should be good for M&S authors and for some of the small publishing firms. You are also bang on in anticipating that there will be a lot of criticism in a lot of quarters. I have come to expect that and don't really worry too much about it, except when I am accused of being an opportunist-nationalist. In truth, I don't consider myself one, but am prepared to concede that it is a complex issue and one can't be too critical of how one is seen by the eye of the beholder. I enclose a recent such piece that appeared in *The Toronto Sun* along with a copy of my reply.[1] As a general rule, I feel that such replies are useless and do no more than extend the bad view, but for some reason I felt that I should make some attempt in this case. The truth is that I have never had any great respect for the militant rantings of the Godfreys, Lorimers, and others—I guess I have always been and still am somewhat midway between their position and the ultimate Richler position, which seems to be that cultural standards must begin and end in London or New York. Oh well, to hell with it.

Hope we will see you soon. All the best.
Cheers!
Jack McClelland

1. This article, titled "Canadian Jack Finds U.S. Jill," written by Connie Woodcock, appeared in the *Toronto Sun* on 8 February 1977. It explains the merger between Bantam and McClelland & Stewart. The article states that McClelland is an "all-Canadian, aging boy wonder who, five years or so ago, was pushing the kind of golly-gee whiz nationalism guff that makes you want to gag. Canada for Canadian publishers was his line then." McClelland replied, "I am still a dedicated and active nationalist. All Canadians should and must be concerned about the dwindling control of our resources and the loss of our right to self-determination. The role of the post-nationalist is to see that our energies are not squandered by misguided zeal or worthless jingoistic notions. As to the 'Bantam solution,' I consider it a brilliant initiative on the part of our Federal Government. It leaves us firmly in control" (Margaret Laurence Fonds, Clara Thomas Archives and Special Collections, 1980-001/014, File 27, Item 1688).

Regent, 16 February 1977

Dear Margaret:

I am sorry about the mistake on the cover of *The Prophet's Camel Bell.*[1] As you will find out in due course—as a Director of the company—policy requires that all such copy be approved by the author—including cover design, etc. but for some reason that is beyond my comprehension, this policy is honoured more in the breach than any other way. I shall see that this is corrected in the next printing.

That is fine re: Seal. I am pleased that you are able to take this attitude. We will proceed on the basis of the $5,000.00 advance. And you are right. You should lose no sleep. I wish to God I had a remotely comparable security. The Manawaka books will be supporting you in style long past the time they stash you away in the old ladies home. You won't have to call on the Canadian Writers' Foundation for support,[2] but what the hell.

I hope you are going to come to the Directors' Meeting on the 28th of February. If it is impossible, I will understand, but I would like you to come to this one if at all possible. We are going to start a lengthy dialogue about publishing policy. I don't know how much progress we will make because as you will see in the next couple of days, the nature of the advance material that is being sent out to the Directors is confused to say the least. There aren't enough hours in the day, but maybe we will sort the whole thing out eventually.

Cheers!
Jack [signed]
Jack McClelland

1. No archival evidence survives to indicate what the "mistake" was.
2. The Canadian Writers' Foundation was founded in 1931, with the objective of supporting Canadian writers when they confront financial difficulties.

Hollinger, 17 March 1977

Dear Jack:

I have been wanting to write to you ever since the Board meeting, but have been journeying here and there and didn't seem to have a minute. Have recently arrived back from Saskatoon, where I took part in a prairie writers' workshop at a high school—great fun, and I saw a lot of old friends, including dear Paul Hiebert, who at about 85 is a lot more sprightly than I will probably be at 60.[1]

Before I talk shop, I'd like to say what a pleasure it was to see your daughter Anne and to talk with her when she came to my place for lunch. Those McClelland girls sure are bright and independent! She told me that Susie[2] has a baby now—great news.

I felt I learned a lot at the Board meeting, even if only that the publishing business was a whole lot more complex than I had ever dreamed. I can see you smiling sardonically and saying, "Maybe that'll teach her not to rush in with lunatic suggestions." Well ... no. I guess it won't. I have to confess that I am bothered by the firm's apparent commitment to a book of photos by Beny on modern Iran. If it could be seriously suggested, as it was, that insurance might be taken out on the project, in case the present regime does not survive forever, then that seems to me to indicate that the firm is on pretty unsteady ground here. As it happens, I did not agree with the criticism levelled at M&S for the first Iran book. It was a romantic portrayal, certainly, but those beautiful mosques and so on really do exist and are one aspect of the country, and I thought it was quite okay to present that aspect. The book was not dishonest—it did not pretend to be anything other than it was, a portrayal of some of the historic and beautiful aspects of Iran. The book on modern Iran, however, seems to me to be quite a different ballgame. It will, fairly obviously, not present modern Iran as it really is. The political prisoners will undoubtedly not get a look-in, for starters. Will it show the Empress looking (as she did on the program on TV in an interview with Isabel Bassett)[3] very sad, evasive, and scared when the interviewer asked her (brave Isabel, in my opinion!) about the Shah's repressive measures and about the necessity of close security for her children, lest they come to harm? I doubt it. I think that a book on modern Iran, commissioned by a ruling regime which—to put it as politely as possible—represents a medieval authoritarian divine-right-of-kings outlook could be a very great embarrassment to M&S, in the long run. I do not think that the firm's reputation will be in any way enhanced by a book of this nature. I believe that it would be morally wrong to publish such a book, but, to put it in the coldest and most practical terms, it would seem to me that the firm stands to lose by the book, whatever happens. If the present regime in Iran does not continue (and heaven knows I do not have any real knowledge of the strength or weakness of that regime), then M&S will have on their hands a real non-starter of a book. If the regime does continue, even for a very protracted period of time, M&S will be accused of taking on a rather dubious commission job, propaganda for the existing regime. Lovely old gardens and mosques are one thing. *Today* is another. Considering the apparent hassles that you, personally, have had in getting Beny there and so on, I think your time could be better spent. You said that these books of supreme photos were a kind of M&S calling card for European publishers and so on. Surely the Beny books on Italy, on Canada, etc. etc., plus his first book on Iran, *plus* the splendid Lighthouse book and Barn book, plus *Between Friends*, are calling cards enough?

Probably this comment will not do anything much. Still, I felt I had to make my own personal position quite clear. I mean to speak about this again at the next Board meeting.

All the best,
Margaret

P.S. I think the whole Seal project sounds great, and also the Canada's Illustrated Heritage series, for which I have just sent Hugh Kane a T.M. (Tender Message) for publicity purposes.

1. Paul Gerhardt Hiebert (1892–1987) was a Canadian writer and humorist best known for his book, *Sarah Binks*.
2. McClelland's eldest daughter, Suzanne.
3. Isabel Bassett (1939–) is a Canadian broadcaster and former politician. Between 1999 and 2005, she was the chair and CEO of TVOntario/TFO, Ontario's provincial public television network.

Regent, 21 March 1977

Dear Margaret:

It was good to have your letter. Anne, by the way, was thrilled by her visit with you. She tells me your house—which I haven't seen yet—is really great. She had a fine time.

I am grateful for your views about the Modern Iran book. There is no doubt about the fact that there is some validity to your point of view. Several of our international publishers have already expressed their reservations. It's my view at the moment, at least, that the concern, while valid in principle, does not necessarily relate [to] what is in effect going to happen.

First, let me speak about the insurance problem. Dan Casey is the former Vice-President of the Bank of Montreal. He was concerned about the first book from the financial point of view. First, he had been told in error that it was not profitable. Dan is a member of our audit committee and, in a review of closing details of the previous year, he was misled about this book. It has been extremely profitable, although it did not appear to be so on an early analysis. That has remained in his mind plus the fact that we waited a long time to receive payment on the first book. He is aware too of the political instability, if it can be called that, in Iran. There is no doubt about it that the Shah is a prime target for assassination, even more so than a president of the United States. Prevailing wisdom in diplomatic circles is that he will be very fortunate to survive for many more years. This does not, by the way, represent any large movement in Iran. It is a matter of international terrorism and Communist infiltration. I could go on about that one at great length. We have, by the way, looked into the insurance aspect of the thing. It would cost us $7,500 to insure the contract. Although no decision has been reached as yet, I doubt we are going to spend that $7,500. It's my personal conviction after having been in Iran eight times in the last three years, not only will the regime survive (whether or not the Shah is assassinated) but also that we are more likely to get payment on this account than from most of our booksellers.[1]

As to the book itself, Margaret, it is not in the sense you think a propaganda piece any more than *Between Friends,* for example, is a propaganda piece.[2] How many elaborate picture books on Canada—*The Year of Our Land,* for example, or any others you want to mention—elaborate picture books on Britain, USA, France or any country contain coverage of jails, political prisoners, etc. It's a nice editorial concept that they should, but the fact is that they don't. These are coffee-table gift-books and they don't purport ever to show all aspects of life in the country. How many such books show unemployment line-ups? How many such books show the slums? I don't say that such subjects are not covered in books. Where they are not covered, however, is in elaborate coffee-table books printed in colour. The fact that it should be done or that it's ever been done is a poorly thought-out liberal notion that bears no relation to the truth. Despite what you say, you have been influenced by Fulford's rather silly comments on the first book.

Let me tell you how the book came about. In her final review of the content of *Persia: The Bridge of Turquoise,* the Empress became concerned that the book was too heavily weighted towards the past. Her interest, by the way, is in history and the past; the Shah's in the present and future. She was concerned about his reaction to the book with such little coverage of the contemporary Iran. She then decided to remove all the contemporary images from the first book and immediately commissioned the second book.

Now, the second book is not going to be a propaganda book. It is a Roloff Beny book. It is essentially dealing with art, culture, and beautiful things. While it may be true that there is torturing of political prisoners in contemporary Iran—which in the context of that country's history I consider to be about as bad as the fact that citizens continue to be brutalized by the Toronto Police Force—under this despotic regime, the arts have flourished. Painters, sculptures [*sic*], dancers, singing groups, etc. have never had it better. There are new universities, new schools, new art galleries, new museums, new slum clearance programs, new workers holiday resorts, new satellite cities, new city centres, everything—dealing with the humanities—in the broadest sense being built. The standard of living is increasing at a rapid rate, and it's my impression that the quality of life is increasing at a similar rate. There are more cars per capita in Tehran than in Rome, Paris, or New York, or Los Angeles. To an outsider, the development in Iran is tremendously impressive.

People complain about Iran. They question why the Shah should be building up one of the most modern air forces, navies, armed service operations anywhere in the world. His answer to that is that his country is not a Communist country, but he is surrounded by Communist countries. He doesn't claim that it's a democracy. It is not, but it is closer to the West than it is to Communist. My view is that it's very sensible of him to concern himself with armed forces. They are also criticised for being very hard on drugs. Kids from other countries [who] are caught going into Iran with even a small amount of marijuana are given lengthy prison sentences. Native Iranians caught with drugs are shot. So they don't have a drug problem in Iran. I'm not sure that I disagree with this policy. Bermuda has one and it's very similar at least as far as outsiders are concerned. They just don't shoot the natives who are caught using or trafficking in drugs; they just put them away for about 20 years. It's a judgment issue.

What about political prisoners? The Shah and his secret police claim there are relatively few of them and that they are Communist infiltrators. Who is going to question that? Not me. If you look at your map, you will see that Iran is the last outpost of Western thinking in that part of the world. Their society is different than ours, their philosophy is different, their values are different. I don't know why we should attempt to impose Western concepts on them. Western journalists have managed to build up a pretty grim picture of Iran. It makes sensational reading. The only problem is that it conflicts very much with what you find on the spot. Visitors are free to go anywhere as they are in Canada. The people seem as happy as they seem in Canada. There is no visible evidence of repression. Certainly, the Shah's children are carefully guarded. So are Margaret Trudeau's children. In that part of the world, they do it a little more overtly. In North America, the Secret Service people walk behind them as unobtrusively as possible. In the east, the philosophy is a show of power is the proper treatment. The guards have to have machine guns and they are extremely visible.

So I really understand if the Beny book on Italy doesn't show the seamy side of Italy, Roloff Beny of Iran is not going to show the seamy side of Iran. The French, the British, the Japanese have all published beautiful picture books on contemporary Iran, why the hell can't a Canadian house do it? The ultimate problem I think is that a lot of nasty things have been said about Iran in the Western press. Certain people, yourself included, have been influenced by these things. I can't say you are wrong. I can't tell you that the Shah claims this is Communist propaganda. From what I have seen first-hand, it may well be. I don't hide the fact that they are tough on political prisoners. They are in many other countries in the world and we are too except that in a democracy rough tactics have to be used very carefully in case they are discovered. In Iran, the secret police are in charge. So that's it.

Hope to see you soon. I am going to be travelling out your way to have a look at Anne's house—which I haven't managed yet—and will let you know in advance and hope to have a visit with you at the same time.

All the best,
Yours sincerely,
Jack McClelland

1. McClelland was not correct in his prediction. Later in 1977, there was significant civilian protest against the shah's oppressive policies, which led to the Iranian revolution and the shah's eventual exile from Iran in 1979. As James King notes, "From Jack's perspective, things had gone very badly: the Iranian government subsidy for the two books never materialized, and thousands of copies of the book—never paid for—vanished" (*Jack* 318).
2. *Between Friends* was published in 1976 by McClelland & Stewart as a gift to the United States on its bicentennial. Prime Minister Pierre Trudeau and Lorraine Monk, the author, presented President Gerald Ford with his own copy in a ceremony in Washington, DC (Lorraine Monk Books).

Regent, 20 May 1977[1]

Dear Margaret:

As a Member of the Board, I received a copy of your circular letter of May 17th.[2] It is an extraordinary document. I have, through the years, developed a standard procedure for dealing with such communications. I have a rubber stamp, which in antique English prints the word "bullshit." The regrettable fact is that I have not yet developed the temerity to use it in dealing either with distinguished authors or Members of our Board of Directors. Pity!

The letter creates several basic problems. The first is: what do I do with it at a Board meeting at which you won't be present; the second is: how do I deal with it personally?

At the Board level, I am sure I will be admonished—if the Board is in good form—with three direct questions. (a) Why did you send out such a stupid letter, (b) why on earth did you ask this lady to join the Board and recommend her so highly when she is proposing to resign before her second appearance, and (c) while we recognise the great things you have done in the past, why don't you realise that it is not in the best interests of the firm to offend unnecessarily our most important author.

To the foregoing I shall probably reply along these lines. (a) It was a privileged letter to our Board of Directors. It was suggested to me before the letter went out that the tone should have been softened. I said "no" because, as always, I want to say exactly what I feel. Her letter was not edited or redrafted. It contained my precise reaction to the T.W.U.C. [Writers' Union of Canada] agreement. (b) I do not believe that Mrs. Laurence will resign from the Board. I sent her, in advance, a letter warning her not to read the document if she anticipated any conflict of interest. I then talked with her on the phone before she had read the document and again warned her. Her reaction was that she would probably be mad as hell, write me a nasty letter—which in fact she has done many times before—and then resolve the problem with me in one way or another. I don't believe that she will resign. If she does, from the purely pragmatic point-of-view, she will be bound because of what has gone before not to reveal a word of the content of the letter to anyone. It's a lousy point. It's a pragmatic point but it is real, and (c) I don't believe the letter or the situation has anything to do with the publishing arrangement between McClelland and Stewart and Margaret Laurence. Her only possible form of retaliation here would be to insist that we sign a T.W.U.C. agreement for her next book. If she did, her agent would shoot himself immediately and, if she did, I would say no. I wouldn't sign that agreement—as a matter of principle—with Jesus Christ if he reappeared and offered us his memoirs.

That could be the way it will go at the Board meeting. In fact, though, I doubt it. I suspect what will happen is that we will table the matter for further consideration at a meeting when you are present. The subject is far too delicate to be dealt with when one of the protagonists is absent. My recommendation, at least, will be to that effect.

Next, I had to deal with the matter on a personal level. I am going to have to tell you several things that you won't like. First, I am going to say that the intensity of your letter has re-confirmed my view that the best decision you have ever made is to acquire an unlisted number, to develop a form-reply to the mail that flows into your place, and to cut off your numerous obligations re: speaking engagements, seminars, committee appearances, consultations, and God knows what else. I believe it is a fact that you have been taking all these things too bloody seriously. You are a writer. You are not den mother or block parent to the whole bloody writing community of Canada. You have been getting too uptight about this whole scene, so I am glad at least that you have taken that step.

Secondly, it seems that you are stunned by the fact that I have imputed motives or ulterior motives to the people that have formulated the draft agreement. Why shouldn't I impute motives? I am sending a report to the Board of Directors of my company. I didn't know who had served on the committee, but it wouldn't have made any difference had I known. I looked at the document and I had to make one of two conclusions. Either that the motive was ulterior or that the committee was inept and incompetent. Frankly, I didn't know who was on the committee. Frankly, too, I couldn't have cared less. Of the two choices available to me, I chose the charge of ulterior motive in preference to incompetence. As you will have read from my evaluation—and here I speak professionally—I felt it to be a very cunning document. Ineptness or incompetence was the furthest thing from my thoughts after studying it. Tell me what the other alternative is.

It seems that you were a member of the committee. It seems that you have been hurt by what I said. Let me try to straighten out the record on a few important points:

1. I have never made a public statement against the interest of the Writers' Union. I have never made a private statement designed to persuade anyone from joining. I have told you and a select company of others that I am by no means convinced of the usefulness of the organization.
2. I have, right from the start, both in writing and verbally, told the Writers' Union that I don't think the standard contract agreement or whatever you may call it—it really doesn't make much difference—is a useful effort. I have consistently instead suggested that a guide to contracts could be useful and constructive. My advice on this matter has been consistently ignored. Fair enough.
3. To the best of my knowledge, either I or someone at M&S, has answered in detail every specific query ever sent to us by T.W.U.C. We have, in fact, gone out of our way to be extra co-operative.
4. Your charge that we have refused to meet with either individuals or a committee representing the contract group is correct. There are, in my view, good and sufficient reasons for that position and I stand by them: (a) we have no single individual in the firm competent or qualified to meet with such a committee. It is that simple. I am the only person fully apprised of our publishing policy, our attitude

and who is fully conversant with contracts. My problem is I am too soft-lined for such deliberations. I am not sufficiently versed on some of the implications of minor technical points. Larry Ritchie has considerable experience with contracts, but is too hard-lined and couldn't represent our policy towards authors. Anna Porter, on the other hand, could represent the latter, but hates contracts and understands very little about them.

Our lawyer, though he is superb from the legal point of view, can hardly be conversant with changes in author relationships and publishing attitudes, even though he has been a member of our Board for more than 20 years. We could have all gone, I suppose, but it took Larry and I on a face-to-face review a total of 16 solid hours to understand the contract. It would have taken a committee three times that which, for all practical purposes, would have meant something like half a year of weekly half-day meetings. We can't afford it. (b) Even if we were prepared to make the foregoing sacrifice, which we were not, and even if we could afford it, which we couldn't, the fact is that we don't believe in the principle of a basic contract. My personal experience with Alma Lee had not encouraged me to think it was a fruitful exercise. My personal experience with Marian Engel has convinced me that it was not. The whole thing is bloody impractical.

I am not trying to be bloody-minded about this thing. I am trying to be practical. I think I care as much about the future of Canadian publishing as any member of T.W.U.C. and probably more. If I care about Canadian publishing, I care about Canadian writers, because the two are inseparable. In a recent letter to Earle Birney,[3] I pointed out that, although some people believe to the contrary, that it was a matter of fact that I had never done anything in 30 years in publishing that was not on the basis of enlightened self-interest. The fact that in many cases it turned out to be unenlightened self-destruction was another matter. That has nothing to do with principles. My principle has always been that publishing survives because of authors and the intelligent publisher serves himself by doing the best he can to look after the best interests of the authors that he publishes. That is paternalistic bullshit. I wish I had the stamp with me as I am dictating this letter.

I can't remember exactly what I said in that long memo. Let me now tell you what my current intention is and what I will, of course, recommend to the Board.

1. That we should not discuss the matter in detail at the Board until you are present.
2. That if you think it is urgent, we can call a special meeting for that purpose.
3. That until such a meeting is held, it will be the policy of the company not to reveal our attitude to T.W.U.C. That policy is not vindictive. It is a policy. It is based on what I have already pointed out to you. We cannot afford to meet with them. There is no one here equipped to do so except possibly myself and the company cannot afford for me to spend my time in that way.
4. That the lawyer that has already been assigned the job will proceed with the preparation of our new contract.
5. That when that has been approved, that we will prepare a standard letter to new authors explaining the rationale of our contract.
6. When that is approved, we will send copies of both to T.W.U.C.
7. That these things proceed on an orderly basis as time permits, but that it be recognized that we have many more urgent and critical items on our agenda. Should we, in the interim, before our standard contract is prepared, be confronted with the issue of an author who insists on a T.W.U.C. agreement, simply say no. Good luck, you can publish elsewhere.

It is not my intention, Margaret, to circulate this letter to any members of our Board. In all truth, I feel they have more important matters to deal with. This one is important to you, because it turns out that you served on this committee and it seems that you may have a fair sensitivity about that. This letter and my previous one will give you some insight into my personal dislike of committees. Generally speaking, I think that most committees are time-wasters. More specifically, I think that committees composed of amateurs, no matter how well-intentioned, who are dealing with highly complex professional subjects, are downright dangerous.

I am going to add a final footnote about committees. I really believe for the most part their results tend to be negative. I am not going to lay the old camel story on you,[4] but the next time we meet—assuming that we have a reasonable amount of time at our disposal—let me tell you how I assess several of the blue-ribbon accomplishments of T.W.U.C. I mean two of the accomplishments in which T.W.U.C.—well intentioned as always—thinks it has accomplished something truly worthwhile. In both cases, it is my assessment that the results have been, or will be before long, proved to be disastrous to the book trade. By the book trade, I mean Canadian authors as well as publishers as well as retail booksellers. Book publishing is a complex, but at the same time a sensitive, commercial mechanism. To me, at least, there are a lot of signs that too many parts of the delicate mechanism are being adjusted by well-intentioned, but not necessarily well-informed, committees. Do I sound like a crotchety old man? Of course I do, but I will be glad to tell you about it.

Love and kisses,
[Jack McClelland]

1. McClelland has put a line through this letter in pen and written "not sent."
2. There is a note with this letter from Laurence to Hodgeman. It reads, "I enclose herewith a Memo to Board members. I would be most grateful if you could have it duplicated and circulated to members of the Board." The memo to which Laurence refers, however, is not attached and does not survive in the archives (McClelland & Stewart Ltd. Fonds, Box 87, File 24).
3. Earle Birney (1904–1995) was a renowned Canadian poet from Calgary, Alberta, although he later moved to Toronto. He published over twenty books of poetry.
4. McClelland appears to be referring to the fable of the Camel's Nose, where a camel managed to work its entire body into the tent of its owner by asking permission to put just one more body part inside. The fable is a metaphor for an apparently innocuous request leading to an incrementally worsening situation.

Regent, 26 May 1977

Dear Margaret:

We agreed in advance that you would be mad. I guess it's a matter of degree. There is always the question of degree. You predicted that you would get mad and send me a nasty letter. How right you were.

Your letter was discussed at considerable length at our Board meeting this afternoon. As a matter of fact, it consumed more time than any other item on the agenda. Considering the fact that members of the Board should have been concerning themselves with why we had such a lousy year in 1976, rather than an emotional note from our newest Director—well, what can I say beyond the fact that your message got through. Your position was ably supported by more than one member of the Board. You will be relieved to know, I'm sure, that reason ultimately prevailed.

The decision in this matter was postponed until the next meeting. This decision was reached for a number of reasons. First, that you were not present; second, because the next meeting will be on June 22nd less than one month away; third, because apart from your letter, only a few members of the Board were familiar with the details—they had not received my memo, etc.; [fourth,] because I was able to muster at least a minority support; and fifth, because I was able to attack your position—and I consider it to be quite unreasonable—without fear of rebuttal from you personally.

On balance, then, I would say that the Board tended to accept your point-of-view and feel that some sort of explanation should be sent to TWUC. Even more important in the order of priority was that some sort of olive branch be offered to you. I am expected to tender the olive branch. The sweetest olives come from the south of Italy. Your suspicion that this [one] comes from the North may not be totally unfounded.

There are a number of things that I must say to you. First, I feel that your letter breaks the ground rules. My memorandum was a privileged document in several ways. First, it was a memo from me to my Board of Directors. Surely, it is my privilege to be honest with the members of the EMS Boards. As a matter of fact, it is my obligation. If I am ever going to question motives, surely this is where I should do it.

With the document, I sent you a memo. I warned of the danger of a conflict of interest and urged you not to read it if you thought there could be a conflict. At the time I was not aware that you had served on the contract committee of TWUC. When Anna Porter read the memo—I use her as a sounding board on a great many matters—she was appalled. She pointed out to me that you had been on the committee. I didn't know that. I said, "screw it." "If I can't be honest with Margaret Laurence, I can't be honest with anybody." I then talked to you. I explained the problem. You said you could deal with it, so you did. I guess you didn't anticipate how mad it would make you.

No problem, Margaret, except that I think your position is a slightly dirty pool, and I think that because you served on the committee, you worked hard on the committee and, although it was in no sense designed for that purpose, my memo upset you.

I think there are several points that are particularly upsetting to you. The first is the matter of motive. Can I tell you in all candor that the thing that interests me least is motive. It simply doesn't interest me. I am aware that the motive of TWUC is not to destroy the publishing industry. I am aware that that is not your motive or the motive of most of the members of the committee. That really is not an issue. My point—and perhaps it was ineptly made in a privileged document—was that the end product, the contract and the end of the contract, was to me as though it had been drafted by a committee with the motive of destroying the publishing industry in Canada. Do you really believe that I think TWUC is out to destroy the publishing industry? Of course you don't, but do understand that I consider the end product of that committee to be so hopelessly inept that I was able to say in all honesty that it would appear to have been put together by a committee with such an objective in mind.

I admit that I have a problem with committees. Although I won't remind you of the camel story, it is fair to say that I don't believe in them. I don't believe that a good bridge would be constructed by a committee of amateurs that co-opted one professional engineer, no matter how good those were who had never built a bridge before. It is a highly professional, legal subject. It needs expertise. Contracts fit into the same category. People use bridges. People use contracts, but that doesn't make them experts. This committee, regardless of its constituency—and that doesn't interest me—lacked expertise or lacked familiarity with publishing problems. I don't know which. It really doesn't matter. I would not favour a committee composed substantially of patients recommending surgical procedures at the Toronto General Hospital. I have a thing about committees.

However, your next point—perhaps in order of the degree to which my memo bothered you—might be our apparent unwillingness to co-operate with TWUC in this matter. I have a few things to say about this. First, I never said an unkind word in public about TWUC. Second, only a few of my good friends, yourself included, are aware that in general terms I consider it to be a fairly useless organization except socially. Third, to the best of my knowledge, we have never received at M&S a direct request or query from TWUC that has not been answered properly in detail. There is one exception. The standard contract or whatever it may be called. Let's have a review of our positions.

Initially, the question of a standard contract was raised by a number of members of the union in discussion with me. I admit that I opposed it. I said, consistently, for the record, that I felt it a waste of time. That what I felt would be useful would be a guide to contracts. TWUC chose to ignore my advice. Fair enough. Why not? I did at least make my attitude clear at the outset.

The contract was then produced. I'll tell you in a minute why we refused to meet with the committee. When a copy of it was sent to us, however, it is a matter of record that I said, "I have had time to read it superficially. There are many things in it that I like. On the basis of a hasty reading, I'm inclined to think it may be acceptable to us, but until we have time to give it a more detailed study, I can't say any more than that." Those are not my exact words, because I don't remember my exact words, although they are probably recorded often enough. It doesn't matter. That is the substance of what I have said from the time we first received a draft of the contract. My statement was sincere. I was not trying to mislead anybody. In fact, a number of people here read the contract and their reaction was similar. Can I tell you that that only underlines the fact that contracts are very complex and very tricky? At least three of our senior people shared my initial reaction to that draft agreement.

But why wouldn't you meet with this committee? Why this lack of cooperation? Why this animosity? Was it a dog-in-the-manger attitude? It was none of these things. How do you tell a committee that has been meeting for months on the subject of a contract that you haven't got either the time to meet with them or people equipped to meet with them. The fact is there is no point in telling them that. They wouldn't believe it. They have been meeting on contracts.

First, Margaret, it is a matter of fact that we had no one who could meet with them. I couldn't or wouldn't meet myself, because I am not a lawyer and because I take too soft a line in these matters, and yet, because I have had about 30 years experience, I am the best person for it. I ruled myself out. The second person would be Larry Ritchie. He knows quite a bit about contracts, but his field is accounting. He is a professional—a professional Chartered Accountant. He takes a harder line on contractual matters than either Anna or I would want the firm to take. The third person might be Anna. She hates contracts in the same way I do and the fact is that she has not had enough experience dealing with them to represent as professional at such a meeting. The only other person who could conceivably represent us would be Bob Martin, our lawyer. As a lawyer, he could represent us. Even though he has been on our Board for 20 years, he could not represent us from the publishing point-of-view, because publisher-author relationships change constantly. I mean none of these people any disservice but none of them could have appropriately represented the M&S point-of-view at any such meeting.

The second point is that we couldn't afford the time. This doesn't mean that we don't consider contracts important. In fact, we consider them to be very important, but we could not afford the idea. I said in my memo that Larry and I spent a solid, concentrated 16 hours reviewing the TWUC contract. I mean it. That was a solid 16 hours without interruption. I spent at least another 2 hours summing up our point-of-view and dictating the memo. Say 18 hours in total. That's with two people meeting. If 6 people are meeting, I guarantee from my experience with committees, that you can triple that time. That's 54 hours or, say, 52. Margaret, that is one-half year of weekly meetings taking 2 hours plus the time to get to the meeting and return. In other words, a full half-year of afternoons or mornings to get even close to an intelligent result and that's leaving out the technical legal side. After 30 years, I know the intent only. I am not a trained lawyer, nor is Larry. After all the time we spent, we still had to defer our comments to a lawyer for careful study.

Does that give you a feel for the impracticality of meeting with TWUC? If it doesn't, it should. Does it give you a feeling for the impracticality of telling the TWUC or trying to explain why we couldn't meet? They were, in fact, meeting. I had already expressed my opinion that it was not a useful exercise.

The third thing that I think troubles you was my expressed wish to "stonewall it" or delay a confrontation as long as possible. I guess that is a reasonable reaction. The only thing is, Margaret, we are still not ready to meet and I don't know when we will be. We don't have a single individual equipped to meet with them and properly represent the firm. Even if we did have such an individual, I'm not sure we can afford that sort of time.

It is even rougher than that. Does it make sense to tell them we don't like their contract without telling them why? We don't yet know how to tell them why. It is a confrontation. As you have seen from my memo, the draft agreement is not even remotely acceptable to us. I consider it to be essentially a dangerous document.

I think it is a dangerous document—apart from the detail—mainly because it sets up an adversary relationship between author and publisher and I think that is wrong. Dead wrong. You talk about paternalism in Canadian publishing. There may be paternalism. If there is, I am unaware of it. Lorne Pierce might have experienced it,[1] we never have. But I will tell you one thing. Because Don Cameron published with Ryerson and they sold to McGraw-Hill, which he didn't like, and because he then published with Macmillan who then sold to Maclean-Hunter[2], which he didn't like, is no reason to draft a model agreement that says publishing houses can't be sold without releasing authors from their contracts. It doesn't make any bloody sense. It may be that a Farley Mowat or a Peter Newman[3] or a Margaret Laurence could get such a clause in a contract, but there is no way for your average author. So it can be argued, as Pierre Berton did at our Directors' Meeting, that everybody in the union knows that they will never sign a contract like this contract. ... That is not its purpose. That is not what it is intended for. Its purpose is to show what the ideal perfect contract would be like. That may have been said. If it was said, it's crap. I will tell you one place it isn't said is in the guidelines. The guidelines are quite explicit.

Does it really make sense to set up a model agreement that is going to make 95% of the authors in Canada feel they are being screwed by their publishers?

No matter how I moderate my tone, do you really want me to go and meet with TWUC representatives and talk the way I am talking? I really consider that contract to be dangerous. Let me give you a current example. I received a letter this morning from a fairly well-known Canadian author, who is a member of the union. We sent her a contract several weeks ago. That contract, in terms of the TWUC agreement, is iniquitous. It relates to a special publishing project and one of our subsidiary companies. It is iniquitous except that it represents the only way in which we can afford to publish her book; make it available; and it also represents the only way she is going to get her book published. She took the contract to the union lawyer, whoever that may be. Great!

The most important issue, of course, was money. She didn't need a lawyer for that and my guess is that we won't sign a contract because of money, even if we had it coming out of our ears, we couldn't sensibly pay her what she wants. But the other two major issues are interesting. She must have copyright in her name. Margaret, that is a joke. I have explained at great length to the TWUC—and invited them to tell me that I am wrong—that this is an American concept. It has nothing to do with Canadian Copyright Law. It has no relevance here and that, in fact, there are many practical reasons why it is not desirable here. We, frankly, don't give a damn. For all it matters under Canadian Copyright Law, one can forget it. It is interesting, though, that under U.S. Copyright Law, it is very important. The other point related, for God's sake, to one of the points that I have been complaining about. The publisher can't assign the agreement. Big Deal. I hope the advice was free. I don't mean disrespect to the lawyer involved. What I do mean is that expediency will always govern most publishing contracts.

So what are we going to do about all this? First, let me tell you what my intention had been:

1. Await the completion of our own new contract. This was started several years ago. A young lawyer spent many long hours preparing a draft. The draft was considered. It was put into abeyance about the time the Union committee was formed. The young lawyer is at work on it again. Working with his original draft, the current draft from TWUC with comments, and our memo on the subject.
2. When that agreement is complete and approved by our executives—and it is impossible to put a date on it—we will then prepare an explanatory comment.
3. When that is complete and approved, we propose to (a) start using it and (b) to send it to the Union for study.
4. If, at that point, they want to meet with our young lawyer to review it, we would be more than willing to arrange it.
5. In the meantime, I don't propose to do anything.

How long will the foregoing procedure take? Margaret, I don't know. It could be two months. It could be six months. It could be longer than that. It is a time-consuming procedure. It is a high priority item because the fact is our new computer program, which we desperately need, must be based on that agreement. It will still take a lot of time.

Now that's where we were before your letter arrived. That's where we will remain until our next Board meeting, which will follow the Annual meeting on June 22nd. I hope you can be at that meeting. If you can't be, I think you and I are going to have to find the time to meet and review the whole matter in detail.

I am sorry to have written at such length. It can't be helped. It is a very important subject. I would be glad to have it settled with TWUC during my lifetime. I wouldn't want it to happen much sooner than that—and you will think I am joking—because of the commitment we have made to the new Translators' Union. We have told them that we can't tackle their standard agreement until we have settled things with TWUC because we consider writers more important than translators. They don't of course and their requirements—at first glance at least—appear to be even tougher than TWUC, which ain't easy. Even though on average translators are making double the income of the original author in Canada, they want a few lovely little items like share of royalties, approval of promotional copyright (in their name). For all I know, they might even have the same lawyer.

I was going to close the letter by giving you some advance information on the new Publishers' Union that I have formed. We have committees on how to prepare manuscripts, writing as a craft, standard agreement with authors, the promotion of publishers including funded tours, a newsletter for the exchange of information about the peccadilloes of authors—and a lot of other grand ideas. The main problem is that John Roberts[4] has thus far refused to fund us on the grounds that we should be publishing, not meeting all the goddamn time, but no, I am not going to tell you about the plans because I just remembered that this letter is being circulated at their request, I think, to all the members of our Board. Board members tend to be very serious people and they may misconstrue any detailed description of the new Union.

Have I responded adequately? I hope so. I don't want to cause trouble between you and Marge and she will be mad as hell if she has to do another long letter like this one.

Cheers!
Jack McClelland

1. Lorne Pierce (1890–1960) was an editor at Ryerson Press from 1920 to 1960. As Sandra Campbell notes, he was "one of the most influential publishers in Canadian literary history." Moreover, "Pierce situated himself as a major cultural nationalist," much like Jack McClelland, who operated albeit in a time period that was different from and subsequent to that of Pierce (4).
2. Maclean-Hunter was a Canadian communications company, which began in 1887. It launched the successful magazine, *Maclean's*, in 1905 and the newspaper, *Financial Post*, in 1907. It was sold to Rogers Communications in 1994.
3. Peter C. Newman (1929–) is an influential Canadian journalist and writer.
4. McClelland was probably referring to the Canadian politician, John Roberts (1933–2007), who at this time was the secretary of state for the federal Liberal government under Prime Minister Pierre Trudeau.

Hollinger, 15 June 1977

Dear Jack:

The olive branch from Northern interior climes is so ice-encrusted that I think I may wait until it thaws a bit before picking it up.

I am sorry that you feel that my letter to the Board members breaks the ground rules. Your memo to the Board members *was* treated by me as a confidential document. I said nothing about it to the union, nor will I.

Surely you cannot have been naive enough to have imagined I would not read your memo? In fact, I did not read it until after the Writers' Union conference. I do not quite understand the term "privileged document" in regard to your Memo to Board members. Does this mean that you are privileged to send such a memo to Board members, but a Board member who is unable to attend a meeting is *not* privileged to respond to such a Memo with another Memo to Board members? I would like this point clarified. As I was unable to attend the last meeting, it seemed to me quite ethical to respond to your Memo in the way I did. If other Board Members had not seen your Memo, that is hardly something I could have anticipated.

I consider your remarks on the union as being a "fairly useless organization except socially" to be insulting and inaccurate. The fact that you have been careful not to make such remarks in public does nothing to heighten my respect for your views.

I appreciate the fact that a contract is a complex document, and I realize that for a representative of M&S to spare the time necessary to meet with the Union Agreement Committee on this matter would not be easy. Nonetheless, I cannot help but believe that you exaggerate the time factor. I still think it was unfortunate that no one from M&S met with the union committee to discuss the final draft of the union Agreement. I believe an important opportunity was lost. I think it also unfortunate that you are not prepared to meet even at this point with representatives of the union.

I am glad to note, however, that you are prepared to meet with the union's representatives upon completion of your contract. However, if you are by that time using the contract, the union's viewpoints will presumably not have the slightest affect [*sic*] upon your contract or upon your willingness to discuss contracts with your writers. If this is not paternalism, what is it? You seem all along to be saying that, as a publisher, you know what is best for the writers whom you publish, and that the writer had better not lift his or her voice at all in the matter of the Agreement. I'm sure this cannot be your view, but this is how you make it sound in your letter. The union has at no time said that our Agreement should be signed in its entirety in any one case. Rather, it is a guide to our members when discussing their Agreements with their publishers. It covers a wide range of circumstances, because, in this country, as I mentioned in my previous Memo, there are many different kinds of publishing houses and many different circumstances when publishing books of various kinds. But we do assume that a publisher will be willing to discuss the matter of the Agreement, either with the writer himself or herself, or with an agent. And of course, in practise, at least for those of us who have agents, this is what does happen. It is still my feeling that much could be gained at this juncture by your lawyer meeting with a representative of the union Agreement Committee. I do not think this would entail months of meetings. I merely believe that some discussion could be profitable to both sides.

As far as your jocular comments on the final page of your letter are concerned, you appear to have a very slight knowledge of the principles of unionism. You have no need of forming a "Publishers' Union," I am happy to inform you. You, as Management, already have your own Publishers' Associations; two of them exist in this country. They are for the benefit of publishers; their aim is, as I understand it, to further the cause of Canadian publishing. You may say that this is the same as furthering the cause of Canadian writers, but I'm afraid this is not always so. The Writers' Union of Canada has been formed for exactly the same basic reason as the publishers' association ... to further the interests, in this case, of Canadian *writers*. You surely cannot claim that no writers in this country have been ripped off by their publishers. As it happens, you can be justly proud that M&S has one of the better contracts in this country and has in general treated its writers pretty well. But I have seen contracts offered by publishers who shall remain nameless that are a disgrace. Writers want better conditions in this country and we have a perfect right to work towards that end, which we shall continue to do so. I think that you may ultimately come to see that your own paternalistic attitudes are shown nowhere more clearly than in your own attitude to the Writers' Union, and it is my sincere hope that you may in time come to modify and change those attitudes. The interests of writers and publishers are by no means always identical, and writers have for too long been low man on the totem pole. It is in fact our labour, which gives you your product, and no amount of public recognition or handsome publicity can obscure the fact that professional writers are entitled to a living wage for their work. The union was formed to try to bring this about through various means. It will not simply go away if you ignore it. Co-operation with the union, therefore, would seem to me to be essential.

I will be attending the meeting next week. If you did indeed circularize the Board with copies of your letter of May 27 to me, then I would be glad if you would have this letter similarly circularized.

Sincerely,
Margaret [signed]
Margaret Laurence

•———

Hollinger, 24 August 1977

Dear Jack:

I was reassured to learn from our phone conversation last week that the selection of the 100 NCL titles will not be done by just one or even two people. However, in the past week I've been thinking about the project, and I confess that I find myself uneasy about several things. Possibly, I am needlessly worried, and possibly I misunderstand the aims of the project, but I hope you won't mind my expressing my concern, and I'd really be grateful if you could take the time to respond to the following points.

1. Re: the initial selection committee: I wonder not only how many of these 10 people are women, but also how many of the younger academics (such as, say, John Moss)[1] are included? I think it is just terribly important that these people be as representative as possible, and that the people who are teaching Canlit *now*, as compared to some years ago, be involved. I also think that both at this stage and later on, with the consultative ballot, some high school teachers of Canlit should be included. I wonder if Malcolm [Ross] has considered this? I can personally supply you with a list of possible high school teachers across the entire country who are knowledgeable in Canadian literature—these were the people who formed work groups to put together the educational guides in Canlit for high schools, the booklets which are being published by the Writers' Development Trust. I would hate to see such a vitally important selection done only by "the old brigade," all men and all academics.
2. I have been having some doubts about the concept of the 100 NCL package. My doubts can be summarized thus:

a) Is this package going to be pushed as "*the* 100 major Canadian novels"? I hope not. Perhaps this is not the case. But, in the first place, I think it would be highly dangerous to present a package of NCL books in this way, as those books will have been selected primarily by a pretty small group of people ... are they setting themselves up to say which are all the major novels of this country? Surely not. Even if the 100 are reviewed every 5 years, what then? Is the number expanded, or is it kept at 100? If it is kept at 100, won't people say "How come X's novel was a major novel in the last lot, and now it's been turfed out to make way for Y's novel?" I can't envisage any updating which would work, or which would not make the series look ridiculous.

b) We discussed briefly your intention of putting some other books into the selection of 100 novels, books published by other publishers. Obviously, if the intention is to present the series as "major Canadian novels," it is going to look pretty silly without such people such as Robertson Davies,[2] Lowry,[3] and many many others. But Davies, for example, is published in paperback by Penguin, if I am not mistaken, and I would guess that M&S's chances of getting Penguin to agree to another paperback edition in NCL would be roughly that of a snowflake in hell. Or look at Adele's *The Sacrifice,* now out in Macmillan paperback. Malcolm tried for years to get NCL rights to that book, and Mac's refused, even before they had their own paperback edition out. They certainly won't agree now, it seems to me. Or look at Atwood's *Surfacing* first published by you but now in paperback. Is General going to relinquish rights? Not on your life.[4]

c) If these 100 NCL titles are presented as a package of major Canadian novels, it seems to me that there is great danger in giving the impression that these 100 books are *all* that are needed to teach any number of Canlit courses in schools and universities. You might persuade some naive teachers of this, Jack, in which case you would be doing them a disservice. But for the most part, it would simply make the firm look ludicrous. There are literally *hundreds* of extremely well-informed teachers of Canlit, at both the high school and university level, who would certainly not buy this presentation of the series.

d) The weeding out of over fifty titles from the present NCL seems in itself to raise great problems. It implies that some titles and writers are being demoted. This would, I believe, not go down well with writers or teachers or even many general readers, who will be dismayed to find that their own favourites are now excluded from the NCL.

Naturally, I admit to a personal concern in all this. It is obvious to me that, if there are only 100 titles, it would be quite disproportionate to include seven of my books. I would be sorry to see some of them go into the new series, however. There would not be the same guarantee of their being kept in print, and, as many of these books are used on courses, this could mean that in future years, when I may not be writing any longer, my income may be sharply reduced, to say the least. The royalties from the NCL volumes aren't going to keep me in luxury in my old age, but they just might mean the difference between a little income and no income at all.

Having declared interest, however, I must also say that I am genuinely concerned about the NCL as a series, for the reason that it has had such an important influence on the formation and on-going quality of the teaching of Canlit in this country. I am wondering if it would not be possible simply to keep *all* the 153 (or however many titles the series now stands at) within the NCL itself, and cut out all this fancy business of selection and demotion and consultative ballots and all that jazz. It would solve a lot of complications and would certainly be far less confusing for the teacher and the general reader. The new series, under new editions, could then possibly include biography and autobiography as well as fiction or anything else you like.

For obvious reasons, I would prefer that this letter be considered only by you and Anna at this time.

Believe me, Jack, I am not trying to criticize you (not this time, anyway!). I am truly concerned about the NCL and the vital role it has played in the teaching of Canadian literature. I would not want to see that role endangered or diminished. I hope you will take these views and suggestions in good part and will let me know your response to them.

All the best,
Margaret [signed]
Margaret Laurence

P.S. Thanks for the promo copy of Templeton's novel.[5] I am now reading it. He keeps his narratives moving right along! Copies to be sold in Canada before Dec 31st, 1977—my guess is—

47,300

If I (and you) win, please send my free copies of all M&S books to the Peterborough School Board![6]

1. John Moss (1940–), a professor at the University of Ottawa and mystery writer, was elected a Fellow of the Royal Society of Canada in 2006 in recognition of his distinguished contributions and career as a professor of Canadian literature.
2. Robertson Davies (1913–1995) was a Canadian novelist, playwright, critic, journalist, and professor.
3. Clarence Malcolm Lowry (1909–1957) was an English writer most renowned for his novel *Under the Volcano*. In 1938, he moved to Vancouver and he is therefore sometimes considered a Canadian writer as well.
4. "Not on your life" is inserted as a handwritten note.
5. Charles Templeton (1915–2001) was a Canadian journalist, cartoonist, and author. The novel by Templeton that Laurence refers to is *Act of God*, published by McClelland & Stewart in 1977.
6. The postscript, including the number within the box, was handwritten by Laurence. Evidently, Laurence and McClelland had a bet about how many copies of Templeton's book would sell by the end of the year.

Regent, 9 September 1977

Dear Margaret:

I think you worry too much—perhaps needlessly. I hope needlessly, by the way, because if not I would have gone totally berserk. In any case, let me try to respond to some of your concerns.

1. Don't worry about that group of 10—in fact, 12 people. This is not a committee and it has nothing to do with the final selection. This group was selected for the purpose of an initial test ballot, solely in order to determine how the final ballot should be. The group is split into two. We are using two test methods. What we are trying to find out is what is the best way of getting an adequate response to the ballot itself. I do know its constitution—at least, I could look it up—but, Margaret, it is not important. It doesn't matter whether it is male or female. The initial inquiry is merely to determine by test rather than by asking, what is the best form in which to send the final ballot.

The actual ballot—which is a consultative ballot and not binding on Malcolm Ross—will go to everyone who is invited to attend the Conference in Calgary. Perhaps I shouldn't say everyone, but everyone who has any credentials for voting on this issue. It will go to all the people who are invited to attend with credentials, whether they attend or not. So, we are looking at a cross-section of 250 at least—scholars, academics, critics, etc. The major people who are involved in the study and teaching of Canlit in this country. We are trying to do the thing well. Women will be well represented in the group. Count on it.

2. (a) Yes, we plan to push the result—if there is a satisfactory result—as the 100 most significant Canadian novels or whatever. That is part of the purpose of the exercise. This group of 100 books is not being selected by a small group of people. It is being selected by a large group of experts, but we are not going to be bound by the results. It is an experimental project to see what the results are. If they are totally

unsatisfactory to us, Malcolm will simply announce them and that will be the end of the project. We are not committed to anything. All I have been talking about and telling you about is our intent re: the NCL. The people who are part of the ballot will not know our intent as it affects the New Canadian Library.

We don't plan to make any decision about the revision of the list of 100 until well after the Calgary conference.[1] It may be that the list should be revised every 5 years. It may be that it should be every 10 years. It may be that the list should be expanded, not kept at 100. I don't know. We have lots of time to settle that. So, these decisions will be made by McClelland and Stewart. Not by the Calgary conference.

(b) I am very conscious of the problem. We have reason to believe that we can obtain rights to the Davies novels, Lowry, Adele Wiseman, etc. if the project works. We are not worrying about it now. We are not making any claims or projections. I am just telling you privately and personally that I believe we can obtain the books if everything fits into place.

(c) Well, I guess I don't agree with you on this one. I speak as a publisher. I don't believe that there are "literally hundreds of extremely well informed teachers of Canlit at both the high school and the university level." As a matter of fact, I disagree with this quite categorically. One of our problems in Canada is that there are bloody few teachers in Canadian schools who know anything about Canadian Lit. There are a lot of teachers who have been influenced by Peggy Atwood's book[2] and I think that book has done a disservice to Canadian Lit. as a whole. It has done a disservice in detail, not in its general promotional push. But migod, Margaret, given our balloting methods, [if] we can't come up with the 100 books which forms all that the high school teachers need to know, then there are many more good Canadian books than I know about. At the university level in post-graduate courses, it is a different matter. But one of our great problems at the moment is that a lot of people teaching Canlit don't know the difference between Arthur Hailey,[3] Sheila Watson, and Richard Rohmer.[4] You don't believe that. If you don't, you probably wouldn't believe that Alistair MacLean's *Ice Station Zebra* is required reading in Calgary schools in the Grade Eleven English course.

(d) As it happens, most of the titles [that] will be weeded out in the selection would not worry you for a minute if you look at the list. For example, there are about 14 Leacock titles in the New Canadian Library. None of them are novels. We will, of course, retain *Sunshine Sketches*. The others will be kept in print, but not under the heading "Great or essential Canadian novels." We are not going to let *Over Prairie Trails* go out of print.[5] We would be crazy to do so, because it is one of the great Canadian books and it sells very well as do some very bad books by Grove, but hell, *Over Prairie Trails* is not a novel. Frankly, Margaret, I am not much worried about the denigration that you anticipate. It won't happen. The other books will be kept in print if they are worth a damn. They will be in an edition that will probably be more attractive. Believe me, I have looked at the list. The problem is apparent, not real, but it is because of this apparent problem that we are not saying to the delegates of the Conference that this is a final democratic process. Malcolm will not feel bound by the results. He may decide to feel bound, but it is a "consultative ballot." There is no dishonesty involved here. It is just that we are not going to make our purposes totally known until we know what we are dealing with.

Incidentally, in passing I have noted your handwritten reference to Atwood's *Surfacing* published by Paperjacks. Of course it is, but it will come back to us. The contract expires in a year or two.

Re: your personal concern, let me be very frank about it. I am certain the four key novels will be retained. If they weren't, we would totally reject the balloting. About the other three, I don't know but my guess is that if four stayed in the NCL and three went into the new series (or vice-versa) both groups would sell better than they are now selling. In other words, the 100 great novels are going to sell better and the books that are not in that particular category are also going to sell better because they will be attractive to a broader segment of the public. Believe me, Margaret, we haven't reached this marketing conclusion off the top of our heads. We know where the NCL helps and where it doesn't.

Let me not go on at great length. There will be plenty of time to discuss this and I would like to have a serious discussion of the subject with you. Let me re-assure you again. There will be no announcement made at the Calgary conference about the New Canadian Library as such. I settled this with Malcolm; mainly for pragmatic reasons we don't want to be saddled with something that we can't deal with. Neither Malcolm, or MS, or the people [who] are organizing the Conference are going to make any announcements about changes in the NCL at this time. We will be publishing a new group of NCLs in January. We know privately that it is the last group in its present form, but, as I say, we are not publicly committed to any action and there is lots of time to consider our intentions. Incidentally, re: Klinck,[6] Malcolm is baffled by his concern. I don't have a copy of the letter that went to the 10 or 12 people involved, but it specified that there were 10 or 12 people involved. In fact, there were 3 people from Klinck's own university, so what the hell.

So, don't worry about it. All is under control. Maybe we can have a drink after the next Directors' Meeting or dinner if you are staying in town, which I presume you are and this would be a much better idea.

Cheers!
Jack McClelland

1. McClelland had organized a literary conference in Calgary in 1978 with the intention of announcing the hundred greatest Canadian novels. Unsurprisingly, the conference caused controversy among many writers and critics, especially since McClelland & Stewart had published many of the writers selected.
2. McClelland refers to Margaret Atwood's book, *Survival*.
3. Arthur Hailey (1920–2004) was a popular and lucrative Canadian writer who published many novels from the 1950s through the 1990s.
4. Richard Rohmer (1924–) is a retired lawyer and writer. He wrote two influential works of nonfiction, *The Green North: Mid-Canada* and *The Arctic Imperative*, and ten works of fiction.
5. Frederick Philip Grove (1879–1948) was a German-born Canadian novelist and translator, renowned for his depictions of prairie life in Canada. *Over Prairie Trails*, a collection of essays, was published by McClelland & Stewart in 1922.
6. Carl F. Klinck (1908–1990) was a prominent Canadian literary historian and academic and editor of *Literary History of Canada: Canadian Literature in English*.

Hollinger, 13 September 1977

Dear Jack:

I'm writing, quite frankly, to ask a large favour of you. Here is the situation. A few days ago, Alan Wilson,[1] who is head of Canadian Studies at Trent University, phoned me. He wanted me to meet Professor G.H. Moore, of Hull University, England, who was visiting briefly and who wanted to discuss Canadian literature with me. I couldn't make it, unfortunately, but I was extremely interested in Professor Moore's situation and I feel I want to do everything possible to help. He is head of American Studies at Hull University, and feels strongly that it is absurd to have American Studies and not Canadian Studies. I couldn't agree more! He wants to introduce a Canadian Studies programme ... it will have to be small at first, as he has virtually no funding. However, he very much wants to begin a course in Canadian literature. He was apparently at York U in Toronto and saw Dennis Lee and others ... I don't know who else. But he has been saying that he doesn't really know a thing about Canlit, and asking people what he should be reading, to begin with. Naturally, to me this is a challenge not to be resisted! I have made up a list of 51 books, and I want to have these sent to him. It is, of course, a highly personal list in terms of selection, and it naturally reflects my own tastes. It is, for starters, almost all contemporary (no, it is *all* contemporary), partly because I think that the most interesting Can writing has been done since 1940, when our writers became de-colonialised. I will, of course, make it clear to him that these are only my own views. I will also make clear: (a) the preponderance of novels reflects my own tastes and is also necessary because I don't know much about poetry, but I'll suggest who he can contact; (b) the selection of 51 books is simply a kind of sampler, but, in terms of contemporary novels, I think these 44 novels could be regarded as core books of a sort; (c) I have not included any background books ... e.g. Susanna Moodie;[2] various history books; etc., and he should get in touch with Alan Wilson about this, as a certain amount of background in our history is obviously necessary.

Anyway, my list includes 5 critical works; 2 poetry anthologies; and 44 novels. It's only a taste, but it's a beginning, perhaps. It could lead to something ... we can only hope so.

Of these 51 books, you will probably not be surprised that 30 are New Canadian Library. I did not do this with any planned intention ... it simply happened this way.

What I want to ask you is this: would you be willing to send the books on the enclosed list to Professor Moore without charge? It would be an awfully nice thing to be able to tell him that you were doing this, and it might even in time lead to a little more knowledge of Canlit in England.

As far as I know, there is only 1 university in Britain at the moment teaching a course in Canadian literature, and that is the University of Edinburgh. Leeds has a Commonwealth Lit department, and does teach some Canadian books. I think the fact that Professor Moore is keen to find out more about Canadian writing is an important thing.

I am ordering the remaining 21 books from Longhouse,[3] and will pay for these myself (shudder! But I do think this is important). I quite realize that none of us could continue to do this kind of thing if interest in Canlit suddenly blooms in England (unlikely). But, for this first time, I think we might well do it. The Writers' Development Trust is sending him a set of course outlines for free. I shall explain (in fact, I've already done so, via Alan Wilson) that these are in no sense suitable for university study, as they are all at a secondary school level, some for lower grades in high school and some for senior grades. But they will at least give him a kind of overview of poetry, novels and plays in this country, as well as other resources such as films, which might be useful for a Canadian Studies Program.[4]

Anyway, I hope you will agree to supply Professor Moore with these 30 NCL titles. I would be most grateful, and I know he would be, as well. If you feel that this isn't possible, I'd like the books to be sent to him anyway, and the bill sent to me. In that case, I'll see if I can get a few friends to help out.

I very much wanted to include Pierre Berton's 2 CPR books and Farley Mowat's *A Whale for the Killing*, but wasn't sure if these were out in paperback or not. If you felt you could include them, it would be super. I could, of course, make a marvellous list of about 300 titles, but have resisted the temptation for obvious reasons!

Could you let me know your response to this request as soon as possible, please? I will postpone writing to Professor Moore until I hear from you. Incidentally, you are the only publisher I'm approaching about free copies, simply because (I tell you in confidence) I don't think the other publishers would take all that kindly to my long explanation of my list of 51 books, out of which theirs amounted to 1 or 2 or 3! This says something, as a sort of random spot check, for M&S' list. (This looks like flattery, but it's fact, really.)

Anyway, I look forward to hearing from you.

All the best,
Margaret [signed]
Margaret Laurence[5]

1. Alan Wilson (1927–) is a historian and was the first head of the Canadian Studies Department and the first chair of the History Department at Trent University. He and his wife, Budge, were close friends of Laurence, particularly during the years in the early 1980s when Laurence served as the chancellor of Trent and on the editorial board of Trent's prestigious *Journal of Canadian Studies*. Budge became an author of children's books, in part through her friendship with and encouragement by Laurence.
2. Susanna Strickland Moodie (1803–1885) was an English-born Canadian author who wrote about her experiences as a settler and pioneer in Canada. Her most acclaimed autobiographical book is *Roughing It in the Bush*.
3. Longhouse Books, on Yonge Street in Toronto, was run by Beth Appledorn and Susan Sandler. See Laurence's letter dated 14 May 1975 for more information about Longhouse Books.
4. This period marked the beginning of Canadian studies programs at universities within Canada and abroad. These programs were interdisciplinary in nature and included studies on Canada in disciplines such as political science, history, and English. While some of these programs remain, funding for the programs abroad was withdrawn under Prime Minister Stephen Harper, starting in 2012.

5. A typed note is attached to this letter, presumably from Hodgeman. It reads, "Margaret called me today. Apparently, she found out that the guy [Professor Moore] was a con man and said not to send the books." McClelland has written "OK" in handwriting on the note. A previous handwritten note from McClelland is also attached. It reads, "Marge 1/ Phone her and say okay. 2/ Place the order. Include ... [blurred]. 3/ Send a letter confirming for the record" (McClelland & Stewart Ltd. Fonds, Box 87, File 24).

Regent, 3 October 1977

Dear Margaret:

Delighted to hear you have won an Award from the Periodical Distributors.[1] They don't tell me what the Award is, but still it is a good thing. I don't know whether you plan to attend or not. Unfortunately, I am going to be in Frankfurt, but the firm will be well represented.

Cheers!
Jack McClelland

1. Laurence won the Periodical Distributors of Canada Short Fiction Award in 1977, as did Margaret Atwood.

Regent, 28 February 1978

Dear Margaret:

You are an absolutely fantastic person. I think you did more personally to make the Calgary conference a success than any other single individual. I don't know where you get your energy, interest, or dedication from. I hope you didn't consider the whole thing too much of a chore, an imposition or a drudgery. God knows everybody was so thrilled that you were there and you seemed to be everywhere at the same time. You are an absolute wonder.

Margaret, my one regret about the whole Conference is that I wasn't able to spend more time with you personally—or you with me, as far as that goes. I guess we both had to do what we had to do. It worked out very well. I thought the Conference was a great success. Gabrielle [Roy] was thrilled to meet you. I think in the long run she really enjoyed the Conference, if only because of that. I felt that your tribute to Malcolm Ross was great and couldn't have been done better. In fact, despite the sad realization that I didn't manage more than two hours' sleep any night during the three nights, I was truly pleased about the whole thing. I was unhappy that the U of C was a bit mickey mouse [*sic*] on a lot of the details, but generally I think the thing was so useful and so important that nobody felt too bitterly about that.

So where do we go from here re: the New Canadian Library? I don't know. We won't make any move at all until I have an opportunity to review it with you in some considerable detail. As I have indicated before, I don't want to destroy it by making it a house list any more than I want to destroy it by continuing to publish books that are of doubtful literary merit and doubtful historic interest. I do want to continue it. I do want to continue to publish even more Canadian books in paperback than we have done in the past. I think it is in this area that you can make a real contribution as a Director of M&S and it is my hope sometime later this spring that your schedule may permit a meeting—not a regular Directors' Meeting—where we can review what should be done. There will be another Directors' Meeting in the interim before I take off for Tehran, but that's mainly financial and if I were you, I would avoid it.

Re: the use of the list itself, I have strong feelings that it should be perpetuated and improved in some form or another. John Moss suggested that it should be annotated and I think that is a very good suggestion. Someone else suggested that we should expand it beyond 100 because there was very little difference between numbers 80 to 100 and number 100 to 120. Malcolm has a good feel for that. I enclose a copy of a letter that I have sent to Ernie Ingles,[1] which will give you some notion as to how I feel on the subject. If you have any strong views about it that you would like to pass on to me, I would be grateful to have them.

Margaret, thanks again for going to Calgary. It was a great sacrifice on your part and just a further indication of your great dedication to Canada and to Canadian letters. It was appreciated by everyone there and I doubt that there was anyone present there that cares more than I do or was quite as appreciative of your sacrifice as I was. How can I thank you?

Love,
Jack McClelland

1. Ernest B. Ingles was the head of the Department of Rare Books and Special Collections at the University of Calgary between 1974 and 1978, and the founding executive director and chief executive officer of the Canadian Institute for Historical Microreproductions between 1978 and 1984. He also served as the president of the Bibliographical Society of Canada.

Hollinger, 7 March 1978

Dear Jack:

Thanks for your letter. I'm glad you felt I did alright at the conference. I enjoyed it, really, and it was marvellous to meet Gabrielle Roy, and also Roger Lemelin,[1] and to see old friends.

However, I have to say I am uneasy on several counts, especially after reading your letter to Ernie Ingles. (Incidentally, if I were Ingles, I would be mad as hell at receiving a letter like that—ye gods! The poor helpless writers did *not* need student guides, for heaven's sake! Surely they are capable of summoning a cab or opening their mouths to ask for directions. The Hospitality Inn looked okay to me—I've stayed in plenty worse, when travelling at the taxpayers' expense. And, as far as the province is concerned, the Ministry of Culture put up a lot of dough, and I don't think it is very nice to complain at this point.) That parenthesis bit is by the way. What causes me considerable anxiety is your talk of using the list in an ongoing way. You say that if the U of Calgary doesn't want it, then perhaps some other institution or publishing company, and maybe—wait for it!—McClelland and Stewart would like to use it. Well, surprise, surprise. I have to admit that I have been for some time worried that this is precisely what you were aiming for with that damned list, and now my worst fears are confirmed. Please, Jack, I beg you to re-think this one. Listen, believe me—I am *trying* to be loyal to you and to the old firm. Please don't make it impossibly difficult for me to support you in public utterances I may make. Let me tell you why I am so much against your using this list:

1. The list, as it was visualized by Malcolm, was, as I said in my letter to *The Globe* (which was printed in tandem with yours), NOT a list of THE HUNDRED BEST OR THE HUNDRED GREATEST. Good god, we don't *have* a hundred "great" novels. And as for "best," well,

that would have been the arbitrary choices of not more than 140 academics, hardly a referendum on a national scale. Malcolm, as he explained, intended the list only as a talking point at the conference, and to show which books were being the most widely used on courses. As several people pointed out, there are far too few translations from French Canadian writers, and also, only books out in paperback can be used in course work, so there are wide gaps in the list in terms of its being representative of the whole of Canadian writing. So a use of the list as "the best" would be a total distortion. I would like to see the list carefully forgotten.

2. A use of the list could only damage the reputation of McClelland and Stewart. There has been a lot of talk, and not idle talk, either, about the nature of the conference. Perhaps no one tells you these things, Jack. I hope you are not going to be offended, but someone has got to let you know about this situation. The fact that *only* M&S writers were there, apart from Yves Theriault [*sic*][2] (whom maybe you have also published for all I know) did not go unremarked. I did not realize until I arrived at the conference and began to look around, that only M&S writers were there. Of course, it was marvellous to meet Gabrielle Roy and Roger Lemelin, and to see Rudy Wiebe, Marian Engel, James Houston,[3] Mordecai Richler, Brian Moore, etc. But then one began to think—where are the writers published by other Publishers? Where, for that matter, are the other publishers? I have since learned that Doug Gibson[4] of Macmillan had to ask for an invitation, and the only other publisher I knew [was] Frances Halpenny of the U of T Press.[5] I know of at least one other publisher who was sent an invite so late it was impossible for him to go. I don't blame you for that, of course—but I can't entirely blame the U of Calgary, either. Ernest Ingles is a very nice and hard-working man, but I don't think he is all that familiar with contemporary Can fiction. *Someone*, however, at some early date, should have made sure that a large number of publishers and writers were invited, not just M&S writers. It did not take much eyesight to spot the lack of representation on the part of other publishers and writers. The

press, naturally, noticed this, as why wouldn't they? This has caused a good deal of hard feeling on behalf of other publishers and, from my point of view, even waves, on the part of writers published by other publishers. Am I supposed to cheer with happiness when my colleagues, published by other publishers, have been totally left out and are understandably annoyed? Am I supposed to chirp with glee when it appears that I am a party to this kind of exclusion, when I didn't know a damn thing about it until I got there? Anyway, forget my role in all this. If you use that blasted list for advertising or other purposes, it will confirm what the press has already noted—the conference was predominantly M&S writers, and the list, naturally, has a huge list of M&S writers, simply because of the very valuable NCL—and full marks to you and Malcolm for the NCL. But you don't need to advertise the NCL in that way—it cheapens it, and it will do your reputation no good. Of that I am sure.

3. I have heard (and I do hear a lot, believe me—Lakefield is not far from *anywhere*, and things filter through like prairie smoke signals) that there is a good deal of rather bitter comment, on the part of (a) academics who weren't invited; (b) writers; (c) publishers; (d) media people—to the effect that a very great deal of Canada Council money (ie. taxpayers' money) was poured into that conference, which, it is being said, was a clever front for M&S (who had conned the U of Calg) to publicize its own books and writers. Well, obviously, the conference was not that—the papers were serious, and for the most part interesting attempts to deal with aspects of our literature; I'm damn sure none of the academics thought they were there to boost M&S (and, heaven knows, it would be terrible, if they ever came to feel they'd been used). But because M&S had such a high profile at the conference, and the other publishers virtually were not given a chance at all, one can see how such feelings could arise in various quarters. I, for one, although naturally I did not say so at the time, felt highly upset by the absence of writers other than M&S writers, and so did some of the other writers. Any use of the list for any purpose of your own would simply serve to confirm people's

suspicions in this direction. It would harm the firm; it would harm your own reputation; it would harm Malcolm; and it would harm all your writers who attended that conference. Jack, I do hope you will take my remarks seriously.

As far as the NCL is concerned, I would be delighted to meet with you at any time to discuss it. I think you are perfectly correct in saying you don't want it to be a house list. I also think you are right in saying that you don't want it to contain novels which might appear more appropriately in some other paperback form. I do feel, however, that it would be a great pity if some of the turn-of-the-century novels were not kept in print, even in small quantities, for the use of scholars. I know you are not in this as a charity operation, but I hope there can be some way found to keep these books available. Also, I would hate to see the NCL simply cut to 100 titles and the list closed forever. I think all these things should be discussed. I quite agree with your idea of some kind of cut-off point—the Everyman Library is a good example of what NOT to do—it got so many titles that they all began to look the same. Anyway, I would really like to talk about the NCL with you, as I believe it is absolutely crucial to the teaching of Canlit in our schools and universities.

But please, I beg you, let the list go. Just let it go. Enough harm and bad feelings have been caused by its being interpreted as some kind of exclusive club. Please don't add to that. It can only put you in a very bad light, and I would hate to see that happen. Believe me, I am not exaggerating the things I have heard. Nor am I exaggerating my profound sense of unease at the apparent exclusive nature of the conference. It's over now—let's for heaven's sake let it be.

All the best,
Margaret

1. Roger Lemelin (1919–1992) was a Quebec novelist, television writer, and essayist. His works include *Les Voies de l'esperence*, *La Culotte en or*, and *Le Crime d'Ovide Plouffe*.
2. Yves Thériault (1915–1983) was a Canadian author. One of his most notable publications was the novel *Agaguk*.
3. James Archibald Houston (1921–2005) was a Canadian artist, designer, children's author, and filmmaker. He was instrumental in the process of introducing printmaking to the Inuit and cultivating attention for their aesthetic achievements.
4. Douglas Gibson (1943–) first served as the editorial director of Macmillan in 1974 and became its publisher in 1979. He was later employed by McClelland & Stewart in 1986 and eventually came to serve as its president and publisher in 2000.
5. Francess Georgina Halpenny (1919–2017) was an esteemed Canadian editor, scholar, and author. She held leadership positions at the University of Toronto Press, was dean of the University of Toronto's Faculty of Library Science, and was general editor of the *Dictionary of Canadian Biography*.

Hollinger, 20 March 1978

Dear Jack:

John Cushman phoned me yesterday. He told me he had talked with you before you went to Iran, and that you had been very helpful. Well, Jack, despite our periodic disagreements and despite my (perhaps) slightly feverish letter re: the Calgary conference (by the way, I see now that there were several more non-M&S writers there than I had thought; also, however, I *was* and *am* sincere in my concern about your reputation and the firm's in absolutely *not* appearing to have masterminded the conference), despite all that, there are many occasions in which we see eye-to-eye, and this has got to be one of them. I think you know my feelings about John. He is an absolutely sterling person, and I owe him a great deal. I want to do anything I can to help. It seems to me that C-B[1] has done a terrible, even if legal, thing.[2] Even to taking his *name* for their new agency in N.Y., obviously in order to retain his authors and take all the benefits from all the work he's done over the years.

Two things I'd like to ask you.

1/ Please make sure that henceforth, until further notice, *all* the royalty cheques coming to me from M&S are sent in their entirety directly to me. I will make sure John gets his 10%. ... I'm damned if I want C-B England (now John Cushman Associates, ye gods) to have that money, as they didn't turn a finger to earn it.

2/ John said you thought that, by Canadian law, authors can change agents and take their old contracts with them. I would, naturally, want to do this and am prepared to do battle to achieve it. When I left Willis Kingsley Wing, which by that time was Collins-Knowlton-Wing, in 1966, to go with John Cushman, I did not (on his advice) take my old contracts with me. They (now Curtis Brown, New York, what a complex puzzle all this is) still handle my books up to and including *A Jest of God*, a fact I've always felt sorry about. I would now like to get those contracts back from them, and all my other contracts back from "John Cushman Associates" (i.e. C-B England) and turn them over to John. Any advice about how this can be done would be greatly appreciated by me.

All the best,
Margaret [signed]
Margaret Laurence

1. The publishing company, Curtis Brown.
2. See Laurence's letter dated 4 June 1966 for more information on John Cushman and John Cushman Associates Inc.

Regent, 6 April 1978

Dear Margaret:

I am sorry about the delay in replying to your two letters, but I have been away. I'll deal with the one of March 20th first. We are in entire agreement with Cushman. He is having a tough time. We are determined to do everything we can to help him, and I am glad that you feel exactly the same way. ...

Re: the general U.S. situation, I did check this out legally and was advised as follows: Under Canadian law when a publisher makes an agreement with an author that includes what is in effect a direction from the author to send royalty reports and make payments to an agent, such a direction is not an integral part of the agreement. It is included in the agreement only as an acknowledgement of receipt of the instruction or direction. It can be changed at any time by written direction of the author. ...

Thus, under Canadian law, you are free to do as you wish, provided you have no written agreement with an agent. This is an interesting point. Such agents—the wise ones I think—do insist on written agreements with their authors. Others, John being one of them, have never had any agreements as a matter of principle. I understand that principle to be belief and a lack of a written agreement indicates the honesty of the agent and indicates, further, that the agent doesn't expect to be retained if the author is not satisfied. It is a traditionally old-fashioned agency practice. I suspect that in these litigious days that unwritten agreements of this sort will soon disappear. Peculiarly enough, though, it is to John Cushman's advantage that Curtis Brown did not insist on written agreements. Did they exist, none of the authors could now move. It is my belief too that you had no written agreement with Collins-Knowlton-Wing.

There is an ethical aspect of all this too. The traditional industry practice, I think throughout the world, has been that when an author switches from one agency to another, they have tended to leave earlier contracts with the original agent. Looking at this legally, however, in Canada at least, there is no reason why they should do so failing a written agreement. I think it is quite appropriate to say that the agent has been well paid for all their initial work, so let's terminate that agreement. There is all sorts of precedent for this. Clearly, it is in the author's best interest to have all their work handled by one agent and the author has to look out for their best interest. And usually, too, when an author leaves, there is some reason for the separation. The agent has no continuing interest in an author once they have left for another agency. It is best to make a clear break. I only regret that I hadn't suggested this to you long ago re: Collins-Knowlton-Wing. It would have made it easier for all of us.

Okay, what should you do now? First, we have received instruction from you that all further royalties and payments on your books are to be made directly to you. We accept that instruction and will do so beginning with the next royalty period. At that time, we shall send an automatic report to John Cushman Associates and to Collins-Knowlton-Wing saying simply that we have received instruction from you that the royalty statement and payment is to be sent directly to you and that this has been done. They may want to quarrel with you at that point. If they do, may I suggest that you get in touch with me or Ann Nelles[1] immediately before you take any action at all. It may be important to get some legal instruction as to the nature of the reply that you might send them. ...

I think that covers the matter, Margaret. The only additional thing you could do—although I don't advise it—is to send a letter to Collins-Knowlton-Wing and John Cushman Associates saying that you are going to do this. This is probably a more polite route. On the other hand, to be practical, it could only cause problems for John, and he doesn't need them at this stage. In addition, by going the other route, you can effectively test whether the direction to the publisher has the same validity in the U.K. and the U.S.A. as it has in Canada. I think it does have, but I am not positive.

I hope this is helpful. Ann Nelles has a copy of the letter. If you have any queries and can't reach me, do call her.

All the best.
Sincerely,
Jack McClelland

1. Ann Nelles managed the finances at McClelland & Stewart.

Regent, 6 April 1978

Dear Margaret:

Now let me attempt to reply to your letter of March 7th which, thank God, was softened slightly by your subsequent letter. You seem to think that I can be guilty of the most horrendous acts. I suspect you are overly impressionable and too easily influenced by the vast number of young authors, critics, editors, etc. to whom you have become den mother or whatever. Maybe you really do detect in me a deep, sinister side that unnerves you from time-to-time.

Let me tell you the absolute truth about the Calgary conference for starters:

1. Yes, I did propose it to them in the first place.
2. Yes, my sinister purpose was really to find a way of honouring Malcolm Ross appropriately and ease the way for his retirement. Initially, Malcolm was to have been the core of the Conference. This was watered down considerably in order to ease the fund-raising activities for the University of Calgary. Dissipation of original purpose was such that I despaired from time-to-time as to whether or not he would even play a central role in the closing banquet. Thanks to you that, at least, was retained. I think the fine tribute that you paid to him was appreciated by everyone present and probably by me more than anyone else.
3. From that point on I had surprisingly little to do with the Conference. I attended the initial committee meeting in Calgary where I outlined a further meeting with Glazier and Ingles in Toronto. Beyond that I had no connection with the committee. There were a lot of telephone calls. A lot of correspondence and we did a lot of work for them, but beyond the overall form of the program—the fact that there was an opening reception and a closing banquet, the fact that

Malcolm made his report on the Sunday morning and that the whole thing was covered by the National Film Board (which I arranged)—almost every suggestion or proposal that I put forward was ignored.

4. It is a matter of fact that beyond supplying a list of living New Canadian Library authors, and living New Canadian Library introducers, I had nothing to do with this invitation list. To this day, I don't know who was invited and who was not invited. It was strictly their Conference, but when they asked me to do something, I did it. When they asked me a question, I answered it. I suggested, for example, that they write and send an invitation to the head of every English Department at every Canadian university, community college and high school.

5. I suggested that they get in touch with both publishing associations. In fact, three including the French and ask them if they would set up book displays and also ask them for suggestions and also ask them to circulate invitations to their members to attend, etc. I also asked that they approach other publishers re: author lists. I then wrote and talked to both associations to take the whole thing seriously, which in the end they did.

   I then leaned on a certain number of authors who they were particularly anxious to have present. Some McClelland and Stewart authors were in this group, including Margaret Laurence, Gabrielle Roy, Roger Lemelin, Margaret Atwood (who as you know was out of the country), Mordecai Richler, James Houston, Sylvia Fraser, to name only a few.

6. Also at their request, I wrote to a number of non-McClelland and Stewart authors and pressed them to attend. That list included Robertson Davies, Northrop Frye,[1] Morley Callaghan, Hugh MacLennan,[2] Richard Wright,[3] Alice Munro, and that's to name only a few.

7. I also suggested the speaker for the closing banquet. He backed out, as you know. I then suggested Claude Bissell and some others. They didn't want them. Because I was afraid that we would end up with Horst Schmidt, I finally agreed that Gertrude Laing would be a suitable person.[4] What a mistake that was.

8. You already know how the list was prepared. It was entirely open and straightforward. The ballot list was prepared by Malcolm's original group of 10. People were invited to add names. The thing wasn't doctored or edited in any way by us. We did prepare the physical ballots. We did mail them out. The tabulation was done by our people. The results were exactly as compiled by the tabulator. I wish now that I had intervened. Quite honestly, Fred Bodsworth[5] would have been included, and there would have been some changes in the last 20. Malcolm was supposed to supply this editorial judgement—to allow for anomalies, ties in the voting, etc.—but he didn't. He simply forgot about it. So there was absolutely no tampering with the list.

This is going to be a long letter, because I want to go on from that point. First, I have no regret about my letter to Ernie Ingles. He didn't like it any more than he liked some of the things that I said to him at the Conference. My attitude is, screw him. They undertook to do this Conference on a first-class basis and they failed lamentably. We put a lot of effort into helping them and they let me down. There is an essential difference between your attitude and mine. Fair enough, I'm a publisher. While you have devoted your career to writing, I have devoted mine to promoting and building up Canadian authors. I believe they should be honoured in this country. I believe they should have been met by students. I believe the Hospitality Inn was unsuitable. I believe the way that authors were treated generally at the Conference was deplorable.

Now before I deal with your numbered sequence re: the list and use of same, let me say one more thing. I did have a second motive for arranging this Conference. Let me say a word about Margaret Atwood. I admire her intelligence and her energy. I think she is a fine poet and a pretty good novelist. I think she is a lousy critic. While *Survival* has in some ways helped Canadian writing and the study of Canadian literature because it has been widely read—it has also done a great deal of damage.[6] I consider it to be uninformed, half-baked and, in some respects, extremely damaging to the main body of Canadian literature.

One of the high spots of the Conference, for me, was when one of the critics on the panel the last day said how appalled he was to find it listed as one of the ten essential books for the study of Canadian literature. He was absolutely right. As a matter of fact, the study of the list of the 100 books indicates the damage that *Survival* has already done.

Why has that book had such an impact? There are a number of reasons. First, Peggy is high profile. Second, the timing was right. Third there was no other contemporary book available—it filled a much-needed gap. That's fine except that it has become the schoolteacher's bible and it does a disservice to Canadian literature. It was my hope that something would come out of this Conference to serve over a period of years to replace that book. This will happen. I couldn't care less whether such a replacement is published by M&S or not. I have absolutely no financial interest in the matter, but I do care about our literature and I do care that some balanced, reliable guide be available to undo some of the damage that that book has done.

Now let me look at some of your specific points as you list them:

1. I agree that we don't have 100 great novels and that this list doesn't represent the 100 best. I think it is a starting point in determining what our 100 best are. The very fact that 140 academics (and almost 600 were invited to respond) didn't perform with particular intelligence after they got through the first two-dozen books is a fair indication that such a list is needed. Why do you say it is nothing like a national referendum? If you go to almost 600 teachers of Canadian literature across the country and over 20% respond, surely to God that is a pretty good poll. It is a more extensive poll than most of those conducted by Gallup or anybody else.

   Next under item #1, you make points that simply aren't valid. You say, "there are far too few translations from French-Canadian writers." While it is true that a lot of outstanding English-Canadian novels have not been translated into French, the reverse, in terms of my experience, is just not true. I think any intelligent French-Canadian publisher would agree with me. The best of French-

Canadian literature has been translated into English. Translation money has been readily available. There are some very recent books that haven't been translated yet. It is doubtful that there are any great ones. ... The Canada Council has, in fact, more money available for translation into French and English than anybody can possibly use.

And then there is this argument about all these great Canadian works that aren't available in paperback. Name one. I challenge you to name one. Conceivably you might come up with a title that could worm its way into the lower quarter of the list, or a book by an author like Willa Cather,[7] who refused to allow her books to be done in paper, but I know of no such book. Migod, Margaret, are you not aware that Malcolm and a whole body of people have been looking for such books for 20 years. They do not exist. It is a matter of fact. Let me quote you back. You say, "so there are wide gaps ... So a use of the list ... would be a total distortion." I really challenge you on this. Name me a book in French or English, exclude please anything published in the last three or four years. Such books should not have been eligible for inclusion in any case.

Well, you softened your position on point #2. The talk about the sinister Jack McClelland at the Conference didn't trouble me then and it doesn't trouble me now. You now know why there were mainly M&S authors present. I worked at it. I even got Richard Wright to agree to attend and then they wouldn't pay for him. As to Doug Gibson having to ask for an invitation, that is straight bullshit. The Publishers' Association circulated all the details about the Conference to their membership. Except for those who actually participated, it was not [a] "by invitation" Conference. I phoned other publishers and asked them to attend. I phoned both Associations and asked them to urge the publishers to attend. As a matter of fact, I even tried to get some French publishers to attend and some American publishers to attend and, in fact, one did.

As I have indicated, neither Anna [Porter] nor I were ever invited. We paid our own way. We happened to have a rep in Calgary, so naturally she attended and looked after our display. Other publishers did have senior representatives there, although not the heads of the houses themselves. That's the choice of the heads of the houses. They don't go to these things. Why should I be criticized for that? Any more than I should be criticized for the fact that a high percentage of the work that can be considered Canadian literature appear[s] in the New Canadian Library? You should be lecturing me on this! I don't believe it.

3. Regarding Canada Council money, Margaret, that has to be a joke. Let me tell you exactly what they did. They put up, I think, something like $4,000.00 to support the book display. How this money was actually spent, I don't know. I don't think the publishers who displayed were reimbursed in any way. Perhaps they paid for the space and the tables and that sort of thing. In addition, according to the best of my knowledge, they put up another $8,000.00, which paid the expenses of participants, by which I mean chairmen, panellists, and authors who were participating. Like, for example, Bill Mitchell and I can't even remember if he was there or not.[8] Certainly he was listed. He announced that he would go, as did Roch Carrier[9]—no, I am not sure about Carrier—but there was another French-Canadian author who was announced and scheduled to appear but didn't appear. But what the hell. They were not M&S authors.

So that's a vast amount of money?

I wonder if it is noticed by any of these detractors that neither Anna nor I spoke at any of the sessions or at any of the events. The same can't be said for Doug Gibson.

There aren't too many other points that I want to make, but there are a few:

1. I have absolutely no regret or remorse about anything I did to create and publish this Conference.
2. If the Conference appeared to be pushing M&S authors and M&S books, it is mainly because the Conference was about Canadian

literature and the Canadian novel, and M&S authors and M&S books just happen to form a very substantial part of what is Canlit.

3. If pushing the list lends support to my detractors and lends credence to the suspicions raised by a lot of small people, I can't for the life of me think why that should trouble me. Margaret, I am not running a popularity contest and have never tried to do so except with the people we publish. To hell with these people who resent M&S.

I have read and re-read your letter. At best, I think you are a reactionary and far too impressionable. I heard nothing at the Conference and I find nothing in your letter that persuades me the list should not be used.

The list may be an embarrassing thing to you, because you are at the head of it. That, in fact, is where you belong. These lists have been prepared in England and France and in fact in most cultured countries of the world. Such lists have been prepared relating to film, relating to plays, relating to art, relating to all cultural activities, in fact all athletic activities. What is wrong with such a list?

You probably know better than anyone else why such a list is needed. The academics don't know what the hell they are talking about for the most part. The teachers sure as hell know very little about Canadian literature, and the public, for the most part, knows far too little. So I should be upset because some frightened academics get nervous, because some critics attack the principle, (perhaps because they weren't invited to vote), because some writers who are perhaps afraid they won't be included get nervous, and some publishers get nervous because some of the books they published in the last five years haven't been accepted as instant classics, this is all bullshit. ...

My job is to try to interest people in Canadian literature. How are they supposed to know what is good in Canadian literature if they don't have any guidelines. If they use *Survival* as their guideline, God help us. I don't say this initial list is a better guideline. It could become that. I don't see why you should get on the bandwagon supporting this anti-list position, unless you are able to explain to me why it is such a terrible thing. I simply don't comprehend that. Maybe a lot of people think it was a bad thing, because it was known to have been my idea. That makes it commercial. That makes it bad? I think Canadian literature should be commercial. It is time we recognized what we have. Frankly, Margaret, I am fed up with Departments Of Education that list *Ice Station Zebra* when they could be listing *Duddy Kravitz*.[10] We need a goddamn list. In fact most of the people who attended the bloody Conference need a goddamn list. Would you believe that there were two works of nonfiction on the ballot form to begin with?

Leaving aside your personal feelings, is it bad for Canada to have *The Stone Angel* recognized as the top Canadian novel of all time? I don't think so. Is it bad to have *The Tin Flute* recognized as a close second? I don't think so. I don't understand all this bullshit.

Perhaps you can straighten me out. Otherwise, I am prepared to be the sacrificial lamb. I push this thing because I believe it is for the good of the country.

John Moss made the very intelligent suggestion to me. What the list really needs is annotation. People should know why the various books are included, and the annotation would show that. This work is included because it is a fine work of literature. This work is included because it is historically important. This work is included, because it is an exceptionally fine regional work. These works are included because this author happens to write better than almost anyone else in the country. Just as Jane Austen appears with a number of titles in a comparable British list. The annotation and explanation would act as a guide. ...

So there it is. It is a long letter, but I am glad that I have done it, even if Marge never forgives me. It has served the purpose—giving the matter all this further thought of reaffirming my faith that I was right to begin with and that I am still right. I won't take any action for the moment. I'll give you some further opportunity for rebuttal. Before I do, let me say this. If in your rebuttal you come up with one solid, sensible, and reasonable reason why such a list should not exist and be used, it will be the first one I have heard. Novels should not be classified? That's a joke. I may be a publisher, but I did study English literature at the University of Toronto. Novels shouldn't be compared with each other? That, too, is a joke. We don't have a large enough body of literature? That's a joke. It is a McClelland and Stewart promotion? To me, at least, that is a joke. Okay, Margaret, give me your best shot.

Re: the NCL, still no plans. We will have to deal with it soon. Are you going to be in Toronto during the next few weeks?

Despite all the foregoing, Margaret, I love you dearly. May I suggest that I leave the writing to you and you leave these much less important matters to me.

Cheers!
Jack

1. Northrop Frye (1912–1991) was a pre-eminent Canadian literary critic and literary theorist, renowned for books of criticism, such as *Fearful Symmetry, Anatomy of Criticism, The Well-Tempered Critic*, and *The Bush Garden: Essays on the Canadian Imagination*.
2. John Hugh MacLennan (1907–1990) was a Canadian writer and professor at McGill University. He was most renowned for *Barometer Rising, Two Solitudes*, and *The Watch That Ends the Night*, and he won five Governor General's Awards for fiction.
3. Richard B. Wright (1937–2017) was a Canadian writer who began his career publishing with Macmillan. His best-known work, *Clara Callan*, was published in 2001, well after these letters were exchanged between Laurence and McClelland. The novel won the Governor General's Award, the Giller Prize, and the Trillium Book Award. Wright became a member of the Order of Canada in 2007.
4. Horst Adolph Louis Charles Schmidt (1933–) is an international trade businessman from Alberta and a former provincial-level politician. He served as a member of the Legislative Assembly of Alberta from 1971 to 1986. Gertrude Laing was an instructor of French at the University of Manitoba before holding positions at the Winnipeg YMCA and the Central Volunteer Bureau. She "became the only woman member on the Royal Commission on Bilingualism and Biculturalism (a seven year task)" and served as "a member of the Canadian Radio and Television Commission, as delegate to the UNESCO General Assembly, and as Western Regional Vice-President of the Canadian Welfare Council" ("Gertrude Laing Obituary").
5. Charles Frederick (Fred) Bodsworth (1918–2012), a Canadian writer, journalist, and amateur naturalist, was most renowned for his book, *The Last of the Curlews*.
6. See Laurence's letter dated 9 March 1973 for more information about Atwood's *Survival: A Thematic Guide to Canadian Literature*.
7. Willa Cather (1873–1947) was an American writer famous for her book, *My Antonia*, set on the American prairies.
8. W.O. Mitchell (1914–1998) was a Canadian writer known for his classic, *Who Has Seen the Wind*.

9. Roch Carrier (1937–) is a Canadian novelist and short story writer, most famous in English Canada for his short story collection, *The Hockey Sweater and Other Stories*.
10. Mordecai Richler's *The Apprenticeship of Duddy Kravitz* was first published by André Deutsch in 1959.

Hollinger, 11 April 1978

Dear Jack:

Thanks for both your letters. First, let us get the list out of the way. I was somewhat reassured by your letter, which did tell me some things (e.g. the Can Council funding amount) that I hadn't known. I am neither reactionary, nor overly impressionable. Nor am I against pushing Can books—in fact, to imply that is a distortion of my meaning; I have been evangelizing for Can literature for a long time. Nor do I question the fact that you have been evangelizing for same for an even longer time. I just think that such lists are bound to some extent to be arbitrary and to create dissention, and I don't like lists that are limited to a neat 100. What is supposed to happen in the future? If, as you say, updating is done, that will be a help. I am in favour, *naturally*, of greater sales for NCL books—why wouldn't I be? They're my livelihood, and, if they were to go out of print, so would I, literally. I don't want to answer your letter in detail—I already have a sore throat and a headache, without entering into a long debate. Suffice it to say: okay, I've had my say; I accept the facts re: the Calgary conference, which you tell me, although I don't agree re: the treatment of the writers, which I thought was okay; if you're going to use the list for advertising, then you'll do so; I can't take such lists very seriously, that's all. Now let's forget the whole damn business.

Thanks for your helpful letter re: Cushman. I have now received a letter from Ann Nelles, enclosing copies of the letters she sent to James Oliver Brown and to Collins Knowlton Wing, informing them that royalties will now be sent direct to me. ... What a mess for [John]. Anyway, thanks for being so cooperative re: this.

All my contracts are between M&S and me, not the agency, and I don't have a written agreement with any of my agents. ... I'm a bit nervous about the income tax bit, as the branch of the income tax dept to which I make my return is Belleville—do you remember that awful woman who wouldn't believe it had taken me 3 years to write *The Diviners*, and you had to write a letter swearing it had? Well, she's still there. I'd hate to have to try to explain anything to her—she is a very difficult and stupid lady. Well, there must be a way.

Guess who is coming to Peterborough on April 28? Anita Bryant,[1] with the Rev. Ken Campbell from Milton, Ont. It is believed that part of their revival meeting will have to do with "porn in the schools" ... here we go again! When I think of a possible repeat of *The Diviners* controversy a year or so ago, I could throw up. This time, however, they'll be touring the country, and it has come to my attention that a good few books apart from mine will come under fire, and already are doing so. Can you believe that in N.S. a group of fanatics are trying to get Buckler's *The Mountain and the Valley* banned! Ye gods, what next? It's very depressing.

So, on this cheery note, I'll end.

All the best,
Margaret [signed]
Margaret Laurence

1. Anita Jane Bryant (1940–) is an American singer and former beauty pageant winner who spoke out and actively campaigned against homosexuality during the 1960s and 1970s.

Regent, 17 April 1978

Dear Margaret,

Thanks for yours of the 11th. Okay re: list. Let's forget it.

Glad to hear John is going to be up on April 29th. If he opens his account, then instead of paying the full royalty to you, we will pay his agent's commission into his Toronto account, so that you won't be taxed. If he doesn't get up to Toronto and if we don't just get the bank account settled, why don't we just, although we have accepted your direction to pay the whole amount to you, we will deduct the 10% and hold it for him here until the whole thing can be resolved. ...

That sounds great about Anita Bryant's visit. We must stamp out these dirty books. I am all for encouraging people because this sells more books. I think it is a great idea to get Buckler's *Mountain and the Valley* banned. These censors are so crazy. This recent censorship of the film [*Pretty Baby*] in Ontario has given this film the biggest boost it could get. I was in Montreal and they were jammed when they opened there. They are going to open in most other provinces of Canada and they will have sell-out crowds for weeks. All the people from Toronto wanted to go and see it so that they could say they had seen it, but I can't believe these people are so dumb. I mean the censors, but I am all for encouraging them (well, not really), but it is a good commercial idea.

All the best and we will see you soon.
Sincerely,
Jack McClelland

P.S. Ann Nelles has already had a sort of threatening response from Curtis Brown but we are dealing with it. There is no doubt that they are going to give you a hard time. I am also satisfied that it is a bluff and nothing else.[1]

1. On 28 April 1978, Laurence wrote again to sort out some tax-related issues, and also to mention an Etobicoke school board that tried to have *A Jest of God* removed from a Grade Thirteen course.

Hollinger, 10 May 1978

Dear Jack:

Further to our telephone conversation today, this afternoon John Cushman phoned me. He told me something that I was not in fact surprised to hear, as I had been having misgivings on the subject. His view, and mine, is that my timing in wanting to get back my five books from Curtis Brown New York (my first five) was all off, because we are going to have to settle the matter with James Oliver Brown *first*. As far as James O. Brown is concerned, we have a strong *moral* case, and this is the matter I must concentrate on. I have no quarrel with Curtis Brown NY—I simply wanted to get all my books under the same roof, mainly for income tax purposes, because things have become so confused tax-wise. But this is NOT the time to do this to Curtis Brown NY. In due course, maybe. But for the moment, all I can and should do is get my previous books away from James Oliver Brown.

I am sorry to change direction once again to Ann Nelles, who is incredibly patient and understanding; this letter is addressed as much to her as to you and I am sending her a copy. I am enclosing a copy of my letter to Curtis Brown NY, and as I only have one extra copy, can you please make sure Ann Nelles sees it? My situation with Curtis Brown NY is this: I have NOT communicated with them at all, except on the income tax matter. I haven't told them I want my books back. I have not, thank God, said a word. For the moment, my line with them is that (and this is true, goddammit!) I wanted royalties sent direct to me so that I would know and have on a T-4 from you the exact amount paid to me by M&S, not just the sums sent direct to me by you, and on the American forms only my American earnings.

So the directive now is this, to M&S, with particular attention to Ann Nelles:

1) On the following books: *This Side Jordan, The Prophet's Camel Bell, The Tomorrow-Tamer, The Stone Angel* and *A Jest of God*. ... 90% royalties to be sent to me directly. The other 10%, agent's fees, to be sent to Curtis Brown Inc., 575 Madison Ave., New York, N.Y. 10022, USA.
2) On all remaining books (*A Bird in the House, The Fire-Dwellers, Jason's Quest, The Diviners* and *Heart of a Stranger*), royalties on all editions, including Seal editions, and also to Bantam Canada for *The Diviners* (can Ann see to this?), 90% royalties sent to me, and 10% held by M&S, or Seal, or Bantam Canada, until such time as we get these things sorted out and John Cushman has those books. I assume that my Bantam Can royalties go through M&S.

I think that I feel a bit better about not taking on 2 battles. They are, after all, separate issues, and I have nothing against Curtis Brown NY.

All the best, and thanks,
Margaret Laurence

Hollinger, 29 May 1978

Dear Jack:

This is further to our phone conversation of a few weeks ago. I've just first received 25 (twenty five, ye gods!), of *The Fire-Dwellers* from Bantam Canada. I have this sinking feeling that this unusually large number of free author's copies is a kind of sop to the fact that the Seal editions may indeed prove disastrous to me.

As I mentioned to you on the phone, when I agreed to have all the Manawaka books brought out in Seal editions, just as when I agreed to have *The Diviners* brought out in Bantam Canada edition, I was concerned that the mass market paperback edition would cut into NCL sales. However, I was assured by you that the two markets would be quite different, the mass paperback being aimed, as its name suggests, at mass market outlets such as airports, drugstores and the like, and the NCL being aimed, always, at bookstores and academic sales. I thought this made sense at the time. Now, however, I learn that Bantam has sent out a catalogue including the Seal editions, and [is] making a big play of having all my Manawaka books in cheap paperback, and has circulated this catalogue throughout the academic world in this country. You said you couldn't prevent them from doing so. But I thought M&S owned a controlling share in Seal Books. In the catalogue, no mention is even made of Seal except the emblem at the end of the catalogue, in a very tiny reproduction. The Bantam and Seal editions of my books sell for $1.95, the NCL for prices ranging from about $2.25 to $3.95. No fanfare whatsoever was made of the fact that, with the publication of *The Diviners* in the NCL, now *all* my fiction is available in that series. With Bantam giving lots of publicity to the Manawaka books in mass paperback editions, what will obviously happen is that these will supplant the NCL editions for use in school and university courses, thus cutting my income on these books approximately in half.

I also worry about the future of the NCL itself, as of course with mass paperbacks I have no guarantee of their being kept in print for any time at all. I don't want to be a nuisance, Jack, but I am genuinely worried sick about all this (among my many other worries of the moment such as my agent—any news on that front?). Very unfortunately, I can't attend the Board meeting on June 1, as my aunt is visiting with me. But I would very much appreciate your letting me know what discussions of Bantam-M&S produce at that meeting. And I'd also like your own comments on what to me is a very unsettling situation.

Best wishes,
Margaret

Regent, 5 June 1978

Dear Margaret:

Thanks for your letter. Sorry you missed the meeting. As you will see from the material distributed, it was a very tough, gloomy meeting—probably the worst one I can recall. Well, that is not an unusually high number of author's copies—it is what the mass-market contracts provide for—I understand your concern and, as I have said before, to some degree I share it, but the truth is that I simply don't know. As some reassurance, let me review a few points:

1. The purpose of the distribution in Seal was to get a far wider distribution. We are not satisfied, as yet, from the reissue of the older book that this is going to take place. The results thus far have been a bit disappointing, but they haven't been in operation long enough for us to know.
2. If it should turn out that Seal distribution does not substantially increase your income, then the Seal contracts will not be renewed. They are short term. I still believe it will increase your income substantially. If it is merely a transfer from a more expensive book to a cheaper book, obviously that won't happen. We can only wait and see.
3. I was not aware in advance that the school promotion was scheduled. That was done by Bantam without Seal being involved. They had every right to do it and every right not to consult in advance. Even had they consulted, I would certainly have told them to go ahead because this is part of the experiment.
4. There is no doubt that NCL sales of these titles will be reduced. I anticipate that, but if the end product is that you make more money and we make more money, I see no reason to be concerned.

5. As I have said before, please stop worrying about the New Canadian Library. It is not being discontinued. It will not be discontinued or abandoned. All that has been decided is that we will not continue adding titles to that Series, on the same basis that we have followed for the last several years. ... The NCL today is about the most profitable thing we do. We are simply trying to find a way to make it more profitable. The Seal experiment is a similar one. If it doesn't end up making more money for you, it won't make more money for us and it won't continue ...

All the best.
Sincerely,
Jack McClelland

Hollinger, 11 June 1978

Dear Jack:

First of all, thanks for your reassurance about the Bantam and Seal editions. That allays many of my fears. Sometimes in my wors[t] moments, I visualize all my books going out of print, and me unable to write another novel, going on the dole not in my old age but right now. What you say makes me feel better. ...

Re: the report on the Board meeting, and your letter to me—I'm terribly sorry that Anna [Porter] is leaving, and hope she may return. It will be a great loss.[1] I'm also terribly sorry that the financial position is so dire. But I must really take issue with your phrase, describing your "long and dreary career in publishing." I hope this was no more than a depression of the moment. "Dreary" is the last word I would have chosen to describe your career. Chequered, perhaps; dreary, No. I like to think you've had quite a bit of fun along the way. Also, you must know how much you have done for publishing in this country. Consider who you have published—a pretty impressive list. Also, although your writers (me included) frequently disagree with you, we do have an underlying sense of real loyalty—surely you know that. So please try to cheer up.

All the best,
Margaret [signed]
Margaret Laurence

1. After Anna Porter was promoted at McClelland & Stewart to executive director in 1970 and editorial director in 1974, she became president of Seal Books, owned by McClelland & Stewart and Bantam, and then founded Key Porter Books with Michael de Pencier in 1979.

Regent, 15 June 1978

Dear Margaret:

I'm glad my letter was reassuring on the Bantam Seal thing and also that the material from the Board meeting did not prove completely upsetting. I appreciate your reaction to the word "dreary." Hell, dear; I'm just in a temporarily depressed, overworked state of mind. Contrast this with the fantasy that I have been living with for some weeks—i.e. that MacLean Hunter were going to buy the goddamn company and you can really understand how I feel. Not only are they not going to buy the company, as you will have seen from the subsequent note, I ain't ever going to do any business with them again. So I'm back trying to sort out the shambles, but I'm in good spirits. And somehow by the end of the year we will have arranged a major upswing in our fortunes. The best tonic I can possibly think of would be for you to complete your new book. ...

As for Anna, well nobody knows. I sincerely believe she will return after Labour Day, but she's not sure and we just don't know. We can live with her absence until then, but, if she decides not to come back, we'll find a solution. I don't expect to find another Anna Porter in the future, but I remember very well that she turned up when I most needed her and that will happen again.

Love,
Jack McClelland

Hollinger, 25 July 1978

Dear Jack:

I received yesterday your notice re: Larry Ritchie.[1] I assume that things have been in another state of upheaval of one kind or another, and, although there does not seem to be much I could do to help, I would simply like to express once again my confidence in the firm and my personal sense of loyalty to you as a publisher. We have frequently disagreed on various matters throughout the years, as I am sure you have with many of your writers (who do tend to be just as stubborn and bloody-minded as you are), but I do hope you know and believe that there are a lot of us rooting for you, when the chips are down, and not only out of our own self-interest, either, but because of all you have done for Canadian publishing and writing. I don't know what the problems are right now, although I suppose they are mainly financial. It seems so unfair that a talented publisher simply cannot get on with the business of *publishing books,* which is what I'm sure you'd rather do than anything. Anyway, even though I can't offer anything much except moral support, please know you've got that.

I hate right now to bother you (again) with my agent problem. I've looked up such contracts as I can find, and as I suspected, the M&S hardcover editions (and Knopf hardcovers) all mention an agent. However, I believe only two books of mine are still available in M&S hardcover ... *The Diviners* and *Heart of a Stranger*. As for the Bantam Canada contract for *The Diviners,* and the Seal contracts for the other Manawaka books, *no agent is mentioned.* The books in the NCL I can't find contracts for ... I wonder if they mention an agent? It seems to me that any contract [that] doesn't mention an agent, I could simply ask James Oliver Brown to return to me; also any contracts on books now out of hardcover print. ...

Best,
Margaret [signed]
Margaret Laurence

1. Laurence refers to McClelland & Stewart's troubling financial situation and the departure of Larry Ritchie, a vice-president and senior financial manager.

Regent, 3 August 1978

Dear Margaret:
That's a very good letter and I do appreciate it. You know, I really think we are going to be okay this time. God knows we are overdue for a little luck. The new man has a wealth of experience and really wants to be our senior financial officer. He came highly recommended by a very good friend of mine, who is about the best-qualified person in financial matters in Canada. [Len] Cummings, too, has the makings of a very good general manager.

I should have done something about Larry Ritchie a long time ago. The sad truth is that he is a very bright guy. Had he wanted to do his job properly, he could have done it as well as anybody I have ever met. He was a very bright guy with figures, but his problem was twofold. First, he was, as they say, too bright by halves and both he and the company became a victim of his machinations. The second problem was that he really didn't want to be a senior financial officer. He wanted to be Jack McClelland. Anna Porter could be Jack McClelland, Peter Taylor could probably be Jack McClelland, and there are other people in the firm who could be Jack McClelland, but never Larry Ritchie and really that's the sad truth. ...

All the best.
Sincerely,
Jack McClelland

Hollinger, 12 August 1978

Dear Jack:

The enclosed thing may seem like a strange thing to be sending to you. It may not be M&S' cup of tea at all, but I want to submit it to you first. The "Note to Parents" will explain the origin of this version of the Nativity story, and the note to Publisher will explain my and Helen Lucas'[1] concept of how the production should be—like a high-class colouring book, really.[2]

Just before Anna departed from M&S, I mentioned this story to her. As I recall, we did not then have the illustrations, although Helen Lucas (who is getting to be a very respected artist) had seen the story and said she would like to try doing pictures. I had thought of her as artist because her work is very beautiful and she was the one artist I could think of who would do the kind of illustrations I visualized. What I wanted to avoid at all costs was the Walt Disney look! Anna said she would like to see the story, so when Helen had done the pictures, I got my son to photograph them and sent the package to Anna. She has now returned it, and says she likes it and thinks M&S should do it. I asked her if she would mind my telling you this, and she said go ahead. Anyway, here it is. I guess I am submitting it more or less as a package deal. I'm not prepared to alter the story, and I would want the pictures to go just as they are. Of course, the photographs at present only give an idea of what the originals would look like. The background in production would be a pale beige or off-white, and the pictures would be really white, if you see what I mean. I don't think production costs would be high, as the pics are black and white.

Jennifer Glossop already has another children's Christmas story of mine, quite a different thing.[3] She thinks it should be expanded, and I think that is probably possible. So if you did by any chance want the enclosed Nativity story, it is ready to go and should be brought out first, with the other one being published next year, I think. Anyway, I'll be interested to hear what you think. ...

I'm really really sorry about the Ritchie business. That was all you needed. I'd like to have a good talk with you sometime. ... Do you think we could meet after or before the next Board meeting? Or have lunch sometime?

I do hope you are feeling less depressed now. What with Iran, and Ritchie, and one thing and another, it has been a hell of a year for you. My Celtic second sight tells me things will get better. And as I said in my last letter, I hope you realize what a large amount of loyalty your writers feel for you and how much we realize what a pioneer you've been in Canadian publishing. So—[Coraggio]—Avanti!

All the best,
Margaret

1. Helen Lucas (1931–) is a renowned Canadian artist who illustrated Laurence's children's story, *The Christmas Birthday Story*, referenced here.
2. In a letter to McClelland & Stewart editor Linda McKnight, dated 8 November 1978, McClelland recounted a phone call he had with Laurence about another one of Laurence's children's books, *The Olden Days Coat*. He stated, "Instead of it being in the form of a colouring book as originally planned by Margaret, the artist, Helen Lucas, will re-do the pictures as pastels in colour" (McClelland & Stewart Ltd. Fonds, Box 87, File 25).
3. Jennifer Glossop is a book editor and author of nonfiction children's books. She began working as an editor with McClelland & Stewart and has freelanced for major publishers for many years.

Regent, 24 August 1978

Dear Margaret:

Thanks for yours of August 12th and the enclosed manuscript. Migod, it sounds very different. I shall get at it over the weekend and be back to you early next week. I must say I am no expert on Nativity stories, but I will do my best to become one.

Thanks for your very good word about the problems we have encountered here. It has not been particularly pleasant and they are not over yet. You will, by now, have received notice of the Directors' Meeting next week. I don't know whether you are planning to come or not. It will be an important meeting, maybe a desperately important meeting, but will deal almost solely with financial matters. Obviously, I would like you to be there, but it is a terrible trip at this time of year and my judgement would be that, unless you can come with great convenience and want to do other things in the city, I would say don't come. I will certainly let you know the outcome of the meeting. I don't think anything of any definitive nature will be decided Thursday.

I would very much like to have that lunch and discussion that you refer to. The next time you are in the city, we can make it lunch or dinner whichever suits your schedule best, but I would really welcome the opportunity to review a lot of things with you.

I still owe you a letter cleaning up some of the other matters and I will speak to Charles and find out exactly what he has been doing. I will try to get back to you early in the week on the subject.

All the best.
Jack

Regent, 11 September 1978

Dear Margaret:

I have now had a chance to read the *Christmas Birthday Story* and to review it with several of my associates. It is very simple and direct, and I think altogether a useful account of the nativity. I am somewhat less certain about the illustrations. Certainly, it is beautifully executed, but I have grave reservations as to whether it will appeal much to the age level for which it is intended. I simply don't know, because I am hardly an expert in the field, but it does seem to me that it is on the highly stylized, sophisticated side for this market and possibly not too practical from the standpoint of the colouring that you envisage except for the most gifted of children. I would like to do an exploration of this; get some opinions from those involved with children at this age level because I judge from your letter that you feel very much committed to Helen Lucas and would not want to proceed without her.

May I then proceed with some sort of exploration? Are you coming to Toronto in the next few weeks? I hope we can have that meeting that you talked about in a previous letter before too long. Let me know your plans. I don't want to bring you up here especially for such a meeting, but I'd very much like to see you and would like then to talk about this.

All the best.
Sincerely,
Jack McClelland

P.S. The Directors' Meeting was a bit of a shocker but we came through and all is okay. I would like to talk about that too when I see you. A pile of material on the meeting will be going out to you shortly.

Hollinger, 4 October 1978

Dear Jack,

In moving back from the cottage, I seem to have lost your letter regarding the Nativity story.[1] I'm pretty sure I haven't answered it, though. Yes, I do feel a strong commitment to Helen Lucas' illustrations, and I don't think they are too sophisticated for children. ... Anyway, never mind. I'd be grateful if you could return the pics and story to me as soon as possible.

All the best,
Margaret [signed]
Margaret Laurence[2]

1. Hodgeman wrote back on 10 October 1978 to inform Laurence that McClelland was "up north trying to get caught up on his backlog" and that he wanted further discussion with her about the Nativity material, *The Christmas Birthday Story*. A copy of his letter, dated 11 September 1978, was attached to her own and is included in this collection of letters (McClelland & Stewart Ltd. Fonds, Box 87, File 25).
2. McClelland wrote "discuss with her" on this letter.

Hollinger, 12 October 1978

Dear Jack:

I am writing to you about a young friend, Leslie Cole.[1] She is tremendously anxious to get into publishing, and would be willing to start anywhere, in any kind of job, to get a foot in the door. She is extremely bright, energetic, and capable. She also has worked in many parts of Canada (including the North-West Territories), is bilingual in English and French, and is knowledgeable in the fields of English Canadian Literature, French Canadian Literature and Canadian Children's Literature.

I hope you don't think it presumptuous of me to write to you about her, but if there was any chance at all of your needing a new young person on staff, I think it would truly be worth your while to grant her an interview. I expect she will be contacting the firm in the next little while.

All the best,
Margaret

1. Leslie Cole is the daughter of Jean Cole, who was one of Laurence's close friends and a local historian in the Peterborough area.

Regent, 22 November 1978

Dear Margaret:

A belated note re: Leslie Cole. We have been in touch with her. Unfortunately, we simply don't have any openings here at all at present. I thought I should mention this just in case it doesn't come up when we meet, because we have so many other things to review and, incidentally, I very much look forward to seeing you on the 30th.

Cheers!
Jack McClelland

Regent, 24 January 1979

Dear Margaret,

As you will see from the attached,[1] we are planning a dinner in Pierre Berton's honour. One of the features of the dinner will be a special souvenir program-menu. We are asking a number of writers and friends of Pierre Berton to contribute short comments, anecdotes, whatever—up to a maximum of 300 words to go into this booklet which will be distributed at the dinner. Be serious; be funny; whatever suits you.

We are hoping very much that you will be willing to contribute a few words. We need it within two weeks. I am sorry about the short notice. Our organisation is somewhat less advanced than it should be.

All the best.
Sincerely,
Jack [signed]
Jack McClelland

1. There is no attachment that survives in the Clara Thomas Archives and Special Collections.

Regent, 5 February 1979

Dear Margaret:

The Ballad of Pierre Berton is really great. He will love it. I can't think of anything that would be more suitable for the occasion. I don't know yet what the program is going to be and whether we can arrange to have it sung, but, if we can, Elsa will be in touch with you very shortly.

I am really delighted you are coming. We have sent the information to Clara for the tickets, etc. It should be a fine event.[1]

All the best.
Sincerely,
Jack

1. He later sent a telegram to indicate he would not be present and to wish her success.

Regent, 28 September 1979

Dear Margaret:

Re: Writers' Development Trust

The Writers' Development Trust has submitted an application for a supporting grant to the Ontario Arts Council. At the last meeting of the executive, it was decided that it could be helpful if we did some lobbying before the meeting. Although we submitted a full application, they have limited funds and it was our conclusion that we should bring as much pressure to bear on them as possible. The WDT desperately needs money.

It would be helpful, then, if you could, within the next few days, send a letter to them saying simply that you understand that the Trust has submitted an application, that you are very much in favour of the Trust, its objectives and its important function and that you hope that the application will be treated with great consideration.

The letter should go to Frank F. McEachren, Chairman, Ontario Arts Council, 151 Bloor Street West, Toronto M5S 1T6.

It is my understanding that the application will be considered in about two weeks. It is important that the letter go forward as soon as possible. We are asking those organizations who are tenants in the Ryerson Street property to send supporting letters. Apart from that, I am writing to about half a dozen major Canadian authors who have been involved in the formation of the Trust. In other words, we are not making a frontal attack. The same letter will go to the others, but obviously the individual letters sent to Frank McEachren should be original and independent.

Sincerely,
Jack [signed]
Jack McClelland

Hollinger, 2 November 1979

Dear Jack:

Re: the copy of the letter sent to June Callwood, re: Bob Weaver—I never heard it suggested that the Writers' Union should nominate Bob Weaver for the Molson Award.[1] I don't know if organizations can nominate, or only individuals? In any event, if anyone is nominating Bob for the Molson, I would be most most happy to support that nomination. If no nomination has been made, I think it is a super idea, and would be willing to nominate him, needless to say. Can you give me any further details?

All the best,
Margaret

1. See McClelland's letter dated 7 January 1960 for information about Robert Weaver. June Callwood (1924–2007) was a Canadian journalist, author, and social activist.

•——

Regent, 6 December 1979

Dear Margaret:

It has always been our policy to keep all McClelland and Stewart titles in print as long as possible. Now, due to inflation, the increasingly high cost of doing business, and particularly because of rising interest rates, we have had to adopt a more realistic policy. Our accountants demonstrate clearly that the cost of a book in our inventory actually doubles if it remains in our warehouse for only two and one-half years.

This has led to some unavoidable policy decisions. We can't afford to keep more than two years of inventory of any title on hand. We can't afford to reprint any titles that will sell less than 1,000 copies per year. Even worse, once our stock of a title drops to the 250-copy level, unless we can schedule it for reprint, we simply can't afford to keep it in stock because of computer cataloguing costs.

We are not happy about these decisions. It is no secret that the Canadian publishing industry receives substantial support from both the Federal Government and from the Ontario Government. Despite that support, the firms that don't face the harsh new realities of the book trade will not survive. We intend to survive.

In the last decade there have been three lamentable trends. More selective retail buying and an increasing emphasis on the bestseller syndrome; the shortening of the life of the average book; and a far more selective retail policy towards stocking backlist titles. Our overall backlist sales had grown at an average annual rate of 15% for as far back as I can remember, until about three years ago when they started diminishing at about the same rate. These new policies will affect different authors in different ways.

In your case, we will be forced to do some "overstocking"[1] on *The Prophet's Camel Bell*, *Heart of a Stranger* and *The Tomorrow-Tamer*. What this means is that if you want to pick up some copies of *The*

Prophet's Camel Bell at about 60 cents, *Heart of a Stranger* at $1.65 and *The Tomorrow-Tamer* at about the same price, do let us know what you would like to have. We will confirm the exact price once we know your quantities. Do let us know by return and by all means use the duplicate of this page for that purpose.

All the best,
Sincerely,
Jack

P.S. We will be keeping all of them in print so fear not. I hope it will look like more retail price-cutting. Things go well—well fair. Have a great Christmas, if I don't see you before.

1. On the copy of this letter, Laurence noted beside this word, "What does this mean?" Further down, after *The Tomorrow-Tamer*, she wrote, "NCL? or, mistake?"

Hollinger, 11 December 1979

Dear Jack:

I enclose herewith a hardbound copy of *The Olden Days Coat*, which I purchased for the sum of $9.95 last Saturday at A Different Drummer Bookshop in Burlington.

Let me explain.

Al Cummings, who is one of the owners of the shops, had advertised my going there to autograph some books, when it was believed there this book would be a hardcover one. He decided, when it turned out to be paperback, to have 50 copies specially bound. This cost him $3 a copy, so he didn't make any extra money on those 50, but he didn't lose, either. Most of the hardcovers were pre-sold by phone orders. The rest went in the first 10 minutes I was there. All afternoon (I was there about 2 hours) people kept expressing disappointment that no more hardcover copies [were] available. Not one person quibbled over the $9.95 price.

Now, do not get me wrong. I can understand why M&S went for the paperback. I know that the firm is in financial difficulties. I know that Lorimer's edition of my other kids' book was going to sell for $6.95, and I surmise that may have influenced M&S' pricing decision. It is also my guess, having seen *Six Darn Cows* (the one I did for Lorimer),[1] which has an attractive laminated cover with the picture on the cover itself, that when M&S decided to drop the class production they had originally planned and go for a paperback, using the erstwhile endpaper design as the paperback cover design, and putting out a paperback with a dust jacket, *that the dust jackets had already been printed.* Otherwise, why not go for a laminated cover, as Lorimer did.... an attractive but also *durable* binding, and, I would guess, less expensive than a *hardbound* edition with a dust-jacket? I can see that if the jackets were already printed, there was no way you were going to throw them away and do a laminated cover. I can understand it. I don't quibble with that decision.

BUT.

There are great disadvantages in the present edition, paperback. The jackets were designed to fit a hardcover edition. They don't fit. They slip off. They will quickly get lost, and the paperback mix binding will then last approximately 2 weeks before getting ripped, torn, etc.

What I am suggesting is this: if the book goes into a second printing (which really means if you decide to put it out again next Christmas, as it is clearly a Christmas book), would it not be possible to put out a bound edition, using the present paperback cover as a base, as in the copy I am enclosing, only do it in the reverse way, so that the butterfly design is on the outside and thus serves as endpapers? Obviously, A Diff Drummer couldn't do this, as the book was already bound, but starting from scratch, why wouldn't it be possible? Or, and this is probably more practical (although it would lose the butterfly design), why not do a laminated cover with the present dust jacket design being on the actual cover?? This could certainly be sold for more than $6.95, and would be made much more durable. If you got a fair number done, presumably the unit cost would be less than the $3 a copy that Cummings paid for the 50 hardbound copies he got. At, say, $8.95 for a book with a laminated cover, I bet you money to doughnuts that you'd sell more. A friend of mine who is head of a library board says that libraries will have to get their copies bound anyway, at expense and nuisance.

I have always made it my inflexible policy never to believe dust-jacket hype. The hype on the jacket says (idiotically, in my view) that it is "destined to become a classic in children's literature" and "will be received with delight by young readers for years to come." Okay, so we all know that is baloney, but if you really believe that it may be received by young readers even next year, and, if [it] go[es] to a second printing, I beg you to consider doing a bound edition in either of the ways I have suggested. I think a laminated would be the most practical, even if you had to leave off the pic that is now on the back jacket and put the blurb there instead.

One more thing. As you probably recall, next year I will be having yet another kids' Christmas book out. This is *The Christmas Birthday*

Story, a retelling of the Nativity story for very young kids (let's say to 6 years) with absolutely gorgeous full-colour pictures by Helen Lucas. As you know, Knopf is doing the production job, and you will be getting that edition with your imprint. If I am still alive and kicking, why could I not once again do book signings in some stores, for *that* book, and also again for *The Olden Days Coat* in a new laminated-cover edition???? "Madam, if you want a Christmas gift for your 5 to 6 year old, this is just the job. If, on the other hand, you want a Christmas gift for your 6 to 10 year old, we have here..." How about it, Jack? Please think about it. And if, as I hope, you view this idea favourably, PLEASE get cracking on getting *The Olden Days Coat* in new bound (laminated form) next Christmas. This year, I did three bookshop signings (and is a lot, for me), and I found that the two books really were not in competition with one another. ... They sold, as it were, in tandem. And some people even bought *The Olden Days Coat* for their grandmothers. I kind of liked that. I really think that if you could bring out the book in some form of hardcover, next year, and price it from about $8.95 to $9.95, it would sell very well in tandem with a Christmas book for smaller kids (which, I suspect, will also be bought for adults themselves, as well, or for older kids). You could present *The Olden Days Coat* as "in new durable binding, with the same magic pictures by Muriel Wood"[2]. ... etc. In these trying times, nobody would really wonder much why you hadn't brought out a bound edition originally; they would just assume that you'd waited to see if the "classic in children's literature" would be around for more than one year. Because the three signings I did (at Stedman's, Children's Bookstore, and A Different Drummer) all went so well, I think I might take my courage in hand and go to some more shops next year. ... After all, there will be a new Christmas book to hustle, so why not hustle this one again, at the same time?

I would be grateful if you would show this letter to Linda McKnight[3] and give it thought. As this is not a book many people are going to be asking for in July, *if* sales on this edition seem to merit it, *please* at least table these suggestions for consideration for the 1980 Fall list.

Best,
Margaret

1. Laurence's children's book, *Six Darn Cows*, was published in 1979 by James Lorimer and Co., a publisher specializing in children's literature.
2. Muriel Wood is a Canadian children's book illustrator who illustrated Laurence's *The Olden Days Coat* and editions of L.M. Montgomery's *Anne of Green Gables*.
3. Linda McKnight has worked as an editor, publisher, and agent. She began working at Copp Clark and was later hired as the educational editor at McClelland & Stewart. She then became managing editor, director of publishing, and, finally, president and publisher (see McClelland's letter dated 11 March 1982). She left McClelland & Stewart in the mid-1980s to work at Macmillan, and then became an agent, director, and president of Westwood Creative Artists. In 2016, she won the Ivy Award for her substantial contribution to Canadian publishing.

Regent, 17 December 1979

Dear Margaret:

Thanks for your letter of the 11th. I am in complete sympathy with your position. However, while such a letter from a normal author would not surprise me in any way, when it comes from a director, that's a different thing. It indicates clearly to me that I have been remiss in not educating you sufficiently well on the intricacies of book publishing.

Let me try to do so. First, the format of the book has nothing to do with our financial problems. Second, the format of the book has absolutely nothing to do with our having printed the dust jackets first because, in fact, that did not happen. Third, I doubt very much whether we will be able to issue it in a hardbound edition, although it is too early to be absolutely certain about that, and I can assure you that we will consider it as carefully as possible. ...[1]

Now, as to the second point: we did consider a straight paperback or, as you describe it, a laminated cover. We opted for something that we thought was better than that and would, in fact, go further to justify the $6.95 price which, despite the colour, is still considered high for such a little book. We decided to opt for a stiff board cover plus a dust jacket. This is a technique that has been used before in various parts of the world and with some success. Unfortunately, the committee that was dealing with the matter ran into a problem that, while it was anticipated, was not expected. The thickness of the cardboard cover that was used was about half the thickness of the one that was pictured to us. We were assured that we would get the thicker cover, but, in fact, we did not. By the time we realized what had happened—and believe me everyone around here was heartsick—it was too late. The books had been bound. There was nothing we could do about it. Our production department was at fault, because it was our production department that assured us they would give us the thick cover. They failed. I am not sure it was entirely their fault, because we really laid the problem on them, but that's the way it came down. It is that simple.

Because I was involved personally in every step of the operation and every decision that was made, I accept the full responsibility and I apologize to you for the fact that the cover is not as good as it should have been. Let me assure you of two things, however. Had the cover been the right thickness, that cover with a jacket on top of it would provide a much more attractive cover than a straight paperback. Let me also tell you that the book is selling really well and people have complained, but it is selling despite this physical lamination and it appears to be selling just as well as we had expected it to sell this year.

I don't agree with your comment on the jacket blurb. We are satisfied that it has been accepted as a children's classic, and there have been a number of reviews that say exactly that including one in the *London Free Press*—and I have just returned from London. There was one snarky review in *The Globe* or perhaps it was *The Star*[2] and that sort of thing is bound to happen, but to hell with them. They don't know a good book when they see it. They don't know a first-class production when they see it and they don't recognize a great text when they see it. Not much we can do about that as long as the general public understands it. When we do a reprint—and we will certainly reprint—we will substitute real quotes for a publisher's blurb.

Then we come to the question of whether we can do it as a hardbound next year. Margaret, if libraries want to bind it up in a cloth binding, that's their problem. Publishers have been pointing out to them for years that rather than do that, they can buy a number of paperbacks and that the paperbacks can be thrown out from time-to-time and they are still ahead of the game financially. The major libraries who care about this sort of thing—they are not going to learn this lesson—can afford to pay for the special binding, so I think we should let them do that. However, there is one possibility: American publication. That hasn't come through as I anticipated yet—at least I don't believe it has—but it will come through eventually. If an American publisher manufactures the book, they do have the binding equipment to do the thing economically in the States and we will buy some copies from them and have a hardbound edition on the market. Certainly, everybody in this company would prefer to be able to offer it in hardbound next year and would have preferred to do so this year, but not at $12.95. The book is just not large enough.

So what more can I tell you? The problem won't exist with *The Christmas Birthday Story*, because we will be manufacturing with Knopf. Not only are U.S. manufacturing costs about 25% below ours for this type of book, but they do have the binding equipment, which makes it even more practical.

So have a great Christmas. I am told that yours is one of the few books on the market this fall that won't be coming back to the publishers in huge quantities come January. I hope it is true. It ain't going to be a great spring for anybody, even if Trudeau becomes our Prime Minister once again.

All the best.
Sincerely,
Jack McClelland

1. McClelland provides details here about why it is not financially viable to publish the book in hardcover.
2. McClelland is referring to "Younger Children," the review by Jacquie Hunt that appeared in the *Globe and Mail* on 1 December 1979, in which she claims the "story is a let-down, the flimsy structure matched only by the insipid prose" (D11).

III | *A Legacy, 1980–1986*

Hollinger, 18 January 1980

Dear Jack,

Please forgive the Xeroxed letter. I felt it was important to get this information to you as soon as possible. As you know, Robert Weaver has been nominated for the Molson Award. In addition to this, he has been nominated to receive the Order of Canada. I have written to the Order of Canada, and have today received word that they already do have a file on him, as a nominee, and that further supporting letters would be helpful.

If you would like to write a letter supporting Robert Weaver's nomination to the Order of Canada, your help would be greatly appreciated. ...

Yours sincerely,
Margaret [signed]
Margaret Laurence

Regent, 23 January 1980

Dear Margaret:

Thanks for your good work on behalf of Bob Weaver. I have sent a supporting letter and a copy is attached.

I apologize for having given Nantel a philosophic treatise in the middle of that letter, but it is something that has troubled me in a theoretical way for a long time. Although I haven't checked the list in too much detail, I think that you, Gabrielle, and Hugh MacLennan are Companions.[1] I don't think anybody in their right mind could question the appropriateness of that. I would also say that I think additions from the writing community should be few and far between. I think the qualifications should be a major body of work, an important work, over a considerable number of years. On a current basis I would, for example, probably exclude Margaret Atwood, because she hasn't been at it long enough, although in other respects she would certainly qualify.

The case I refer to, a very recent one, was Mordecai Richler.[2] I think his decision was the right one. I think the committee of whoever makes these decisions has shown very good judgement in most cases, but the danger is there and, in Richler's case, I think he has been discriminated against. Probably through ignorance of his real stature.

Two other people that trouble me—and they are both Officers—are Farley and Pierre. Farley, of course, lacks academic support, which privately bugs the hell out of him. I tell him that it is partly because he has continually played the clown, but he will have his reward 100 years from now when his work is still being read. Berton is another case. He is ultimately writing in a commercial field and, while he is the best we have in that area, I don't think that is quite good enough. On the other hand, in terms of his contribution to the country, the national spirit and just about anything else you can think of, well hell as you know he, too, is a giant. There may be a few others who belong up there—although damn few—maybe Callaghan, but I think he rejected the Order,[3] probably because he was graded and just possibly Layton, although he is very controversial.

One of these days, perhaps you and I could talk about this and even do something useful about it, since your motives would be recognized as absolutely pure and my only bias would be towards M&S authors, but in a quiet way we just might be able to do something, if you think it is important. Ed Schreyer is a friend [who] might not do any harm.[4] Think about it.

The funny thing about all this is that Mordecai loves Bob Weaver. I also think that Mordecai is a big enough person to applaud it, if Weaver became a Companion, but hell Margaret, I really wouldn't want to have his circuits loaded with that one. Richler is a major creative genius—and, by the way, his new novel certainly re-affirms that[5]—while Bob is a self-effacing, dedicated guy who has worked very hard in the vineyard. Do I worry too much about unimportant things?

Love and kisses,
Jack McClelland

P.S. God, I am grateful to the Writers' Union for getting all that great publicity for us in Bill French's column.[6] Don't comment on that one. I know that June [Callwood] was well intentioned.[7] At least, I think she was. It is just that William French ain't overly bright.[8]

1. McClelland cites the three writers from the fold of McClelland & Stewart who had already been made Companions of the Order of Canada. Laurence was awarded the distinction in 1972, and Hugh MacLennan and Gabrielle Roy in 1967. Farley Mowat and Pierre Berton, referenced later in this letter, were made Officers of the Order of Canada in, respectively, 1981 and 1976. The Order of Canada is a national honour that recognizes significant lifelong contribution in a career and acknowledges an individual's outstanding service to the country.
2. Mordecai Richler received the Order of Canada in 2001, although he refused it on two other occasions. McClelland might refer to one of those two occasions here.
3. Claude Ryan and Morley Callaghan both declined the award in 1967.

4. Edward Richard Schreyer (1935–) is a Canadian politician and diplomat who served as the twenty-second Governor General of Canada from 1979 to 1984.
5. The novel McClelland refers to is Richler's *Joshua Then and Now*.
6. McClelland is referring to book critic William French and his column in which he decried the censorship of Laurence's novel, *The Diviners*. He likely meant the article titled, "The Centre Held in Publishing, but the Plot Was a Little Too Frangible," which appeared in the *Globe and Mail* on 29 December 1979, in which French addressed how the Writers' Union of Canada was pivotal to addressing censorship along with the Book and Periodical Development Council (E10).
7. June Callwood was one of the founders of the Writers' Union of Canada (Moore).
8. Between this letter and the next one, Laurence wrote to Hodgeman on 7 April 1980: "Is himself [McClelland] still recovering from mushing down Yonge Street in the freezing rain and mud, clad in a toga? I get these reports from all my spies, Marge, and I sit here in the warmth of my village house and wish them all well, thanking heavens it ain't me!" (Jack McClelland Fonds, William Ready Division, Box 87, File 26). McClelland was notorious for going to great lengths to promote his authors' books. Wearing a toga on Yonge Street was one of his publicity stunts.

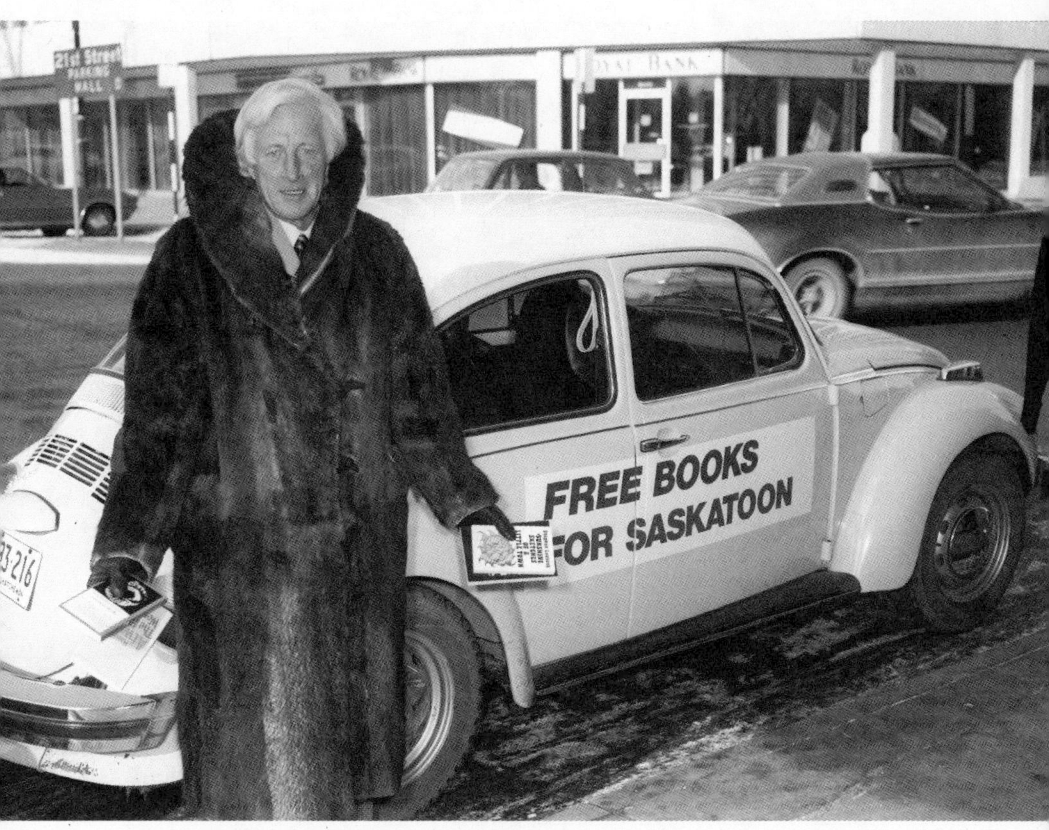

Jack McClelland was known for his outrageous publicity stunts. Here, he is giving out free books on the streets of Saskatoon, wearing a coat made of raccoon fur.

[Courtesy of Saskatoon Public Library—Local History, CP-1797-2]

Hollinger, 20 May 1980

Dear Jack:

Thanks for your letter to members of the Board, regarding the responsibilities of Directors.

I have been agonising, on and off, about my presence on the Board since our last meeting, and indeed for some time before that. I feel I must resign from the Board, but I do want to explain my reasons and my feelings.

The possibility that the Directors might under some circumstances be liable to creditors is certainly a consideration, but not my main one, as it would seem from your note that the likelihood of this situation is a remote one. In fact, I really can't see it happening. But if it ever did, it would be pretty ironic, not to say disastrous, for me if I were—as a writer—not paid royalties due, while as a director were liable for, let's say, staff salaries. However, as I say, this is not my prime consideration, because I can't really see that happening.

My main and growing concern about my presence on the Board is that I do have a conflict of interests. As my whole professional life is tied up with McClelland and Stewart, and as most of my income for some years now has come from royalties on books published by the firm, it is obviously in my interest that those books should remain in print during my lifetime—even if they are not selling more than 1,000 per year. It is obviously in my personal interest for the firm to survive in its present form. There are, now, and will be issues upon which the Board must vote, and I do not feel I can vote in any unbiased way. The alternative—not to vote on these issues—does not make me feel comfortable, either. Unlike Pierre [Berton], I do not have shares in the firm, and I also do not have his business acumen in the wider world of business. Within the area of my own life and work, I think I am a pretty fair business woman, but, in terms of a more general and a wider business knowledge, I am only one step away from being ignorant. In other words, I don't feel at this point I am much use on the Board, and I feel that my personal involvement as a writer makes me unsuitable to discuss dispassionately certain problems the firm has to deal with at this time.

I also feel that the fact that I do not live in Toronto means that I have not been able to attend some Board meetings, or I go in as I did last time (owing to no one's fault) insufficiently prepared.

I have been trying, as you know, to get into another novel.[1] I work slowly at this stage, but I think I am beginning to get somewhere. Quite frankly, I think I may be able to do myself and the firm more good by trying to produce another novel.

I am very concerned, however, that you should take my resignation as it is meant—not as a gesture of withdrawal or as a lack of faith in the firm *at all*, but rather as a sense of where I can most effectively act at this time. We have had our ups and downs over the years, Jack, but these spirited exchanges of letters and differences of opinion from time to time have only served to confirm in my mind the fact that I have been fortunate enough to have a writer/publisher relationship with you and the firm that has consistently been one of mutual respect and professional concern and caring on both sides. I hope it is a relationship that will continue as long as I'm writing anything that is worth publishing. My sense of loyalty to you personally and to the firm is very strong, perhaps stronger than you realize, and I know that many M&S writers feel the same. In my own case, it is no small thing to have had a basically very sound relationship with my Canadian publishers for twenty years. You published my first novel in 1960. This year, with the publication of a children's book in the fall, you will have published 12 of my books, seven of them books of adult fiction. I not only owe you and the firm a great deal—I also am well aware of this fact.

I feel that the firm will weather these storms, and when haven't there been storms? One can hardly underestimate the importance of M&S to the publishing scene in Canada, and to the whole area of our culture. I wish there were more I could actively *do* to help in the present crisis.

But I feel that what I should be doing is to be concentrating on my writing, and, in the end, that may be the best course. I am sure you will understand. I just want to make sure that you also understand that my support for you, despite our many differences of viewpoint throughout the years, is as always unswerving. I need hardly say that any information that I have received in confidence, as a Director, will remain confidential.

All the best, and in hope,
Margaret Laurence

P.S. If you wish to show this letter, or any part of it, to the Board, you have my full permission.

1. At this time, Laurence was trying to write a novel, which she titled "Dance on the Earth"—the same title she later gave to her memoir. The novel was never finished, and the unfinished manuscript resides in the archives at McMaster University. Nora Foster Stovel discusses this unfinished novel in *Divining Margaret Laurence*. Stovel notes that Laurence discusses her inability to complete this novel in the preface to her memoir. "It has finally become clear to me," Laurence states, "that the novel I thought I wanted to write was simply not there to be written" (qtd. in Stovel 265).

Regent, 23 May 1980

Dear Margaret:

I thank you for your letter of May 20th. I can't say that I was delighted to receive it—that would be untrue. How could one ever be delighted to have Margaret Laurence resign from their Board? Your contribution has been a valuable one and your name has lent great prestige to the firm.

Having said that, however, I hasten to tell you that I am pleased with your decision. I think you have made the right judgment, and the only thing I deplore is the existence of the circumstances that make it the right decision and the right judgment. Those circumstances are not going to disappear in a hurry—well, hell, I'm not sure of that. They now may well disappear very quickly—but I am very sensitive to the problem and I am also very much aware that you can contribute more to the firm by writing.

I know it has been a difficult letter for you to write. Our friendship has been a long and valued one and will continue to be so long as we can be honest with each other. You have reached an honest decision. I recognise it as a necessary decision, so let's put that behind us.

As to the future of the firm, Margaret, I don't really know what to expect. I've called a tentative Directors' Meeting for Friday morning of next week—and I will present your resignation along with some others at that time. My current anticipation is that my own will probably be included. There has been much political scurrying around over the last week, but, if my spies are to be believed, we are heading for a tough and possibly unfriendly confrontation with the ODC[1] on Thursday. It is possible that there will be political intervention before then, but I am doing nothing to encourage it. The intimidation tactic has gone on too long. If the terms and conditions are sensible, I will stay on. If they are not—and the indications are that they are not going to be—then, with the full blessing of my family, I am simply going to walk away.

Obviously, the part about this that I don't like is that some of our authors—particularly those with books coming this fall—will be hurt in the process. Well, that may or may not happen. I have some fairly strong cards that I can play to protect the interests of the authors and I am certainly going to play them.

In the meantime, don't worry too much [about] the situation. I realize that [it] is easier to say it will be all resolved by next Friday and either Marge or I will phone you with the results one way or the other. The meeting itself will be a very brief one and may, in fact, be cancelled.

I could go on at great length, but I won't. Let's keep our fingers crossed and see how things work out.

We will keep you informed.

Love,
Jack [signed]

1. The abbreviation ODC likely refers to the Ontario Development Council.

Regent, 4 July 1980

Dear Margaret:

This letter, which is mainly for the record, is to let you know that at the meeting of the McClelland and Stewart Board of Directors yesterday, July 3rd, your resignation was formerly [*sic*] accepted with great regret.

The motion was unanimously passed thanking you for the very substantial contribution that you have made since joining the Board. Your interest, your counsel, and your personal presence were much appreciated by the Board as a whole, and you will be very much missed.

The resignations of Sam Orenstein and Dan Casey were formerly [*sic*] accepted at the same meeting. So much for the formality. I think I have already conveyed to you my personal appreciation and thanks for your very great contributions. You really are going to be missed but, given all the circumstances, I feel that decision to resign was for the best.

As to M&S, things are okay. Our credit lines have been renewed for a year and our revised cash-flow indicates that we can operate reasonably well within those limits. A committee has been formed to find a solution before the end of the year for the long-term financing of the company. I don't know what the solution is going to be. I am certain only that we will find one and that the company will continue to operate as it has in the past for many years to come.

Thanks again and best personal regards.

Sincerely,
Jack McClelland

P.S. So much for the formality. I love you dearly.

Regent, 31 July 1980

Dear Margaret:

The attached from Gwen Curry[1] is self-explanatory. Would you like to see the manuscript? Do you have any feeling pro or con re: her approach? Would you rather not be involved in the decision?

All the best.
Sincerely,
Jack [signed]
Jack McClelland

P.S. Bantam have come up with some lovely illustrations—at least I think they are—for *Jason's Quest*. They will be sending some photocopies of them on to you for approval shortly. My guess is that we should do a hardcover reissue using them, but I will be in touch before very long about that.

1. McClelland is referring to a letter he received from Gwen Curry, who wrote "Journeys toward Freedom: A Study of Margaret Laurence's Fictional Women," a 370-page manuscript that served as her PHD thesis at Indiana University. She approached him about publishing her thesis because, she noted, it was "written from a feminist perspective" and "comes to some genuinely new conclusions." However, McClelland & Stewart did not publish her book (McClelland & Stewart Ltd. Fonds, Box 87, File 26).

Hollinger, 9 August 1980

Dear Jack:

Thanks for your letter of July 31st, regarding Gwen Curry's manuscript on my work. I know Gwen and Ralph—they are, in fact, coming for dinner next week—and I like them a lot. I've got the greatest respect for Gwen's perceptions and intelligence. But I really do not want to be involved in the decision as to whether you should publish or not. (Needless to say, you will not impart this information to her.) I just do not know how economically viable critical works of this nature are, nor do I feel I am necessarily the best judge of the critical works written about my writing. To tell you the truth, and I tell you this in STRICT CONFIDENCE, I really can no longer bring myself to read all the articles, theses etc. on my work, which in bulk now must total far more words than I myself have ever written. It all seems a bit odd to me. I don't object to it, heaven knows, if it means my books are being read, and what is more, *sold*. And I think some of these critical analyses can be extremely good in making novels or whatever more accessible at higher reading levels to some people. But it sure is strange to see oneself as a kind of growth industry; meanwhile here am I, beating my brains out trying to get into a new novel and trying to deploy my financial resources in such a way that I won't die in the poorhouse. It is probably a very good thesis, would be my guess, and she could certainly trim it and rewrite it for a more general audience, unlike some academics whose published PHD theses read just like that. So—over to you.

I am *very* interested to learn that Bantam has some new pics for *Jason's Quest*. I didn't know they were going to do that. (Nobody ever tells me anything—the plaintive writer's cry. ... I speak in jest). Actually, I'm pleased. When the book was first published in 1969, I liked the pics a lot, but I think they were more suited to an English readership than a North American, and now they look a bit dated, if such is possible with a work of fantasy. Also, in the Can and Amer edition[s], some of the pics were reproduced smaller than in the Eng edition, and thus came out looking rather smudged. So new pics will be good, but I hope to heaven they haven't made them look like Walt Disney, a style I loathe and abhor. Anyway, I will be very interested to see them. I suppose when you say they'll be sending some photo-copies for my "approval," it just means I get to look at them before publication, not that I have any real say in the matter. Well, they can't be worse than some of Bantam's/ Seal's jackets—but what the hell. This is not a matter over which I propose to lose many nights' sleep. I think it is super that they are reprinting the book, and I am surprised and delighted about that.

I hope you have been able to get away for a holiday. How are things? Now that I am no longer on the Board (and thanks, by the way, for your very nice letter re: that), I don't expect a detailed reply, but would just like to know in general how things are and how you are. That gal who wrote the profile of you in *Toronto Life*, or whatever it was, managed to shaft you while appearing to be sympathetic. Rats to the media. It's not those people as individuals; it's what the structure of the media appears to do to them. Incidentally, I was glad to see your recent letter in *The Globe*,[1] concerning that really nutsy article by Joyce [*sic*] Fielding, whoever she is. I thought you showed great tact while at the same time pulling no punches, if you see what I mean. It was about four years ago, if memory serves, that I learned why Anna has a large and (to me) absolutely terrifying dog. Rejected manuscripts apparently lead their genius writers into some very uncivilized stances. I don't suggest that this Fielding babe would go so far as to phone in a dire manner, or whatever, but really—Anna shouldn't have to take that kind of shit. My admiration for her has grown throughout the years. In my opinion, *The Mermaid Tavern*[2] in *The Globe* goes from bad to worse. Today's, by Jim Christy, suggests that it doesn't matter if the Big Blast comes because our world is so rotten. This, from a writer who purports to be a responsible human being? Well, enough of this or my blood pressure will rise. I actually have normal blood pressure, a fact that has always astounded me.

All the best,
Margaret [signed]

P.S. I have just received my author's copies of *The Christmas Birthday Story* from Knopf. The production job is really beautiful. About 6 pics have been added since the first pics were done, and they are really impressive. Your prophecy (which I read at the last meeting I attended as a Board member) is probably right—critical acclaim, but won't make money. However, the little book *may* be condemned by the same rednecks who condemned *The Diviners* as blasphemous, because Mary and Joseph don't care whether their child turns out to be a girl or a boy. Actually, I hope that doesn't happen—what a hell of a way to sell books. I've had enough of being called nasty names. Never mind. We press on.

1. Joy Fielding (1945–), who evidently had a manuscript rejected by McClelland & Stewart, wrote a letter to the *Globe and Mail* to denigrate McClelland & Stewart and specifically Anna Porter. McClelland responded by writing a letter to the *Globe and Mail*, which was published on 9 August 1980. McClelland defended Canadian publishers and stated that Porter was "one of the most intelligent, dedicated, and talented stars in the Canadian publishing industry and indeed, by international recognition, in any publishing industry anywhere" (Jack McClelland Fonds).
2. The Mermaid Tavern was a pub in London during Elizabethan times. It was known as a place where writers such as Ben Johnson met to gossip and discuss literature. Canadian poets Duncan Campbell Scott, William Wilfred Campbell, and Archibald Lampman collaborated on a literary column, titled At the Mermaid Inn, for the *Toronto Globe* between February 1892 and July 1893. Here, Laurence seems to refer to literary gossip written in the *Globe and Mail*.

Regent, 18 August 1980

Dear Margaret:

As always your letter of August 9th was great and very helpful. I always have a terrible guilt complex when I receive a letter from you because [I] can't help but feel what a terrible waste it is for you to be writing letters when you should [be] spending that time on the novel, but what the hell.

Re: M&S, since you asked, things are okay. For the moment I am not sweating the big picture too much—at least on a day-to-day basis—because there are too many small and pressing problems. Our cash position is better than it is supposed to be. I don't have an Executive Committee of the Board to bug me (when Casey and Orenstein resigned, we abandoned it) and, while I loved Sam, Dan was beginning to get on my nerves, because he is so nervous, but I consider that positive. We are supposed to have a long-term financial solution by the end of the year—and we work with a government committee towards that end—and that isn't proceeding all that quickly, but it will work. The Fall season looks okay but not great. It really is difficult to comprehend the economy, the rise in the stock market, the decline in the dollar, in interest rates, inflation, the increase in unemployment—all these things. Who the hell knows what is going on? I don't think anybody does.

So I guess the answer is I assume we are okay and we are going to survive one way or another, and I am concentrating on problems like the long term future of the New Canadian Library, Seal books and that sort of thing. We are working ahead on this issue and I'll be calling you or come out to see you about it sometime in the next 6 weeks, but, essentially, I think we are okay.

Thanks for the help re: Gwen Curry. I don't know what our decision will be, but your comments are very helpful. Re: *Toronto Life*, the new issue is out, so no problem. As to Joy Fielding however, I am glad you approved. I didn't know *The Globe* had done the latter. I am delighted by your comment re: Anna. There was a lot of flack from a lot of people during the early years about Anna because she is so beautiful. She may have been hired because she was beautiful, but that's not why she got promoted and moved to the top. She is a person of extraordinary dedication and ability. Well, hell, Margaret, I really appreciated the note. Don't reply to this. I will be in touch with you before you know it, because I really want to talk about what we are going to do about The New Canadian Library.

Love,
Jack [signed]
Jack McClelland

Hollinger, 9 October 1980

Dear Jack:

I'm terribly sorry, but I have had second thoughts about the Writers' Devel Trust thing on Oct 30. I hope this won't upset your plans too much, but I have decided I can't go. Two reasons. First, I did go to a dinner that one time before, and that was, to put it bluntly, an ordeal. You may say this one will be different and maybe it will, but all that sort of thing is an ordeal for me, whatever it's like. Second, I have not done any writing all summer because people won't leave me alone—of course, it is I who have agreed to see so many visitors, but it is hard to refuse when they are, e.g. academics from universities in U.S., France, Italy, as well as Canada, who are trying to get Can books on courses. I also have a huge correspondence, and answer up to 50 letters per week, most of them requests for me to do something or other, and, even if I refuse, it takes time to answer. My unlisted phone must be known to everyone in the country by now. It is one damn thing after another, and from time to time I can feel hysteria mounting, as I despair of ever being able to write a novel and see my life being frittered away in all manner of good causes and warding off all manner of demands and requests and damned interruptions. I am my own housekeeper, cook, secretary, etc. If this sounds a bit churlish, please forgive me. I don't mean it to. But I do get desperate. I have agreed to do five book autographing things for this new little book, and I dread facing them. One session in T.O., also, is in fact two days out of my life. So please try to understand. I really am sorry, but I just have to be more self-protective, and goodness knows it is difficult.

All the best,
Margaret [signed]

Regent, 14 October 1980

Dear Margaret:

You may be the only person in the world that I would let off the hook as far as the Writers' Development Trust dinner is concerned—but I do let you off the hook completely. You do far too much. You are used by far too many people. I don't want you to ever feel used by me. Your health and your book are far more important than the dinner. Don't give it another thought.

My only regret is that I am anxious to have a talk with you, and, at the moment, I just don't seem to be able to get away. I am going to find out when your autographing parties are and maybe we can organize a meeting at that time.

Love,
Jack [signed]
Jack McClelland

Regent, 12 November 1980

Dear Margaret:

Thanks for your letter re: Al Purdy.[1] That is no imposition. I love the man. It is a good suggestion and I have written Mr. Bartlett as per the attached.[2]

I also have your second letter to Marge. Migod, two letters on two successive days. I am impressed. Well, today a copy of the Templeton novel has been sent and six more of *The Christmas Birthday Story* will be sent as soon as they are received.

That was a lousy review. I don't know who Jacquie Hunt is.[3] Screw her. We will get her eventually. Don't worry about it. I don't think it will really affect sales.

Re: *The Globe* doing it on Christmas Day, we have agreed.[4] It will probably become an annual event. As far as I am concerned, it won't help the book much, but it is found money. How can we lose? It is a strange fall season. Yours seems to be the only book that is in demand. If you really want to know, I am getting terrified. I am told it is going to snow soon and all will be okay.

Please, dear Margaret, get back to your typewriter. Don't write any more letters to me or to anybody else. Just write novels.

Cheers!
Jack [signed]
Jack McClelland

1. The letter from Laurence to which McClelland refers does not survive in Laurence's or McClelland & Stewart's papers.
2. Hodgeman attached a note, dated 12 November 1980, to this letter. She stated, "I am feeling deathly so will send you a copy of the Bartlett letter when I get it transcribed. Am going home to try and survive this bloody virus I have picked up." McClelland's letter to David Bartlett, dated

13 November 1980, was also in the archives: it is a letter of support for Al Purdy as "a most suitable recipient of the Molson Award." Apparently, George Woodcock had suggested to McClelland that Purdy was a worthy candidate (McClelland & Stewart Ltd. Fonds, Box 87, File 26).

3. Jacquie Hunt reviewed Laurence's *The Christmas Birthday Story* and Susan Musgrave's *Hag Head* for the *Globe and Mail*. About Laurence's book, she claimed Laurence "reduced the Nativity to a simpering domestic drama": "The prose, which should be limpid is simply limp. And most unforgivably, a tone of didactic condescension creeps into the narrative" (D15). For Laurence, the story was about privileging the "female principle in Christian faith" (Cohen 103), an indirect way of attacking those who had tried to censor *The Diviners* and who had not comprehended her own feminist inclinations.
4. *The Christmas Birthday Story* was, in fact, published in the *Globe and Mail* on 25 December 1980.

Regent, 24 December 1980

Dear Margaret:

It is December 24th. I have been trying for several days to get you on the phone with no luck. Maybe you are away—I hope down South in the warmth. In any case, I just send this note to let you know that I was thinking about you and wanted to wish you a very Happy Christmas.

Sincerely,
Jack [signed]
Jack McClelland

Regent, 2 April 1981

Dear Margaret:

Congratulations on the Canada Council Senior Arts Grant. That should help to keep the wolf away for a while. Marge tells me you are hard at work on the novel, which is good news. I hope it goes smoothly this time.

All the best.
Sincerely,
Jack [signed]
Jack McClelland

Hollinger, 21 May 1981

Dear Jack:

Probably Linda McKnight has told you about all this stuff, but here it is, in writing, from me.

The CAA [Canadian Authors Association] wants to give me a Special Award for my contribution to you-know-what. I just cannot be in Montreal at that time. I understand that you will be there—lucky you—to take part in their conference. So I'd be grateful if you would pick up the Scroll for me, eh? I have told them that I would be unable to be there because of a long-standing previous engagement.

Somewhat to my embarrassment, the CBA [Canadian Booksellers Association] has apparently named me Author of the Year. I certainly don't know why, as I haven't published an adult novel in years, but I suppose it is the reissuing of some of my books in paperback plus the kids books. Anyway, this particular award carries with it $1,000, which is better than a slap across the face with a wet fish. So, natch, I'll go to Vancouver to collect it, July 19th. Mr. Titheridge, President of the CBA, said in his letter that he understood that my publishers would arrange my travel. I don't know what the hell this means. I phoned Linda, and she said she thought it meant you'd pay. I really don't see why you should, unless you can get some mileage out of this. Anyway, let me know.

If anyone from M&S will be going to Vancouver for the CBA conference, maybe we could arrange to travel together. Usually, I prefer to make my own travel arrangements, but we will see. Of course, you know that I will *never* travel with you, as you tend to get to the airport very late and I tend to get there very early.

Boss, I'm really trying to write a novel. It is not easy. But it will happen; however, it may turn out. It would be awfully nice if everyone would leave me alone, but apparently they won't.

From what I've heard, the NFB film on Farley is great.[1] I'm so glad.

Best,

Margaret Laurence

1. *Ten Million Books: An Introduction to Farley Mowat* was produced by the National Film Board and directed by Andy Thomson in 1981.

Regent, 25 June 1981

Dear Margaret:

It was a great honour to accept your Award at the Canadian Authors Association dinner. I am sending you herewith the scroll that was presented. May I tell you that I learned at that dinner that the four Awards for the books that the CAA have decided are the best published in the current year each receive not only a very handsome medal, but a $5,000.00 cheque. Migod! I was stunned. I received one for Pierre. I mean, the CAA (financed by Harlequin[1]) is in the big league. I had, of course, long forgotten they originally administered the Governor General's Awards. I would like to bring them together with that award again and make it $10,000.00 for each of the winning books.[2]

In any case, I told them what a great lady you were. You were very much missed. They were delighted to be able to honour you as the scroll indicates.

Cheers!
Jack [signed]
Jack McClelland

1. Harlequin Romance Enterprises, owned by Mills & Boon since the 1970s, is a publishing company specializing in paperback romance novels. The company started in Winnipeg in 1949 and was founded by Richard Bonnycastle. It is one of the most lucrative publishing houses in the world.
2. The Governor General's Award in 2016 was worth $25,000. Finalists in that year received $1,000 and publishers of winning titles received $3,000 to promote the book.

Hollinger, 5 December 1981

Dear Jack:

I'm encouraged to know that the NCL will continue and that a few selected books will be put into the series. I'd like to suggest one—and I've suggested this one before to Malcolm Ross, who is, I think, in agreement. It is Mort Forer's novel *The Humback*.[1] M&S published it originally, as you know. I rank it with such novels as Sinclair Ross' *As For Me and My House*, sinking without a trace at the time of publication, only to surface years later as classics. I don't know of any better novel that deals with the Métis, but doesn't "deal" in a didactic sense. ... I mean in the sense of making some characters come alive and letting the reader know and feel how it was with those people. I really hope you'll consider putting this novel into print, once again, in the NCL. If I may make a suggestion ... if you do put Forer's novel into the NCL, I would certainly be honoured to write an Intro. I think it's an important and a very moving novel.

All the best,
Margaret [signed]
Margaret Laurence

1. Laurence's suggestion that *The Humback* be added to the NCL's roster clearly met with some favour. McClelland wrote to Forer on 16 November 1984 that he had "no doubt" that he would "hear in the relatively near future that *The Humback* [would be] added to the New Canadian Library" (McClelland & Stewart Ltd. Fonds, Box 112, File 25). However, although the novel was published by McClelland & Stewart in 1969, it was ultimately not included in the NCL Series.

Regent, 11 March 1982

Dear Margaret:[1]

Because I consider you a very good friend and because you are one of the relatively small group of people whom I love and admire—and if that sounds like a form letter, it ain't—I want to tell you about an event that will take place on March 18th. We have a Board meeting that day—I wish you were still on that Board. I shall resign as President of the company. Our new President and Publisher will be Linda McKnight.

I want you to know that I have thought about all this for a long time. I think the change is not only in my best interest personally, but I think it is in the best interest of the company. Linda has had a long and useful apprenticeship. She is one of the most reliable people I have ever met in the book world. She is totally dedicated. She has a great feeling for what is important. She recognizes what M&S has tried to stand for. She recognizes that the author is the most important person in the publishing equation. She will, I believe, run the company effectively. I don't mind admitting, too, that, in the year 1982, I am particularly delighted to be appointing a woman to head Canada's most prestigious publishing house. I am not a woman's libber by any sense of the word, but at the same time I think it appropriate and right that a woman should take over as boss of our company.

She is not going to be a fake boss; she will be the real boss. I will be here. I will be Chairman of the Board and will work on a lot of projects and I intend to retain a direct connection with a small handful of people who I care about, like Farley, and Pierre and Mordecai and Margaret—but not all that many. I am going to work on other projects—all publishing related—and I will back Linda up when she needs it, but she is going to be the operational head of the company.

I don't think that this will usher in a new era in Canadian publishing. If I thought it was going to do that, I wouldn't have appointed Linda

McKnight. I want her to do a better job than I did—and, quite honestly, I think she will do a better job than I have done in recent years. I want her to improve the internal management of the company. I haven't the slightest doubt that she is going to do that because I have been too bored to pay much attention to that. Promotional flair is not her strongest point, but she knows enough about promotional flair to hire people who will be able to do that for her, but I think she is smart enough to realize that she had better be the central core of that, and I think she will.

So, I wanted to share this information with you. I think you know Linda and respect her. I wish you were at the Board meeting Thursday. They are hearing it for the first time—well, except for members of the small executive committee, but I wanted you to know it before you saw the public announcement. I hope you will applaud the decision. Believe me, Margaret, I wouldn't be doing it if I did not think it was better for Jack McClelland and also better for McClelland and Stewart. I am not walking away, I am just walking into concentration on other things.

I love you dearly. I want you to know that the preparation of the new edition of *Olden Days Coat* is well in hand and it will appear this fall. Once the plan is fully materialized, it will be presented to you for approval. Apart from that, what can I say? I hope you are well. I hope the new novel is going very well and I hope to see you again before too many weeks go by.

Cheers!
Jack McClelland

1. This letter appears in Solecki's *Imagining Canadian Literature*.

Hollinger, 16 March 1982

Dear Jack:

Thanks very much for your letter, which I received two days ago. This is my third attempt to answer it! It's difficult to say exactly what I mean.

I do approve of your decision to make Linda McKnight President and Publisher. I have known her a long time and I respect her efficiency and her ability to work with writers. I've given a statement to this effect for the PR in connection with the announcement of her appointment. I'm also very glad that you will remain Chairman of the Board. You are very much needed there.

The announcement will obviously cause quite a stir in Canadian literary and publishing circles, and you will probably get some flack, but then, you are used to that, if anyone can ever be said to get used to that kind of thing. So I wanted to let you know my own personal feelings on the matter.

The main reason I approve your decision really has to do with you yourself. You have worked far too hard, frequently under terrible pressure, for a long time. You have kept the firm afloat mainly owing to your determination, willpower, and tremendous sense of caring. I think you bloody well have earned the right to simplify your life to some extent and to have sufficient time for various projects that truly interest you. Never fear, your life will continue to be busy as hell, because that is the kind of person you are. But you have paid your dues many times over. The day-to-day operation of the firm, and day-to-day decisions *should* be handed over to someone else at this point, not because you can't do them, but because I think you owe it to yourself and your family to take life a bit easier from now on.

I made a similar kind of decision about my own life two years ago. I felt the need to simplify and to quit running as hard as I had been doing for more than 20 years. I sold my cottage.[1] I sorted through all my papers (in case I kick the bucket suddenly, and also for—let's face it—a certain amount of money). I got a form letter, which I often use now to refuse invitations for readings, etc. etc. etc. (I enclose a copy for your amusement—I really am asked to do all those things!)[2] I still answer stacks of mail,[3] but I'm trying to make it as easy as possible for myself. I'm trying to keep fairly regular writing hours, but the fact that the thing is coming very slowly no longer bothers me a great deal. There are ways in which I, too, have paid my dues. Not that my life will ever be boring or overly quiet—I'm not that kind of person, either.

But I must take friendly issue with you when you say Linda will be able to do the job better than you have in late years. Rubbish. She will do a splendid job, but so did you, throughout very trying times. Please do not *ever* underestimate what you have done in your years as publisher, Jack. Damn near singlehandedly, you transformed the Canadian publishing scene from one of mediocrity and dullness to one of enormous interest and vitality. Had it not been for M&S, I wonder if a whole lot of people such as myself, Mordecai, Al Purdy, Farley, Pierre, Peggy Atwood, and on and on and on, would have found the wide audience of readers that we have. I doubt it. Your great talent has always been your ability to spot good writers and your willingness to take a chance on them. Lots of people who now think of some of us as household names, or at least, in Mordecai's words, "world famous throughout Canada" (!), forget that there was a time when we were all beginning and unsure of ourselves. At least this is true of myself, anyway, and I'm sure it must be true of others. You and Malcolm dreamed up the NCL, and that series in itself has revolutionized our publishing industry and made it possible for Canlit to be taught in our universities and high schools. (By the way, I love the new format. … very classy).

I've known you as my publisher and friend for 23 years now. Seems impossible but there it is. I first met you in 1959, when M&S had just accepted my first novel, *This Side Jordan*. You certainly took a chance on that one, as it was set in Africa (indeed, was one of the first books about Africa at the time of a country's independence and transition).

This was before the upsurge of African writers themselves and also before books about the "new" Africa became popular subjects. In those 23 years, you have published 12 of my books—all of them, in fact, except a small book of Somali translations published years before, and my book on Nigerian writing, which I did not expect you to publish in any event.[4] I have not forgotten, also, that it was very largely through your efforts that Knopf was persuaded to take on my books, and that was a major turning point in my career.

I recall also some of our magnificent battles, usually through letters. The battle over the title of *The Fire-Dwellers*, which was *not* through letters at that time. You visited Elm Cottage in England briefly that year, and I sat you down in my study and talked at you for about three hours, explaining in boring detail just why my title was the right one! At the time, I didn't realize that the firm was in dire straits financially and you had a hell of a lot more on your mind than the title of one author's book. I also recall the famous battle over the Writer's [*sic*] Union contract, when I angrily wrote to all the Board members. Ye gods, I now think the union contract is far too ambitious and complicated and needs to be simplified and made more realistic (I think this is being done). Also the fight re: the Iran book. Nostalgiasville, at this point.

Well, we have disagreed a lot, throughout the years, Jack, but the main thing is that I have always felt I could express my views and that, although you might disagree with them, you would always take them seriously. I know quite well that a great many other M&S writers feel the same way.

It has been a long association, and a valuable one, I think, to both of us. That association won't end now, of course. But I just wanted to say some of these things, and to wish you all the best in whatever new ventures you'll be undertaking.

God bless—
Margaret [signed]
Margaret Laurence

P.S. Of course, I still do some of the things mentioned in my form letter, but not very often any more.

P.S.2 This letter is marked "Personal." That doesn't mean it's Confidential—that's up to you.[5]

1. Laurence owned a cottage on the Otonobee River, which, as she mentions here, she sold in 1982. She also owned a home in Lakefield, Ontario, where she lived for the remainder of her life.
2. The enclosed letter, in part, states, "I must tell you that I cannot undertake to do any of the following," and then proceeds to list twenty-one activities. These include "read manuscripts, do book reviews, give quotes for book jackets, give readings or conduct seminars, participate in writers' workshops or panels, give interviews, judge writing contests," and so on.
3. It should be noted that even into the year 1985, Laurence was responding not only to "stacks of mail" with regard to business letters but also to her fans. On 9 March 1985, for instance, she responded to a social worker, Karen Moncur, who wrote to her in support of her books and against censorship. Laurence wrote, "If ever you stop breaking your heart, every single day of your life, over the terrible injustices in this world, then you will cease to be you. ... If you do not know the pain of the world, you cannot know the joy either, or such is my belief. Take heart, young daughter: And God bless you" (Margaret Laurence Fonds, William Ready Division, Box 11, File 3).
4. Laurence has written beside this sentence, "also, that one little kids' book I did for Lorimer."
5. The two postscripts are handwritten.

Regent, 23 March 1982

Dear Margaret:

All things considered, I guess that is the nicest letter that I have ever received and I thank you for it. There is a lot of fiction in your assessment but one expects fiction from Canada's greatest novelist. Dear Margaret, I thank you for what you have said. Our association over the years is one of the things that I value most in any retrospective of my life as a publisher, which in effect was the course of my life.

I feel everything worked very well. The Board gave Linda a strong vote of support, and I think she was pleased by that. The staff thus far has reacted with overwhelming support and enthusiasm. The timing of Peter Taylor's departure—not entirely coincidental but nothing to do with Linda—was probably unfortunate, but she has already found a strong and extraordinarily able person to replace him, which is fortunate. His name is Larry Dent. He is an experienced publisher, and I think is well liked by everyone who meets him and he will do a very good job.

The press, too, has reacted more-or-less as expected. Bill French, despite his usual number of key errors, was fine, as was the *Star*, and *Maclean's*, with an extra day to deal with it, will probably handle it more positively.

I wish I could believe that today was the start of a new life—it ain't, but it is the start of clearing up a backlog and eventually not a new life, a slightly different one, but you are quite right. We are both the same in that respect. It is possible to disengage in some areas, but it is not possible to disengage entirely.

I hope I see you very soon and thanks again.

Cheers!
Jack McClelland

P.S. I am told that *Olden Days Coat* meetings are proceeding and you will, of course, be consulted before the design is finalized.

P.P.S. I love your piece on the John Moss.[1] I have passed it and, in fact, a copy of your letter on to Linda and I think she will want to circulate the McCloud piece at least to John Moss' editor.

1. McClelland is referring to Laurence's playful response to the fact that, in John Moss's *A Reader's Guide to the Canadian Novel*, Vanessa's surname, "MacLeod," had been misspelled as "McCloud." Vanessa MacLeod is the protagonist in *A Bird in the House*.

Regent, 17 June 1982

Dear Margaret:

I think I have not responded to your letter about the Writers' Development Trust Dinner. I am now about to respond. Let me say this. I lay very few personal trips on you. This time I am laying a real personal trip on you. I want you to come to the dinner. In fact, I insist that you come to the dinner.

I want you at the dinner so much, Margaret, that I will, if necessary, drive to Lakefield and pick you up and bring you back, take you to the dinner, have you live at my place. I will do all that or part of it—or whatever. It is one night and we need you.

A few things you should remember. First, you were one of the founders of the Writers' Development Trust. Second, it is in financial trouble. Third, in order to save it, I have put my reputation and my energy on the line, and we are going to save it. In order to raise a lot of money, we need Margaret Laurence at the dinner. It really is that simple.

Your presence has been sold to Donald Early, who has bought a table so that he will have Margaret Laurence as the guest. You may not remember Donald Early, but I hope you will. He is the Chairman of the Executive Committee at McClelland and Stewart. You have met him at board meetings in days gone by. A very charming man. He is a partner in Greenshields and Company. You will like the people with him. It will be old-home week. It will be a very pleasant evening.

Who else is going to be at the dinner—a lot of people that you like. Farley, Pierre Berton, Peter Newman, Mordecai Richler, on and on. Well, they are sold as you are, but I am doubly committed. I am committed to selling 100 tables and I am also committed privately in not embarrassing any authors. In other words, I don't want anybody left out. It is going to be a fantastic night, but Margaret, we really need the stars, and you are the top star in the whole Canadian galaxy and I have got to have you.

I don't want to be a real shit and embarrass you, but let me tell you that another star, not in your galaxy at all, but another star, can't be there. She is going to be in Australia. Her name is Margaret Atwood, but would you believe what she is doing. She is making a goddamn Atwood effigy.[1] I enclose a description of it. I mean this is a total commitment thing.

Margaret, I love you, but my reputation depends on you being at the bloody dinner, and it is not too big a price to pay. I would love to have you stay at our place in Kleinburg. It really is very comfortable and you would enjoy it. You will go to the dinner with Elizabeth and myself, and you will come back with us. It will be easy. You will love our new place and, quite literally, I will drive down and pick you up and drive you back if necessary. So help me God, I want to issue a press release saying that Margaret Laurence will be there. You are a modest lady and don't understand how many people that will attract. Believe me, that is what the whole thing is about and we need Margaret Laurence. Think back how many times I have laid a trip on you. Not very often. This time, I am laying a real trip. Come.

Please phone Marge on receipt of this letter and say, okay, tell the boss or old Jake that I will be there. I will be there reluctantly, but I will be there.

It is, after all, September 29th. Clara[2] told me that you almost came down for her party for godssake. I went to it, by the way. It was sort of fun. Claire Pratt and her mother were there and Clara was in good form and there were a number of people who you would remember. I told Clara I went to the party, only because I wanted to find out why anybody would be idiotic enough to write a book about that old bastard Bill Deacon. Since then I have finally read the book, and I am going to write her about it, but it is a helluva good book, even though I had no great respect for Bill Deacon.[3] So, I love you, dear, and please do phone Marge and say yes. It is not just $1500.00 for the Writers' Development Trust, it is the whole style, ambience, and success of the dinner. Can

I really tell you how it is? I want it to be a major success. It is a simple fact of life that the dinner can't even come close to my aspirations, unless Margaret Laurence is present. I have conned Farley into coming all the way back from Cape Breton on the same pretext—well, I phoned him. The reason I have written you rather than phoned you is that I like getting your letters and besides our mutual correspondence is saleable at both ends. I sell your letters. You should be selling mine.

Cheers!

Jack McClelland

1. In response to this fundraising dinner organized by the Writers' Development Trust, Atwood sent a life-sized effigy of herself, "a 'Peggy' doll that was set up at the dinner" (York 122), because she was on a lecture tour in Australia. Lorraine York, citing Barbara Righton, adds that a tape was hidden in the effigy's purse, "on which was recorded the following half of her conversation: 'Oh, you're a novelist too.' (Pause) 'Oh, I wouldn't really have the time to do that right now. I'm writing my own novel'" (122).
2. McClelland refers here to Clara Thomas.
3. Clara Thomas and John Lennox wrote *William Arthur Deacon: A Canadian Literary Life*, published by the University of Toronto Press in 1982, to which McClelland refers here. Deacon (1890–1977) was the literary editor of *Saturday Night* from 1922 to 1928, and, later, the *Globe and Mail* from 1936 to 1961.

Hollinger, 28 June 1982

Dear Boss:

Your letter, as I told Marge, is the closest thing to blackmail as I have ever encountered. Yeah, I'll go to the damn dinner if it kills me, and it probably will. Marge is going to send me the details, as I filed your original letter away and now it is lost forever until I sell that particular set of papers. My filing system is by way of being like the tombs of the pharaohs ... only to be opened by future generations. ... I certainly can't find anything and don't try! Anyway, I won't accept your kind offer to come to L'field and pick me up. ... Jack, you know how nervous a passenger I am, and let's face it, you drive like a demented bat out of hell. So I'll go by bus. Will probably go directly to the place where the dinner will be held, but that poses the problem of where to change my clothes. Never mind. ... I'll work that out. I'd love to go out to your place at Kleinburg that eve, but would Elizabeth please do the driving?!! Actually, much as I would really love to see your new place and to have a chance to chat with you and Elizabeth, it might just work out that it would be better for me to check into a hotel, preferably the Windsor Arms, and go from there to the dinner, and that would also mean I'd be close to the bus station to get home the next morning. Or, I could stay with a friend, and for the sake of frugality will probably do just that. I *would* like to see your place, but it's a long haul, relatively, from K'burg to the bus station and that would get me back home pretty late. Sorry to be so difficult. ... I think I am turning into a semi-hermit (not really). So let's put it this way, for now. ... I'll make my own way in; will get myself to the dinner; will stay with a friend. ... There are several possibilities. ... I have a couple of friends who live centrally in T.O. and with whom I can usually stay, so that will simplify things. You'll have enough on your plate without worrying about transport for me. Also, I kind of like to be independent in these matters. I can visit your new place another and quieter time, if such there will ever be for any of us.

Naturally, I remember Don Early very clearly, and am extremely pleased that the table has gone to him. I must say you had your damn nerve selling that table before I agreed, but I forgive you. Atwood's idea seems super to me ... maybe I'll copy it for ALL future public appearances! I don't think I'd have my effigy saying (albeit sarcastically) "how interesting" ... I think mine would say something like, "Well, you may have a point there, but more important issues are at stake ..." and there would follow a pitch for the many good causes I believe in, together with telephone numbers and addresses to which contributions could be made, rather in the style of the awful TV evangelists.

So—okay. The hard sell approach has worked this time, Boss, but don't you ever try it again, eh?

All the best,
Margaret [signed]

Regent, 9 July 1982

Dear Margaret:

I love you and thank you for your good letter. Don't worry about my driving and don't worry about changing. First, we will have rooms where you can change at the Sheraton, so that is no problem. Second, we won't be driving, neither Elizabeth nor and I. I am going to have a limousine reserved and you, Elizabeth and I, plus probably the Mowats, plus probably the Bertons will go back to Kleinburg in style.

No problem the next day. The bus station is actually only about 40 minutes drive from Kleinburg. I will be sober by the next morning and will deliver you safely to the bus station well before noon, so you will be home in good time.

No, I promise never to try the hard-sell again. God knows I am really trying it on this dinner, though not only on the authors but on potential sponsors. The Trust desperately needs money. I don't like to see it in that condition. The current Chairman, David MacDonald, is a very charming man but not a good administrator, and the whole thing is in disarray. I want to leave them with a fair amount of money, so the new Chairman, Harry Boyle, will be able to do something useful. So my attitude is, this is my final effort on the Trust. They will never see me again after this dinner, but somehow—come hell or highwater we are going to raise $100,000.00 for them—and, in fact, I now begin to hope that we may raise much more. I think we now have 43 tables actually sold. My target is 100, but I think if we get to 100, we may easily get to 125.

Also, thanks for sending me the note re: the mistake in *The Stone Angel*. I am now the boss at Seal, so I will look after that directly.

Love and kisses,
[Jack McClelland]

Hollinger, 13 August 1982

Dear Jack:

Your letter was a great relief to me.

Thanks for being so understanding re: my desire to stay at the Sheraton Centre. I also feel much reassured re: the band and its purpose.

I would really like someone to come up with the books and posters, so I could sign them in advance. It won't be difficult to manage a time ... I'm pretty flexible in that way.

I'm interested to hear that you are not keen on these big parties. That is not what many people believe about you. Well, I think you're a spartan to be doing all this.

All the best,
Margaret

Hollinger, 15 September 1982

Dear Jack:

Have just read *The Globe and Mail,* and have phoned Marge! Wow! Terrific!! Swell! And the Molson Award is TAX FREE![1] CONGRATULATIONS! That is just marvellous, and much much deserved. God knows you have sweated your guts out for years in the cause of Can publishing and writing, and it is about time that your tremendous contribution to this country was recognised in a *tangible* way! All of us who have reason to be grateful to you, over many years, will be rejoicing! I am just delighted.

All the best,
Margaret

1. The Molson Prize of the Canada Council for the Arts was awarded to Jack McClelland in 1982.

Hollinger, 2 October 1982

Dear John:[1]

This letter is for you, Jane Cushman, Jane Wilson and the folks at the office, and NO ONE ELSE. You will presently see why. I am writing another letter to you, about business thing[s], but will do it separately.

First things first. I phoned Jane Wilson to thank her for the Martini Stones, but had not then tested them. Well, I have now. THEY WORK! The greatest dry martini in the world! ...

Well, John. The Night of a Hundred Authors. Thank God I had lunch with you that day ... that was the only good thing that happened. What follows is confidential, because Jack McClelland worked so hard, not to say insanely, over this idiotic project, and I do not at the moment want him to know my true response. I will write to him later, in cool fashion, and say I will never take part in this kind of farce again, under any circumstances. But not right now. He's tired; he's exhausted. I hope Elizabeth gets him up to Muskoka for a week or so, but I wouldn't bet on it. At the end of the evening, I told him it had been a smashing success ... the lies one tells for the sake of people one cares about, I guess. But next week I will write and will give him a low-key but true outline of what really happened to me. I do hold him to some extent responsible, but what the hell. No use in staging a tantrum, and I won't, of course.

John, you know about the Authors' Cocktail Party beforehand. Thank heavens I had signed these 250 posters a week before. Nice to see old friends and so on, but ye gods do I ever hate standing on my feet for an hour, drinking 1 glass of very diluted scotch and water.

Worse was to come. Little did I know. John, you know about the cocktail party, so-called, but you do not know what followed for the Hundred Authors.

It was GRUESOME. It was HORRIBLE.

Dear friends and loving hearts, I have taken part in quite a few university convocations, and I understand how the marshalling is done. You get the people in line ... and no time lost. Alas, this was not done at the Event. We milled around ... and you know me. ... I longed to organize the whole show but naturally just waited until things happened. The one person who was the best organizer was not consulted re: the organization at the eleventh hour, namely Marge Hodgeman, who had worked her butt off, but who did not have control over the last-minute presentations. I talked to her the next day and she felt v. worried because of the shambles, which was certainly not in any way her fault. I hope I reassured her.

Governor General Edward Schreyer and Her Excellency Lily Schreyer, who are good Manitoba people, showed up on time. They proceeded to the dining room. The patrons of various tables were already there. Some of the tables were patronized by ANONYMOUS, according to the program. I later discovered that Anonymous really meant that no one put up $1500 for a six-person table, so the tickets were sold individually. I think I could have written the program better, if I may say so. Anonymous, indeed.[2]

After the authors' cocktail party, we, the authors, were led as lambs to the slaughter, into what was apparently a long basement corridor connecting one kitchen with another and also housing the hotel's sizeable furnace. The corridor was airless, hot, without windows, and without a place to sit down. We lined up, alphabetically, being guided by bewildered and worried young helpers, who obviously thought we were all strange creatures from outer space. We were to be taken into the dining room and introduced individually. Never has L seemed so far from the beginning of the alphabet. Thank God my name does not begin with a Y.

We stood and we stood and we stood.

My feet hurt. I got more and more irritated. Had I been organizing the hash, I thought (oh perfect organization when one doesn't actually have to do it) I would have marched the authors in, all hundred of them, seated them, and then, with a wandering mike, introduced each and had them stand up.

After 45 minutes on my feet in that steamy dungeon, my Scots anger took sway, er, I guess, I got a little bit insane.

"If this line does not move soon," I proclaimed, "I AM GOING HOME."

Of course, one never gets to complain to the people in command. Instant panic among the young marshalling people, who did not know me well enough to know that OF COURSE I would not march out and let J.G. McC. down. One should never pull rank for this reason. "I think," said partially insane ML, "that I am going to faint."

I have never fainted in my entire life, and I probably never will. But flutterings went on, and a young man who was one of the marshalling kids, who would ultimately escort me in to the SCENE, came up to me and said, "Oh, Mrs. Laurence, if you're really so troubled, we'll take you in right now, before anyone else."

Oh John.

"Are you out of your head?" I yelled at him with, as I now see, almost perfect absurdity, "I'm a socialist!"

Finally, we all got into that dining room. I was escorted to the table that had been bought by Don Early, who is really a very good guy, and who is on the Board of M&S.

THE TABLE WAS EMPTY.

Mine host, Don Early, was very late. A woman from a nearby table came in to keep me company until mine host and his guests arrived. She was, as it turned out, the daughter of a guy who owns a chain of hotels. We talked a while about her problems ... the chief one being that if you own two homes, that's okay, but one really must get rid of the third one, because that can be a bore. Not a problem most of us have had to deal with.

She *was* kind and came in when I was alone at that goddamn table, so I should NOT knock her. However, she said she had read ALL my books, ALL THREE OF THEM. She liked Hagar in *The Stone Angel* best of all my heroines (she did not know the word "protagonist"), because Hagar could "GIVE GIVE GIVE and I mean GIVE! Yer other heroines don't know how to GIVE!" Well, I thought she had read some other book or books, certainly not mine.

Mine host arrived. "Don," I said, "what the hell has happened, and where are the others?"

"I will tell you," said he, "when these introductions of writers are over."

We were then proceeding through the alphabet and were then at about S.

He then de-camped to Pierre Berton's table where he stayed for 20 minutes, leaving me with the rich lady who by then was telling me that she was also an author [see "Footnote to P.2." at the end of this letter].

Early was obviously thinking up reasons to tell me why he was not only late, but had not invited guests and not even his wife was there.

He told me that he had bought the table months ago and thought that J.G. McC would invite the six guests. Well. I think what happened was that Jack McC sold the table for $1500 to Early, saying that he (McC) would get me (ML) as guest, and McC then wrote to me saying I had to agree because Early had bought a table with ML as guest, and I agreed, out of loyalt[y] to McClelland.

Early obviously forgot about the whole thing. Was probably reminded that day by someone phon[ing] from the Writers' Trust to tell him where he could pick up his tickets. But he didn't want any tickets ... he hadn't invited anyone! Not even his wife.

The rustlings went on, and I was not supposed to notice, so I pretended not to. Finally, the ML table was filled up with Writers' Trust and M&S people, etc., including one of J.G. McC's daughters, who is a sweetheart, and who 10 years ago stayed with us in Elmcot. Mine host talked to me from time to time but mostly went off in search of his business buddies.

The dinner was awful, John, as you will have noticed. Thank heavens, I had the smoked salmon with you at lunch. The "pheasant soup" tasted like one Bovril cube. The beef was cold and tasteless. Yuk.

Never mind. It is over.

You will recall, no doubt, the way in which the Big Band (The Spitfires, ye gods) opened up after dinner and blasted everyone's eardrums. My rich lady said to me, when I had politely refused to dance with mine host and with Roger Lemelin, who is a good guy, "Oh, you must dance with my husband. ANYONE can learn to dance, if they dance with MY HUSBAND." I said to her ... "Look, it isn't that I do not know how to dance. ... I in my time was a great dancer. ... it is just that I do not wish to do so now." "Oh," she said, "my husband has perfect rhythm. ... Anyone can learn to dance with him."

Thank God my mother brought me up to be a lady. I did not smash her in the teeth.

"I'm sure your husband is a marvellous dancer," I said, "but actually, I have this lower back problem."

The band at that point was LOUD. I hate loud. Except for the bagpipes.

I do not know when you escaped. I escaped at 12:30 [A.M.], having told J.G. McC it was all great. I will, however, write to him in a week or so, saying please do not ever do that to me again. With calm and cool.

I phoned Joe the next day (having got home and slept 12 hours. ... I slept only 1 hour in that damn hotel). Poured it all out and said this was in confidence. Which it is, and to you people as well. Got back home and got a letter from my son with pics of San Miguel and a pic of himself taken by himself ... he has a beard now and a mustache and it really suits him; he looks great.

Well, John, good things did happen that day ... we had lunch and talked and got caught up on the news, and I got from Jane Wilson the Martini Stones. The dinner ... we should forget it.

With love to you all,
Margaret Laurence

P.S. Business letter follows.

Footnote to P.2.
** "Oh," said I, "do you write fiction?" "Oh no," said she, "my book (she did not tell me if it had been published or not) is on HOW TO SCREW."

"Mm," said I. "It is adding to a genre of already considerable proportions, then."

"What?" said she. Giving me a bewildered look.

"Men are persons," she said.

Revelations all around.

1. Although this letter is addressed to John Cushman, Laurence sent a copy of it to McClelland to explain why her experience at the fundraising dinner was miserable. Her letter dated 4 October 1982 confirms that she sent him a copy of this letter.
2. Laurence wrote in the margins of this paragraph "or so it appeared to be."

Hollinger, 4 October 1982

Dear Jack:

I received your note this morning, and once again agonized over whether to send you a copy of my letter to John Cushman or not. It has been on my mind all weekend. I was going to write to you in a week or so, and just briefly say what went on that evening, from my viewpoint. Then I began to think that I should send you a copy of my letter to John. It was written very shortly after the Event, and it represents my feelings at the time, both of humour and of anger. Also, it was not intended, originally, to be seen by you and therefore expresses very honestly (with no soft-soaping) my concern for you and my loyalty towards you. Those were the only factors, really, that made me agree to attend the dinner and that made me not walk out (especially when I found myself alone at the table ... pretty humiliating). At first, when I got home, my feeling was that because you'd put so much into the Event, I shouldn't tell you about my experiences. Of course you and Early got together on your stories that night, but I am not quite a dumbbell.

Anyway, I then thought that you *should* know.

The dinner wasn't as bad as I say. ... but, by then, the staff had had to keep it hot for about two hours longer than expected. The whole affair, from most people's viewpoint, was undoubtedly a great success. I hope it made a lot of money for the Trust. My own experiences were less felicitous than most, no doubt. ...

I hope you will understand that I am not angry, but I was, understandably I believe, fairly upset at the time.

Best,
Margaret [signed]

Regent, 8 October 1982

Dear Margaret:

I hope I will have reached you on the phone before this letter arrives. I must say that any satisfaction that I may have taken from whatever success the dinner did achieve, was more than overcome by the belated realization that you were embarrassed and justifiably angry at what happened. In all truth, had it not been for your letter and a subsequent investigation, I would never have learned about it and that would have been most unfortunate.

When something of that sort happens, [there] is no way of undoing the harm and the hurt: and no degree of explanations or excuses serve[s] a useful purpose. Certainly, there is a valuable lesson in it for me because it indicates that, no matter how careful one considers the planning, some things are going to go wrong. That something should have gone wrong in relation to your table and your peace-of-mind on an evening that we both already knew was going to be painful for you, was a real horror-story that shames and embarrasses me.

I was aware during the evening that no one was at Pierre Berton's table or your table when you were taken there. But I thought, until now, that it was a very short-lived embarrassment, longer for Pierre than for you. Because I was near the door when a group consisting of Mrs. Phillips, Pierre's host and Donald Early, yours came in, I didn't speak to Donald at the time but I did speak to Mrs. Early, who did not know where she was or why exactly, which baffled me a little bit but, by and large, I considered unremarkable in relation to that lady and I spoke too to Mrs. Phillips who was all apologies and was truly embarrassed. She phoned me the next day to apologize again and sent me a note. I assumed that all was under control from that point and that the only thought, apart from momentary embarrassment, would be that people at surrounding tables—with the introductions still going on—would have thought these people were very rude and discourteous.

I have heard no explanation from Donald and, although I will get one in due course, I have never known him to be rude and discourteous, although I have known him to be late for meetings, to miss meetings entirely and on occasion to arrive on the wrong date for a meeting. Margaret, I thought our routine and cautionary checks for this dinner were foolproof. Obviously not.

I explained the dinner to Donald and sold him the table personally. He agreed to buy a table provided you were the author. When I was finally able to convince you to attend, I wrote Donald, explained to him that I thought the only reason you had agreed to go was because he was your table host. Meanwhile, the Trust sent him two routine follow-ups in the mail, plus a telephone call in the last week, first as a reminder, second to explain that the Governor-General was going to be present and they had to be in the room before the Governor-General entered, to find out who the specific host would be and to ask the host to sit at the right of the author, so that the escort could introduce the author to the host.

That was the routine that was established. It should have been foolproof, but obviously it wasn't.

Several things I did learn from the dinner. The first was that I did not have sufficient time available to administer such a function. The logistics were too complicated. I was still reducing the length of the author introductions until about 6 o'clock the night of the dinner itself. It was a full-time job for many weeks but, even at that, the Trust does not have the depth of staff or volunteers to do things quite well enough. We added several top people from full time for the last week, plus a daily statistical back-up and still there were other horror stories—CP Air, who flew Roloff Beny first class from Rome and back for the event, were given a table, with two batons at their table, at which they couldn't even see the stage or the introductions—none of the horrors were shocking to me as your experience.

Well, hell, Margaret, I am sorry. If I ever try to talk you into anything against your will again—and I hope I never shall—say no automatically. I thought it would be okay; it should have been okay, but it wasn't. I am sorry.

Sincerely,
Jack McClelland

Hollinger, 9 October 1982

Dear Jack:

Oh Boss. Sigh. I got your letter today, and it told me precisely why I had hesitated over sending you a copy of my letter to Cushman describing the Event. You must not ... repeat NOT ... let my experience diminish your sense of success re: the Dinner. It *was* a success. If all the tickets were sold, I estimate that, after expenses, the Trust must have received some $100,000. By me, that is success. You worked terribly hard on the whole deal, as did many others, but you especially, and Marge was as usual a heroine. I was glad Pierre said what he did about your efforts, because I was planning how to do the same but he got there first. Also, what I wanted you to understand in my letter to you was that my attending the Dinner really was an expression of my loyalty to you ... which the Event did not diminish in any way. We don't always agree, Jack, and have had some royal disagreements, as you will recall, but you have been my publisher for 22 years, and not only do I owe you a deep debt of gratitude ... damn it, I like you! I also thought I had got across the fact that it was in no way your fault that that incredible mix-up took place. Lord knows what happened, and it doesn't matter now. I don't think you should approach Don Early about the subject. ... I suspect he is embarrassed and doesn't quite know how to handle it. Let's let it drop. I am not *la grande dame* and, I assure you, I'm not wounded in the heart or anything like it. I just felt I had to let you know what happened. As my letter to Cushman suggested, I hope, the whole thing decidedly had its humorous side. I did in my letter express concern to you, because you had worked like a fiend and I just hoped that Elizabeth would get you to go to Muskoka for a few weeks. Also, as I said in my letter to John, I loved seeing your daughter Susie, who is great. I got a note from ... Lovat Dickson a day or so ago, saying, among other things, that he thinks you're a genius for having got the Event together. So, for heaven's sake, don't feel badly. You have no need to. And as far as I am concerned, the annoyance departed quite quickly, leaving only the amusement. I did *not* feel rejected. ... I'm much more confident than that! But, as a writer, I could not resist writing it up and saying what had happened and how I felt. That's all. So not to worry.

Best,
Margaret [signed]

P.S. Don't you think the best line of the evening, delivered spontaneously and not ever to be made public, was when I yelled at the young escort who offered to take me in first, "Are you out of your head? I'm a socialist!" Even as I spoke the words, I thought, "Heavens, how crazy can you get?" In retrospect, quite a lot of funny things happened. One that I didn't mention in my letter was that the Director (or whatever) of Harlequin Books came over to talk to me and proudly told me that their romances are doing well translated into Arabic, and they (Harlequin Books) have to get separate vetting in a whole lot of Arabic countries, but so far they have had very few problems with the censorship laws in these places! I refrained from saying "who's surprised?" It says something about his line of books. "They don't go much for books in these places," he said, "but these Arab ladies are eating up our books." I did not mention that in long ago years, before the advent of strict and lunatic fundamentalist Muslim regimes, *The Arabian Nights* stories (which I read many years ago in the translation by Sir Richard Burton) and other books were so specifically sexual and erotic that the translations were banned in Victorian England! Harlequin indeed.

Regent, 15 October 1982

Dear Margaret:

How can I respond to your letter of October 9th? It was totally unnecessary—in fact it should have been, but I couldn't reach you on the phone. In any case, I love you dearly and I look forward to seeing you at, would you believe, Simpson's[1] on November 9th.

You know the truth of the matter is that I really regret you people have to do what you have to do. Why in Christ do you have to be at Simpson's on November 9th? It is good that you will be there. It will help the book and it will help all sorts of things. But, believe me, Margaret, I deplore that as much as you do.

On the other hand, I understand the other side of the coin very well. Gabrielle Roy said to me almost exactly 35 years ago, if you want the books, then you will publish them, you will promote and sell them—but I won't. Don't ever expect me to assist you in the promotion of one of my books. She never has, and the closest she came to anything of that sort was her appearance in Calgary, which you remember very well. A marvellous lady and, in all truth, I have been in love with her for 35 years. But migod, Margaret, what the effect of that decision has had on the sales of her books has been appalling. Her books continue to sell very well. The quality has continued to be miraculous, but the sales now are down to less than 20% of the base she established back in 1947. You know and I know that it shouldn't work that way.

On the other side of that coin, one of the reasons I love you dearly—is that Richler was supposed to be at our horrendous evening. He cancelled out because of his back, but he knew and I knew about his back, but nobody could or ever will be able to prove anything, but it is an educated guess that his back was causing him about as much trouble as mine was that evening.

So you interpret that I let him off the hook finally. I admit that to you, but I did for only two reasons. The first is that we didn't absolutely need him. The second is that, although I love him dearly, I knew the people at his table would have [had] an appallingly bad time. So why did I not let you off the hook, Margaret? We needed you and, as it turned out, without you despite the unpleasantness that you experienced, without you the evening would not have succeeded as it did. It is that simple.

Why did I tell you that story about Richler? Let me explain. Now I know very well and probably better than almost anybody else—that you can't categorize authors and writers as a group. It is a weird world. Atwood, on behalf of the Union, keeps complaining that publishers are selling books on the backs of authors and that has got to stop. I keep saying, okay, Margaret let it stop, but remember Gabrielle Roy.

Then I get a call from dear Mordecai. Guess who is reading from his new novel at Harbourfront next weekend—yes, Mordecai Richler. I was sort of stunned by that. He calls to tell me about it and to arrange lunch, and I don't comment. I say, okay fine. But I am stunned. Why wouldn't he come to THE NIGHT OF ONE HUNDRED AUTHORS, and he will go and read his goddamn unfinished novel at Harbourfront? Well, I found out why. Marge tells me I am to appear on Friday on the *Morty Shulman File*.[2] That's fair enough, because Morty wants to stick in the knife, because he wasn't one of the authors sold for the dinner until 24 hours before and then he refused to appear. So I don't blame him and I told him so, but it is my job to appear on his show, and then I suddenly find out the reason for the show is not just to stick the knife into me (the reason for my appearance) but the reason is that it is The International Authors Festival at Harbourfront this weekend.[3] I mean really major figures like Toni Morrison (and I don't denigrate her, in fact I really respect her but I am making a point) and a few others like that, so Richler—who funnily enough I really like and whose work I really admire—drops everything to read at sleazy Harbourfront. Hell, I don't know what I am going to say. What I am going to say, I guess [is] that it is a very strange world.

I thank you for being so forbearing and, if I don't see you before, I will certainly see you on the night of November 9th and, one further thing, Margaret, I have had no involvement in the production of the new edition of your book. All I can say is that it had better well be superb, because one of my last directives as President of M&S was to say that the new edition of this book is an atonement—it better be very bloody good.

Cheers!

Jack McClelland

1. McClelland is probably referring to Simpsons department store, since he often did publicity events at large retailers. Much like Eaton's, Simpsons was known for its mail order catalogue, as well as its stores across the country. The first incarnation of the store opened in 1858 in Newmarket, Ontario, as the Robert Simpson Company; in 1952, it merged with Sears to become Simpsons-Sears Limited. Sears went out of business in October 2017, after sixty-five years in Canada.
2. *The Shulman File* was a talk show on City-TV, which featured confrontational interviews and was hosted by Dr. Morton Shulman (1925–2000) between 1977 and 1983.
3. The Harbourfront Centre in Toronto has hosted the annual International Festival of Authors since 1974. The event attracts international novelists, biographers, short story writers, and playwrights.

•———

Regent, 7 May 1984

Dear Margaret:

It was, as always, a great delight to talk to you, and I would like to start by saying I have absolutely no problem with your decision re: the WDT [Writers' Development Trust] function. You are right and you should not attend.

It is also true, however, that we should have some time together very soon. It has been far too long and there is a lot to talk about. To be clear about that, I am not and will never pressure you to write another novel.[1] You know a helluva lot more than I do about writing a novel and if, after trying, you don't want to write another novel—then you shouldn't. I have no problem with the book that you are writing and we have agreed on that. If when you are ready, you want it—then we will certainly want to publish it—unless we think it is wrong for you, and I will have no hesitation in telling you if I think it is wrong for you. If you say I am wrong and yes it should [be] published, then we will publish it. I mean that is the way that is. I would not have done that with Al Purdy. I presume M&S turned down that book—or Al did not have the nerve to submit it to us, which may even be more likely. What I also want to talk about is the kid's book idea—I want to see three more—related to *The Olden Days Coat* (i.e. basic Canadian traditions), and I would really like to talk that one out.

But, apart from that, I really want to see you. My suggestion is that you come in and stay with us for a weekend in Kleinburg. I would like to have a small party one night and one night when we won't. The weekend I suggested is June 9th to 11th—and I know I will be here on the night of the 11th because of the goddamn WDT function, but it could be another weekend that is more convenient to you. Ideally, you would come to Toronto on either the Friday or the Saturday and stay for two nights. I don't know how you come in—I presume by bus or train—and I'll meet you and drive you to Kleinburg. It will all be very easy and we will have a great time. I really want to do this, Margaret. You will be with old friends and there will be absolutely no pressure or anything of that sort and the WDT thing is totally buried. So I will call you in a week and we will definitely then confirm the date.

With great affection.
Cheers!
Jack

1. As James King explains, when Linda McKnight became president of McClelland & Stewart in 1982, "it was agreed that Jack would still continue to deal with some of his major authors" (*Jack* 359). Laurence was one of them.

Regent, 1 October 1984

Dear Margaret:

I had a call from Jim Wade of Crown Publishers telling me that a special fund has been set up in New York to make sure that John Cushman's son, Tom, is able to complete his university education.[1] I think this is important. I hope you will too.

They are inviting authors, publishers, and associates to contribute. The amounts don't have to be large. Anything could be appreciated. The cheques should be made out to The Thomas C.S. Cushman Special Account, and they should be mailed with a note so that a proper thank you can follow, to James Wade, who is coordinating the whole program. He is at Crown Publishers Inc., One Park Avenue, New York 10016.

All the best.
Sincerely,
Jack

1. As noted earlier, in Laurence's letter dated 4 June 1966, Laurence's literary agent, John Cushman, passed away suddenly in 1984, at fifty-seven years of age.

Hollinger, 4 October 1984

Dear Jack,

Got your letter today re: the Thomas Cushman fund, and have sent $500 Canadian. This will probably be about $450 American, if that. But it is important. Jane Cushman will run that agency, with the help of Jane Wilson, just so well. But Tom wanted to go into the family agency, you know, and he and John discussed it some time before John died. As I said to Jane, in a letter and in phone calls, and to James Wade in my letter, I think this is wonderful and hopeful, *but* if Tom changes his mind and wants to do something else, that will be okay, too. I like the thought that he will be sure to be able to complete his university training, but I don't like the thought that there will be any strings attached. I am sure you will know what I mean.

I hope and know that Marge gave you my message when the whole thing re: M&S came up. Jack, frankly, although you and I have had some dust-ups, my loyalty to you and to the firm will never be in question. I understand from the press that some writers were beginning to look for new publishers. I wasn't one of them. I was, however, approached by some agents in Canada who (a) knew that Cushman had died and (b) knew that M&S were in trouble. Frankly, I didn't bother to reply to them. The vultures were gathering, and I say the hell with them. I was so delighted to learn that the Ont. Gov. kicked through, as well they might. All will be okay, Jack, or so I hope. Anyway, I am not yr prolific writer who turns out yr book a year, as you know. But my books, or some of them, do keep on selling in the NCL and Seal. Old friend, I'm with you.

Best,
Margaret Laurence

Regent, 12 October 1984

Dear Margaret:

That is a very nice letter for which I thank you. First, I am delighted with what you have done re: the Cushmans. It had not occurred to me that Tom might change his mind and want to do something else—you make a very good point. However, I suspect that in this contemporary world, a literary agent with a university degree is a helluva lot better off than one without a degree. Either way they are very nice people—and my guess is that they will turn the agency around the corner with all the help that is being offered by authors, publishers and, funnily enough, other agents. One thinks of New York as a dog-eat-dog sort of place—but after watching what happened after John Cushman's death, I am much less certain that it is. He was, of course, extraordinary.

Re: M&S, all appears to be under control. It was a long and very tough struggle. The real story has not yet appeared. The government was extremely supportive of course. The interesting thing, though, was that the private sector finally came through and came through very effectively. We have an impressive new Board, a new Sales Director, a new computer wizard, and I haven't any doubt that the firm has a great future. My new role will be essentially one of observer, policy maker, and sort of watchdog for the new investors. It is amazing how that can change one's attitude. In the past few years, I have concerned myself from time-to-time about our lack of profitability. Now, out of deference to the private investors, that becomes more or less a full time activity. One of these days, I will tell you a horrendous story of what has come down since we have last talked.

I am really grateful to you for your letter of support. As you know, you are one of a relatively small group of authors who have made my life possible.

Sincerely,
Jack

●——

Regent, 31 May 1985

Dear Author:[1]

To the best of my knowledge, this is the first—and I hope the last—that I have addressed "Dear Author." I have said for almost 40 years that authors are our most important people and our number one priority at M&S. In the interest of practicality and time, however, this is addressed "Dear Author."

Recently, *The Globe and Mail* ran a campaign against McClelland and Stewart,[2] and me personally, that I consider to be not only unfounded, but irresponsible on their part and I have told them so. As you will read in the material attached, I don't intend to sue them, but I don't intend to give up this battle.

Authors—and I have talked to many of you—have been very supportive and I want you to be informed. I enclosed for your information a series of press releases we have issued since that strange attack began.[3] We are also placing an open letter to booksellers in the CBA issues of *Quill and Quire* and *The Canadian Bookseller,* which I hope you will read. If you have concerns, complaints or anything you want to have a report on, please put it on that toll-free number mentioned in the booksellers' letter and you will get a very fast reply, from me if at all possible.

I am a believer in what you do and what we do, and I hope you will continue to have faith in this company.

Finally, you may have seen in the national edition of *The Globe* on May 30th a story about a new arrangement made between Apple Canada Inc.—and their Macintosh computer—and M&S.[4] We will be talking I hope in the very near future to all of you about Macintosh word processors because we think they are terrific.

My best regards.
Sincerely,
Jack McClelland

1. This letter was written by McClelland to many of his authors, not just Laurence.
2. McClelland refers to a series of articles that include, for example, one titled "President Resigns from Tottering McClelland & Stewart," written by David Oliver, John Partridge, and Paul Taylor, and which appeared on the first page of the 10 May 1985 issue, and another titled "McClelland Returns as President of Troubled Publishing Company," written by the same authors, and which appeared on 15 May 1985. This latter article refers to McClelland as "the mercurial book publisher" (M1). McClelland responded on 17 May 1985 to denounce Oliver, Partridge, and Taylor as writing stories that "have been damaging to our company and to me personally" ("McClelland Denounces Globe" 1).
3. McClelland enclosed four press releases. On 9 and 14 May 1985, he issued press releases announcing the resignation of Linda McKnight as president and publisher of McClelland & Stewart, his own appointment as president of the company, and other appointments of senior executives. On 10 May 1985, he issued a press release responding to the article titled "President Resigns from Tottering McClelland & Stewart," referenced in the previous note. He stated, "The story in the *Globe and Mail* today is without foundation except as it related to the tendered resignation of our president. ... The company is financially healthy and currently preparing for a major fall book season." On 16 May 1985, he issued a six-page press release, an angry and detailed response to the *Globe and Mail* articles and the notion that the company was not financially stable. This article was published as "McClelland Denounces Globe," referenced in the previous note (Margaret Laurence Fonds, Clara Thomas Archives and Special Collections, 1986/006/ 016, File 690).
4. The advertisement was titled "Announcing the Retirement of Canada's Most Famous Typewriters." It featured a photograph by Yousuf Karsh that included Veronica Tennant, Charles Templeton, Peter C. Newman, Jack McClelland, Ben Wicks, Margaret Atwood, and Harold Town. The accompanying text revealed that the entire McClelland & Stewart organization would soon be operating its business on the "Macintosh Office network of hardware and software products" (9).

Photo from the Globe and Mail *advertisement for the Macintosh computer, 30 May 1985. Above the headline "Announcing the retirement of Canada's most famous typewriters," the caption read, "Macintosh and seven of its newest devotees." From left to right: Veronica Tennant, Charles Templeton, Peter C. Newman, A. Macintosh, Jack McClelland, Ben Wicks, Margaret Atwood, Harold Town. [Yousuf Karsh, Library and Archives Canada, accession number PA-207438. Used by permission of Karsh.org]*

Regent, 19 September 1985

Dear Margaret:

It was good to hear your voice. I was stunned to hear about the eye problem—no one had told me—but I suspect the truth is no one had the nerve to tell me. Whatever I may have been in the past, I have become in recent months a rampant curmudgeon. People only tell me good things—they are afraid to tell me anything that will make me sad or mad.

In any case, I am delighted that you are making such a super recovery. I would judge that it is a much rougher experience than you indicated. Strangely enough, the only part of me that continues to work is my eyes, although they are failing rapidly along with everything else.

Well, I had four questions and we have dealt with the first one—namely, how are you surviving and are you well. And I am delighted that you are. Then there are the other three:

First, I don't understand why I can't give you a Macintosh. For one who has moderate typing skills, it is easily the best piece of equipment that I have ever encountered. The truth is, Margaret, I don't type, although I used to and I took a typing course for one summer, but I don't type. Nonetheless, I find the Macintosh a totally useful and entertaining piece of equipment. It will do just about anything that you want it to do provided you have faith. It takes no more than an hour's instruction to do all the obvious things and from that point on, yes one has to work to achieve but it really is, as they say, a user-friendly machine.

Why do I want to [give] you one? Truthfully, if you don't want to use it, I couldn't care less. But, I can give you one—value $7500.00 with no tax implications—[as] a straight gift. Apple may or may not want you to pose in a picture similar to the earlier one. I don't think they will, but I don't know that.

What they will do is have a dealer in Lakefield or Peterborough deliver it to you directly. All the equipment. Install it. Give you an hour's instruction, and then they will give you half a day's instruction if you want it, but the truth is that if you don't like the machine you can give it to one of the kids and they will love it. That, at least, has been my experience. I have one at home. I use it much less than Rob, but if I typed memos, I would use it constantly. It is super equipment. However, if you don't want it, that is that.

Second, my daughter Anne has been working with the Board of Education of Toronto on an author project for next April. Specifically, it is authors reading in the schools—12 of them. They will read in high schools and they will come to Toronto for a two-day stint of two sessions. She has lined up a pretty impressive group of authors: Tiff Findley,[1] Bill Mitchell, Earle Birney, David Donnell,[2] etc. etc. etc. 12 in all. However, what they want is a super author to deal with their super students of all the high schools. The top English students in the Metro Toronto area. All your expenses will be paid, and it will be made very easy for you and you will not even have to prepare a speech. You will just have to appear and talk to these bright kids.

You don't have to do it, unless you think it would be fun. There is no big issue on this one, except that I think you are very good with bright young kids—and I realize you do far too much in the public interest—they will have read your books and you will get intelligent questions, and I think it would be a very easy thing and I think it would be good for Canadian writing. It is a pilot project for the Toronto Board. It will happen during Canadian Book Week or whatever they call it now. It is very much in the formative stage at the moment, so I can't really give you any more details. I could dredge up a specific date or dates. You would have to stay overnight at their expense but they will not pay a fee. What it might do is keep your celebrated position in the minds of students ... well, I don't know.

Third, I asked you if you are going to have a book finished for next year. You explained that you will not. That's fair enough. I don't have any argument. [You] also explained why my idea re: pre-seasonal books relating to *The Olden Days Coat* was a bad idea. I think you are wrong—but I am not going to argue that one.

Finally, I am going to see you at the Convocation function—if I have the energy to go. Honorary Degrees are about as high on my list of priorities as Toronto high school kids is on yours. But I may be there. I hope that the strange film crew that is doing the NFB documentary of the Life and Death of Jack McClelland[3]—I hope they are going to become convinced that they have to go to Lakefield to film the two of us having a drink together. What more can I say?

Cheers!

Jack [signed]

1. Timothy Findley (1930–2002), nicknamed "Tiff," an acronym of his initials, was a Canadian writer best known for his novels *The Wars*, *Not Wanted on the Voyage*, and *The Piano Man's Daughter*.
2. David Donnell (1939–) is a Canadian writer who has written both prose and poetry. His first collection of poetry, *Poems*, was published in 1961. He won the Governor General's Award in 1983 for his poetry collection titled *Settlements*.
3. This 1986 documentary was written and produced by Bay Weyman and James Weyman of Close Up Films, in association with the CBC and Telefilm Canada. Its title is *Against Reason: A Portrait of Jack McClelland*.

Hollinger, 22 September 1985

Dear Jack:

Thanks very much for your letter. Surprise, surprise ... I have decided to accept your offer re: the Apple word processor!!! Upon mature consideration (meaning that a couple of friends yelled at me, "Accept the offer! Don't be an idiot. Etc. etc. bla bla bla!") and, after reading your letter, I think that possibly I don't stand to lose in any way. I will probably continue to write first drafts in longhand as I have done all my life, but the processor might prove to be useful in transcribing and editing and rewriting. I do not have "moderate" typing skills. ... I have EXCELLENT typing skills. I have been a touch-typist since I was 14 years old, and, believe me, Boss, that was about 200 years ago! I have now become totally proficient with my relatively new electronic typewriter (which has a memory of 48 characters), so perhaps I can master the Macintosh. After all, I don't need it to do everything it can do. ... I don't need it to talk to me or teach me tap dancing. This electronic typewriter can do a bunch of stuff that I don't need, but so what. It does what I want it to do, and I will undoubtedly continue to use it for writing letters. But I am now prepared to give Apple at least a good chew.

There will be no dealer in Lakefield, but there will be in Peterborough. If Apple wants me to pose, draped elegantly (ho ho) across the table from the little charmer, I will hardly be able to say "No." It would make all my friends and acquaintances fall off their chairs in astonishment, but never mind.

I know one should not look a gift horse in the mouth, but I am too old to believe in free lunches (how is that for a mixed metaphor?). Why are you giving these fancy pieces of equipment to M&S writers? How come you have these machines to give away? I can see that Macintosh would benefit from the pics of Atwood and Newman and Town and

McClelland and Old Uncle Tom Cobbley [*sic*] and All,[1] posed with the Machine, in circumstances of such elegance as no writer or publisher ever worked in. But what is in it for you? And why do you want me to accept an Apple, but don't really care if I use it much or at all? Boss, I, too, am a canny Scot, and am curious about these matters. If you can give me some information, I will be grateful, and, if necessary, maintain the matter in confidence. If it does THE OLD FIRM some (preferably both legally and morally acceptable) good, I am all for it.

Second, I just cannot go out to read in High Schools, although I applaud Anne for this project. Jack, I LOVE High School Students, and a hell of a lot of them are very very bright. Yes, I get on well with them. And I have had so many sessions with them, in various parts of this country but mainly in Ontario throughout the last 11 years, that I just don't think I can do any more for the next few years. Not to mention the hundreds and hundreds of letters to which I have replied, letters from students who are writing papers on my work and want information from me. I have tried to do my best, but I am getting worn out and I honestly think I have paid my dues for a while. Give Anne my best wishes and tell her, please, that I just can't do it.

Third. re: my having another book ready for next year ... [or] ever. I think it is time that I gave you a Progress Report. I would appreciate it if you would treat this as confidential. I do not require pity and I abhor same. For the past 11 years, since I moved into my house here, I have published very little, as you know. A couple of kids' books, which, frankly, I loved doing, and a book of essays, *Heart of A Stranger*. For the past 5 years, nothing. I have not been sitting on my butt doing nothing—I have done a lot of work with anti-nuclear and pro-peace groups;[2] I was Chancellor of Trent for 3 years and took that job seriously; I have written numerous articles on disarmament and on censorship, published here and there; I have talked with innumerable high school and university students; I have answered 1200 letters a year; etc. Well, no big deal. But the thing that only my kids and my closest few friends know is that I have also made about 5 or 6 false starts on a novel that proved just not to be there, or not for me. For me, a novel is not an intellectual decision

… it has to be in some way "given," a necessity to write. This wasn't. I suppose I have thrown away hundreds of pages. I prophesied this at the end of *The Diviners* (and NO, this was NOT a self-fulfilling prophesy), but I did not know that if it happened to me, as I felt it might, it would be terribly painful.

It [has] been. I rejoice. … I really do … in the work of my inheritors; I mourn my apparent lack of ability to do another novel. Maybe it will again happen to me and maybe not. It is not, I assure you, for lack of trying. But I will never write a mock-up of a novel, even though I recognize at this point I probably have the skills to be able to do just that. It is not possible. So, Jack, under this mostly cheery exterior these past years has been a person with some considerable anguish. No … not Poor Me. … I have such a heck of a lot to be grateful for, and I am. I read an interview recently with Mordecai in which he said … every writer writes one novel too many. Hell, no, not everyone. And I'll bet he won't, either! I spent quite a long time trying to write my memoirs … what a travesty! I knew that there were large areas I wasn't prepared to deal with. Also, I got myself to about age 18, and I got really bored. I knew what was going to happen next, unlike a novel. More hundreds of pages in the garbage.

Perhaps, just perhaps, I may finally have found what I must write. Don't hold your breath waiting for it. And, if it is ever completed, it won't, I think, be a very popular or even acceptable subject. (And yes, I know, I thought that when I began to write *The Stone Angel* some 20 years ago. … I should be so lucky again!) But I am trying, once more. We shall see. Expect nothing. I think I owe it to you to tell you all this. We have, after all, been colleagues for more than 25 years.

The eye operation is okay, but I am very very bored with not being able to see properly. As the implanted lens gets better and the eye gets more used to it, so do my present glasses in the right eye lens get worse, naturally. My glasses I have to wear all the time to protect the eye until it is totally healed. But the implanted lens and the glasses lens are totally unsuitable for one another, hence quite distorted distance viewing. I hope I will get my new glasses next week. I feel I have been virtually grounded for 2 months. Thank heavens, I am a touch typist and do not have to look at what I am typing; my hands know when I have made an error ... amazing.

Jack, I know exactly what you mean about Honorary Degrees. But please be there. Or, if you think you can't, let Trent know NOW. They have all their announcements out and so on. Universities don't give them *in absentia,* as you know. It is all kind of peculiar, and the recipients of honorary degrees feel, I suppose, as I have often felt (having 13 of the things) that we are there to add a little colour to Convocations, and that only. But this view is not right, Jack, from the viewpoints of the universities. We, the recipients, are there for other reasons ... not only to accept the university's "honouring" of this one and that one but to affirm the value of a university in a wider community. (Wow, how is that for preaching?). Please be there if you can. I am only sorry that I am not Chancellor of Trent any more ... it would have been great (and ironic) for me to able to confer the D. Litt. on you! I did give Malcolm Ross the D. Litt. ... even more ironic and pleasurable. I will not be at the Convocation ... I have sat through TOO MANY convocations, but I will be at the luncheon beforehand.

All the best,
Margaret Laurence

1. Laurence uses the English colloquial expression, "Old Uncle Tom Cobley and All," to mean "and everyone else."
2. As Davis explains, during the 1980s, "Laurence became an advocate for the PPAC (Public Petroleum Association of Canada) and supported Energy Probe and the Council for Nuclear Awareness" ("Margaret Laurence's Correspondence" 61). In addition, during these years, Laurence dedicated herself to political causes such as the contemporary women's movement and the fight against war (Davis, "Margaret Laurence's Correspondence" 72), as is evidenced by the plethora of letters to and from various organizations in Laurence's papers at York and McMaster.

Regent, 30 September 1985

Dear Margaret:

It was great to have your letter. That is a super decision you have made re: the Macintosh. You have it, dear. It will be delivered to you before you know. You will hear from someone in Peterborough and then you have the machine.

Will they want to photograph you receiving it from the dealer in Peterborough? Hell, I don't know, but it is not a bad idea. They just may and I will urge them to do it. Remember you suggested [it] as a possibility. You will have no regrets about getting a Macintosh machine. That I promise and if your friends, relations, whatever are appalled, just remember, it is a super machine and you can use it and if you can't, pass it on to Jocelyn.[1] Frankly, though, I think you will use it.

Okay, you want to know why. Let me tell you exactly the precise nature of our deal with the Apple people. They have problems, as you have read in the paper [M&S] has problems. I am trying to return to total viability. What else can I do. We deserve to have total viability or maybe we don't, but my job is to strive for it. You want to know what the deal means to M&S. It means this year approximately $260,000.00 in the asset column free. They are giving the machines to us in return for that first picture—which they promoted widely—my willingness to speak at several of their conventions and future publicity. We own the machines. Out of the 35, we will have 10 at M&S and 25 to authors, and it is good for them and it is good for us and good for writers. If I didn't believe the machine was super for writers, I wouldn't be involved in this, but it really is and it is a gift. Well, it is on long-term loan, with no really serious conditions attached, but we own the machines. We get a big write-off. We continue to own the 35 machines, but they are in the hands of our writers. I mean, what could be better? Do you think there is something sinister about this? I don't. If it is sinister, it is no more sinister than anything I have done ever before in my life. It is a question of keeping alive and trying to help writers and help book publishing. The whole goddamn thing. If the Apple people can benefit so much the better.[2] I actually like their equipment and can use their equipment. I would not have done it otherwise. In fact, we had an earlier deal with the Phillips Micom, but I couldn't work it and my people couldn't work it, and I found them impossible to deal with. I like the Apple people and I hope you will. They won't bug you.

I have no problem with your unwillingness to read in high schools and the Toronto trip that I suggested. Forget it. It simply is not a problem. My daughter Anne may never forgive you or me—but that is not an issue. Margaret, this sort of shit you do not have to deal with.

As to writing another book—don't feel any pressure about that, particularly if you are talking about another novel. You said, and I knew, and I agreed with you back so many years ago that you might not write another novel. You said it. I have no problem with it (although I secretly hoped it wasn't true), but I have no problem with that. I do come back and say to you, though, that I think you should write—apart from what you want to write—three more children's books. I think you should make that a classic tradition. What you did for Canadian winter—which will be remembered long after we are both dead—I think you should do for the other three seasons of the year. I have kept telling you that. I stand by that. I think you can do it and I think you should. You have celebrated one season of the year we, as Canadians know, why not the other three? The non-writing of another novel—you warned me about that many times and I don't have any problem with that—why in the hell should you but, shit, dear the writing of another seasonal kid's book is something that you should be able to do without great stress. I mean, hell—we do as Canadians have four distinct seasons. Each one has its traditions. God, I do want to talk to you about that, because if there is anything that I can feel attuned to, it is the four seasons. You have done one of them in a way that nobody has ever done it before, and you have made it magical. God, Margaret—I don't know why I keep inserting that comma—the other seasons are so clear and so distinct and so different and so important—and I mean so important in terms of our total heritage—well, hell, let's leave it until I see you, which will be in about three weeks anyway.

Of course, I will be there for the Trent thing. Of course, it is super for you to appear at the lunch and I would be appalled if you stayed beyond that. Don't, and don't even think about it.

As to the eyes—well, by the time you get this letter you will be seeing again very well. It is a funny thing, Margaret, that my father was told—because he had a hemorrhage in one eye in his early sixties—that he would never be able to see again. This practically put him out of business. A book publisher who couldn't read, see or do anything like that or do anything in his profession, it almost destroyed him. But I now understand. I haven't had that problem, although I have had many others, but he had to live with the prediction—he and my mother and the children had to live with it—it was very difficult for them—we the children didn't understand it, totally. I understand that as a book publisher. I don't have any problem with the prediction that I would be dead next year or two years from now, but being blind would totally destroy me. You have come back from that one. I think that is great. I am thrilled that I won't see you during the period when you won't see.

Look, Margaret, we are at a sort of uneven period in our lives. You, in my opinion, owe me exactly zilch. I, in turn, owe you a great deal. That is how I feel. That is how I will always feel. Let us leave it that way. We are friends. We have been friends for a great many years. Let's continue to be friends, and Apple or no Apple—it is totally irrelevant—we will see you at Trent for lunch.

Much love and cheers!
Jack [signed]
Jack McClelland

1. Jocelyn Laurence (1952–2015) was Margaret's first child. When Margaret Laurence wrote her memoir, *Dance on the Earth*, she was dying of cancer. Because she was not well enough to type

the manuscript, Laurence spoke into a tape recorder. Jocelyn transcribed the memoir and took over its project management with McClelland & Stewart. Jocelyn Laurence worked in Toronto as a writer, editor, and project manager, and held editorial positions with *Fashion Magazine*, *Toronto Life*, *Canadian Art*, and *Green Living*. She died of cancer in 2015, at the age of sixty-two (Fitterman).

2. The Apple computer company began in 1976 and was a relatively small company when McClelland wrote this letter. He could not have anticipated the worldwide success the company would become. In March 2017, Apple was worth $750 billion (La Monica).

Regent, 28 October 1985

Dear Margaret:

You were in great form. It was marvellous to see you. The Convocation, funnily enough, was swift and not bad because John Holmes[1] made a very good speech. The reception after and then the dinner, they were all great, and we had a fine evening, and we finally got to bed about 3:30 in the morning. That's the story of my life.

I thought you looked terrific and in great form. I hope fairly soon we are really going to talk about the book you are writing. There is no pressure. No hurry. We will do it when time permits. In the meantime, do the book. Love the Macintosh and then we will get serious about doing another *Olden Days Coat*. I love you dearly.

Cheers!
Jack [signed]
Jack McClelland

1. In the fall of 1985 John Holmes and McClelland both received honorary Doctor of Laws degrees from Trent University, Holmes for public service and McClelland for arts and publishing.

Regent, 24 December 1985

Dear ~~author~~ love,

It had been my intention to send you a personal and confidential letter on December 24th announcing the forthcoming sale of the controlling interest in this company. Through a speculative news leak, that opportunity was pre-empted.

I attach a copy of a press release that we do hope to issue on December 30th.[1] If that happens, it should mean a Happy New Year for all of us. In the meantime, it is still confidential.

Sincerely,
Jack McClelland

Will call you shortly. Hope are ok.

1. A copy of the press release was not found with the letter.

Regent, 24 July 1986

Dear Margaret:

It was really good to talk to you. I really have been trying to reach you for about two weeks but finally decided that you were either visiting somewhere or on a trip. Congratulations on the 60th birthday. I usually think of it in terms of commiserations rather than congratulations but since you enjoyed it—so be it. So you are 60 years young. I must say I think the idea of 60 gifts was a great one.

I was delighted by your confirmation of the rumour that you finished the first draft of the memoir. That really is good news—particularly as it was a week early. Fore mother's concept seems a good one, whether or not you retain the play on words.[1] If you want a year for a working draft—who is going to argue. I may even survive to see it. Great God, I meant to tell you that I am now on day 26 without a drink. Strangely enough, it was self-imposed, because I had really reached the stage physically where I lived for the next drink to pick me up. I feel particularly buoyant at the moment but how long that will continue, I am not predicting. Whatever, it helped me get out of the total depression that inevitably followed the selling of the firm.[2] Now I have no second thoughts about it. It was the right thing to do and believe me, I did it at the right time.

What I am really writing about, though, is October 29th, which is the night of THE GREAT LITERARY DINNER PARTY. We changed our pattern from the evening you and I won't soon forget. This time, there are individual dinner parties right across the country and including Tokyo, Hong Kong, Paris, London, New York, Washington and L.A. Each dinner raises a minimum of $1200.00 clear for the Trust. That will be doubled by the Ontario fund, so each dinner represents $2400.00—and given the fact that some dinners will be larger than minimum, we really are looking to raise $300,000.00 net for an endowment fund that will keep the WDT [Writers' Development Trust] going permanently, and, once it is achieved, I will be able to sever all connections for all time with the WDT. You can do the same.

The Canada Council plans on having two dinners—probably one French-Canadian and one English. Their problem is who can they honour without making other people mad. I have pointed out that if Margaret Laurence would agree—everyone would think it eminently fitting and suitable.

So, why should you do it? Well, for the Trust is one thing. The other would give you a free evening to tell the senior Canada Council people what you think is good and what you think is bad about their programs, with speeches, a gourmet dinner. It is really one evening. If you want to make a day of it, you can (and don't need) to go to a cocktail party for the authors being given by David Peterson.[3] You can in the morning or in the afternoon sit down with 10 gifted English students from a Canadian high school and speeches and get a substantial tax credit. There are other things you could or could not do that day. It is the dinner that I care about. If it makes it any easier (or worse), you can stay with the McClellands in Kleinburg and the Canada Council can wine and dine you in one of the glorious restaurants in this area—or, for that matter, if you prefer it in Peterborough. I know of at least one really super restaurant.

I won't be able to join you for dinner personally—Elizabeth could—because I am having dinner alone that evening. I am having dinner with the memories of Gabrielle Roy, Sheila Burnford, Ernest Buckler, Marian Engel, Roloff Beny, and Gordon Sinclair[4]—all of whom have departed the scene since the last dinner four years ago. I am hoping to God I don't think of anyone else, because it is going to cost me $200.00 a plate. Now there is a real grabber for you. That is how much I care. If that doesn't at least make it difficult for you to say no—what will? So, it is over to you.

Cheers!
Jack

P.S. Even if you say no, I would like to get a letter from you. That helps my tax credit at McMaster.[5] Don't send a form letter.

P.P.S. I think the *Journal* is a good idea.[6] If it doesn't make a book, I will be amazed.

1. Laurence's memoir, *Dance on the Earth*, published posthumously in 1989, was structured with sections on her relationship with each of her "four mothers": her birth mother, her aunt, her mother-in-law, and herself. This is why McClelland refers to the play on words (fore/four).
2. McClelland sold McClelland & Stewart in 1985 to real estate developer and philanthropist Avie Bennett (1928–2017). In 2000, Bennett donated 75 per cent of the company to the University of Toronto and sold 25 per cent of it to Random House Canada, "which acquired M&S outright—for a single dollar—in 2012" (Medley). Elaine Dewar's book, *The Handover: How Bigwigs and Bureaucrats Transferred Canada's Best Publisher and the Best Part of Our Literary Heritage to a Foreign Multinational*, articulates and analyzes details regarding M&S's acquisition by Random House in 2012.
3. David Peterson (1943–) was the premier of Ontario from 1985 to 1990.
4. Gordon Sinclair (1900–1984) was a Canadian writer and journalist.
5. McClelland deposited his letters and archival materials at the William Ready Division of Archives and Research Collections at McMaster University.
6. No surviving letter indicates to what idea McClelland refers, though it may refer to the personal diary that Laurence kept at this time and that she considered publishing. It is possible that more discussion of the idea was transmitted by telephone.

Hollinger, 30 July 1986

Dear Jack:

Thanks for your letter. I was all prepared to say NO to your request re: The Great Literary Dinners. You know how much I love that kind of thing, even had the last one (Night of 100 Authors) not turned out, from my point of view, to be such a disaster. (Actually, after you phoned, I had a pleasing fantasy of saying I would attend, only if the gentleman who bought the Margaret Laurence table last time would put up a lot of money for a table with me this time. I would then NOT TURN UP.) Anyway, Jack, if my performance could be staged in Peterborough, I would be willing to do it. Then, it would truly be one evening instead of two days out of my week, which would happen if I went to Toronto. By the way, I am agreeing much more for your sake than for the Writers' Development Trust. ... I severed ties with them long ago. So you can keep me posted, please, about arrangements. I don't want to have sessions with students, or listen to speeches, or go to cocktail parties given by the premier. I have done all that sort of thing so often; I think I have paid my dues by this time.

I hope to get started on typing out my memoirs after I return from Alberta, Aug 11. My brother is very ill, and I am going out next week to be with him and his family for a while.

Congrats on your willpower! That's really great. Also, glad to hear that you have gotten over the depression re: selling firm. I also hope, as I have been telling you for years and years, that you accept how much you have done for publishing in Canada and for our writers.

All the best,
Margaret Laurence

Regent, 15 September 1986

Dear Margaret:

My first reaction on receiving your letter of September 10th[1]—it reached me on Saturday morning—was to phone. I [hoped to] have been able to connect. Then it was to write, which I am doing. You have told me not to rush to Lakefield. I wish I could do that, but I am off to Vancouver on a commitment that I cannot get out of.

The news is easily the saddest that I have received in a very long time. For you, it is totally grim. I know you can cope with it, but I wish I could believe that that sort of inner strength that you have could make it easier. I can't believe it is going to be very easy.

For friends, it is going to be rough. I am certainly one of them, but I have got to tell you, Margaret, that I don't know of anybody who has more friends who care, because the fact is that you have done more for people than anyone else I know. I hear about it constantly. The number of well-known writers, unknown writers and aspiring writers that you have helped is beyond calculation. God help us all. It will be very rough on you, and it won't be too easy for the multitude of us who love and care about you so much.

If it were that simple, it would be easy in a way. One of my two brother-in-laws died about 10 days ago. It wasn't a pleasant experience for any of us and particularly my sister and the children. But we are dealing with something much tougher than that. We are dealing with a projected medical death sentence for a person who has done more for Canada, has meant more to Canada than any writer I can think of during my lifetime. Margaret, you are modest, and I know you very well—and you are going to think this is bullshit—but it is not. You are the most important, most respected, most admired writer in Canada of our lifetime. Goddamn it, you are our most important citizen. If the medical projection is right, your death will be a bloody national day of mourning. You are to Canada what Dickens and Thackeray and Jane Austin [*sic*] and Laurence Sterne were to the U.K., what de Maupassant and Balzac were to France—well, I don't have to go through that litany, but I think we both have to talk about this and think about this and think how it all should be handled.

You will probably prefer that I talk to Jocelyn about this, and I will, but the fact is that this is not going to be a secret, and it is already not a secret. Certainly, you are off the hook for October 29th, but if you think I am not going to proceed with a major dinner in your honour in Peterborough that night—forget it. Margaret, it does not matter whether you are able to attend or not. I am determined that they will have a great dinner in your honour.

I know you don't want to read a long letter from me, and, in fact, you don't have to but, God, you have so much to be proud of including the children and everything else—that if anyone should feel pleased about what they have accomplished in their relatively short period on the face of this earth, it is Margaret Laurence.

Funnily enough, what catches me at this particular moment is that I wish to God I could write. I would like to write you such a superb letter that it would enchant you and enrich you and support you through whatever the months ahead have to impose on you. I just don't have that gift [or] skill—the one in the world that I admire more than any other.

Well, count on it that I will be up to see you at the earliest date that is permissible at your end. I have a terrible feeling that you may not want me to do that, but do let me do it. I will be on my best behaviour, and we will have a good time. Meanwhile, hang in with great faith. The doctors may be right or they may be wrong. My total life experience gives doctors about a 50% batting average (in baseball parlance .500). They are right as often as they are wrong. They are like book publishers. My batting average is about the same. But thanks to you and a handful of others—it is fair to say that, when I have been right, I have been very, very right. That is the way it is with doctors but, hell, Margaret, I am old enough to have become philosophic on the subject. The [world is] not going to get better with each succeeding year from now on. They simply are not. So if we are cut short or cheated out of a few more declining years—does it really matter? I don't think it matters.

My dear, we have had our best years. If we don't have too many more, that may not be all bad.

With love,
Jack [signed]
Jack McClelland

1. Laurence's letter to McClelland dated 10 September 1986 is not available in Laurence's or McClelland's archives. It is the letter in which Laurence informed McClelland that she was dying of cancer.

Regent, 10 December 1986

Dear Margaret,

As promised, I am writing to you as soon as possible after reading *Dance on the Earth*—a great title by the way and eminently appropriate thematically—to give you my reaction while the reading experience is fresh in my mind.

First, I loved the manuscript and found it not only moving but, aside from some minor caveats that will follow, I found it compelling reading. To tell you the truth, I received the manuscript—thanks to Jocelyn and Marge—Monday evening and it kept me up until 4 A.M. I read the last third of it on Tuesday.

I now understand what you have meant when you have described it as not a standard autobiography or memoir. It is anything but. What emerges from the manuscript is the real Margaret Laurence: determination, the conviction, the courage, the caring, the love, and the commitment (I hope that is the proper use of the colon)—I am now inhibited.

My one broad concern would be that in the overall balance I think you may be unduly harsh on the male sex. It is not that the points you make are not valid and well presented—my concern would be in the area that a male would benefit a great deal from reading this book and many may not do so because they may be put off in advance by reviews and even by word of mouth. I am not in any sense suggesting the toning down of what you say. I wonder, however, if there mightn't be some bones tossed here or there. This is done in the latter part of the book, of course, but it is something you may want to think about.

You told me that several of the early readers had expressed the opinion that more detail and fleshing out is needed. I am not in agreement with that in principle, although I could be in terms of minor specific areas. In other words, I think you have done what you set out to do and, as one reader, I would favour judicious cutting here and there and for two different reasons. There is some repetition—a minor editorial problem. There are other places where I think you occasionally carry on too long after making the point with great eloquence. Again, this is a relatively minor editorial problem.

I have marked such places in my Xerox of the manuscript, but I am not going to enumerate them here, because I don't think it is advisable to have too many cooks in the broth. If Jocelyn is going to be the editor, then I think those comments should go to her when she is ready for it.

There is another suggestion I would like to throw out—speaking as a publisher, publisher's consultant, or whatever. My question is does the AFTERWARDS [*sic*] belong in this book? There are two points I would make. First, because it is a patchwork, I think it could be done separately as a small book. It is mainly poetry, press articles. I presume it has been winnowed already and it could be a little longer. The point here, Margaret, is not the obvious one of giving the publishers another book to sell. Rather I would propose it in the interest of keeping *Dance on the Earth*—in these days of high book prices—at a slightly more attractive retail price.

In addition, I think there should be a more substantial difference in your thoughts re: cancer and the hell you have been going through. I realize, or assume, that this will be very much a part of the Diary,[1] but I don't think the lifting, at least of some of the philosophical thoughts on the subject, would take anything away from the Diary and since everybody is aware of your situation—well, hell, I just think that something of it is going to be expected here and if you can bring yourself to do it, I think it should be here. You have a brief reference. Your concern may be ending what is essentially a happy book is preponderantly a celebration of life ending [*sic*] on a downer but, Christ, Margaret, it is a very honest book and I think you should say what you want to say, even if it is only two or three pages.

So what can I add to the foregoing but congratulations on an accomplishment. It takes one helluva book to keep me up until 4 o'clock in the morning these days, especially when I am on an enforced health retreat.

I will call you in a few days after I know you have received the letter.

Love,
Jack [signed]
Jack McClelland[2]

1. McClelland refers to the personal diary Laurence kept during the latter years of her life. In the diary, which is housed under restriction at the William Ready Division of Archives and Research Collections at McMaster University, Laurence indicated that she was interested in having it published. It was, however, never published.
2. This is the last surviving letter between McClelland and Laurence. Margaret Laurence died on 5 January 1987, at the age of sixty-one. After years of ill health following a stroke, Jack McClelland died at his home on 14 June 2004, at the age of eighty-one ("Canadian Publisher Jack McClelland"). In a tribute to Laurence, written on 13 January 1987, McClelland made the following statement: "Margaret Laurence was probably the greatest gift to the literary community that Canada has ever known. ... The country has lost a great citizen, whose spirit will endure through the books she has left us. I feel privileged to have touched her life" (Jack McClelland Fonds, Box 87, File 27).

Works Cited

"About the BPC [Book and Periodical Council]." *Book and Periodical Council: The Umbrella Organization for Publishing in Canada,* www.thebpc.ca/the-publishing-industry/about-the-bpc/.

"Anna Porter: Brainy Beauty." *Toronto Sun,* 19 Sept. 1982, p. G17.

"Announcing the Retirement of Canada's Most Famous Typewriters" [Advertisement for Apple computers]. *Globe and Mail,* 30 May 1985, p. 9.

Association of Canadian Publishers Fonds. Simon Fraser University Archives, www.sfu.ca/archives2/F-57/F-57.html.

"The Atlantic Monthly." *Encyclopedia Britannica,* www.britannica.com.

Atwood, Margaret. Margaret Laurence Lecture Series, 2007. *A Writer's Life: The Margaret Laurence Lectures,* edited by The Writers' Trust of Canada, McClelland & Stewart, 2011, pp. 315–28.

——. *Survival: A Thematic Guide to Canadian Literature.* House of Anansi Press, 1972.

Berton, Pierre. *The Last Spike: The Great Railway, 1881–1885.* McClelland & Stewart, 1971.

——. *The National Dream: The Great Railway, 1871–1881.* McClelland & Stewart, 1970.

Besner, Neil. "*The Double Hook.*" *The Canadian Encyclopedia,* 2006, www.thecanadianencyclopedia.ca.

Blondal, Patricia. *A Candle to Light the Sun.* 1960. Oxford UP, 2013.

Brockie, Ian. "Case Study: Coles Notes." *History of the Book in Canada,* edited by Carole Gerson and Jacques Michon, vol. III, 1918–1980, U of Toronto P, 2007, pp. 232–33.

Buckler, Ernest. *The Mountain and the Valley*. McClelland & Stewart, 1954.

Campbell, Sandra. *Both Hands: A Life of Lorne Pierce of Ryerson Press*. McGill-Queen's UP, 2013.

Canadian Authors Association, Toronto Branch, 1921–1954. Manuscript Collection 101, 3 Boxes (description of "History" introducing the papers). Fisher Library, University of Toronto, fisher.library.utoronto.ca/sites/fisher.library.utoronto.ca/files/cdn_authors_assoc.pdf.

"Canadian Publisher Jack McClelland Dead at 81." *Globe and Mail*, 14 June 2004, https://www.theglobeandmail.com/news/national/canadian-publisher-jack-mcclelland-dead-at-81/article22507223/.

Canadian War Museum. "Doing Justice to History:" Canada's Second World War Official Art Program, www.warmuseum.ca/cwm/exhibitions/artwar/essays/canada_worldwar2_art_program_e.shtml.

"Cannonballs from the Educators." *Globe and Mail*, 10 Feb. 1976, www.globeandmail.com.

Castaldo, Joe. "Douglas & McIntyre May Have Published Its Last Book." *Canadian Business*, 12 Nov. 2012, www.canadianbusiness.com/business-news/industries/media/douglas-mcintyre-may-have-published-its-last-book/.

"City Woman Writes Book on the Birth of Ghana" [Review of *This Side Jordan*]. *Vancouver Sun*, 23 Mar. 1960, p. 19.

"Claude Bissell." *The Canadian Encyclopedia*, www.thecanadianencyclopedia.ca/en/article/claude-bissell/.

Cohen, Mark. "In Defense of Censorship: Margaret Laurence." *Censorship in Canadian Literature*. McGill-Queen's UP, 2001, pp. 88–118.

Davis, Laura K. *Margaret Laurence Writes Africa and Canada*. Wilfrid Laurier UP, 2017.

———. "Margaret Laurence's Correspondence with Imperial Oil: An Anti-Imperialist at Work." *Journal of Canadian Studies*, vol. 44, no. 1, 2010, pp. 60–74.

Derrida, Jacques. "Structure, Sign, and Play in the Discourses of the Human Sciences." *Modern Criticism and Theory*, edited by David Lodge, Longman, 1988, pp. 108–23.

Dewar, Elaine. *The Handover: How Bigwigs and Bureaucrats Transferred Canada's Best Publisher and the Best Part of Our Literary Heritage to a Foreign Multinational*. Biblioasis, 2017.

Djwa, Sandra. *Professing English: A Life of Roy Daniells*. U of Toronto P, 2002.

Downey, Donn. "Writer's Women among Most Memorable in Canadian Fiction." *Globe and Mail*, 6 Jan. 1987, p. A11.

Duncan, Robert, writer and director. *Margaret Laurence: First Lady of Manawaka.* National Film Board of Canada, 1979, DVD.

E.J. Pratt Library Special Collections, University of Toronto.

Engel, Marian. "It's the Grit: Laurence Is Unforgettable Because She Is Us" [Review of *The Diviners*]. *Globe and Mail,* 19 Apr. 1975, www.theglobeandmail.com.

Fielding, Joy. [Letter]. *Globe and Mail,* 9 Aug. 1980, p. 7.

Fitterman, Lisa. "Jocelyn Laurence Brought Out the Best in Writers." *Globe and Mail,* 5 July 2015, www.theglobeandmail.com/arts/books-and-media/jocelyn-laurence-brought-out-the-best-in-writers/article25308929/.

Forer, Mort. *The Humback.* McClelland & Stewart, 1969.

French, William. "The Centre Held in Publishing, but the Plot Was a Little Too Frangible." *Globe and Mail,* 29 Dec. 1979, p. E10.

——. "Colorful Tales of Modern Africa" [Review of *The Tomorrow-Tamer*]. *Globe and Mail,* 1 Feb. 1964, p. A14.

——. "If People Were Nourishing Nougats..." [Review of Sylvia Fraser's *The Candy Factory*]. *Globe and Mail,* 22 Mar. 1975, p. 32.

——. "Just Blame Enthusiasm for Flaws" [Review of Ernest Buckler's *The Rebellion of Young David and Other Stories*]. *Globe and Mail,* 5 Apr. 1975, www.globeandmail.com.

——. [Review of *The Fire-Dwellers*]. *Globe and Mail,* 3 May 1969, p. A17.

Friskney, Janet. "Case Study: McClelland and Stewart and the Quality Paperback." *History of the Book in Canada,* edited by Carole Gerson and Jacques Michon, vol. III, 1918–1980, U of Toronto P, 2007, pp. 233–37.

——. *New Canadian Library: The Ross-McClelland Years, 1952–1978.* U of Toronto P, 2007.

Fulford, Robert. "A Literary Reputation Made Overnight." *Toronto Star,* Dec. 1964, p. 19.

General Publishing Inc., www.generalpublishing.co.uk/index.html.

"Gertrude Laing Obituary." *Ottawa Citizen,* 7 Jan. 2006, www.legacy.com/obituaries/ottawacitizen/obituary.aspx?n=gertrude-laing&pid=16232372#sthash.9W60Toa6.dpuf.

Horn, Michiel. "Academic Freedom." *The Canadian Encyclopedia,* www.thecanadianencyclopedia.ca/en/article/academic-freedom/.

Hunt, Jacquie. [Review of Margaret Laurence's *The Christmas Birthday Story* and Susan Musgrave's *Hag Head*]. *Globe and Mail,* 1 Nov. 1980, p. D15.

——. "Younger Children" [Review of Margaret Laurence's *The Olden Days Coat*]. *Globe and Mail,* 1 Dec. 1979, p. D11.

Irvine, Dean. *The Canadian Modernists Meet.* U of Ottawa P, 2012.

Jack McClelland Fonds. William Ready Division of Archives and Research Collections, McMaster University, Hamilton.

Jane Rule Fonds. Special Collections, University of British Columbia.

John Cushman Associates Records, 1965–1978. Columbia University Libraries Archival Collections, Rare Book and Manuscript Library, www.columbia.edu/cu/lweb/archival/collections/ldpd_4078675/.

Kadar, Marlene, et al. *Tracing the Autobiographical.* Wilfrid Laurier UP, 2009.

King, James. *Jack: A Life with Writers.* Knopf Canada, 1999.

——. *The Life of Margaret Laurence.* Knopf Canada, 1988.

Kroetsch, Robert. "On Being an Alberta Writer." *Canadian Literature in English: Texts and Contexts,* edited by Laura Moss and Cynthia Sugars, vol. 2, Pearson, 2009, pp. 327–31.

La Monica, Paul R. "Apple worth $750 billion. Next stop? $1 trillion." CNN Money, 21 Mar. 2017, money.cnn.com/2017/03/21/investing/apple-stock-all-time-high-three-quarters-trillion/index.html.

Lampman, Archibald. "Two Canadian Poets: A Lecture." *Canadian Literature in English: Texts and Contexts,* edited by Laura Moss and Cynthia Sugars, vol. 1, Pearson, 2009, pp. 420–23.

Laurence, Margaret. *A Bird in the House.* McClelland & Stewart, 1970.

——. "Buckler's People Possess Strength and Dignity" [Review of Ernest Buckler's *The Rebellion of Young David and Other Stories*]. *Montreal Gazette,* 17 May 1975.

——. "The Christmas Birthday Story." *Globe and Mail,* 25 Dec. 1980, p. 25.

——. *The Christmas Birthday Story.* McClelland & Stewart, 1980.

——. *Dance on the Earth: A Memoir.* McClelland & Stewart, 1989.

——. *The Diviners.* McClelland & Stewart, 1974.

——. *The Fire-Dwellers.* McClelland & Stewart, 1969.

——. *Heart of a Stranger.* McClelland & Stewart, 1976.

——. "Ivory Tower, Or Grassroots? The Novelist as Socio-Political Being." *A Political Art: Essays and Images in Honour of George Woodcock,* edited by W.H. New, U of British Columbia P, 1978, pp. 15–25.

——. *A Jest of God.* McClelland & Stewart, 1966.

——. *Long Drums and Cannons: Nigerian Dramatists and Novelists, 1952–1966.* Edited by Nora Foster Stovel, U of Alberta P, 2001.

——. "Novelist Wants Copyright Changed Now to Combat US Books" [Letter]. *Globe and Mail,* 7 Feb. 1975, p. 7.

——. *The Olden Days Coat.* McClelland & Stewart, 1979.

——. *The Prophet's Camel Bell.* McClelland & Stewart, 1963.

——. "Richler's Tender, Two's Magic, and So's Fang" [Review of Modecai Richler's *Jacob Two-Two Meets the Hooded Fang*]. *Globe and Mail,* 26 Apr. 1975, p. 37.

——. *This Side Jordan.* McClelland & Stewart, 1960.

——. *The Tomorrow-Tamer and Other Stories.* McClelland & Stewart, 1964.

——. *A Tree for Poverty.* British Somaliland Protectorate, Eagle Press, 1954.

——. *A Very Large Soul: Selected Letters from Margaret Laurence to Canadian Writers.* Edited by J.A. Wainwright, Cormorant, 1995.

LeBourdais, Isabel. *The Trial of Steven Truscott.* McClelland & Stewart, 1966.

Lennox, John, and Ruth Panofsky, editors. *Selected Letters of Margaret Laurence and Adele Wiseman.* U of Toronto P, 1997.

Lewis, Jules. "Scott Symons." *The Canadian Encyclopedia,* www.thecanadianencyclopedia.ca/en/article/scott-symons/.

Lorimer, Rowland. *Ultra Libris: Policy, Technology, and the Creative Economy of Book Publishing in Canada.* ECW Press, 2012.

Lorraine Monk Books, lorrainemonk.com/books.html.

Ludwig, Jack. "Doting on Derek: Judy Martin Loves Derek Sanderson." *Maclean's,* Apr. 1972, pp. 39–40.

——. "The Unreal Derek Is Unreal." *Maclean's,* Apr. 1972, pp. 37–38.

——. *A Woman of Her Age.* McClelland & Stewart, 1973.

MacLean, Alistair. *Ice Station Zebra.* Fawcett Crest Books, 1963.

MacSkimming, Roy. *The Perilous Trade: Book Publishing in Canada, 1946–2006.* McClelland & Stewart, 2007.

Mannoni, Octave. *Prospero and Caliban: The Psychology of Colonization.* Translated by Pamela Powesland, Praeger, 1950.

Margaret Laurence Fonds. Clara Thomas Archives and Special Collections, York University, Toronto.

Margaret Laurence Fonds. William Ready Division of Archives and Research Collections, McMaster University, Hamilton.

McClelland & Stewart Ltd. Fonds. William Ready Division of Archives and Research Collections, McMaster University, Hamilton.

McClelland, Jack. "Book Invasion" [Letter]. *Globe and Mail,* 7 Feb. 1975, www.theglobeandmail.com.

——. "McClelland Denounces *Globe*" [Letter]. *Globe and Mail,* 17 May 1985, p. 1.

Medley, Mark. "What Happened When a Beloved Book Publisher Changed Hands." *Globe and Mail,* 10 June 2017, pp. R1, 7.

Moore, Christopher. "The Writers' Union of Canada 1973–2007." The Writers' Union of Canada, www.writersunion.ca/content/history.

Morra, Linda M. *Unarrested Archives: Case Studies in Twentieth-Century Canadian Women's Authorship*. U of Toronto P, 2014.

Moss, John. *A Reader's Guide to the Canadian Novel*. McClelland & Stewart, 1981.

Mowat, Farley. "Foreword." *This Rock Within the Sea: A Heritage Lost*. McClelland & Stewart, 1976.

Mowat, Farley, and John de Visser. *This Rock Within the Sea: A Heritage Lost*. McClelland & Stewart, 1976.

New, W.H. "Politics and Bedfellows" [Review of David Lewis Stein's *Scratch One Dreamer*]. *Canadian Literature*, vol. 33, 1967, pp. 75–77.

Oliver, David, et al. "McClelland Returns as President of Troubled Publishing Company." *Globe and Mail*, 15 May 1985, p. M1.

——. "President Resigns from Tottering McClelland & Stewart." *Globe and Mail*, 10 May 1985, www.theglobeandmail.com.

Ouellet, André. "Book Dumping" [Letter]. *Globe and Mail*, 5 Apr. 1975, p. 6.

Panofsky, Ruth. *The Literary Legacy of the Macmillan Company of Canada: Making Books and Mapping Culture*. U of Toronto P, 2011.

Peterman, Michael. "Quite a Presence: Margaret Laurence Would Visit Trent Campus to Discuss, and Sometimes Defend, Her Novels." *Peterborough Examiner*, 21 Jan. 2015, www.thepeterboroughexaminer.com/2015/01/21/quite-a-presence-margaret-laurence-would-visit-the-trent-campus-to-discuss-and-sometimes-defend-her-novels.

Powers, Lyall. *Alien Heart: The Life and Work of Margaret Laurence*. Michigan State UP, 2003.

"President's Remarks" and "Results of Ballot on Proposed Changes to the Constitution." ACCUTE *Newsletter*. Department of English, University of Alberta, Dec. 1991, pp. 2–3, 7.

Purdy, Al. *The New Romans: Candid Canadian Opinions of the US*. St. Martin's Press, 1967.

——. *Storm Warning: The New Canadian Poets*. McClelland & Stewart, 1971.

——. *Storm Warning 2: The New Canadian Poets*. McClelland & Stewart, 1976.

Read, S.E. "The Maze of Life: The Work of Margaret Laurence." *Canadian Literature*, vol. 27, 1966, pp. 5–14.

Renault, Mary. "Review of *This Side Jordan*." *Saturday Review*, 10 Dec. 1960, pp. 23–24.

[Review of *The Fire-Dwellers*]. *Time*, 28 Mar. 1969.

Richler, Mordecai. *The Apprenticeship of Duddy Kravitz*. McClelland & Stewart, 1959.

Robert Weaver Fonds. Library and Archives Canada, Ottawa.

Scobie, Stephen. *Sheila Watson*. ECW Press, 1985.

Scott, F.R. "The Canadian Authors Meet." Canadian Poetry Online, University of Toronto Libraries, canpoetry.library.utoronto.ca/scott_fr/poem3.htm.

Sim, Donald F. "Compulsion, Not Censorship, Seen Issue on Laurence Book" [Letter]. *Globe and Mail*, 13 Feb. 1976, p. 7.

Smith, Russell. "How to Publish a Book in Canada." *Globe and Mail*, 4 July 2015, p. R3.

Solecki, Sam, editor. *Imagining Canadian Literature: The Selected Letters of Jack McClelland*. Key Porter Books, 1998.

Steel, Jamie. "Lakefield Print Shop Closing after 50 Years in Business." *Lakefield Herald*, 2010, www.lakefieldherald.com/2011/08_12_2011/pat.html.

Stovel, Nora Foster. *Divining Margaret Laurence: A Study of Her Complete Writings*. McGill-Queen's UP, 2008.

——. "Introduction." *Heart of a Stranger*. U of Alberta P, 2003.

Tausky, Thomas E. "Henry Kreisel." *The Canadian Encyclopedia*, www.thecanadianencyclopedia.ca/en/article/henry-kreisel/.

Thacker, Robert. *Alice Munro: Writing Her Lives*. McClelland & Stewart, 2005.

——. "*Robert Weaver: Godfather of Canadian Literature*" [Book Review]. *Canadian Literature*, vol. 198, 2008, canlit.ca.

Thomas, Clara. *The Manawaka World of Margaret Laurence*. McClelland & Stewart, 1975.

——. *Margaret Laurence*. McClelland & Stewart, 1969.

Thomson, Andy, director. *Ten Million Books: An Introduction to Farley Mowat*. National Film Board of Canada, 1981, DVD.

Toye, William. *Encyclopedia of Canadian Literature*. Oxford UP, 2011.

Weeks, Edward. [Review of *The Fire-Dwellers*]. *Atlantic Monthly*, June 1969, pp. 112–13.

Weyman, Bay, and James Weyman, writers and producers. *Against Reason: A Portrait of Jack McClelland*. Close Up Films, in association with CBC and Telefilm Canada, 1986, closeupfilms.ca/Films/Against_Reason.php.

Wiebe, Rudy. *The Tempations of Big Bear*. McClelland & Stewart, 1973.

Wigmore, Donnalo. "Margaret Laurence: The Woman Behind the Writing" [Interview with Margaret Laurence]. *Chatelaine*, Feb. 1971, pp. 28–29; 52–54.

Wiseman, Adele. *Crackpot*. McClelland & Stewart, 1974.

——. *Old Woman at Play*. Clarke, Irwin, 1978.

——. *The Sacrifice*. Macmillan, 1956.

Woodcock, Connie. "Canadian Jack Finds U.S. Jill." *Toronto Sun*, 8 Feb. 1977.

Woodman, Dianne. Personal interview. 10 Oct. 2015.

Woolf, Virginia. *A Room of One's Own*. 1929. Broadview Press, 2001.

Xiques, Donez. *The Making of a Writer: Margaret Laurence*. Dundurn Press, 2005.

York, Lorraine. *Margaret Atwood and the Labour of Literary Celebrity*. U of Toronto P, 2013.

Zander, Michael. "The Case of Steven Truscott." *Guardian*, 24 Mar. 1966.

Index

Illustrations are indicated by page numbers in italics.

Other Titles from The University of Alberta Press

Long Drums and Cannons

Nigerian Dramatists and Novelists, 1952–1966

MARGARET LAURENCE

NORA FOSTER STOVEL, *Editor*

Long Drums and Cannons is a classic of early postcolonial criticism, of interest to Laurence's wide readership and to anyone interested in African literature.

Challenging Territory

The Writing of Margaret Laurence

CHRISTIAN RIEGEL, *Editor*

How can we approach Margaret Laurence's writing in a postcolonial and postmodern age? *Challenging Territory* is a collection of essays that examine positionality across the range of Laurence's writing.

Heart of a Stranger

MARGARET LAURENCE

NORA FOSTER STOVEL, *Editor*

Between 1964 and 1975, Margaret Laurence wrote this collection of essays chronicling her travels and revealing how they inspired her fiction.
A volume in cuRRents, a Canadian literature series

More information at www.uap.ualberta.ca